Mesoamerican Archaeology

BLACKWELL STUDIES IN GLOBAL ARCHAEOLOGY

Series Editors: Lynn Meskell and Rosemary A. Joyce

Blackwell Studies in Global Archaeology is a series of contemporary texts, each carefully designed to meet the needs of archaeology instructors and students seeking volumes that treat key regional and thematic areas of archaeological study. Each volume in the series, compiled by its own editor, includes 12–15 newly commissioned articles by top scholars within the volume's thematic, regional, or temporal area of focus.

What sets the *Blackwell Studies in Global Archaeology* apart from other available texts is that their approach is accessible, yet does not sacrifice theoretical sophistication. The series editors are committed to the idea that usable teaching texts need not lack ambition. To the contrary, the *Blackwell Studies in Global Archaeology* aim to immerse readers in fundamental archaeological ideas and concepts, but also to illuminate more advanced concepts, thereby exposing readers to some of the most exciting contemporary developments in the field. Inasmuch, these volumes are designed not only as classic texts, but as guides to the vital and exciting nature of archaeology as a discipline.

Mesoamerican Archaeology

Theory and Practice

Edited by

Julia A. Hendon and
Rosemary A. Joyce

Blackwell
Publishing

350 Main Street, Malden, MA 02148-5020, USA
108 Cowley Road, Oxford OX4 1JF, UK
550 Swanston Street, Carlton, Victoria 3053, Australia

First published 2004 by Blackwell Publishing Ltd

Library of Congress Cataloging-in-Publication Data

Mesoamerican archaeology: theory and practice / edited by Julia A. Hendon and Rosemary A.
Joyce.
      p.   cm. – (Blackwell studies in global archaeology)
Includes bibliographical references and index.
    ISBN 0-631-23051-3 (alk. paper) – ISBN 0-631-23052-1 (alk. paper)
    1. Mayas–Antiquities.   2. Mayas–Material culture.   3. Mayas–Social life and customs.   4.
Indians of Mexico–Antiquities.   5. Indians of Central America–Antiquities.   6. Excavations
(Archaeology)–Mexico.   7. Excavations (Archaeology)–Central America.   8. Mexico–Antiquities.
9. Central America–Antiquities.   I. Hendon, Julia A. (Julia Ann)   II. Joyce, Rosemary A., 1956–
III. Series.

F1435.M557 2004
972.81′016–dc21

                                                                                          2003001667
A catalogue record for this title is available from the British Library.

Set in 10 on 12.5 pt Plantin
by SNP Best-set Typesetter Ltd., Hong Kong
Printed and bound in the United Kingdom
by MPG Books Ltd, Bodmin, Cornwall

For further information on
Blackwell Publishing, visit our website:
http://www.blackwellpublishing.com

Contents

Series Editors' Preface

This series was conceived as a collection of books designed to cover central areas of undergraduate archaeological teaching. Each volume in the series, edited by experts in the area, includes newly commissioned articles written by archaeologists actively engaged in research. By commissioning new articles, the series combines one of the best features of readers, the presentation of multiple approaches to archaeology, with the virtues of a text conceived from the beginning as intended for a specific audience. While the model reader for the series is conceived of as an upper division undergraduate, the inclusion in the volumes of researchers actively engaged in work today will also make these volumes valuable for more advanced researchers who want a rapid introduction to contemporary issues in specific sub-fields of global archaeology.

Each volume in the series will include an extensive introduction by the volume editors that will set the scene in terms of thematic or geographic focus. Individual volumes, and the series as a whole, exemplify a wide range of approaches in contemporary archaeology. The volumes uniformly engage with issues of contemporary interest, interweaving social, political and ethical themes. We contend that it is no longer tenable to teach the archaeology of vast swaths of the globe without acknowledging the political implications of working in foreign countries and the responsibilities archaeologists incur by writing and presenting other peoples' pasts. The volumes in this series will not sacrifice theoretical sophistication for accessibility. We are committed to the idea that usable teaching texts need not lack ambition.

Blackwell Studies in Global Archaeology aim to immerse readers in fundamental archaeological ideas and concepts, but also to illuminate more advanced concepts, exposing readers to some of the most exciting contemporary developments in the field.

Lynn Meskell and Rosemary A. Joyce

Preface

This book is intended to be useful for anyone teaching Mesoamerican archaeology, whether as the sole subject of a course, or as one case study among others in courses dealing with archaeology of the Americas, complex societies, or other topics. We also expect that it will be of interest to any reader who wants a sample of contemporary research on the major time periods and societies that are the focus of Mesoamerican archaeology. Because this book is a departure from other models for introductory texts, it is appropriate for us to briefly explain what it is, and is not, and to suggest how we hope it might be incorporated into the classroom.

We both teach material from the field of Mesoamerican archaeology, in basic introductory courses and more advanced offerings. As active field archaeologists with our own research projects, we find ourselves struggling to provide students with a sense of the research process. In particular, we think it is important for students to see that changes in archaeological understanding (or differences in opinion, as illustrated by some of the essays included here) are a constructive part of the research process. They reflect the mechanisms through which our discipline debates explanations, puts them to the test against existing and new data, and gradually revises them. Too often, we find that students (and people outside the academy interested in archaeology) have the impression, from media coverage of archaeology, that changes in interpretation result from violent rejection of earlier ideas, represented as poorly conceived, foolish, or examples of bad practice. We do not think that representing archaeology as a kind of winner-takes-all contest is very true to the reality of the constant hard work, only occasionally accompanied by moments of transformative insight, that we experience as field researchers. Nor does the metaphor of a contest accurately represent the way that new research builds on and acknowledges older ideas, even in the process of modifying, extending, or disagreeing with those ideas.

We have both found that our teaching is most successful when we base it on a diversity of articles, written by scholars with different points of view. The juxtaposition of many different, but credible, arguments helps us make clear to students that there is not now, and never has been, a consensus about how to understand Mesoamerica's prehispanic history, what the important questions are, and what the best way to investigate intriguing questions might be. Using research papers written by practitioners active in field and laboratory analyses brings the research process to life. It enables students to engage in critical thinking about how explanations of the past are produced, verified, and disputed. This engagement has the potential to promote a greater mastery of content and principles, and a more enduring understanding of the archaeological process.

But there are also difficulties with this approach. Foremost among them, articles written for professional audiences assume a great degree of shared background knowledge. They begin in the middle of an ongoing research dialogue, where even everyday words can have very specific meanings. To use research articles in teaching requires us to spend substantial effort on explaining specialist terms and assumptions. And even when this is done, there remains the fact that professional articles are written for particular contexts, often as part of edited volumes dealing with specific themes or issues. To make these articles effective outside their original setting, it is necessary to place them back in context through lectures, orienting notes, or annotations. We have both been successful teaching from thematically focused edited volumes, where the context of all the articles is the same, and the repetition of conceptual vocabulary reinforces our background discussions. But there are very few edited volumes that cover the full chronological and geographic breadth of Mesoamerican archaeology.

We realized that our ideal would be to have a single volume containing new papers written with a non-specialist reader in mind. By selecting contributors who are actively engaged in research on key time periods and topics in contemporary Mesoamerican archaeology, this volume could provide what we have been piecing together from existing resources, but with an important difference. Written self-consciously as explanations of current issues in specific archaeological research areas within Mesoamerica and orientated towards the student or other non-specialist, these papers could provide the equivalent of a casebook optimally suited for teaching. As editors, we undertook to provide the general orientation necessary for the volume as a whole, and to provide a glossary of terms that might be unfamiliar to nonspecialist readers.

The response to our invitation to participate gratified us immensely, as extremely dedicated, busy researchers took the time to prepare new essays for this volume. Where possible, we sought to provide dual approaches to important time periods and places, hoping that these juxtapositions would illuminate the way that research problems framed differently call for different methods of investigation and interpretation. We balanced contributions taking macroscale approaches with those examining the microscale that begins with the individual actor and extends outward to households, communities, and regions. We deliberately invited researchers whose opinions on the relative importance of economic factors and ideological factors varied. The one thing we sought in every contribution was self-conscious attention to how problems were framed and what the effects of problem orientation were on research outcomes.

The resulting volume therefore considers research employing many different kinds of materials, highly diverse methods, and many strands of theory. Many of the contributors share with the editors an interest in questions of individual and group identity and agency, and are exploring the implications of practice theory for Mesoamerican archaeology. Contributors who do not explicitly use concepts from practice theory nonetheless take seriously the same kinds of questions about how individual people who are raised in a specific cultural, social, and natural environment continue the traditions in which they were raised while also subtly modifying them, so that, to modern observers, they can be seen as participants in sequences of social change. All of the contributors examine particular practices, perceptible to modern researchers because they left material traces, and consider the significance these practices had in the formation and re-formation of Mesoamerican societies over a long historical trajectory.

We have included sufficient orienting material in this volume to ensure that students and other interested readers will understand the chronological and geographic frameworks of the Mesoamerican tradition, and will recognize key issues in its history. Because this volume includes an introduction explicitly sketching out the contexts necessary to understand Mesoamerican archaeology as a subject, it can also serve to contextualize other research articles that might be used to complement the contents included. As a casebook of theoretically explicit studies, it should serve as a resource for comparison with archaeologies from other world areas. Our goal was not to be exhaustive, but selective. We do not attempt to replace comprehensive syntheses of Mesoamerican prehistory, but to complement them with a volume that takes understanding *how* we know as central to understanding *what* we know. Finally, we hope that this volume gives all of its readers a sense of the exciting developments in the contemporary theory and practice of Mesoamerican archaeology, and encourages them to delve further into the original research cited by all of the contributors.

Julia A. Hendon
Rosemary A. Joyce

Acknowledgments

The editors would like to thank Jane Huber, Sarah Coleman, Annie Lenth, and other staff at Blackwell, and Lynn Meskell, co-editor of Blackwell's Global Studies in Archaeology, for their support for this project. This work was partially prepared while Rosemary Joyce was a Fellow at the Center for Advanced Study in the Behavioral Sciences, with financial support provided by Grant 2000–5633 and the "Hewlett Fellow" Grant 98-2124 from the William and Flora Hewlett Foundation. A pretenure leave to Julia Hendon from Gettysburg College provided time to develop the project.

List of Figures

List of Contributors

Wendy Ashmore is Professor of Anthropology at the University of California, Riverside. She has conducted field research in the Maya lowlands in Guatemala, Honduras and Belize, and pioneered research in household archaeology and landscape archaeology.

Elizabeth M. Brumfiel is the John S. Ludington Trustees' Professor in the Department of Anthropology and Sociology at Albion College. Her research on the Aztec state is based on extensive fieldwork in Central Mexico. Her analyses of gender relations in centralizing states are fundamental texts in the archaeology of gender.

John E. Clark is Professor of Anthropology at Brigham Young University. A leading scholar in lithic analysis and the study of Formative societies of Mesoamerica, he collaborates in fieldwork in coastal region of the Mexican state of Chiapas.

Julia A. Hendon is Associate Professor in the Department of Sociology and Anthropology at Gettysburg College. She has conducted fieldwork in the Maya lowlands of Belize, Guatemala, and Honduras, developing analyses of social agency, gender, and household economic organization.

Arthur A. Joyce is Assistant Professor of Anthropology at the University of Colorado, Boulder. His fieldwork in Oaxaca contributes to the study of state organization and environmental impacts of the development of states.

Rosemary A. Joyce is Professor of Anthropology at the University of California, Berkeley. She has conducted fieldwork in Honduras on sites ranging in age from the Formative through the Postclassic. Her research contributes to the study of social identity and difference, particularly age and gender.

Richard G. Lesure is Associate Professor of Anthropology at the University of California, Los Angeles. His fieldwork on the Formative period societies of Mexico's

Pacific Chiapas Coast and highland Department of Tlaxcala is complemented by global comparative work, particularly on the significance of gender representation.

Linda Manzanilla is Investigador of the Instituto de Investigaciones Antropológicas of the Universidad Autónma de México. Widely recognized for her innovative research on households at Teotihuacan, she holds a doctorate in Egyptology from the Sorbonne.

Deborah L. Nichols is the William J. Bryant 1925 Professor of Anthropology at Dartmouth College. She has carried out extensive fieldwork in the Southwest United States and Central Mexico, exploring issues of craft production and cultural ecology.

John M. D. Pohl is an independent researcher affiliated to the Fowler Museum at the University of California, Los Angeles. He has conducted field research in Canada, the United States, Mexico, and Central America, and is a noted authority on Postclassic Mexican codices.

Cynthia Robin is Assistant Professor of Anthropology at Northwestern University. She has conducted fieldwork at a number of Maya archaeological sites in Belize, and also carried out ethnographic fieldwork on farming in the Maya lowlands.

Saburo Sugiyama is Professor of Archaeology in the Faculty of Foreign Studies, Aichi Prefectural University, Japan. He has conducted long-term research at Teotihuacan investigating the symbolism of state government, in collaboration with both the Instituto Nacional de Antropología e Historia of Mexico and Arizona State University, where he is an adjunct research professor in anthropology.

1

Mesoamerica: A Working Model for Archaeology

Rosemary A. Joyce

The essays in this volume provide insight into the range of theoretical issues and topical debates of concern to archaeologists currently studying the Mesoamerican societies that flourished in Mexico and Central American prior to European contact and Spanish conquest in the sixteenth century. But what is meant by the term *Mesoamerica*, and why do we group together essays on widely separated sites, distinct groups of people, and vastly different time periods?

In this introduction, I will explore some of the meanings of Mesoamerica that have supported its use as an organizing framework for archaeological debate for over 50 years. In the process, I will make explicit a number of background assumptions shared by the contributors to this volume, and will specify some of the common knowledge that contributors have that readers may not share. Along the way, I will review some of the major theoretical and methodological approaches to Mesoamerican archaeology that have historically been important, many of which are mentioned in the chapters that follow. This discussion also touches on the complex relationships between the practice of archaeology and broader social and political developments, dramatized by the significance of archaeological materials in the development of nationalism in the region.

I also address where Mesoamerican archaeology stands today, introducing some of the critical concepts in contemporary archaeology shared by authors who have contributed to this volume, and some of the productive differences in their approaches to developing an understanding of the early history of the region through the study of material remains of past human action documented in context (a rough definition of archaeology as practiced by all the contributors).

Mesoamerica as an Object of Archaeological Research

Although it is sometimes treated as a spatial unit that can be delimited by northern and southern frontiers (Fig. 1.1), Mesoamerica is not really just a geographic

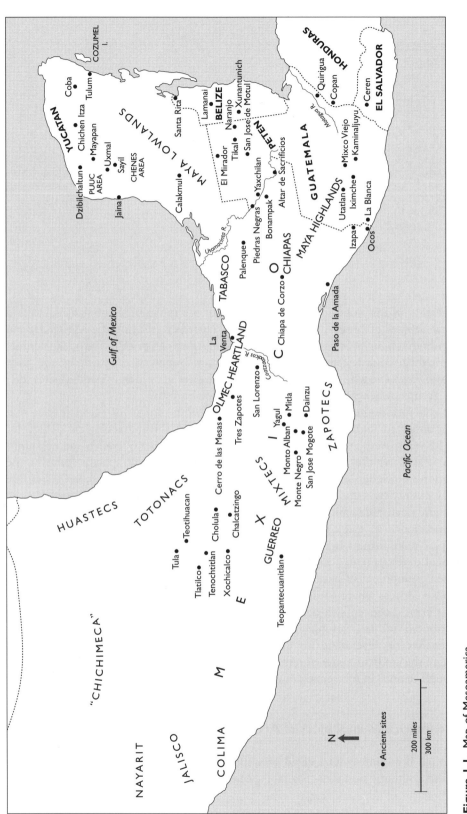

Figure 1.1. Map of Mesoamerica

region. It is mainly a cultural and linguistic concept that anthropologists find useful as a way to refer to groups of people who lived within a defined geographic region over a long period time and who shared certain cultural and linguistic features. These shared features coexisted with and cross-cut social, linguistic, ecological, and political boundaries. The only viable social mechanism to explain the development of Mesoamerica as a cultural tradition, cross-cutting all sorts of other boundaries, is a long history of intensive interaction among social groups in the region.

In this sense, the term "Mesoamerica" is analogous to the term, "Western civilization." Both suggest the existence of various kinds of historical connections among a set of interacting societies that led to shared values, practices, and institutions, despite variation in language, political structure, religion, and cultural practices (Joyce 2000c; see also Clark and Pye 2000; Pye and Clark 2000). Meosamerican peoples had far less intensive and enduring interaction with the societies to their north and south, making it possible for archaeologists and ethnographers to discern boundaries to the area of intense interaction we call Mesoamerica. To understand Mesoamerica, we must consequently attempt to understand the development of networks of interaction between its distinct peoples over long periods of time. When archaeologists do not take the existence of Mesoamerica for granted, they are in the ideal position to provide an exploration of the historical development of these networks of interaction, their limits, and variation within the Mesoamerican tradition.

Mesoamerica as a culture area

Mesoamerica was originally defined as a culture area based on a checklist of traits ranging from basic religious concepts to minor details of costume (Kirchhoff 1968[1943]). The mere compilation of a trait list is now rejected by archaeologists as too crude a way to identify likeness or to group societies or archaeological sites because it treats all similarities as being of equal importance and provides no way to explain how such connections came into being or why. Archaeologists still find the concept of Mesoamerica useful, however, because it allows them to group together cultures which, through extensive interaction, developed a common set of values and practices that continued to develop over a long period of time, some 3,500 years before European contact. From this perspective, we can replace the Mesoamerican trait list by shared *practices* in a number of distinct social domains.

The most important of these practices are (1) a basic structuring economy, (2) beliefs about how the world works and the practices related to those beliefs, and (3) material signs of social stratification (Fig. 1.2). Mesoamerican peoples were agriculturalists, living in socially differentiated communities, understanding themselves to exist in specific kinds of relations to other people, in a natural and supernatural world with specific kinds of features. Although the details of beliefs varied, the basic elements of a Mesoamerican worldview were among the longest-lived Mesoamerican *structures*.

Arena of practice	Traits from original definition of Mesoamerica
subsistence production	agriculture based on corn, beans, and squash, dependent on human labor using digging stick agricultural intensification including raised fields (*chinampas*) plants raised for specialized uses: cacao, amaranth, *maguey* corn processed by soaking with lime and grinding on *metates*
long-distance exchange	valuables such as obsidian, cacao and jade

cosmology and ritual	numbers 4, 5, 7, 9, 13, and 20 significant
	 shared calendars:
	     solar year of 18 months of 20 days plus a set of 5 final days;
	     260-day ritual cycle of 13 day names combined with 20
	     numbers
	 use of writing and positional mathematics to record astronomy and calendar, in paper and deer skin books (*codices*) and more permanent media
	 ritual warfare, special warrior costumes, and human sacrifice
	 specialized architecture for ritual:
	     ball courts, temples, observatories, including use of stucco

social stratification	status expressed in costumes, including gender specific forms of dress, role-specific headdresses, warrior outfits, and ornaments such as lip plugs, pyrite mirrors and polished obsidian mirrors and ear plugs

Figure 1.2. Archaeologically identifiable defining traits of Mesoamerica, organized according to social and cultural practices

The production of structures and their reproduction over time does not happen automatically. They are the result of conscious and unconscious actions carried out by people as part of social groups. The active process of socialization and reproduction of values results from people acting as social *agents*. People in these societies reproduced and transformed social structures through their choices among the possible ways to act that they saw open to them. In the process of exercising agency and reproducing and transforming structure, people create and add to individual and group histories, shaping the constraints and possibilities of agents in succeeding generations. What we see today as a continuous tradition is actually the result of generations of practices by people working within the bounds of what they understood to be both possible and desirable. Both the continuity in the Mesoamerican tradition and its changes over time can be understood from the perspective of the transformation and reproduction of social structure by agents through practices.

A historically situated view like this implies that Mesoamerica, as a cultural tradition, had a beginning point, a period in the history of the indigenous societies of Mexico and Central America when the practices and beliefs we recognize as Mesoamerican are first identifiable. Gordon R. Willey (1966:78) long ago identified the emergence of archaeologically identifiable Mesoamerica with the time period around 2000 B.C. when village life dependent on corn agriculture took form. This volume also begins coverage of Mesoamerica at this moment. This is also the time when, in early villages, social stratification first becomes evident (see Chapters 2 and 3). Many of the practices that archaeologists have identified as typical of Mesoamerican culture are expressions of social differentiation, and these practices first take shape in the early villages of Mesoamerica. The high number of specifically Mesoamerican practices that relate to cosmology and ritual underlines a point made by many authors in the chapters that follow: in Mesoamerica, social stratification was intimately bound up with propositions about the nature of the universe and the relations people had to other forces and beings. The centrality of certain economic practices to Mesoamerica is equally important. The agricultural economy of Mesoamerica provided surplus production that supported the development of distinctively Mesoamerican social complexity.

Mesoamerican societies are linked by continuity in the use of particular materials as items of wealth and standards of value, reflected in economic, social, and political practices. Craft specialists worked obsidian, jade and other greenstones, and feathers into signs of distinction; scribes, astronomers, and calendar specialists developed and recorded indigenous wisdom; and a select body of people who claimed legitimacy in exercising powers of governance consumed these and other forms of "high culture" (Joyce 2000c; see below). Concepts of social order, manifest in Mesoamerica as early as the Formative period, structured the actions of later social agents by providing them with particular ideas of value and legitimacy within which people carried out practices.

Craft production thus had both practical value and specific importance in the reproduction of a specifically Mesoamerican way of doing things. At the same time, the vast majority of people organized and carried out the work of cultivating fields, hunting, gathering, processing, and preparing foods, creating useful and beautiful objects for household consumption, and educating new generations in the traditions and practices that constituted Mesoamerica. Archaeological evidence demonstrates that most Mesoamerican villagers relied for subsistence on a combination of maize (corn), beans, and squash, complemented by chili peppers and supplemented by a wide variety of wild and cultivated fruits and tubers. Among the most important alternative staple crops in the dry highlands were other seed-bearing plants, amaranth and chenopods, including *chia*, used by the Aztecs to make images of supernatural beings displayed and consumed in ritual. In some parts of the wetter lowlands root crops, particularly manioc (or yuca) were cultivated.

Beverages prepared from certain plants were widely used in religious rituals and social ceremonies: cacao, made from chocolate beans (products of a tree growing in wet lowlands), and an alcoholic drink the Aztecs called *pulque*, made from fermented hearts of maguey, a succulent plant cultivated in drier areas. Native stingless bees were kept in lowland areas, and honey was used by the lowland Maya to brew another ritual alcoholic drink, *balche*.

Other than bees, domesticated animals were limited to the dog and turkey, the latter introduced rather late in Mesoamerican history from further north. The primary sources of animal protein suggested by archaeological remains of animal bones were land animals such as deer and peccary, hunted with blowguns, snares, and nets; birds, especially waterfowl such as ducks; and fish. In the absence of large domesticated animals, all agricultural work was provided by human labor. With the work of subject populations, Mesoamerican societies built complex systems to intensify agriculture, improving production through irrigation, the construction of terraces on slopes, and raised fields built in swampy areas.

The combination of these traits of subsistence production characterizes Mesoamerican peoples, but was not unique to them. The same kinds of agricultural systems were found in North and South America. Corn, beans, and squash were raised throughout the Americas. But cultivation of the specialized plants raised in Mesoamerica and used for ritual purposes did not extend to other areas, and techniques of food processing, preparation, and serving that developed in Mesoamerica constitute a distinctive cuisine (Coe 1994). What was made of maize agriculture was a defining part of Mesoamerica: the elaboration of the maize- and chili-pepper-based cuisine, and of mythologies in which the survival of maize gods was attributed to the actions of nobles and the supernatural beings they claimed as their predecessors (Monaghan 1990; Taube 1985, 1989).

Myths about maize were part of a specifically Mesoamerican set of beliefs and practices concerning the relationship between human beings, supernatural beings, and ancestors. Mesoamerican peoples shared a view of the universe as composed of three levels, a supernatural underworld and overworld, between which was located the natural world of humans (see Chapter 7). Each level had four sides, the four world directions, conceived of not as the cardinal points of western European tradition, but as a segment of the sky traced by the annual movement of the sun. East and west were marked on the horizon by the northern and southern extreme positions of the sun on the solstices in December and June, and the midpoint position of the sun on the equinoxes in March and September (see Aveni 1980). The directions between east and west seem sometimes to have been thought of as north and south, and other times to have been thought of as up and down, two additional points in the daily path of the sun, across the sky during the day and through the underworld at night.

In Mesoamerican belief, contact could be made directly with the supernatural world, which was inhabited by personified supernatural forces. Access to the supernatural world took place through rituals, using certain pathways, particularly holes into the underworld (caves, wells) and mountains and trees which rose up into the upperworld (Gillespie 1993). Mesoamerican rituals, founded on shared cosmological ideas, took place in specially constructed architectural spaces. Such ceremonial or ritual centers were constructed according to cosmological concepts. Buildings were often placed in alignment with unmodified features of the landscape that were pathways to the upperworld, such as the alignment of the Temple of the Moon at Teotihuacan with the mountain Cerro Gordo (see Chapter 4). Buildings with distinct functions, such as ancestral temples and everyday residences, might be placed in regular directional relationships, although precisely which direction was appropriate for which activities varied (see Chapter 7). Architectural centers, from the earliest to the latest periods known, incorporated buildings which were stages for typically Mesoamerican rituals: ball courts, temples, and astronomical observatories. Timing of rituals performed in these locations was based on calendrical and astronomical information, recorded in written texts, of which only examples recorded on durable stone monuments have survived from the earliest Mesoamerican societies. Among the repeated ritual actions represented in images, recorded in texts, and detectable from material traces, were the burning of incense, dances, games, and other dramatic performances, and also human sacrifice, often paired with militaristic symbolism.

The people who built these ceremonial centers lived in varied shapes, sizes, and styles of houses. Settlements in Mesoamerica were often composed of residential compounds large enough to house multiple generations of related families, or multiple families related as patrons and clients. Here, people lived and carried out the activities necessary for their subsistence and more specialized production. Here also they carried out rituals, especially those marking changes in the status of members of the group. Most evident in the material remains that archaeologists study are rituals transforming living members of the group into ancestors following death.

Formal tombs and less formal graves placed under the courtyards or house floors, and caches (unique deposits, containing particular parts of skeletons) are known at different Mesoamerican sites. The range of ways of treating the dead body in preparation for burial is extremely varied, from binding bodies in seated positions, so they form bundles, to laying the dead body out as if asleep. The bodies of the dead were sometimes carefully dressed in elaborate costume, and set in the ground with a wide array of objects (see Chapters 3, 4, 5, and 6). In other cases, dead bodies were apparently burned, as suggested by images in Postclassic Mixtec codices and texts written about the Aztecs in the sixteenth century A.D. Archaeologists have argued that conserving the bodies or body-parts of deceased members of a group might have been a means for Mesoamerican people to create historical continuity between generations (Gillespie 2001, 2002; McAnany 1995). Distinct practices of disposing of the dead employed by separate groups within each society would have contributed to differentiation within the community, like that noted between residents of individual household compounds at Teotihuacan (Chapter 5; see also Hendon 2000; Joyce 1999).

The social commemoration of other points in the lives of inhabitants of house compounds involving feasts, a practice attested in the latest periods through written descriptions created using the European writing system, is evident archaeologically in the remains of vessels and food consumed (see Chapters 10 and 12). House compounds in many areas incorporated special architectural features that were sites for household ritual (see Chapter 5). These were not merely places to live and work. They were imbued with the same cosmological structures as major architectural groups. The same kinds of principles associating directions with different activities affected the use of space within the everyday confines of house compounds. The integration of cosmological beliefs in everyday life at an intimate scale was critical to the reproduction of the structures of Mesoamerican societies (Joyce and Hendon 2000).

Household compounds were also sites of the structural reproduction of Mesoamerican economies and polities through the organization of domestic labor (Hendon 1996, 1997). Every community had to have its own agricultural base;

because of the reliance on human labor for transport, in general, it was not feasible to move significant quantities of food long distances (but see Chapter 7). Within Mesoamerican villages from the earliest times, some degree of craft specialization was also supported. The highest number of crafts, and the greatest intensity of production, has been documented in or near the larger and more lavish compounds that are interpreted as residences of rulers and other nobles (see Chapters 2, 3, and 6). In the most highly stratified Mesoamerican societies, craft specialization was shared by residents of groups of neighboring house compounds or whole communities (see Chapters 5, 8, and 11).

Products of specialized crafts (such as pottery, stone tools, and woven textiles) were presumably redistributed within the local community and beyond through a combination of social ties and markets. Exchange from particular craft-producing households and communities has been reconstructed using compositional analyses that create a chemical profile of the raw materials used in craft production (such as obsidian, iron ore, and jade) or the mixtures of clay and other materials that characterize pottery workshops (see Chapters 2, 10, 11). Craft production carried out within residential compounds was more than simply a source of subsistence. It helped define a person's place within his or her society. Throughout the history of Mesoamerica, participation in craft production as part of a group was intimately related to the constitution of personhood (see Chapter 12).

Many of the traits making up the original definition of Mesoamerica refer to objects used as markers of different kinds of personal and group status. As a historically linked series of socially stratified, economically differentiated, complex societies, the way people were placed in relation to each other was fundamental to the distinctive character of Mesoamerica. Long-distance exchange, one of the practices through which intensive interaction between different peoples within Mesoamerica was fostered, was centrally concerned with obtaining materials used for marking distinctions between commoners and nobles (Hirth 1992). Costume, a major means of marking distinctions between different kinds of people in Mesoamerica, and for signaling the roles of different people, was typically composed of textiles woven of cotton or maguey fiber. Feathers, polished mirrors, and carved greenstone ornaments were all important components of costumes indicating special status and rank.

The development of Mesoamerica, defined in the traditional manner, is centrally concerned with the ways distinctions in social status developed over time and were marked in the network of complex societies that made up Mesoamerica. The majority of the traits archaeologists have used as diagnostic of Mesoamerican civilization were part of a common "high culture" promulgated by individuals and groups, including elders within household groups, local community authorities, and political and religious leaders, who were interested in marking out differences between themselves and others in their communities (Joyce 2000c). The exclusive practices of cuisine, dress, and architecture through which select social groups at many scales distinguished themselves from others were supported by specific kinds of economic practices, including the production of agricultural surplus that supported some members of society as part- or full-time craft specialists. The use of calendars

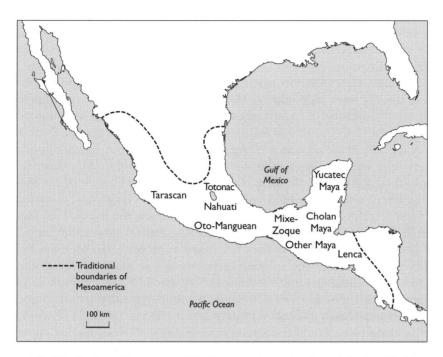

Figure 1.3. Distribution of languages within Mesoamerica at the time of the Spanish Conquest

and writing to record patterns of social relations among diverse kinds of people through time was also part of Mesoamerican "high culture" (see Chapters 6, 7, 8, 9, and 12).

The shared use, across linguistic boundaries, of technologies for counting days, recording time, and representing texts through writing, inevitably affected the nature of the languages spoken by the peoples that were part of the Mesoamerican tradition. Intensive communication between different communities engaged in long-distance economic exchange and social relations would also have encouraged the spread of speech practices between speakers of unrelated languages. A second way of defining Mesoamerica as an object of study is based on such effects on language of the dialogues across linguistic boundaries over long spans of time that were part of the Mesoamerican tradition.

Mesoamerica as a linguistic area

The traits which are our evidence for the Mesoamerican tradition, and the practices they imply, extended across major language barriers (Fig. 1.3). Three major language families, Mixe-Zoque, Totonac, and Mayan, are composed of languages spoken only by Mesoamerican peoples (Campbell 1976). Another major family, Oto-Manguean, includes some languages in neighboring parts of Central America.

Nahuatl, the language of the Aztecs of central Mexico, is a branch of a language family extending through northern Mexico to North America. Smaller numbers of people in Mesoamerica spoke apparently isolated languages: Huave, Tarascan, Xincan, and Lencan.

These major Mesoamerican language families are entirely independent of each other, as distinct from each other as German is from Chinese. Despite the lack of genetic relationships between languages spoken by different Mesoamerican people, linguists note a variety of shared features in Mesoamerican languages. Such shared features are not found among all languages in a group, but rather those whose speakers were part of societies in intense interaction within Mesoamerica. For example, these features are found in Nahuatl, but not in its close northern Mexican relatives. Because they are found only in Mesoamerican languages, these features must have developed historically in that region. Because the features are found in unrelated languages, they must result from intensive contact between speakers of different languages. These patterns have been used to propose that Mesoamerica is a linguistic area: a zone in which, through intensive interaction, speakers of unrelated languages adopt common linguistic features (Campbell 1976; Campbell, Kaufman, and Smith-Stark 1986). Historical linguistic studies suggest that the Mesoamerican language area had taken its present form by about 1000 B.C., when a series of loanwords for important cultural concepts spread throughout Mesoamerica, apparently from a Mixe-Zoque source language (Campbell and Kaufman 1976).

Mesoamerican languages share features of grammar, sounds (phonology), and meaning (semantics). The shared phonological features mean that Mesoamerican languages sound similar to each other even when unrelated. This suggests that speakers of different languages adapted to each other's manner of speech. Grammatical and semantic features reflect the shared practices that resulted in the Mesoamerican tradition. Number systems based on 20 (in contrast with the western European decimal system, based on 10), and numeral classifiers, special forms used in counting different categories of things, are widely shared features of Mesoamerican languages. These are linguistic traces of the common use of calendar and mathematics that are a major part of the Mesoamerican tradition (compare Chapters 2 and 4).

Poetic aspects of speech are among other features found in unrelated Mesoamerican languages. Shared poetics hint at the ceremonial, ritual, and courtly contexts within which cross-language communication would have been most likely, as guests in other communities, including noble visitors, were entertained socially. Mesoamerican formal speech typically employs metaphors arranged in paired couplets. Many of the specific metaphors are shared by unrelated Mesoamerican languages. Locative words are often derived from parts of the body, for example the word "stomach" meaning "inside." Common figures of speech include calling the door of a building its "mouth," the bark of a tree its "skin," and the eye of a person the "seed of the face." Such verbal metaphors can be related to visual representation, for example, the construction of an image of an animal head surrounding doorways of Classic Maya temples, with the door to the temple located at the mouth of the animal.

The process through which independent, unrelated languages grew to resemble each other must be thought of as a historical process of mutual translation, like the process through which post-conquest speakers of Yucatec and Spanish clerics together created a new form of Yucatec (Hanks 2000). This documented historical process provides a useful model for thinking about the situations in which a Mesoamerican linguistic area could have taken form. Given the diversity of different languages spoken within a relatively restricted area, it is possible that many Mesoamerican people learned and spoke multiple languages. The Mesoamerican people pressed into service as interpreters for the first Spanish invaders certainly were fluent in several unrelated Mesoamerican languages. For those Mesoamerican people from one region who traveled to or lived in other areas, like the foreigners living in distinct neighborhoods in Teotihuacan (see Chapters 4 and 5), multilingualism would have been the norm. From the earliest periods for which archaeological evidence of human behavior is available, multiple opportunities for interaction across linguistic boundaries would have been created as members of different Mesoamerican societies sought materials only to be found in other places within Mesoamerica's complex geography.

Mesoamerica as a geographic space

From a geographic perspective, it is easy to define the Mesoamerican core (Fig. 1.1). The Isthmus of Tehuantepec, where Mexico reaches its narrowest point, serves as a major pivot for Mesoamerican geography. It divides western Mesoamerica, completely contained within Mexico, from eastern Mesoamerica, encompassing eastern Mexico, Guatemala, Belize, and parts of western Honduras and El Salvador. At the Isthmus of Tehuantepec, the Maya-speaking societies of eastern Mesoamerica abutted the territories of diverse non-Maya peoples of western Mesoamerica, often collectively referred to as Mexican: speakers of languages such as Zapotec, Mixtec, Totonac, and Otomi. At the Isthmus of Tehuantepec the territory inhabited by speakers of Mixe-Zoquean languages crosses from the Gulf coast of Mexico to the Pacific Coast of southern Mexico and Guatemala.

East and west of Tehuantepec, the contrast between lowlands and highlands structures Mesoamerican geography, but the balance of these two kinds of settings is profoundly different in the Maya and Mexican zones. In western Mesoamerica, the Mexican highlands are extensive, with a series of upland basins and valleys, extending from the Basin of Mexico to the Valley of Oaxaca, the home territories of distinct Mesoamerican societies. The lowlands of western Mesoamerica, located along the Gulf and Pacific coasts, are narrow strips formed by a series of rivers originating in the highlands.

In eastern Mesoamerica, the lowlands are much more extensive, and were the site of the development of the interconnected Classic Maya city-states. The Yucatan peninsula, a vast expanse of limestone, extends far into the Caribbean, surrounded on west, north, and east by ocean, navigable along an extensive coastline. Rainwater percolates through the porous limestone of the northern Maya lowlands, and surface rivers are found only on the edges of the peninsula. Where the limestone sheet meets the base of the Maya highlands, composed of volcanic and metamorphic rocks, impressive tropical rivers run along the zone of contact. The Usumacinta river system on the west, and the Motagua river on the east, formed important corridors of population and communication, with tributaries reaching up into the highlands. The better-watered southern Maya lowlands, centered on the Guatemalan Department of Peten, and the drier northern Maya lowlands had distinct environmental conditions and histories of occupation.

Despite the ease of identification of the Mesoamerican geographic core, it is more difficult to define precise edges for Mesoamerican geography. Historically, maps of Mesoamerica have used the approximate location of an ecological boundary with more arid lands populated by mobile groups relying on gathering and hunting to demarcate the northern Mesoamerican frontier. This boundary-marking should imply that these hunter-gatherers lived outside the bounds of Mesoamerican society. But it is unlikely that these groups had no significant contact with the residents of city-states that were their southern neighbors. Central Mexican histories of the sixteenth century describe significant historical ties between the ancestors of the Aztecs and northern groups, whom the Aztecs collectively described as "Chichimecs." Aztec myths describe the origin of the founders of Tenochtitlan as a place called Aztlan, also said to be located to the north. Archaeologists do not treat these traditions as literal truth, since there is abundant evidence suggesting that the Aztec state developed from roots in place in the earlier Basin of Mexico (see Chapter 11). But these traditions should alert us to the fact that people of the Mesoamerican core did not view their northern neighbors as outside their social and historical world. Archaeologists working in northern Mexico and the US Southwest have repeatedly documented suggestive evidence of interaction between residents of sites in these areas and places in Mesoamerica.

The difficulty of defining a boundary for Mesoamerican geography is even more acute on the southeastern periphery of the core area. Here, the immediate neighbors of eastern Mesoamerican peoples were not mobile hunter-gatherers, but farmers, many organized in stratified societies that were important trading partners for Mesoamerican states. Objects made in the Maya area have been recovered archaeologically as far south as Costa Rica, and gold ornaments of Costa Rican or Panamanian style have been found in sites in the Maya lowlands. Definition of a southern boundary for Mesoamerica has thus been extremely arbitrary. Based on a review of relatively sparse archaeological data on distributions of selected settlement features and artifacts, the Ulua and Lempa rivers of Honduras and El Salvador were identified as the eastern geographic boundaries of Mesoamerica (Lothrop 1939). More recent archaeological research has shown that even the most complex settlement features proposed as diagnostic of Mesoamerica, ballcourts, were constructed in regions east of these river valleys (Joyce and Hendon 2000). From the lived perspective of local peoples themselves, it would seem that the rivers identified as boundaries of Mesoamerica were not edges separating people, but routes joining them together.

Mesoamerica as a lived place

Rather than being overly concerned with the identification of the edges of Mesoamerican geography, it might be more useful to take just such a lived perspective on the geography of the region. The juxtaposition of highland valleys, basins, and plateaus with lowland regions with markedly different environments and natural resources creates the potential for significant movement of natural resources between starkly different environments (Sanders and Price 1968). A major environmental contrast exists between the drier, cooler highlands and warmer, wetter lowlands. Steep mountain chains parallel both coasts, with active volcanoes on the Pacific side producing flows of lava, used for grinding stones, and of volcanic glass, used for cutting tools.

Marked wet and dry seasons affect the highlands and lowlands differently, and create varying conditions within each zone. Seasonal rainstorms move in across the coast, shedding most of their moisture where they first cross the drier, hotter land surface. As a result, rainfall decreases from east to west across the Maya lowlands and Gulf Coast of Mexico. Along the Pacific Coast, rainfall drops off sharply from the coast to the steep edge of the mountains. Heavy rainfall allowed the development of wet tropical forest in the southern Maya lowlands, eastern Yucatan peninsula, and Gulf Coast of Mexico, and in places along the coastal strip of the Pacific lowlands. Here, high canopies formed by tall trees screen the ground surface, so little undergrowth develops. In these tropical forests, a high number of plant and animal species are found, scattered over the area so that in any area there is a low number of individuals of each species. The ceiba tree and native fruit trees such as nance, sapote, and avocado grow in wet tropical forests. In western Yucatan, the Motagua river valley, and dry upland basins with less rainfall, dry tropical forests develop, also characterized by high species diversity. Lower forest canopy allows more undergrowth to develop. Dry plant communities include plants such as nopal cactus and maguey. In the highest mountain ranges, tropical forests give way to upland pine forests. These are the home of the quetzal bird, prized for its long green tail feathers, and of unique plants such as the bromeliads that grow clinging to the branches of other trees.

Mesoamerica's highlands and lowlands contrast in the distribution of a wide array of natural resources. The volcanic mountains that parallel the Pacific Coast include a series of obsidian flows used at different times by different groups within Mesoamerica. Guinope and La Esperanza in Honduras, Ixtepeque, El Chayal, and San Martin Jilotepeque in Guatemala, Tepeapulco, Pachuca, and Zinapecuaro in Mexico were all heavily exploited by Mesoamerican people, and the material and tools produced were traded over long distances. Distinct rock formations produced a variety of green stones, precious stones used for ritual implements and costume. Major serpentine resources are known in west Mexico and the upper Motagua valley in Guatemala, the sole confirmed source of jade, used for artifacts produced and consumed throughout eastern and western Mesoamerica (Lange 1993).

The lowlands have fewer mineral resources. In some areas, locally available chert and limestone were exploited in place of obsidian and lava. But lowland peoples also obtained minerals from the highlands through exchange for more perishable lowland resources. Precious substances employed in important Mesoamerican practices, including bird feathers used for costume, and cacao, used for a beverage with ritual and social importance, were products of the lowland tropical forests. Animals such as deer, tapir, peccary, jaguar, monkey, and crocodile, abundant in the wet tropical forests, were also exchanged with highland societies. Access to the coast provided lowland peoples with marine resources, including shells, stingray spines, and salt. The movement of local resources back and forth between highlands and lowlands, and within each zone, were among the practices through which diverse societies were integrated into a single Mesoamerican world. Such exchanges are already evident in the earliest phases of village life documented by archaeologists.

Time in Mesoamerican Archaeology

There is no single archaeological chronology that is employed by all archaeologists for all of Mesoamerica, but a broad division into Archaic, Formative, Classic, and Postclassic periods is generally recognized. (In Maya archaeology, Preclassic is often, but not always, used in place of the term Formative, which we use throughout the present volume.) Precise beginning and ending dates given for any of these periods vary with the region and often with the specific author. The contributions to this volume are no exception (see Figure 1.4). With slight differences, however, the contributors have conformed to a single chronological framework for the major periods (Fig. 1.5).

The words used to name these spans of time are significant; they demonstrate that this chronological framework comes from a particular theoretical perspective, one associated with the idea of cultural evolution. From a cultural evolutionary perspective, the history of a region like Mesoamerica is also the story of the gradual development of a cultural peak from its initial roots, and of the decline after that peak. The Classic period was seen as the development of highest cultural value or complexity. Every other period either led up to this peak (from Archaic beginnings, though Preclassic or Formative progressive development) or fell away from it (the Postclassic). Each of these spans of time had a particular character and a characteristic level of development. In the Archaic, people lived as mobile hunter-gatherers. The Formative was initiated by the advent of the first settled villages of farmers. While some Formative villages had leaders in ritual, war, and other activities, these forms of leadership were not codified into permanent, inherited statuses. With the Classic period, fully developed forms of permanent status, and extreme divisions among people, were realized in cities. The breakdown of the Classic cities was followed by the reorganization of new urban societies that were less impressive, smaller, more secular, or otherwise disadvantageously compared to their Classic predecessors.

Period	Dates	Chapter cited
Archaic	8000–1600 B.C.	3
(late)	2400–1600 B.C.	2
Early Formative		
Initial	1600–1200 B.C.	3
Late	1200–900 B.C.	3
Middle Formative	900–400 B.C.	3
	850–300 B.C.	8
Late Formative	400 B.C.–A.D. 100	3
	300 B.C.–A.D. 100	8
Terminal Formative	100 B.C.–A.D. 200	8
Classic	A.D. 250–1000	7
	A.D. 200–800	8
Early	A.D. 200–500	8
Late	A.D. 500–800	8
	A.D. 600–1000	6
Terminal	A.D. 800–1000	12
Postclassic	A.D. 800–1521	8
	A.D. 950–1519	9
Early	A.D. 900–1100	10
Early-Middle (transition)	A.D. 1100–1200	10
Middle	A.D. 1200–1430	10
Late	A.D. 1430–1521	10
	A.D. 1350/1400–1521	11

Figure 1.4. Chronological periods cited by contributors

Dates in years	Period
8000–1600 B.C.	Archaic
1600–900 B.C.	Early Formative
900–400 B.C.	Middle Formative
400 B.C.–A.D. 250	Late Formative
A.D. 250–600	Early Classic
A.D. 600–1000	Late Classic
A.D. 1000–1521	Postclassic

Figure 1.5. Summary chronological framework for Mesoamerica

These broad time-spans, in other words, were not simply periods of abstract time, but rather stages of cultural development. Stages are diagnosed by specific features, which are adopted at various dates by different peoples. As a result, despite using the same broad categories, different researchers assigned slightly different dates to each of these stages, depending on the date of introduction of agriculture, pottery, settled villages, hereditary status, cities, and the like. The beginning of the

Classic period in the Basin of Mexico was correlated with the maximum development of the great city of Teotihuacan. In the Maya area, it was tied to the first use of writing and calendars on public monuments.

Despite a general move away from the underlying assumptions of this early form of cultural evolutionary theory, Mesoamerican archaeology is stuck using an inherited framework of time periods that are really stages. Characteristics that were supposed to define the beginning of a stage are now found to have begun before the initial date of the period of the same name. In the Maya area, for example, written texts and dates on monuments, though rare, are occasionally found in Late Formative sites. In general, archaeologists today treat these names as labels for arbitrary time segments. But they still are concerned with the correlation of developments at different sites, and much theoretical and methodological discussion has been devoted to a better understanding of chronologies across the region.

From superposition to relative chronology

Understanding why different dates are assigned to time periods with the same names in different regions introduces a range of topics often taken for granted by specialists: how archaeologists generate dates for *events*; how these are generalized to time-*spans*; and how theoretical assumptions have affected the development of regional chronologies. In order to construct sequences of events, archaeology is dependent on a number of techniques to establish the *relative* age of material traces: which came first, and which followed after. The fundamental principle of *superposition*, stressed in every introductory textbook as the key to relative dating, brings to mind an image of layers, one on top of another, corresponding to distinct time periods, with the most deeply buried being oldest and the others following in order. In reality, part of the process of establishing relative chronologies does depend on superposition, but in Mesoamerica, superimposed deposits are usually more discontinuous and fragmentary than the layer-cake image presented in most textbooks. In many parts of Mesoamerica, major architectural monuments were rebuilt multiple times, and the layering of stages of construction has been a key to establishing local chronological sequences (see Chapter 4, for example). But fine-grained histories of construction at particular buildings cannot be directly applied elsewhere, even in the same site: the layers superimposed in one place have to be tied to layers superimposed in another.

In the history of Mesoamerican archaeology, the main means of linking together different construction histories has been the identification of distinctive types of artifacts, especially ceramics, found in different layers at different locations within sites and across regions. Artifacts, and especially ceramics, were treated like the "index fossils" of geology, on the assumption that, like natural organisms, styles of pottery had histories with well-defined beginnings and endpoints. In actual practice, archaeologists are used to things being more messy, with examples of pottery types popular at different times becoming mixed together as human beings remodeled buildings and reoccupied previously abandoned terrain. But in each region where any significant amount of work has been accomplished, sequences have been established in the introduction, popularity, and abandonment of groups of pottery types. Such pottery complexes, in combination with superimposed architectural sequences, have been the fundamental basis for local chronology-building. By convention, local units of time derived in this way, called *phases*, are given names unique to particular sites or regions: Barra, Locona, Ocos, and Cherla in the Mazatan region (Chapter 2) and Cuanalan, Patlachique, Tzacualli, Miccaotli, Tlamimilolpa, Xolalpan, and Metepec at Teotihuacan (Chapter 4), for example.

Once such sequences were established in one area, they could be used to help establish sequences in other regions, where items of known relative date had arrived through exchange. Even when items of exactly the type used to create the original sequence were not found, similarities between different regions could be attributed to contact between them, and local sequences coordinated on that basis. The assignment of pottery with Olmec motifs made in distinct local traditions to the period between around 1200 and 900 B.C. (Chapters 2 and 3) is precisely this kind of coordination of different local sequences, not by the presence of an actual "index fossil," but by the common preference for particular ways of making pottery, or other artifacts distinctive of a specific period in time (see Chapter 12).

But this step of correlating different regional sequences raises a problem that Mesoamerican archaeologists continue to grapple with today. The assumption that has to be made is that sites with a shared artifact type or trait are (roughly) contemporaries. This is fine as long as the goal of chronology-building is getting places aligned in a common framework of general equivalence on the scale of centuries. This was the procedure of Mesoamerican archaeology through the first half of the twentieth century, when it was dominated by the approach now called "culture history." Culture historians aimed to establish the distributions across time and space of different traits, understood as part of sets of traits characterizing distinct cultures. This was viewed as a first step required before more anthropological questions could be formulated and addressed, a position critiqued as early as 1948 (Taylor 1948).

The assumption of contemporaneity required to align chronological sequences is particularly problematic if the questions archaeologists want to explore deal with interaction at a human scale, where understanding the direction of interaction from one place to another will depend on finer-grained distinctions in chronology. When chronologies are aligned based on shared relative position and the necessary assumption of rough equivalence, it becomes difficult, if not impossible, to ask or answer questions like "Did the suite of practices recognized as 'Toltec' develop at Chichen Itza, or was the site rebuilt following a Mexican pattern originating earlier at Tula, Hidalgo?" (see Chapter 12). Even within single sites, the correlation of events across different contexts, which may be critical to understanding how the exercise of human agency affected different social segments or institutions, is made more difficult by the homogenizing effect of constructing chronological sequences composed of blocks of time, even relatively short ones like those recognized at Teotihuacan (Chapters 4 and 5). The issue is not simply that the blocks of time are too large; the problem is that the construction of chronologies as blocks of time cuts into segments what may be better thought of as ongoing sequences of events.

In saying things like "hereditary social inequality developed in Oaxaca during the Middle Formative (850–300 B.C.)" (Chapter 8), archaeologists understand that the development described took place sometime during the block of time between the boundary dates. The actual date of the first successful institution of inheritance between generations of wealth, titles, and positions of power might have happened at a human scale during the lifetime of people living early in this block of time, or late. The change in social relationships that allowed such intergenerational transfers and legitimized them may have happened repeatedly during the chunk of time, so that in one village, hereditary social inequality "developed" around 800 B.C., in another around 600 B.C., in another only at 300 B.C., and in yet another, never happened during this span of time.

Archaeologists understand that the use of time segments to organize their discussions is a claim that a particular event or events of interest happened sometime during the block of time, not that the event lasted for the whole period. Archaeologists excavate and analyze the remains of a series of "depositional events," human and natural actions that resulted in the deposit or transformation of material traces of past human activity. Depositional events, including erosion and removal of previously deposited materials, are continuous, but we excavate discontinuous identifiable depositional units in contact with each other at surfaces that may represent substantial gaps in time.

The amount of time it took to create the sediments included in a depositional unit can vary from a very rapid interval to a longer period of time. The amount of time it took to erode or remove deposits, creating interfaces between units, is equally variable. It is as if the layers of the simple model of superposition were created at different speeds. Part of the archaeologist's craft is narrowing in on the length of time that it took to create a particular depositional unit, while simultaneously identifying the relative segment of time within which the activities resulting in that unit occurred. This dual movement is a fundamental requirement for archaeologists who are interested in interpreting large-scale depositional events, like the construction of monuments, in terms of human decision-making and action (Chapters 2 and 4). Knowing the relative order of things, and even the coordination of different relative orders across space, is not enough: the sequence has to be complemented by *measurements* of real time elapsed.

Measuring intervals of time

A number of methods have been used to tie relative chronologies to measured (chronometric) dates. Archaeologists working in areas of Mesoamerica where historical texts with dates are available have taken advantage of these unique resources. Accounts of Maya archaeology often refer to specific years and sequences of events happening over periods entirely encompassed within a named period, such as the Late Classic. This approach is made possible in the Maya area by the presence of monuments with inscriptions using the Long Count calendar, for which scholars agree on a calibration with European calendars (see below).

We cannot assume that the dates inscribed on Classic Maya monuments are necessarily contemporary with the use of the sites where they are found, since historical texts can and do record earlier events. But most dates in Maya texts do appear to fall in the time-spans expected on other grounds. They consequently promise the possibility of interpreting sequences of development in precisely measured intervals, down to a day, for the specific constructions with which they are associated (see Chapter 7). The political histories of Postclassic Mixtecs (Chapter 9) also allow definition of events and spans of history measured in absolute terms. But in this case, the histories are not physically tied to the archaeological deposits, as Classic Maya inscriptions form part of the archaeological sites themselves. Determination of the chronometric dates represented in Postclassic codices helps single out likely candidates for the places that were sites of the events recorded, and provides further support for the definition of beginning and ending dates for specific intervals of time achieved with other archaeological methods of chronometric dating.

These other methods of providing chronometric dates for periods, phases, and depositional events can be applied more broadly, wherever the raw material necessary for analysis is found. Chronometric methods take advantage of natural processes of change that occur at known or precisely measurable rates and that affect common materials found at archaeological sites. A prime example is the use of the known rate of decay of radioactive carbon to produce estimates of the time elapsed from the death of plants or animals, by measuring the ratio between different types of carbon in organic materials that are the remains of these plants and animals. While radiocarbon dating is the most widely employed scientific method supporting Mesoamerican chronologies, other methods have been applied to other materials. Obsidian hydration has been employed at a number of sites, including Copan. This method exploits the natural tendency of volcanic glass to absorb water from the atmosphere, creating a "hydrated" rind on fresh glass surfaces exposed when tools were created. Specific rates of hydration have to be measured for obsidian from different sources used in sites with different environments, and fluctuations in climate over time have to be considered, but the method has the potential to provide estimated dates from material that is abundant in most Mesoamerican sites. Obsidian hydration is particularly promising because the *event* dated is the action of a human being making a tool, presumably for use at a time close to when it was made. This tie to human action is not always obvious, even when a chronometric method produces a precise date.

Chronometric methods produce estimates of an interval of time during which it is highly likely that a specific event took place. In the case of obsidian hydration, that event is the exposure of the fresh surface of obsidian. In the case of radiocarbon dates, the event is the death of the organism from which the carbon sample came. This introduces a series of potential problems well known to archaeologists. A sample could come from a plant that died long before it was used by human beings, or that was reused much later (as when a large piece of timber might be recycled from one building to another). Because trees grow by adding layers of living tissue over dead tissue, even different parts of the same log from a long-lived tree can produce different age estimates. Any sample can be recovered from a deposit created long after the event that would be dated, for example, when trash containing obsidian tools and scraps of plant material was swept up and used as part of the construction fill when a building was remodeled. A single chronometric determination is, consequently, of uncertain significance. Archaeologists seek multiple samples from the same deposits, so that samples that do not belong will stand out.

For each sample evaluated, the possible date of the event that began the process on which the method is based is calculated as a relatively precise estimate. Those estimates are reported by the specialist labs that carry out these analyses as intervals around a central number. For example, Beta-129129, a sample from Puerto Escondido, a site in Honduras where I have excavated since 1994, was reported as 3320 +/− −40 BP ("Before Present," conventionally A.D. 1950). The reported date brackets an interval of 80 "radiocarbon years," and there is a 95 percent probability that the plant providing the carbon sent for analysis died sometime in that interval. Originally, many radiocarbon dates used to measure the beginnings and endings of phases and periods were translated by the archaeologists using them by a simple process of subtraction, essentially counting backward from A.D. 1950. Using that approach, this sample from Puerto Escondido would be presented as equivalent to the date 1370 B.C., plus or minus 40 years, or an interval from 1410 to 1330 B.C. All of the authors who have contributed to this volume use time frameworks that were originally based on this simple process of counting back in radiocarbon years from A.D. 1950.

Unfortunately, this simple conversion procedure is inaccurate, because it was based on the assumption that the concentration of different forms of carbon in the atmosphere has not changed over time. Specialists in chronometric dating have prepared highly detailed graphs showing the divergence between the simple radiocarbon age and the real calendrical age, based on adjustments for fluctuations in atmospheric carbon. For many dates, the effects of this adjustment can be substantial. The sample from Puerto Escondido discussed above actually corresponds to 1690–1510 cal. (calibrated) B.C. Even when the shift in dates seems relatively minor, not calibrating radiocarbon dates can misrepresent the *length* of an interval of time. Sample Beta-129125 from Puerto Escondido was dated 1530 +/− −40 BP, or A.D. 380–460 in radiocarbon years. The actual calibrated date range was cal A.D. 430–625. Not only does calibrating change the date from Early Classic to Late Classic, it greatly increases the span of time within which the event most likely occurred, from 80 to 195 years.

The effects of calibrating do not vary in any single predictable way. Puerto Escondido sample Beta-129126, at 2730 +/− −40 BP, would correspond to the span from 820 to 740 B.C. in radiocarbon years. The calibrated date of cal. B.C. 940–810 shifts the interval earlier (instead of later as in the previous example) and tightens up the interval of highest probability to 70 calendar years (from 80 radiocarbon years). These effects matter when archaeologists are interested in understanding the rate of change and timing of actions within a society. The consistent bias in Early and Middle Formative radiocarbon determinations, where radiocarbon ages are more recent than calibrated ages, has a particularly marked effect on discussions of the earliest village societies in Mesoamerica (Chapter 2). Use of radiocarbon ages also can be expected to create disjunctions with other forms of measuring time in calendar years, including indigenous calendars like those used on Classic Maya monuments and in Postclassic Mixtec codices. As archaeological interests shift to microscale understanding of the actions of agents operating at the scale of human lifespans and generations, divergences like these will have to be resolved.

Indigenous calendars and mathematics

Indigenous calendars in use when the Spanish arrived in Mesoamerica in the early sixteenth century shared a basic structure. All were based on counting sets of individual days. The universal sign in different Mesoamerican writing systems for the number 1, or a single day, was a dot. In the written texts of the sixteenth-century Mexican highlands, larger numbers were represented by rows of dots, sometimes linked by lines. In the Postclassic Maya codices, in contrast, a second sign stood for the number 5. Represented as a solid bar, this sign can be recognized in Classic Maya monuments, as well as in monuments from the Mexican Gulf Coast and Pacific slope of Guatemala dating to the Late Formative period. It also appears in the monuments from Classic and Late Formative Oaxaca. In some examples, the bar is drawn as a thumb, suggesting it stood originally for counting five fingers.

Using these two symbols, numbers could be expressed through combinations of dots (standing for one digit) and bars (standing for five). One dot (1), two dots (2), three dots (3), four dots (4), one bar (5); bar and dot (6), bar and two dots (7), bar and three dots (8), bar and four dots (9); two bars (10), two bars and dot (11) two bars and two dots (12), and so on, went the mathematical notation used by Postclassic Maya, until, after three bars and four dots (19) it reached a full set of 20, the base of the Mesoamerican mathematical system.

Rather than expressing 20 as a set of four bars, the Maya independently developed the use of place notation, including a third mathematical symbol that could serve as a place holder, like the zero of European math. This third symbol allowed Mesoamerican mathematicians to record multi-place numbers. Because the base of the Mesoamerican number system was 20 (rather than the familiar base 10 of European decimal mathematics), each place in pure Mesoamerican math recorded multiples of 20: 20, 400 (20 × 20), 8,000 (20 × 20 × 20), and so on. Sixteenth-century manuscripts recording the tribute paid to the Aztec empire used units of measurement of 20, 400, and 8,000. It is likely that, in addition to being used to measure time, Mesoamerican mathematics had roots in economic transactions (Freidel 1993). But the earliest use of Mesoamerican numbers for which we have evidence is recording dates on monuments, beginning by the late Middle Formative, when a date in the 260-day ritual calendar was carved on San Jose Mogote Monument 3 (Chapter 8).

The 260-day ritual cycle was still in use when the first Europeans arrived in Mesoamerica, and in some Maya communities continues in use today. The cycle combines a sequence of 13 numbers with a series of 20 day names. Beginning on the same date, the shorter cycle of 13 numbers has to restart seven days before the longer cycle of 20 day names. Because the two series are offset from this point on, the second set of 20 day names begins again with the number 8, the third set with the number 2, the fourth with the number 9, and so on, with sets of 20 day names beginning with the numbers 3, 10, 4, 11, 5, 12, 6, 13, and 7. Once 13 sets of the 20 day names are counted, a cycle of 260 days (13×20) is complete, and the two counts return to their first positions simultaneously. Every one of the 260 days can be uniquely specified by its combination of number (from the series of 13) and day name (from the set of 20).

Among the Aztecs, this cycle was named *tonalpohualli* or "count of the days," and was used by diviners to assess the prospects of all manner of proposed projects (see Chapter 11). Most central to every person's life, the tonalpohualli allowed divination of individual life chances, based on birth date (Monaghan 1998). Many Postclassic Central Mexican people used their birth date in the 260-day calendar as a name. The close association of the 260-day calendar with individual birth dates is also evident in much earlier Mesoamerican societies. The inscription on San Jose Mogote Monument 3 has been interpreted as the use of birth date as a name. Later Classic and Postclassic Oaxacan monuments and codices used the 260-cycle positions as personal names as well. Even when the birth date was not used as a name, as on Classic Maya monuments, anniversaries of birth and death were calculated using the 260-day cycle. The close association of the cycle with human fate has led some scholars to propose an origin in human life cycles, as an approximation of nine lunar months, a rough estimate of the length of human pregnancy (Aveni 1980). Other scholars view this cycle as an abstract development, the mathematical product of multiplying two sacred numbers, 20 (a complete cycle) and 13 (a number associated with levels of heavens among sixteenth-century Maya and Aztecs).

While the 260-day cycle is the oldest for which we have direct evidence from inscriptions, it is highly likely that the Mesoamerican solar year was equally ancient. Both calendars likely long preceded the first preserved monumental records of their use. Measurements used to lay out the Early Formative ceremonial center of Paso de la Amada were spaced in multiples of 13, 20, 260, and 365 units, suggesting that already both the 260- and 365-day cycles were calculated (see Chapter 2). The 365-day solar year, in use from Central Mexico to the Maya area when the Spanish arrived, was also based on the fundamental complete unit of 20 days, further subdivided into groups of five days. To approximate the solar year, 18 complete cycles of 20 days and one incomplete cycle of five days were required. This cycle of 18 "months" of 20 days, with a period of five extra transitional days, was the basic civil calendar of the Aztec and Postclassic Maya states. Community-wide ceremonies were scheduled in it, many with clear associations with an annual agricultural cycle.

The combination of the 365-day calendar and the 260-day ritual cycle was the basis among Central Mexican peoples in the sixteenth century of records of periods of 52 years. The measurements recorded at Paso de la Amada suggest that the

52-year cycle was already important in the Early Formative (Chapter 2; see also Chapter 4). Because the beginning points of the two cycles did not coincide until 52 solar years had passed, every single day within a 52-year cycle could be uniquely distinguished by naming its position in the 365- and 260-day cycles. This system was employed in the Postclassic codices from Central Mexico and Oaxaca. Because the entire cycle repeated every 52 years, a date in this system was fixed only relative to other days in the 52-year cycle. By combining the 365- and 260-day cycles with a third cycle, recording changes in the visibility of the planet Venus every 584 days, it was possible to create a double cycle of 104 years, with each date uniquely specified. But the main way that individual cycles of 52 years could be placed in order in Postclassic Mexican historical codices was through their relationship to the genealogical connections of major historical characters over successive generations (Chapter 9). Dates with the same names, based on their position in the 365-day and 260-day cycles, could be distinguished because they were associated with the lives of different public actors.

The earliest records of dates in the 365-day solar year are carved stone monuments dating to the Late Formative period, found in an area extending from the Gulf Coast of Mexico to the Maya highlands of Guatemala. They are combined with records of the 260-day cycle. In addition to the evidence these early monuments provide for the use of the fundamental Mesoamerican 52-year cycle, they also employ a separate continuing time cycle. Most familiar from its extensive use in Classic Maya monuments, scholars call this system the Long Count. The basic unit of the Long Count is a single day. Using the zero symbol and place notation, Long Count dates can record any number of days. Normally, the numbers in the Long Count are arranged in a column, with the lowest place at the bottom and higher places above them. The lowest place records the numbers from 1 to 19 that can be written out using bar and dot alone.

The second place in Long Count dates records multiples of 20 days. This coincidence with the basic 20-day unit of the solar calendar perhaps motivated a slight departure from strict place notation and base 20 math in the third position of Long Count dates. Instead of recording multiples of 400 days (20×20), it records multiples of 360 days (20×18). With this innovation, the first three places in the Long Count correspond to units of a day, a cycle of 20 days (the length of a solar year "month" or 260-day cycle day name series), and an approximation of the solar year (360 days).

As a result of this innovation, each higher position in the Long Count records approximate multiples of years. The fourth place records 20 cycles of 360 days; the fifth, 400 cycles of 360 days. The majority of Long Count dates use only these five positions. In base 20 mathematics, the use of these five positions allowed Mesoamerican people to precisely date any event within a span of almost 8,000 years – far more time than their cultural tradition, or any continuous cultural tradition known anywhere in the world, lasted. In a few extraordinary instances, Classic Maya scribes recorded Long Count dates using positions above the fifth place, arriving at calculations of millions of years.

The use of the Long Count established a common historical frame for those Mesoamerican peoples who employed it. The oldest inscribed Long Count dates discovered so far, from the Late Formative period, have the number 7 in their fifth position. Archaeologists conventionally refer to these as Cycle 7 dates. Early Classic Maya inscriptions feature dates in Cycle 8, those of the Late Classic Maya carry dates in Cycle 9, and the beginning of the Maya Terminal Classic period is conventionally equated with the first dated monuments recording Cycle 10. Once the logic of the Long Count was understood, Mesoamerican scholars realized that the fact that the Long Count calendar is a fixed, absolute dating method promised the possibility of establishing an absolute relation to European calendars. What was required was a date recorded both in the Long Count and in the western European calendar.

Unfortunately, the Maya of the Postclassic did not generally use the Long Count calendar. Instead, they employed a cycle of groups of 20 periods of 360 days (*katun* in Yucatec Maya) in indigenous texts like the Books of Chilam Balam (see Chapter 12). While these katun cycles shared the same positional logic as the Long Count, based on counting days, periods of 20 days, and periods of 360 days, they were not related explicitly to the beginning point that had anchored dates recorded in Cycles 7, 8, 9, and 10. The story of the development of the now widely accepted correlation of western European and Maya Long Count calendars is too complex to cover here (see Aveni 1980:204–210). Records of dates in Maya calendars mentioned in the post-conquest Maya documents, placing the ending of a 360-day period and a katun in the sixteenth century near A.D. 1540, provided one source of evidence for possible correlations. Another key came from the identification of records of astronomical events on Classic Maya stelae and in the Postclassic Maya Codex Dresden. Because the dates for these universally observable astronomical events were known in the European calendar, they provided points of potential correlation. In the Codex Dresden, some of these astronomical events were related to Long Count records.

Using this and other information, specialists were able to narrow in on a few likely correlations between the different calendars. The correlation used today places the first entry of the Spanish into Yucatan in Cycle 11. Based on this correlation, the base date of the Long Count was in 3113 B.C., long before the first settled villages known in Mesoamerica. The dates for Cycles 7, 8, 9, and 10 calculated with this beginning point are generally consistent with the measured dates independently derived from radiocarbon samples from sites with monuments inscribed with Long Count dates. With this correlation as a basis, events in indigenous Mesoamerican texts created during the Late Formative and Classic periods can be reconstructed in absolute time reckoning, opening the door for understanding how the actions of people, described in indigenous historical texts, are related to the larger-scale developments perceptible through archaeological research.

Writing in the Mesoamerican Tradition

Writing was a fundamental part of Mesoamerican culture in the sixteenth century. The use of writing had a long history, extending back at least to the end of the

Middle Formative period. While several specialized writing systems were created and used by different Mesoamerican societies, they shared a number of fundamental features. Foremost among these was the strong relationship between writing and other forms of representing information graphically. Mathematical records are among the earliest examples of written texts known from Mesoamerica, and a uniform set of numeral signs was used throughout the history of the different societies, regardless of other differences in the way they used writing. A dot is the numeral 1, everywhere; it does not change its value, and no Mesoamerican writing system requires use of a different symbol for the numeral 1.

This uniform graphical numeral system is combined with other systems of signs that stood for whole concepts, words, or sounds. These vary from one language and writing tradition to another, which makes sense given the vastly different languages being recorded in different Mesoamerican societies, each with different sounds and grammatical structures. All Mesoamerican systems of signs for text are to some degree pictographic: the signs are derived from drawings of things. Over the long history of individual writing systems, like that of the Maya (extending from at least 200 B.C. to the mid-sixteenth century A.D.), the graphic images that formed the basis for text signs might be highly conventionalized, making it difficult for a modern viewer not steeped in the original visual environment to initially see the representational relationship between a sign and the sound, word, or concept for which it stood. But it is possible in many cases to demonstrate how an image was transformed into a textual sign. Some writing systems, such as those employed at Teotihuacan (Chapter 4), in the Postclassic Mixtec codices of Oaxaca (Chapter 9) and by the Aztecs (Chapter 10) use pictographic signs that are consistently clear images of objects.

Defining a sharp boundary between writing and other forms of graphic visual representation in Mesoamerica is sometimes very arbitrary. In practice, there was a complex relationship between the graphic signs for numbers, words, and sounds, and other graphics that formed images juxtaposed to texts. Texts were placed beside, above, or below images, on monuments, portable objects like pottery vessels, and bark paper or deerskin books. Texts formed part of the overall design of pictures. Individual text signs could be placed within drawings, forming elements of a picture, for example, embedded in the drawing of a headdress or other part of costume. Texts could be laid out so that in order to read them, a viewer's gaze passed through an image. Parts of the picture could be drawn intruding into the text. Text signs themselves were closely related, both in their forms and their use, to non-textual graphic images. The drawing of an object, such as buildings sketched in Postclassic Maya codices, might have the same form as the sign representing the word for the object.

For example, the abstraction of some designs carved on Early Formative pottery (Chapter 3) can be seen either as extreme conventionalization of a common image, or as the kind of abstraction that was the basis for converting some images to service as text signs. Researchers identify groups of abstract, conventionalized, pictographic images as texts in later Mesoamerican societies specifically because they follow rules for arrangement of signs in a linear reading order. Scholars see the linear order of signs in texts as intended to represent a sequence of words whose grammatical order helps to convey meaning. To ensure that a *sequence* of signs would be reproduced, graphic devices that coached viewers to review text signs in a particular order were necessary, so that actors, actions, and the objects of actions could be made clear, without the visual context that makes these relationships clear in a drawing showing an event.

In the Maya writing system, for example, texts were arranged in columns, double columns, or rows, within a regular grid structure joining signs in reading order. Once a reader learned the rules of order, he or she could follow the signs in any Maya text. On carved monuments, texts might be further set off by being raised in higher relief or incised in lower relief. In drawings, including those in the Postclassic Maya codices, texts might be separated from each other by lines outlining a text and related image. In Postclassic Mixtec codices columns of images and texts were separated by lines that led readers down, across, and up the pages which folded out, one after another, into a single continuous sheet.

Earlier Formative images have no apparent linear reading order, and so are not interpreted as texts. But they, and later non-text images, can still be "read" as conveying messages, as *iconography* (literally, writing with images). All Mesoamerican images are arrangements of conventionalized visual elements. The key difference is that images that can be interpreted iconographically have no set reading order, and provide relatively subtle guidance for a viewer's eye. Sequence is less significant in understanding a Mesoamerican image than other relations among elements, like relative prominence in the visual field, signaled by greater size, frontality, placement at a higher elevation within a composition, and greater complexity of detail. The roots of Mesoamerican writing may be seen in the steps through which, in the Formative period, conventionalized graphic signs were added to clarify details not otherwise evident in an image, and abstracted signs were arranged in standard reading order rather than left open to multiple reading orders.

Conventionalization and abstraction of graphic signs was commonplace on the monumental sculpture, carved pottery, and incised jade works of the late Early Formative and early Middle Formative. The animals depicted on pottery vessels could be reduced to elements such as a motif representing a hand or paw, incised alone, recognized as a name-like reference to the crocodilian creature whose foot was represented in the same way (see Chapter 3). Unique elements represented in the headdresses of Gulf Coast Olmec monumental portrait heads can be identified in headdresses of human figures on other Gulf Coast monuments, suggesting these signs stood for a name-like personal or group identification (Grove 1981). While the relative positions of actors, actions, and objects of action can be represented with little ambiguity in non-textual visual images, the specific identity of an actor, a place, or a date is less obvious. The social context within which an image was produced and circulated might initially make these items clear, but as social scale grew, and images remained in view over longer periods of time, the possibility that a viewer would not know the identity of the actor, the time of the action, and where it took place, would grow.

The earliest recorded uses of text-like signs, such as unique headdress motifs on Gulf Coast Olmec monuments, appear to specify precisely this kind of fleeting information without expressing any grammatical intention requiring a specific reading order. The earliest unequivocal texts known, such as the 260-day cycle position recorded next to a human figure on San Jose Mogote Monument 3, have the same effect of recording information about the context of an event that would not be obvious from the picture, but add a linear reading order: the day-number-day sign sequence of the 260-day cycle position. It is in the recording of dates that early Mesoamerican people first impose linear reading order in visual representation, a requirement for the successful understanding of place notation numbers.

The most obvious early instances of the incorporation of text signs into linear order are the earliest inscriptions beginning with Long Count dates, Cycle 7 monuments from sites such as Tres Zapotes and La Mojarra in the Gulf Coast of Mexico. The juxtaposition of abstract signs in a linear order was extended to non-calendrical signs in other late Middle Formative to Late Formative visual media. La Venta Monument 13, a circular stone carved in low relief, shows a single striding human figure. At the left side of the image, a single footprint could be seen as either a naturalistic detail showing the direction from which the figure traveled, or a text sign. A row of three signs in a column ending with a bird head on the right side can be identified as identifications of the person, not unlike the headdress motifs of earlier Formative period sculptures from the Gulf Coast. The whole image suggests a text with linear reading order, from left to right, noting the movement of the named and depicted person.

With the exception of deerskin and bark paper codices of Late Postclassic date, all the written texts known from Mesoamerica are on durable materials that could survive centuries of exposure to the tropical climate. Carved stone monuments are the largest group of objects with written texts known, with some individual Classic Maya sites yielding over one hundred (see Chapter 6). Texts were also recorded on the painted walls of buildings and tombs, with examples surviving from the Maya lowlands, Oaxaca, and Teotihuacan. The content of those texts that have been interpreted deals, as might be expected from their monumental scale and placement in places of assembly within site centers, with political events such as warfare, records of succession in office, visits between rulers of different sites, and the birth, maturation, death, and burial of members of the ruling nobility. The inclusion in many of these public monuments of records of ceremonies, including sacrifices, visions, and dedications of buildings and monuments, has led scholars to see service as ritual specialists as a fundamental role of governing groups throughout Mesoamerica's history.

Texts have also been recorded carved or painted on pottery vessels and other portable objects, including metal, bone, jade, and other stone ornaments. The texts on many such objects can be understood as recording histories on objects that circulated as heirlooms, connecting nobles across generations (Joyce 2000b), including references to the same kinds of ceremonies and public actions mentioned on monuments. Images on painted Maya pottery vessels show what appear to be

fan-fold books very much like the surviving Postclassic codices, but none of these
have survived in legible condition from earlier periods. As a result, the range of
topics covered by known written texts is likely to be skewed toward matters of public
governance and ceremony.

The Postclassic books that have been preserved include content similar to that
of earlier public monuments, such as the histories conserved in Mixtec codices
(Chapter 9). But other Postclassic books include material not represented in
monuments, such as records of astronomical observations and what appear to be
ritual almanacs for use in carrying out rituals or divination (Chapter 12). There is
no way to know what was recorded in the now lost bark paper and deerskin
books from the Classic period or earlier. Allusions in Classic Maya texts to the
deeds of supernatural beings in the far distant past suggest that written books
might have contained mythology, as did the post-conquest texts created by lowland
and highland Maya (Chapter 12). It is also likely that lost perishable texts recorded
economic information not unlike the tribute lists that were created in a hybrid style
in Central Mexico after the Spanish Conquest to represent the economic relations
of the Aztec empire (Chapter 10). What is indisputable is that one way that
Mesoamerican structures were reproduced over time, including after the events of
the Spanish Conquest, was through the reproduction in texts of immense amounts
of historical tradition. Mesoamerican societies were not only literate; they were self-
consciously historical, invoking precedents from the past as grounds for present
action.

The kind of historical precedents typical of Mesoamerica, recorded in European
writing after the Spanish Conquest, have conventionally been called cyclical,
and contrasted with a purported linear sense of time supposedly typical of
western European societies. At times, this emphasis on the cyclical nature of the
Mesoamerican sense of history has led to a characterization of Mesoamerican
people as fatalists, doomed to repeatedly experience the same kinds of events. The
significance of divination in sixteenth-century Mesoamerican societies has been
offered as evidence of this. But the same texts that tell us about Aztec birth-date
divination also record that parents could delay the recognition of a child's birth to
avoid a birth day with bad associations. Classic Maya rulers contrived spectacular
coincidences between the dates of ceremonies, such as inauguration in office, and
astronomical phenomena associated with mythical events. Far from being fatalists
doomed to repeat time cycles that determined their lives, Mesoamerican peoples
appear to have been able to strategically create equivalences between recorded
events and present circumstances, giving meaning to the events of their lives and
the histories of their societies. The histories they drew on had precedents for everything likely to happen, including the invasion of the region by foreign people speaking strange languages and lacking knowledge of the basic forms of civilized life. The
cyclical evidence of their historical tradition assured them that no political regime
lasted for ever.

Mesoamerican historical traditions of the sixteenth century were varied, and each
had specific features. The histories of the most recent centuries recorded in Postclassic codices (Chapter 9) and post-conquest texts like the Books of Chilam Balam

and Popol Vuh, contain records that can be related to archaeologically documented events, such as the abandonment of Mayapan in Yucatan, the battles between Quiche and Cakchiquel Maya in highland Guatemala, and the War that Came Down from Heaven in Oaxaca. Many Mesoamerican historical texts contain descriptions of earlier idyllic societies, often credited with founding institutions such as the calendar, or with inventing crafts and social institutions. The Aztecs identified early innovators as the Toltecs, the people of a great city-state called Tollan.

Apparent references to prestigious Toltec predecessors to Postclassic city-states are part of historical traditions throughout Mesoamerica (Chapters 9, 10, 11, and 12). Archaeologists have long identified these traditions with an archaeological site north of the Basin of Mexico, Tula, Hidalgo, but there is relatively little evidence that this site had the kind of impact across Mesoamerica necessary to inscribe itself in the historical imagination as a kind of Rome (Gillespie 1989). An earlier Mexican archaeological tradition that identified Teotihuacan as the historical model for Tula in Central Mexico may be more correct. Teotihuacan was the first great city-state to have an effect on political affairs over an area reaching to the ends of eastern and western Mesoamerica (see Chapter 7). It is also possible that there were multiple real models for the Toltecs of Postclassic historical tradition. In the Postclassic Maya lowlands, Chichen Itza may have had the same kind of reputation as Teotihuacan had in Central Mexico, as a city much more powerful than any that followed in the late historic period.

Postclassic Mesoamerican historical traditions traced the innovations of governance to mythical cities whose most likely models flourished in the Classic period. The peoples of the Classic period who left recorded traditions of history linked their rulers to supernatural beings active in the first days of time, before the sun rose, when the world was dark like the background color of Maya painted pots interpreted as images of these mythical times. The same imagery is found in post-conquest histories, many of which describe times before the calendar was in use, before the sun rose for the first time. The most elaborate of these post-conquest traditions detail cycles of creation and destruction of the world and living beings before their current era. These traditions are not segregated from the histories of the first great city-states, or from the detailed records of the actions of particular noble and ruling families. They testify to a broadly shared sense of Mesoamerican history. In that broad Mesoamerican historical imagination, common history began when time could be counted with the calendar. The deeds of early heroes and gods prepared the way for human beings. Human beings created great cities which were destroyed, from which the later peoples dispersed. Individual royal and noble histories were validated by connection to these great city-states. Specific local events, institutions, and practices were linked to earlier times. Mesoamerican people practiced "indigenous archaeologies" (Hamann 2002) and created connections to the past through the use of material from earlier cultures, going all the way back to the Olmec (Joyce 2000b). In broad terms, the historical scenarios archaeologists reconstruct were also known to and valued by Mesoamerican peoples.

What Happened in Mesoamerican History?

Because it was an interconnected network of societies, there were historical developments common to all Mesoamerican peoples. Late Archaic hunting and gathering groups in different areas adopted new subsistence practices that required them to schedule cultivation of plants, particularly maize, in their annual round, and provided them with more predictable yields from cultivation. Exchange of materials, including obsidian and plant products, between mobile Archaic peoples had already created connections between the groups that established the first year-round settlements at the time of the late Archaic to Early Formative transition. Repetition of contacts reinforcing shared values, disseminating common practices, and leading to the linguistic and cultural identities across political, linguistic, and social boundaries implied by the term Mesoamerica took place along established routes of social and material exchange among these maize-cultivating, obsidian-working, early villages.

Distinctive material features of Mesoamerican culture developed in some Early Formative sites by 900 B.C. (Chapters 2 and 3; see also Joyce and Grove 1999). They include certain kinds of public architecture, notably monumental platforms and ballcourts; the employment of relief carving as a medium for public and semi-public political imagery; and the use of a restricted range of materials (especially jade or other greenstones) to produce costume ornaments and sumptuary goods. They were unprecedented innovations, a punctuated shift in practices. No later polity recognizable as Mesoamerican lacked its own variants of these features. These developments in the Early Formative circumscribed the choices open to later Mesoamerican peoples (Joyce 2000c; Joyce and Grove 1999).

Early Formative villages in which social differentiation is evident also have evidence for the beginnings of skilled craft production, including obsidian blades from prepared cores, textiles, iron ore ornaments, and pottery vessels (Chapters 2 and 3; see Clark and Blake 1994; Clark and Gosser 1995; Hendon 1999; Joyce 1999). Patronage of social ceremonies accompanied by feasts created occasions on which the products of patronized household craft production were displayed. This contributed to the creation of distinctions between different social groups living within these villages. Simultaneously, the construction of monumental architecture in some villages created different spaces within sites, forming more exclusive groups of people with special access to these non-domestic spaces (see Chapters 2, 3, and 4). Monumental art created at this time represents human actors as mediators crossing boundaries between the everyday world and supernatural world, represented as a cave-mouth of a supernatural being with animal features like those of the crocodile-like species found throughout the lowlands of Mesoamerica. The abstraction of signs standing as personal identifiers reinforced the identification of people in art as specific members of these early societies. Representation in this medium was not open to everyone, another form of exclusiveness. All or most women, children, and older adults were not represented in monumental art (Joyce 2000a).

In Middle Formative Mesoamerican societies, the number of places employing monumental architecture and art to inscribe social differences within individual communities grew. The execution of related imagery on jade objects conflated value (jade) with exclusivity (representation in art), marking a small group of individuals as privileged at multiple sites (Joyce 2000c). The same symbols, forms of objects, and raw material were used throughout Mesoamerica, so it is clear that the marking of exclusivity within these communities was the result of practices that extended throughout the area. The people buried in pyramids at Los Naranjos, Honduras, Chalcatzingo in the Mexican highlands, and La Venta in the Gulf Coast, wear the same kinds of ornaments, even though other characteristics of these sites are quite different (Joyce 1999). By the end of the Middle Formative, writing and calendrical notations were being added to some monumental sculptures, further specifying the historical identities of the persons who monopolized the privilege of being represented.

Mesoamerican societies with evidence of Early and Middle Formative development of social distinction appear to have been unable to integrate social distinction and larger social scale into stable new communities. Across Mesoamerica, the chronological boundary between the Middle and Late Formative is associated with shifts in site histories. Distinct developmental trajectories are found in each region. Some societies (such as those in the Valley of Oaxaca and Maya area: Chapters 6, 7, and 8) employed writing and historical monuments in public spaces. Others (notably Teotihuacan: Chapters 4 and 5) emphasized monumental architecture without display of dated texts.

Sites that flourished starting in the Late Formative grew to much greater sizes than their predecessors, and featured complex internal differentiation between rich and poor, politically powerful rulers and the commoners they ruled, along with specialization in crafts and other social roles. These city-states continued to develop throughout the Classic period. They were linked together by complex social, economic, and political ties. Teotihuacan, in particular, seems to have been a center whose status was acknowledged by nobles as far away as the Maya lowlands (Chapter 7). Exchange of material goods among Classic cities apparently accompanied social exchanges, including religious pilgrimages, marriages between nobles, and other ceremonies initiated by events in the lives of individual people. Exchanges between ruling nobles reinforced common structures of value with deep histories in Mesoamerica, while increasing the divide between rulers and those they ruled.

In every region studied to date, the transition from the Classic to the Postclassic period involved disruptions in some existing city-states. This includes evidence for burning and defensive works at Teotihuacan and sites in the Maya lowlands, and malnutrition, ill-health, and population decline at sites where there is evidence for environmental damage, such as Copan (Chapters 4, 7, and 12). But other city-states flourished at the same time, sometimes clearly at the expense of declining cities like Teotihuacan, whose neighbors Xochicalco and Tula grew in the early Postclassic.

Across Mesoamerica in the Early Postclassic, nobles of many newly founded or newly prominent city-states shared a complex of material practices that distinguished them from the people they ruled in household culture and public ritual (Chapter 12). The cosmopolitan preferences for the same luxury goods on the part of Early Postclassic nobles fueled development of new craft centers for the production of metal ornaments and luxury pottery. The city-states dominated by Postclassic nobles emphasized militaristic imagery, and may have featured the first permanent standing armies in Mesoamerica. The histories of these city-states included complex political, social, and military negotiations (Chapter 9).

Early Postclassic cities gave rise to the first tribute states in Mesoamerica's history, culminating in Central Mexico in the growth of the Aztec tributary state (Chapters 10 and 11). At the end of the sixteenth century, Mesoamerica was organized in a series of highly urbanized city-states, with institutionalized government, inherited social distinction, and high degrees of social stratification. But it was also still an area bound by shared values, shared calendars and traditions of literacy, and shared historical consciousness traced back to the time when Olmec sites of the Gulf Coast of Mexico first took form. It is no accident that an Olmec jade mask was among the objects placed in pits under the foundation of the Aztec Great Temple. Mesoamerican states shared a sense of history reinforced by practices ranging from the everyday, taken-for-granted routines of daily life to the events timed by the common calendar, aimed at marking relationships between humans, supernatural beings, and the natural world.

What Happened in the History of Mesoamerican Archaeology?

The study of Mesoamerican archaeology has not been static. From beginnings in nineteenth-century antiquarianism, nationalism, and imperialism, archaeology has been institutionalized in both North America and Latin America, where the majority of contemporary researchers are based. Major theoretical developments in Americanist anthropology have affected the development of the field, as did the complex currents of the cultural heritage industry and tourism in the twentieth century. Space does not allow thorough discussion of any of these topics (see Chinchilla 1998; Hervik 1998; Oyuela Caycedo 1994). But some major intersections with the contributions to this volume should be singled out for comment.

Spanish colonial accounts of the complex societies of Mesoamerica fell into historical disuse in the late seventeenth and eighteenth centuries. By the beginning of the nineteenth century, it was news in Europe and North America that there were ruins of a great civilization, rivaling that of the Classical Mediterranean, concealed in the tropical forests of Central America. Speculation concerning the origins of the people who built these ruins included claims of connections to lost civilizations buried beneath the ocean, and to the ancient Egyptians.

But many scholars in the eighteenth century worked on the assumption that the ancestors of the native peoples in the region had been the builders of the great pyramids of Teotihuacan, Chichen Itza, and Copan. Antiquarians from the US, France, Germany, and Great Britain traveled throughout the region after independence was declared from Spain, collecting archaeological objects, historic documents, and ethnographic materials, sometimes in conditions of dubious legality. From these roots modern scholarship of Mesoamerica grew, fostered in North America by newly founded anthropology museums in New York, Washington, and Chicago, and at Harvard and the University of Pennsylvania.

For the social elite of the newly independent republics of Mexico and Central America, the material remains of prehispanic cities were a legacy that provided a means to promulgate distinctive national identities rooted in the region. Familiar today from the works of Mexican writers such as Octavio Paz, and Guatemalan authors such as Miguel Angel Asturias, nineteenth-century nationalists developed the ideology of *mestizaje*, an origin through mixture of the strength of indigenous and Spanish cultures. (As has often been remarked, mestizaje leaves no place for the modern peoples of African descent present throughout the region as a result of the institution of slavery. Skin color becomes complexly mixed with markers of identity potentially more open to manipulation or even personal choice, such as language and dress.)

Two refrains that run through nineteenth- and twentieth-century ideologies of mestizaje are intimately related with archaeology. First, in mestizaje ideologies, the great prehispanic past was a fallen past, in one way or another. The Classic Maya had collapsed and disappeared, and the modern Maya-speaking people were at best their highly degraded descendants, the purest being the Lacandon people, represented as pre-agricultural. The Aztec, while the dominant polity in the sixteenth century, were cruel and corrupt, having built an empire on savage conquest and unbridled human sacrifice. Second, mestizaje ideologies represented the future of the region as one of inevitable cultural mixture, as if the distinct native peoples were disappearing and being assimilated. The rhetorical image for this was Doña Marina (or La Malinche), the native woman who translated for Cortes, and whose children were, it was claimed, the "first mestizos."

From the perspective of mestizaje, archaeological sites and objects were a national patrimony, representing the cultural history of an emerging mixed population with all of its "hybrid vigor." In each country, different archaeological sites became the symbol for a singular indigenous heritage. In Mexico, archaeology of Central Mexico was emphasized, with Aztec sources providing the basis for reconstructing prehispanic Mexican history. As a consequence, the names of Aztec deities were employed throughout the region, regardless of local languages and differences in religion and belief. In Guatemala, beginning already in the 1830s, selected highland archaeological sites were subjected to investigation: Utatlan, Mixco Viejo, and (transgressing national borders) Copan (Chinchilla 1998). Honduras emphasized its Maya heritage, represented uniquely by Copan.

For North American researchers, the significance of the Central American sites was somewhat different. They constituted an alternative to the Greco-Roman heritage of Europe, supporting the concept of the Americas as a "new world" independent of the religious and political traditions of European monarchies. Literacy was key in this discourse, since the relative status of researchers dedicated to the study of the past was linked directly to what was considered the degree of advancement of their subjects, which in turn was measured by the mastery of writing by the people being studied (Hinsley 1985). With the largest body of texts, including complex mathematical and astronomical calculations, the Maya quickly became the favored subject of study, without respect to new boundaries between the Central American republics. Those Maya sites with limited use of writing, including all Postclassic sites, many Highland Maya sites, and sites in the southeastern Maya lowlands of Honduras, were not of interest, except for comparison.

By World War I, researchers from North and Central America with these (and other) agendas had succeeded in sketching the outlines of a basic cultural evolutionary sequence enshrined in the chronological periods or stages discussed above. The sixteenth-century Mesoamerican societies were understood as great empires, militaristic and secular successors to Classic city-states. These Classic city-states in turn had developed from simpler societies of farmers, perhaps sharing roots with the complex societies of South America. The framework of Preclassic, Classic, and Postclassic, while as yet not firmly associated with absolute dates, already was well developed.

World War I, and the closely coincident Mexican Revolution, brought a hiatus to archaeological research in the area. At about the same time, archaeological research in North America had been transformed by institutionalization in academic departments of universities. These institutions dominated the succeeding growth of Mesoamerican archaeology. They approached the field with quite different concerns than their museum-based antiquarian predecessors. North American archaeologists, trained in the few existing anthropology programs in the country, shared an interest in developing space-time distributions of cultural traits, the hallmark of cultural history. They emphasized cultural particularism and, while maintaining the cultural evolutionary framework they had received, treated it more as a set of time periods than as cultural stages. Mexican archaeologists developed similar archaeological projects under a more explicit cultural materialist theory of social evolution, often explicitly identified as Marxist. Regardless of theoretical orientation or institutional base, the archaeologists operating in this period emphasized the same primary cultural identifications, of Mexican archaeology with the Aztecs and their immediate predecessors in Central Mexico, and Central American archaeology with the history of the rise and fall of Classic Maya society.

For researchers working between the world wars, indigenous Mesoamerican people were a reservoir of conservative traits, physical, cultural, and linguistic, that were in danger of disappearing, and overlaid with layers of superficial Spanish culture that could be peeled back like layers of an onion. Archaeologists worked closely with, or even as, ethnographers, documenting cultural practices that were believed to be in the process of disappearing, as a way to explain and interpret prehispanic archaeological sites. No recognition was given to the possibility that living indigenous people might have particular interests in archaeological sites, different from those of other members of national populations. Even when independent Maya attempted to communicate their unique interests in specific archaeological sites, such as Tulum and Chichen Itza (Sullivan 1989), scholars did not apparently see this as a different kind of claim on the past.

World War II again interrupted the course of Mesoamerican archaeology. At the same time, Americanist anthropology was beginning to experience changes, leading to renewed concern with the processes of cultural change. Walter W. Taylor (1948) famously called Mesoamerican archaeology, particularly that of the Maya, to task for sterile cataloguing of things with no attempt to explain how they worked (functionalism) or how they were related to each other (structural functionalism). In the post-war era, archaeology throughout the Americas saw a renaissance in terms of degree of effort, new intellectual programs, and new methodological approaches. In the US, university education was newly available to men who had served in the army, and university departments of anthropology began to expand. By the early 1960s, new sources of funding existed for anthropological archaeology. Technologies such as carbon dating and the use of air photos were applied to Mesoamerican archaeology.

One development probably deserves more credit than any other for changing the emphasis of North American archaeological research in the region: the appointment of Gordon R. Willey as Bowditch Professor at Harvard University in the 1950s. With archaeological experience in North and South America, Willey was a graduate of Columbia University where he was a protégé of W. Duncan Strong. He approached Mesoamerica from the perspective of Julian Steward's cultural ecology, a theoretical model that argued that different levels of cultural complexity were linked in regular, but not deterministic, fashion to environmental conditions, including the human environment provided by past societies and contemporary groups. Willey developed and applied a regional approach to archaeology in order to obtain the kind of information that would be necessary to employ this approach. His settlement survey of the Belize river valley inspired methods still standard today.

Settlement survey took as its focus a region, not a site. All the sites in a region were considered to be part of a system of interlocked economic and social units. Differences in the size of sites would be indications in differences in economic power within a region, and probably of social prominence and political authority. Settlement patterns would provide the basis for selecting sites for excavation that would allow the archaeologist to explore the full range of social activity. The influence of Willey's approach was profound. William Sanders, his first Ph.D. student, applied the approach, and with his colleagues, refined it, in the landmark Basin of Mexico survey project (see Chapter 11).

In the Maya area, researchers following Willey's Belize Valley Project identified the smallest repeated unit of settlement with the fundamental economic unit of society, the household, and argued that understanding this basic unit would be a key to understanding society as a whole (Flannery 1976; Wilk and Ashmore 1988). Coinciding with the rise of processual archaeology in North America in the 1960s and 1970s, the development of household archaeology was concerned with formulating research problems so that they could be tested scientifically. A link was made between the house compound (a group of buildings, exterior space, and external features like storage pits) and the ethnographically identifiable household (a group of people sharing the labor of carrying on from day to day and perpetuating themselves through bearing and raising children). This was a bridging argument that allowed archaeologists to formulate assumptions, for example about the division of labor by sex and age, and specify what characteristics in a site would lend support to, or disprove, their assumptions.

The combination of settlement survey and household archaeology became the fundamental approach of North American archaeologists working in the area. Settlement surveys often started with the definition of an area around a highly visible site, labeled a political or ceremonial center, and proceeded to explore the distribution of other sites presumably related economically, politically, and socially. Major sites central to regional settlement survey projects were the focus of extensive excavation in projects like those of the University of Pennsylvania at Tikal, the multi-institutional Basin of Mexico project at Teotihuacan, and the University of Michigan in the Valley of Oaxaca.

The assumptions made in settlement pattern surveys about the regional influence of larger sites reinforced other existing biases toward the excavation of major sites. Antiquarian interests in excavation as a means to acquire museum specimens for foreign institutions were replaced by nationalist interests in building museums within the countries in the region. The newly excavated sites became important points for national histories drawing on the prehispanic past. By the late 1970s, archaeological sites in the region were explicitly understood as cultural heritage, and archaeology was practiced as often because sites were caught up in development projects as because of an abstract academic interest in ancient societies or cultures. Archaeological sites and museums started to play a larger role in the economies of the region, as mass cultural tourism began to develop. Major projects at sites like Copan were launched in the late 1970s specifically to improve the visitor experience.

This was not the first time that archaeological research had responded to the imperatives of visitation. Archaeologists working at Chichen Itza starting in the 1920s, and at Copan in the 1930s and 1940s, were among those who explicitly worked to restore architectural monuments in the Maya area for later visitors. In Mexico, Leopoldo Batres engaged in extensive restoration at Teotihuacan even earlier (see Chapter 4). But, beginning in the 1970s, international financing was targeted to this purpose. The entry of Mesoamerican archaeological sites into the World Heritage Register of UNESCO paralleled the rise of development-funded projects. Mexico invested substantial funding in creating tourist zones, including those on the east coast of Yucatan that now serve as gateways for international tourism to Maya archaeological sites.

The focus of development archaeology was in some ways a return to the nineteenth-century emphasis on sites and objects as isolated antiquities. Archaeologists working with such development and tourism projects have adapted their research projects and questions to the kind of extensive clearing and consolidation required to prepare sites for visitation. Extensive excavations of noble residences at Copan, funded by such projects, have provided an unparalleled body of information about the particulars of life in a specific residential neighborhood (see Chapter 6). These results have influenced the research approaches of subsequent projects,

even when there is no direct requirement for tourism rehabilitation. Extensive clearing of residential groups has become a key method in many areas of Mesoamerica
(see Chapter 5). New methods have been applied, including soil chemistry and
residue analyses, to derive maximum information about past human behavior from
such broad area excavations. This in turn has re-emphasized the diversity of activities carried out in what earlier were regarded as interchangeable basic units of
society, and has been one spur to new interest in practice theory and human agency
among some archaeologists.

Other currents of contemporary research have also raised issues of action and
agency in Mesoamerican archaeology. Among the most significant have been
advances in interpretation of writing and art, and the development of interest in
archaeologies of subjectivity, beginning with approaches to gender. Both theoretical currents take a perspective pitched to individual human actors, the subjects,
authors, and patrons of art and texts, and the positioned subjects of gender archaeology. Many of the people who have developed approaches to the archaeology of
gender have drawn on art and texts (see Chapters 6 and 12, for example). But the
two approaches also differ in important ways. An account of their similarities and
differences positions Mesoamerican archaeology now, at the beginning of the
twenty-first century.

The Mesoamerican Subject

From its beginnings, Mesoamerican archaeology has been intensely concerned with
the social position of the people under study. Initially, this was framed in terms of
group identity, particularly ethnic identity. The concern was to link ancient sites
with living peoples, to allow researchers to use extensive observations of living
people to fill in their static picture of the past. The assumption was that each group
of people had a unique ethnic identity, coincident with their styles of material
culture and language. The influence of ideas of nationalism current in the nineteenth century was obvious.

But at the same time researchers were aware of, and interested in, social differences within these complex societies. While all the residents of Tenochtitlan might
be Aztec, only some were nobles, and only one was the *tlatoani* ("speaker," the title
for the maximum political authority). Archaeologically, some people were more perceptible than others, and some people's actions were likely to have had more visible
effects than others. Some had been warriors, others craft workers, and archaeologists could identify differences between people with different life courses in their
excavations. Burials, especially, forcefully suggested highly individualized statuses.

The identification of specific human actors in visual images was a tool of these
early forms of archaeological research into different human subjectivities. A. M.
Tozzer's study of the art of Chichen Itza identified different ethnic groups, occupational groups, and social status groups represented by figures carved throughout
the site (Tozzer 1957). Once Tatiana Proskouriakoff (1960) established that Classic
Maya art and inscriptions were histories of the lives of individual people, the door

was opened for the development of detailed interpretations of Maya Classic texts as genealogies of specific nobles and rulers. Similar efforts have been made in other literate traditions in Oaxaca (Chapters 8 and 9) and even in art lacking formal texts from the Gulf Coast of Mexico (Chapter 3).

The explanations of ancient social reality based on analyses of art and writing at times have the appearance of "great man" history, in which individual rulers cause wholesale societal change. This is most obviously due to the necessary reliance of researchers on a selective sample of material, writing in the form of public political monuments and royal courtly regalia. Most glaringly, these media tend to represent relatively few women, and almost no young or elderly people. More subtly, of course, they are records only of a segment of politically powerful wealthy social groups.

The modern archaeological interest in gender is generally traced to the early 1980s. But in Mesoamerica it would be more accurate to credit Proskouriakoff's (1961) article on the identification of women in Classic Maya art. Other scholars followed her lead in identifying noble Maya women, even reigning women, through iconography, the interpretation of texts, and burial analysis (e.g. Coggins 1975; Marcus 1976). Starting in the 1980s, a flood of publications documented the presence and actions of women in various Mesoamerican traditions, from the Olmec to Aztec, the Maya lowlands to Oaxaca. At the same time, scholars actively engaged in household archaeology began to question the assumption that the interests of all members of a household were the same, and started to create models of the dynamics between men and women within households (for example, Hendon 1997). These researchers, while drawing on representations of individual women and men in art, were not limited to this form of evidence, and could reach down to the lowest social strata sampled archaeologically.

Both lines of research, the study of actors recorded in historical texts and images, and of actors with different subject positions, including gender, age, and social status, converge on the issue of the place of social agents in making their own world. Issues of agency and practice theory underlie many of the contributions to this volume. The roots of practice theory in archaeology lie in social anthropology since the 1960s (see Ortner 1984, 2001). Practice theories posit that the focus of social analysis should be on the ways that human agents work within structures to which they are habituated while growing up in a particular society. Structures are not abstract entities outside individual people; they are embodied by human actors, and come to be naturalized as givens about the world. Actors can become aware of structures, but never completely recognize the structures that influence their actions and are reshaped through them.

In these theories, actors engage in performances that are more or less routinized, with both expected and unexpected outcomes. Among the outcomes of action are the reformulation of structures, their reproduction over time, always with change. When actors choose their actions from among multiple options that they perceive as possible, we can say that they are exercising agency. Not all action is an exercise of agency. A requirement of agency theory is that agents understand themselves to have choices (although they need not be correct in this understanding, nor need they know all the options available to them). This knowingness places them in a position to consciously intend some outcome which may reinforce or change structures. But even when exercising agency, an actor is as likely to produce unintended consequences as those he or she intends.

In contemporary archaeology, issues of defining the exercise of agency occupy center stage (Dobres and Robb 2000; for Mesoamerica, see Clark 1997, 2000; Gillespie 2001; Hendon 2000; A. Joyce 2000). Debate exists over whether agency is always a property of an individual, or can be exercised by a group (such as a household, a craft group, or a military society, to give a few Mesoamerican examples). But there is general consensus that agency and practice provide archaeologists with a set of tools with which to bridge the gap between the traces of individual action we can see archaeologically, and the questions we have, as social scientists, about how societies come to have an appearance of coherence over space and time – in Mesoamerica, for example.

REFERENCES

Aveni, A. F., 1980 *Skywatchers of Ancient Mexico*. Austin: University of Texas Press.

Campbell, L., 1976 Middle American languages. In *The Languages of Native America: Historical and Comparative Assessment*. L. Campbell and M. Mithun, eds. Pp. 902–1000. Austin: University of Texas Press.

Campbell, L., and T. Kaufman, 1976 A linguistic look at the Olmecs. *American Antiquity* 41, 80–89.

Campbell, L., T. Kaufman, and T. C. Smith-Stark, 1986 Meso-America as a linguistic area. *Language* 62, 530–570.

Chinchilla M. O., 1998 Archaeology and nationalism in Guatemala at the time of independence. *Antiquity* 72, 376–387.

Clark, J. E., 1997 The arts of government in early Mesoamerica. *Annual Review of Anthropology* 26, 211–234.

——2000 Towards a better explanation of hereditary inequality: A critical assessment of natural and historic agents. In *Agency in Archaeology*. M.-A. Dobres and J. Robb, eds. Pp. 92–112. London: Routledge.

Clark, J. E., and M. Blake, 1994 The power of prestige: Competitive generosity and the emergence of rank societies in Lowland Mesoamerica. In *Factional Competition in the New World*. E. M. Brumfiel and J. W. Fox, eds. Pp. 17–30. Cambridge: Cambridge University Press.

Clark, J. E., and D. Gosser, 1995 Reinventing Mesoamerica's first pottery. In *The Emergence of Pottery*. W. K. Barnett and J. W. Hoopes, eds. Pp. 209–221. Washington, DC: Smithsonian Press.

Clark, J. E., and M. E. Pye, 2000 The Pacific Coast and the Olmec question. In *Olmec Art and Archaeology in Mesoamerica*. John E. Clark and Mary E. Pye, eds. Pp. 217–251. Studies in the History of Art 58. Washington, DC: National Gallery of Art.

Coe, S. D., 1994 *America's First Cuisines*. Austin: University of Texas Press.

Coggins, C. C., 1975 Painting and drawing styles at Tikal: An historical and iconographic reconstruction. Doctoral dissertation, Department of Art History, Harvard University. Ann Arbor: University Microfilms.

Dobres, M., and J. Robb, eds., 2000 *Agency in Archaeology*. London: Routledge.

Flannery, K. V., ed., 1976 *The Early Mesoamerican Village*. New York: Academic Press.

Freidel, D. A., 1993 Jade Ahau: Toward a theory of commodity value in Maya civilization. In *Precolumbian Jade: New Geological and Cultural Interpretations*. F. W. Lange, ed. Pp. 149–165. Salt Lake City: University of Utah Press.

Gillespie, S. D., 1989 *The Aztec Kings: The Construction of Rulership in Mexican History*. Tucson: University of Arizona Press.

——1993 Power, pathways, and appropriations in Mesoamerican art. In *Imagery and Creativity: Ethnoaesthetics and Art Worlds in the Americas*. N. Whitten and D. Whitten, eds. Pp. 67–107. Tucson: University of Arizona Press.

——2001 Personhood, agency, and mortuary ritual: A case study from the ancient Maya. *Journal of Anthropological Archaeology* 20, 73–112.

——2002 Body and soul among the Maya: Keeping the spirits in place. In *The Space and Place of Death*. H. Silverman and D. B. Small, eds. Pp. 67–78. Arlington, VA: American Anthropological Association.

Grove, D. C., 1981 Olmec monuments: Mutilation as a clue to meaning. In *The Olmec and their Neighbors: Essays in Memory of Matthew W. Stirling*. E. P. Benson, ed. Pp. 49–68. Washington, DC: Dumbarton Oaks Research Library and Collections.

Hamann, B., 2002 The social life of pre-sunrise things: Indigenous Mesoamerican archaeology. *Current Anthropology* 43, 351–382.

Hanks, W. F., 2000 *Intertexts: Writings on Language, Utterance, and Context*. Lanham, MD: Rowman & Littlefield.

Hendon, J. A., 1996 Archaeological approaches to the organization of domestic labor: Household practice and domestic relations. *Annual Review of Anthropology* 25, 45–61.

——1997 Women's work, women's space, and women's status among the Classic-period Maya elite of the Copan valley. In *Women in Prehistory: North America and Mesoamerica*. C. Claassen and R. A. Joyce, eds. Pp. 33–46. Philadelphia: University of Pennsylvania Press.

——1999 The Preclassic Maya compound as the focus of social identity. In *Social Patterns in Pre-Classic Mesoamerica*. D. C. Grove and R. A. Joyce, eds. Pp. 97–125. Washington, DC: Dumbarton Oaks Research Library and Collection.

——2000 Having and holding: Storage, memory, knowledge, and social relations. *American Anthropologist* 102, 42–53.

Hervik, P., 1998 The mysterious Maya of National Geographic. *Journal of Latin American Anthropology* 4, 166–197.

Hinsley, C., 1985 From shell-heaps to stelae: Early anthropology at the Peabody Museum. In *Objects and Others: Essays on Museums and Material Culture*. G. W. Stocking Jr., ed. Pp. 49–74. History of Anthropology 3. Madison: University of Wisconsin Press.

Hirth, K., 1992 Interregional exchange as elite behavior: An evolutionary perspective. In *Mesoamerican Elites: An Archaeological Assessment*. D. Z. and A. F. Chase, eds. Pp. 18–29. Norman: University of Oklahoma Press.

Joyce, A. A., 2000 The founding of Monte Albán: Sacred propositions and social practices. In *Agency in Archaeology*. M. Dobres and J. Robb, eds. Pp. 71–91. London: Routledge.

Joyce, R. A., 1999 Social dimensions of pre-classic burials. In *Social Patterns in Pre-Classic Mesoamerica*. D. C. Grove and R. A. Joyce, eds. Pp. 15–48. Washington, DC: Dumbarton Oaks Research Library and Collection.

——2000a *Gender and Power in Prehispanic Mesoamerica*. Austin: University of Texas Press.

——2000b Heirlooms and houses: Materiality and social memory. In *Beyond Kinship: Social and Material Reproduction in House Societies*. R. A. Joyce and S. D. Gillespie, eds. Pp. 189–212. Philadelphia: University of Pennsylvania Press.

——2000c High culture, Mesoamerican civilization, and the Classic Maya tradition. In *Order, Legitimacy, and Wealth in Ancient States*. J. Richards and M. Van Buren, eds. Pp. 64–76. Cambridge: Cambridge University Press.

Joyce, R. A., and D. C. Grove, 1999 Asking new questions about the Mesoamerican Preclassic. In *Social Patterns in Pre-Classic Mesoamerica*. D. C. Grove and R. A. Joyce, eds. Pp. 1–14. Washington, DC: Dumbarton Oaks Research Library and Collection.

Joyce, R. A., and J. A. Hendon, 2000 Heterarchy, history, and material reality: "Communities" in Late Classic Honduras. In *The Archaeology of Communities: A New World Perspective*. M. A. Canuto and J. Yaeger, eds. Pp. 143–160. New York and London: Routledge.

Kirchhoff, P., 1968 Meso-America: Its geographic limits, ethnic composition, and cultural characteristics. In *Heritage of Conquest*. Sol Tax, ed. Pp. 17–30. New York: Cooper Square Publishers.

Lange, F. W., ed., 1993 *Precolumbian Jade: New Geological and Cultural Interpretations*. Salt Lake City: University of Utah Press.

Lothrop, S. K., 1939 The southeastern frontier of the Maya. *American Anthropologist* 41, 42–54.

Marcus, J., 1976 *Emblem and State in the Classic Maya Lowlands*. Washington, DC: Dumbarton Oaks.

McAnany, Patricia A., 1995 *Living with the Ancestors: Kinship and Kingship in Ancient Maya Society*. Austin: University of Texas Press.

Monaghan, J., 1990 Sacrifice, death, and the origins of agriculture in the Codex Vienna. *American Antiquity* 55, 559–569.

——1998 The person, destiny, and the construction of difference in Mesoamerica. *Res* 33, 137–146.

Ortner, S. B., 1984 Theory in anthropology since the sixties. *Comparative Studies in Society and History* 26, 126–166.

——2001 Commentary: Practice, power and the past. *Journal of Social Archaeology* 1, 271–275.

Oyuela Caycedo, A., 1994 Nationalism and archaeology: A theoretical perspective. In *History of Latin American Archaeology*. A. Oyuela Caycedo, ed. Pp. 3–21. Aldershot: Avebury.

Proskouriakoff, T., 1960 Historical implications of a pattern of dates at Piedras Negras, Guatemala. *American Antiquity* 25, 454–475.

——1961 Portraits of women in Maya art. In *Essays in Pre-Columbian Art and Archaeology*. S. K. Lothrop, ed. Pp. 81–99. Cambridge, MA: Harvard University Press.

Pye, M. E., and J. E. Clark, 2000 Introducing Olmec archaeology. In *Olmec Art and Archaeology in Mesoamerica*. John E. Clark and Mary E. Pye, eds. Pp. 9–18. Studies in the History of Art 58. Washington, DC: National Gallery of Art.

Sanders, W. T., and B. Price, 1968 *Mesoamerica: The Evolution of a Civilization*. New York: Random House.

Sullivan, P., 1989 *Unfinished Conversations: Mayas and Foreigners Between Two Wars*. Berkeley: University of California Press.

Taube, K., 1985 The Classic Maya Maize God: A reappraisal. In *Fifth Palenque Round Table, 1983*. M. G. Robertson and V. Fields, eds. Pp. 171–181. San Francisco: Pre-Columbian Art Research Institute.

——1989 Maize tamale in Classic Maya diet, epigraphy, and art. *American Antiquity* 54, 31–51.

Taylor, W. W., 1948 *A Study of Archeology*. Menasha, WI: American Anthropological Association.

Tozzer, A. M., 1957 *Chichen Itza and its Cenote of Sacrifice: A Comparative Study of Contemporaneous Maya and Toltec*. Harvard University, Memoirs 11 and 12. Cambridge, MA: Peabody Museum of American Archaeology and Ethnology.

Wilk, R. R., and W. Ashmore, 1988 *Household and Community in the Mesoamerican Past*. Albuquerque: University of New Mexico Press.

Willey, G. R., 1966 *An Introduction to American Archaeology*, vol. 1: *North and Middle America*. Englewood Cliffs, NJ: Prentice-Hall.

2

Mesoamerica Goes Public: Early Ceremonial Centers, Leaders, and Communities

John E. Clark

Some of the probable causes for the rise of Mesoamerican civilization still stand as its most enduring and spectacular effects – its proud architecture and expansive plazas. Public buildings and communal space have been identified at some of the earliest villages in proto-Mesoamerica, centuries before any developments there of complex societies. Construction of these public spaces and framing structures involved visionary village leadership and volunteered social surpluses, all of which led to the historic accident now revered as Mesoamerican civilization. These non-domestic structures and spaces figure prominently in explanations of Early Formative developments, as either integrative or divisive features of a built environment, and such buildings and their implied coordinated labor are also implicated in recent proposals for the origins and manifestations of social and political inequality. In this chapter I present evidence for early public architecture and plazas and evaluate recent models linking them to the emergence of hereditary leaders and semi-civilized society.

The basic pattern of Mesoamerican civilization and stratified society was clearly in place by 1300 cal. B.C. among the Gulf Coast Olmecs. Therefore, any consideration of developmental trajectories leading up to pristine civilization must focus on earlier histories. Because formative developments in the Gulf Coast are poorly attested, I consider developments outside the Gulf region in the Valley of Oaxaca and the Mazatan zone of Chiapas, Mexico (Fig. 2.1), the only regions of Mesoamerica for which adequate diachronic data are available for pre-1300 cal. B.C. settlement patterns, public architecture, and domestic practices. Local histories of each region have attracted speculation and model-building. The most recent crop of models involve what Richard Blanton, Gary Feinman, Stephen Kowalewski, and Peter Peregrine (1996; see also Blanton 1998; Feinman 1995, 2000a, 2000b, 2000c, 2001; Feinman et al. 2000; Peregrine 2001; cf. Rosenswig 2000) dub "corporate" and "network" strategies or modes of political economy. In bringing together the most recent data for Oaxaca and Mazatan, it is appropriate to address

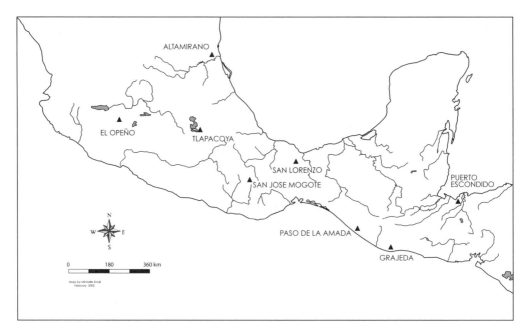

Figure 2.1. Map of Middle America showing the location of Early Formative sites

recent claims concerning collective organization, types of leadership, and societal evolution in early Mesoamerica.

At 2000 cal. B.C., the area of Middle America that would become Mesoamerica was sparsely inhabited by tribal horticulturalists; a millennium later, Mesoamerica's first civilization had already collapsed after three centuries of dominance. Evidence indicates that a major shift occurred in settlement and subsistence practices during the terminal Archaic, with groups becoming more dependent on horticulture and cultigens. There is pervasive evidence of large-scale forest burning and use of corn and manioc, indicative of slash-and-burn agriculture, about 2400 cal. B.C. (Clark and Cheetham 2002; Zeitlin and Zeitlin 2000). In the Valley of Oaxaca, only one minor occupation in a rockshelter has been identified for this period (Marcus and Flannery 1996), and on the Chiapas coast the only secure evidence comes from shell middens in the coastal estuary (Clark and Cheetham 2002; Voorhies 1976, 1996). Late Archaic hunters, fishers, and gatherers were seasonally mobile collectors, and they employed simple technology and engaged in some long-distance exchange of obsidian (Nelson and Voorhies 1980).

The Early Formative represented a fundamental shift from preceding Archaic practices, the most obvious being the adoption of ceramic technology, the creation of sedentary villages, and presumed changes from horticulture to agriculture and from achieved egalitarian ways to pampered privilege. The end of the Early Formative saw the emergence of Olmec civilization in the Gulf Coast lowlands. San Lorenzo was arguably a true city there by 1200 cal. B.C. and accommodated thousands of inhabitants and sprawled over $5 \, km^2$ (Clark 1997; Cyphers 1996; Symonds et al. 2002; cf. Flannery and Marcus 2000). The central portion of this city was an elevated, ostentatious place with large, elaborate residences, monumental sculptures of rulers and supernatural beings, formal terraces, and probably public plazas (see Coe and Diehl 1980; Symonds et al. 2002). San Lorenzo clearly had high chiefs or kings, attendant nobility, patronized artisans, merchants, and a servile class. In short, the Early Formative period was truly revolutionary, with fundamental changes occurring in technology, subsistence, domestic life, political practices, public rituals, art, beliefs, and personhood, among others.

My principal research concern for this period is the emergence of hereditary inequality, the fundamental antecedent social transformation that made Meso-american civilization possible. Critical developments all occurred during the middle centuries of the second millennium B.C. after the advent of sedentism, village agri-culture, and the appearance of ceramic technology. I accord greater attention to the Mazatan case because I know it better, and critical data for early developments there of social inequality have not been previously published. The basic facts of the Oaxaca case have been widely disseminated for the past few decades by Kent Flannery and Joyce Marcus and their collaborators (see Flannery 1968, 1976, 1999; Flannery and Marcus 1976a, 1976b, 1983, 1990, 1994, 2000; Flannery et al. 1981; Marcus 1989, 1998, 1999a, 1999b; Marcus and Flannery 1994, 1996, 2000). The utility of comparing these two local developments is strengthened by their ecolo-gical and historic differences. The Valley of Oaxaca is semi-arid highlands, and Mazatan is a lowland, tropical zone. Some differences in their regional histories and developments, therefore, may be due to divergent ecological possibilities for har-vesting and deploying surpluses (Marcus and Flannery 1996) or to contrasting political strategies (Rosenswig 2000).

I propose that necessary events leading to the emergence of hereditary inequal-ities and political offices were the development of self-perceived communities from dispersed villages and concomitant shifts in personal identities between elites and commoners (see Hill and Clark 2001). These shifts in private and public percep-tions of "being" and "belonging" were wrapped up with the construction and use of public spaces and formal centers. The earliest known ceremonial center in Mesoamerica is Paso de la Amada of coastal Chiapas, Mexico (Blake 1991; Clark 2001, forthcoming; Hill et al. 1998; Lesure and Blake 2002). Due to fortuitous cir-cumstances of site history and preservation it is the only Early Formative center for which there is information on community design (Clark forthcoming). Rank society there developed about 1600 cal. B.C., partly as a consequence of creating formal, public space (Clark 1994; Clark and Blake 1994; Hill and Clark 2001).

Models of Early Leadership, Organization, and Political History

One of the analytically challenging aspects of working with the origins of hereditary inequality is that the data are generally ambiguous, by definition, and can be validly interpreted in multiple ways. Interpretive difficulties concern the archaeological signatures for various kinds of inequality, archaeological signatures for processual or historic changes, and analytical concepts of socio-political conditions and processes that correspond to the formation of personal and public identities. The three most reliable datasets for monitoring differences in socio-economic statuses have traditionally been burials and their offerings, the relative elaboration of domestic structures, and the relative labor investment in public architecture. The archaeological record, however, has long proffered the challenge of societies that look complex and unequal on one or more of these dimensions but not on others.

The shared assumption connecting universal models with recent explanations for social and political developments in the Valley of Oaxaca and Mazatan is that agents and agency matter. Adoption of action theory represents a major shift from earlier, human ecology explanations for the evolution of complex society in these regions (see Coe and Flannery 1964; Flannery 1976; Flannery et al. 1981; Flannery and Marcus 1983). The two archaeological cases are difficult to characterize and have been interpreted in divergent ways (Lesure and Blake 2002). The earliest evidence of rank society and hereditary inequality for highland Mesoamerican societies comes from the site of San Jose Mogote in the northern arm of the Valley of Oaxaca (Fig. 2.1) for the beginning of the San Jose phase, 1350 cal. B.C., or 1150 B.C. in radiocarbon years (Flannery and Marcus 2000:3). San Jose Mogote was the largest village in the Oaxaca Valley during the Early and Middle Formative periods. The transition there from egalitarian to rank society is evident in changes in settlement patterns, the form and size of public architecture, the first evidence of elite residences, and differential mortuary practices (Marcus and Flannery 1996:93–110).

For the Mazatan zone of Chiapas, Mexico, the best evidence for a transition from egalitarian to rank society places the transition at about 1600 cal. B.C. and consists of special residential architecture, settlement hierarchies, differential consumption and production of special goods, and possible differential mortuary practices (Clark 1994; Clark and Blake 1994). Given small sample sizes, these data are not yet compelling. Changes in residential architecture and settlement patterns constitute the best evidence for the emergence of rank society (see below), while data for different burial treatments remain inadequate, although suggestive (Clark 1991, 1994). In a comparative analysis, Marcus and Flannery (1996:91) interpret a large, elevated residence at Mound 6 at Paso de la Amada, Mazatan (Fig. 2.1), as a public structure and, consequently, as evidence of communal institutions in an egalitarian society. In their view, the large building identified as a chiefly residence by Blake (1991; see Hill and Clark 2001; Lesure and Blake 2002) served a function analogous to public buildings reconstructed for early San Jose Mogote (see below). They opine that the processes for the emergence of rank societies in Mesoamerica were broadly parallel for the inhabitants of each region (Flannery and Marcus 2000). Lesure and Blake (2002) consider Marcus and Flannery's proposal, as well as others, and present cogent arguments for identifying the early platforms at Paso de la Amada as foundations for domestic residences rather than for public/ritual structures.

As judged by archaeological configurations, neither the Oaxaca nor the Mazatan case fits the predictions of recent corporate/network models (Lesure and Blake 2002:21). Differences in residential architecture and consumption patterns are minor, as are differences in mortuary offerings and burial treatments. The public architecture identified to date is also rather modest and differed in character, history, and its impact on socio-political developments in each region.

In a model for the origins of rank society in Mazatan, Michael Blake and I (Clark and Blake 1994) proposed a suite of environmental and social circumstances involved in the emergence of hereditary inequality. The crux of our proposal was that, of the numerous conditions favoring the emergence of hereditary inequality, certain kinds of agents with specific propensities would also have been necessary. We baptized these individuals "aggrandizers" – agents who aggressively pursued fame and fortune through culturally acceptable means within the constraints of an egalitarian ethos and practices. I have since emended the original model (Clark 2000; Hill and Clark 2001) to accord greater sensitivity to different kinds of agents and their motives as well as to negotiated identities. But the model still features motivated individuals and deployments of resources of various sorts toward self-serving ends, as evaluated from the perspectives of situated agents.

Blake and I never considered aggrandizers as a stage of leadership, but rather as a type of agent. We portrayed hypothetical aggrandizers as frenetic and single-minded individuals – descriptive excesses involved with initial stages of model-building (see Clark 2000). We have not knowingly written of aggrandizer "strategies," only motives, options, and chosen courses of action within parameters set by cultural practices and their histories. Aggrandizers "pushed the envelope" of the permissible in their pursuit of personal renown, and many were innovators. Some of their conjectured activities include ritual feasting and drinking, sponsor-ship of craft specialists, long-distance exchange, gift-giving, competitive sports, and communal construction projects (Clark 1997, 2000; Clark and Blake 1994; Hill and Clark 2001). In our view, the development of rank society, ascriptive leader-ship, and rudimentary government were unanticipated consequences of changes in cultural practices and perceptions that arose from competition among aggrandiz-ers within the Mazatan region. The most recent explanation for the origins of rank society in the Valley of Oaxaca bears strong similarities to an aggrandizer model. Marcus and Flannery (1996:88) argue for the necessary presence of certain kinds of agents and actions during this transition. They see the transitional stage of egal-itarianism at San Jose Mogote and its environs as one of groups organized around competing, charismatic leaders (analogous to New Guinea big-men) that evolved into rank systems similar to those reported ethnographically for highland Burma.

The proposed explanations for developments in Oaxaca and Mazatan see special kinds of agents as *necessary but insufficient conditions* leading to the transformation of egalitarian society. Important differences in the models concern the types of activ-ities undertaken by the dominant agents and their supporters, and detractors, as well as the antecedent conditions set by the local environment and societal histo-ries. The ability of aggrandizers to move and shake their societies depended on access to resources of various sorts, and their continued success at such tactics had to do with benefits ostensibly delivered to supporters. One activity that peoples in both regions engaged in was collective building projects. These required the consumption of stored foodstuffs to feed workers. As Saitta (1994a, 1994b, 1994c, 1997, 2001) argues, the surplus process is critical for understanding social organization and its transformations. The problem of how surplus may have been stockpiled in each region, however, is not my present concern. The potential for surplus production in each region is described by various authors (Blake et al. 1992; Clark and Blake 1994; Feinman 1991; Feinman and Nicholas 1987; Marcus and Flannery 1996). For current purposes, I assume surpluses were available and used. In the remainder of this chapter I consider the use of social surpluses in the construction of public works.

Early Public Buildings and Spaces

The construction and use of public spaces and buildings are thought to have been critical in the historic transition to rank society in both Oaxaca and Mazatan. I consider similarities and differences between regional developments here as they pertain to questions of public architecture and site planning. Claims for "public" spaces and buildings are not equivalent in meaning in different models. In the Oaxaca model "public" means "non-domestic, supra-household, or non-private," or "restricted use, vicariously for a broader public" for the pre-rank period. In subsequent periods there "public" is used to mean "open to common view," "common access or shared usufruct rights." The Mazatan model considers "public" in the sense of "open commons" and as "use entitlements." A comparison of distinct, regional histories suggests that the demarcation of communal space and erection of different kinds of public buildings may have been a key element in both the conservation of egalitarian village society (Oaxaca) and its subsequent transformation (Mazatan).

Public buildings at San Jose Mogote

The Oaxaca story largely concerns the village of San Jose Mogote during the period 1700–1100 cal. B.C., or the Tierras Largas phase and the first part of the San Jose phase. The story begins after major shifts to sedentism, maize agriculture, and ceramics had already occurred at the close of the Late Archaic. San Jose Mogote is located in the northern arm of the semi-arid Oaxaca Valley, in the middle of the highlands (Fig. 2.1). It was by far the largest village in highland Oaxaca during this period, and it grew to become an early center by late San Jose times. By the end of the Tierras Largas phase (ca. 1350 cal. B.C.), there were at least 19 villages and about 700 (463–925) inhabitants in the greater Valley of Oaxaca (Marcus and Flannery 1996:78), representing an estimated population density of less than 1 person/km^2 (Feinman 1991:242). Most people lived in widely dispersed hamlets 1–3 ha in size, while San Jose Mogote extended about 7 ha (Marcus and Flannery

1996:79). Early residents at San Jose Mogote lived in "nine discrete residential areas," with an estimated population of 170–350 people (Marcus and Flannery 1996:78–79). Outlying hamlets consisted of 5–10 comfortably spaced, small house-holds of 4–5 people, each household with its own yard and storage pits. Over 50 percent of valley population, however, clustered around San Jose Mogote in the northern branch valley, the location of the most favorable soil and ecological con-ditions for farming as well as the best access to a variety of raw materials and food-stuffs from adjacent mountain slopes (Marcus and Flannery 1996:81–82).

By the end of the San Jose phase (ca. 950 cal. B.C.), San Jose Mogote was clearly the ritual and civic center of a chiefdom. The village center had expanded to about 20 ha in extent, with adjacent barrios extending the greater community to 60–70 ha, with population estimated variously at 700 (Marcus 1989:165), 1,000 (Marcus and Flannery 1996:106), and 791–1,976 inhabitants (Marcus and Flannery 2000: 364). The number of villages in the valley had doubled by this time, and the number of persons had trebled, half of whom lived in San Jose Mogote (Marcus and Flannery 1996:106). There was also evidence of a privileged elite, as mani-fested in burial offerings and differences in domestic architecture. The nature of public buildings had also changed to larger, more visible platforms on formal, stone-faced terraces (Flannery and Marcus 1976a, 1976b; Marcus 1989; Marcus and Flannery 1996). But these changes followed the transformation to chiefdom society rather than preceding it. The main story of public architecture at San Jose Mogote concerns the earliest buildings constructed during its heyday of village egalitarianism.

Near the western edge of the San Jose Mogote village cluster, overlooking the Atoyac river, Flannery and his co-workers discovered in a $300\,m^2$ area eight one-room buildings, dating to Tierras Largas and early San Jose times, that they believe were used sequentially (Flannery and Marcus 1976:210–211). The build-ings' special construction, form, features, orientation, evidence of periodic replas-terings, and hyper-cleanliness distinguish them from contemporaneous domestic structures. Marcus and Flannery (1996:87) interpret these sequentially rebuilt buildings as ancient Oaxacan equivalents of Men's Houses, "initiates temples," or *kivas*, known ethnographically, in which ceremonies were carried out by a select group of villagers for all the rest. "Periodically each such building was razed, and a new one was built on virtually the same spot. Measuring no more than $4 \times 6\,m$, these buildings could only have accommodated a fraction of the community" (Marcus and Flannery 1996:87). They may have been used as "limited-access struc-tures where a small number of fully initiated men could assemble to plan raids or hunts, carry out agricultural rituals, smoke or ingest sacred plants, and/or com-municate with the spirits" (Marcus and Flannery 1996:87). As characteristic of their chosen ethnographic analogs, these buildings are thought to have served an inte-grative function that promoted social solidarity. In short, they are a classic example of what Blanton and his colleagues (1996) consider a corporate "strategy." The rites conducted in these confining structures might have served to dissipate social ten-sions (at least among a segment of the adults in the community) and promote social cohesion.

The argument that these buildings were used for non-domestic functions is strong, but considerable doubt remains over the claim for sequential rather than concurrent use. In Flannery and Marcus's descriptions, the implication is that the eight special buildings represent a superimposed series of structures on the same spot, with the argument for a temporal sequence being a necessary inference derived from superimposition. Flannery and Marcus mention eight examples of small, one-room, plastered buildings built on low "platforms," but thus far have provided partial floor plans, profiles, and excavation coordinates only for Structures 3, 5, 6, and 7, with Structure 6 being the most complete and most widely illustrated (Drennan 1983:48; Flannery and Marcus 1976a:209, 210, 1976b: 379, 1990:24–27, 1994:32, 34, 124, 127, 129–132, 290–291, 358; Flannery et al. 1981:69; Marcus 1989:159, 160, 162, 1998:80, 87, 1999a:60, 1999b:72; Marcus and Flannery 1996:87, 2000:363). In the published examples, the "platforms" are really just wide wall foundations, with an outside step up, which enclose a sunken floor on the same level as the living surface outside the building; "it would be more accurate to say the building was 'surrounded' by a platform rather than 'set on' a platform" (Marcus 1999a:61). The main features in the interiors of these buildings were a step (sometimes called an "altar" in earlier statements) down to the sunken or "recessed" floor and a small, cylindrical hole near the center of the floor, sometimes filled with powdered lime. Flannery and Marcus illustrate the central lime pits for Structures 6 and 15 (Flannery and Marcus 1990:26, 1994:130; Marcus 1989:161), but additional details for Structure 15 have not been published. Information for the other three public buildings also remains unpublished.

Recent release of excavation coordinates for Structures 3, 5, 6, and 7, and of the excavation grid for Area C of San Jose Mogote, shows that these structures do not represent a superimposed series of buildings, and, in fact, there is no stratigraphic overlap of the Tierras Largas phase buildings (Flannery and Marcus 1994: figs. 9.2, 11.1, 11.5, 13.1–13.4; see also Figure 2.2). The limited plan and profile drawings reveal that no public buildings were erected over Structures 3, 6, or 7, and we do not know what lies beneath the well-preserved, sunken floor of Structure 6 because it was "consolidated for posterity" (Flannery and Marcus 1994:129), but the north–south profile (Flannery and Marcus 1994: figs. 13.1–13.4) shows that it rests on the same Stratum G as do Structures 3 and 5. Although it does not show up on the long profile, Structure 7 must partially overlie Structure 5. All of the buildings appear to be slightly different, at least with the orientation of their probable entrances. Of special interest, the differing orientations of entrances of these different buildings makes them appear as planned sets rather than the strict recreation of a standard building type. The plans, profiles, and different orientations suggest that a plausible interpretation of these structures may be that groups of them saw concurrent rather than sequential use.

The ambiguities in the descriptions for sequential buildings in the 300 m² "public" area of San Jose Mogote, coupled with the long phases, raise the real possibility that some buildings were used concurrently, side by side. If so, an important modification to the explanatory model for these buildings will be necessary. One of the most remarkable features of some of these buildings is that they were

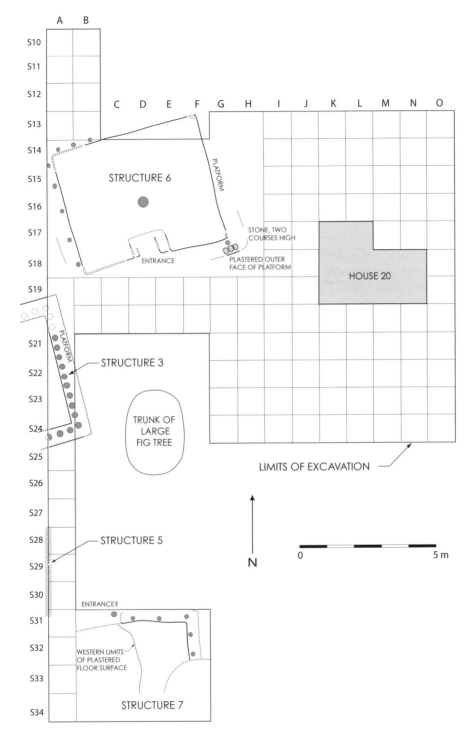

Figure 2.2. Excavation grid for Area C at San Jose Mogote, Oaxaca, Mexico, showing the locations of Structures 3, 5, 6, 7, and House 20. House 20 dates to 1700 cal. B.C. (the Espiridion complex) and is the earliest structure known at the site and the only evidence of a pre-Tierras Largas occupation. The gray squares indicate units that had remnants of floor rather than the shape or orientation of the structure. (Assembled and redrawn from Flannery and Marcus 1994: figs 9.2, 11.1, 11.5, 13.3, 13.4, and 18.1)

deliberately razed – but by whom, and why? The implication in Flannery and Marcus's descriptions is that virtually identical buildings were placed nearly directly above the footprint of demolished predecessors, but this was clearly not the case for the four structures for which plans and profiles have been provided, so the destruction of one and erection of another cannot be linked in any tight chronology or to any single episode of collective labor, as implied in current explanations.

There remains ample reasonable doubt concerning building contemporaneity to leave open the possibility of some concurrent use. If concurrent use occurred, then the various identified "public" buildings could each have represented different segments of the greater community and could have served competitive ends rather than integrative ones. Alternatively, different buildings could have served different functions. If so, the destruction of these buildings would have had a different significance. Add to this the usual proviso, given the small area excavated at San Jose Mogote, that other examples of such buildings could still be found in other sectors of this site. Marcus and Flannery's (1996:87) chosen ethnographic analogs (men's houses, kivas, and initiates shrines) are particularly interesting in this regard because such ritual facilities can and do occur in multiples in single villages, where they serve lineage or cult functions rather than community-wide ones.

Only a select segment of the village ever had access to the hypothesized rites carried out in these dark structures. Each building could only accommodate about two dozen adults under cramped conditions, and they would have had to stand, sit on the floor, sit on the inner lip of the wall foundation, or to have brought their own stools. The one-room structures may have served a supra-household, perhaps lineage function, but they were not "public" in any sense of "in common view" or "for common use." Public spaces for later Mesoamerican centers were "stages" for public performances. The buildings at San Jose Mogote, following this thespian metaphor, were more like changing rooms for costuming rather than venues for public displays. In fact, it was not until after the emergence of rank society about 1250 cal. B.C. that these cubicles were eventually replaced by larger, open structures and platforms that appear to have served the community as a whole. These latter public buildings were erected in a different area of the site, with Area C being converted into a residential zone. Domestic houses were built over the pancaked remains of the early public buildings (Flannery and Marcus 1994:291).

A strong case can be made that the new forms of public architecture at San Jose Mogote were adopted from trade partners in conjunction with other cultural practices of ascriptive rank (see Clark 1997; Lowe 1989, 1998; Symonds et al. 2002). What is particularly interesting in the Oaxaca case is what is thought not to have happened. Practices associated with rank society showed up late there and corresponded to broad changes coeval with the early Olmec horizon (see Chapter 3). As long as the secretive, club houses or lineage houses were the predominant supra-household buildings, this large village appears to have remained egalitarian. The shift in the public architecture program, and the community planning it implicates, appear to have been consequences of changing political organization adopted by locals from foreigners in a broader interaction network. The public spaces at Mazatan reveal a different history.

Paso de la Amada as a ceremonial center

My argument for the origins of rank society in Mazatan rests on inferences concerning the past use of early buildings at Paso de la Amada (see Blake et al. n.d.; Lesure and Blake 2002), and on a new claim presented here that it was a ceremonial center in the full sense of the term. Early Formative villages are thought to have been clusters of households of related kin, with a focus on subsistence pursuits and domestic rituals. My use of "ceremonial center" signals the earliest known case of a site that served this additional function on a community-wide scale, the earliest known so far for Mesoamerica. Those of us involved in the Mazatan Project have consistently portrayed Paso de la Amada as a large, rustic village in our previous work – but we have been guilty of a naturalistic bias and of underestimating the achievements of these early villagers. Heretofore, we have accorded Mother Nature and lazy (efficient) agents too much credit for the configuration at this site. Our early maps embraced the presumption that domestic residences were constructed on natural rises and that these were especially favorable locations for staying above rainy-season floodwaters (cf. Lesure and Blake 2002:4, fig. 1). But Paso de la Amada evinces too much structure and evidence of planning to have been an ad hoc configuration of huts dictated by a haphazard dispersal of elevated ground. Numerous excavations have also shown that our assumptions about high ground were incorrect; many early houses are found a meter below the current, level ground surface, well below the level of mound summits, and all excavated mounds have proved to be man-made platforms. Finding a ballcourt in 1995 was the final stroke that undermined our naturalistic bias. I think the evidence is convincing that Paso de la Amada was planned and constructed as a formal center dating back to at least 1650 cal. B.C. Evidence for regional settlement for this same time period demonstrates a spatial pattern of similar settlement segments, each with its central village and satellite hamlets. Paso de la Amada was the largest, central village of the region.

The Mazatan story benefits from a tighter chronology than is available elsewhere in Mesoamerica (see Blake et al. 1995: table 1). The earliest villages in Mazatan date to the Barra phase (1800–1650 cal. B.C.), with the earliest and best evidence for rank society dating to the beginning of the following Locona phase (1650–1500 cal. B.C., equivalent to early Tierras Largas times in Oaxaca). The most important site was Paso de la Amada, and it is the site for which we have the most adequate information from excavation, survey, and continuing urban disturbance (see Blake 1991; Ceja 1985; Clark 1994; Lesure and Blake 2002; Lowe 1977). Paso de la Amada was abandoned at the time of major Olmec contact, about 1250 cal. B.C., and a rival center elsewhere in the Mazatan zone became the capital (see Clark 1997; Clark and Pye 2000).

Based on analysis of ceramic collections, 31 Barra-phase sites have been identified in survey and excavation in the Mazatan zone. Paso de la Amada extended over 10 ha during the late Barra phase. During this time, and at the beginning of the following Locona phase, there "appear to have been at least ten units of comparable size in the village cluster. The various pockets of occupation, with their associated special residence, appear as neighborhoods or barrios and could possibly represent groups of related kin" (Clark 1994:380). I estimate population for Barra phase Paso de la Amada at 270–380 people, and for the 200 km^2 Mazatan region over 600, a population comparable to the late Tierras Largas population of the Valley of Oaxaca, but 300 years earlier and in an area a tenth its size. In Locona times Paso de la Amada and the population in Mazatan increased more than tenfold, reaching a population density of about 30 persons/km^2 (Clark 1994:212); greater Paso de la Amada reached its maximum extent of about 140 ha. Of the 256 sites thus far recorded for the district of Mazatan, 162 have known Locona occupation.

These are "analytical" sites, recorded for convenience in survey, rather than "natural" ones. By "natural" site, I mean a site that may have been recognized by its occupants as a natural social or political unit. Natural sites, which consist of one or more analytical sites, are shown in Figure 2.3. We have previously published Paso de la Amada as an analytical site extending about 50 ha (see Lesure and Blake 2002:4, fig. 1). The site, as originally defined, is the zone of the tallest and broadest mounds and thus encapsulates what we consider the formal ceremonial center. If we designate "greater" Paso de la Amada as the continuous distribution of Locona settlement, it is at least 140 ha, and could be considerably more depending on how far apart settlement clusters have to be to be considered separate. If 200 m is sufficient for separation between sites, then greater Paso de la Amada is comprised of the analytical sites of Mz-7, Mz-160, Mz-169, Mz-170, Mz-250, Mz-251, and assorted finds between these components (see Clark 1994: appendix 5).

In earlier studies (Clark 1994; Clark and Blake 1994) I avoided these messy problems of site definition and calculated site populations based on the number and extents of known components for the analytical sites and their summed hectares. Thus, intervening "empty" areas within natural sites were eliminated from any calculations. I am now attempting to determine "natural" site boundaries per phase. "Natural" boundaries of a site can only be determined by assessing its extent in any given phase. For Mazatan, this could only be done after surface collections were thoroughly cleaned. Field conditions are such that most surface ceramics look like undifferentiated crud ware until cleaned. In essence, I have treated the Mazatan zone as one large site and have collected it carefully by small components of about 30 to 50 meter squares. I have reassembled these components to determine the most likely natural boundaries. The pattern shown in Figure 2.3 represents natural clusters of settlement for the Locona phase.

A combination of fortuitous environmental circumstances, site history, and investigation decisions allows us now to reconstruct the configuration of the Locona phase community at Paso de la Amada. This site is located inland and so has avoided deep burial beneath river alluvium, unlike its contemporaneous Locona centers located along the margins of the Coatan river, thus some of its former configuration is still visible on the surface. Equally important, Paso de la Amada was abandoned about 1250 cal. B.C. and never again reoccupied. Given the history of dense settlement for the Mazatan zone, the conservation and avoidance of the early mounds there must have been a conscious decision to not disturb this once early center. Even after the past six decades of plowing following the deeding of this land

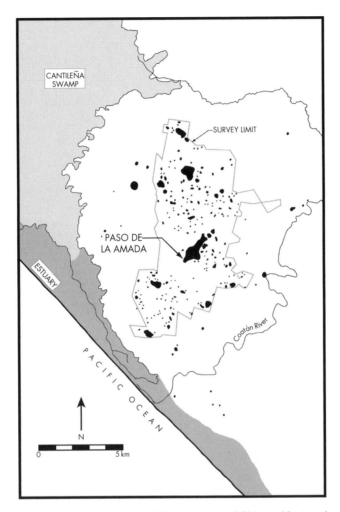

Figure 2.3. Locona phase settlement in the Mazatan zone of Chiapas, Mexico, showing the location and size of natural sites. The boxed area represents 100 percent survey coverage

to an agrarian cooperative, some of the mounds at the site are still substantial. In his initial pace-and-compass map in 1974, Jorge Fausto Ceja (1985) identified 43 mounds, and he tested seven of them, as well as areas between mounds. In the process he demonstrated the site's early date. Gareth Lowe (1977:211) described Paso de la Amada as having a formal plaza, an impressionistic claim we have tried to falsify in our investigations which began in 1985. From 1985 to 1995, Michael Blake (1991; Blake et al. n.d.) supervised extensive excavations in the largest mounds of the southern sector of the site, and test and trench excavations also continued in a dozen others. With the exception of Warren Hill's recent discovery of a clay-surfaced ballcourt at Mound 7 (Hill 1999; Hill et al. 1998; Hill and Clark 2001), all other excavated mounds at Paso de la Amada appear to have been domes-

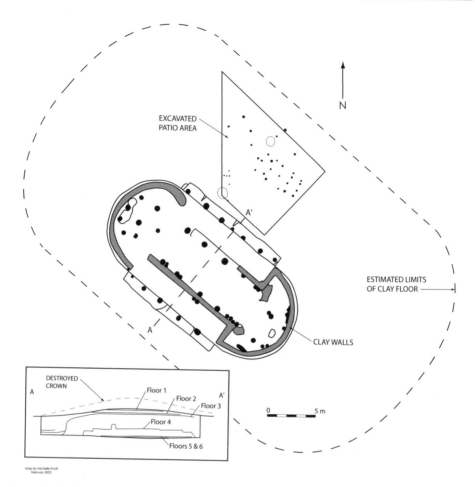

Figure 2.4. Structure 4, Mound 6, Paso de la Amada, Chiapas, Mexico. The northeastern court-yard for this structure was discovered in the last field season and has not been previously illus-trated or discussed. The cross-section shows the sequential floors found in this mound

tic structures (Blake 1991; Blake et al. n.d.; Clark 1994; Lesure 1997a, 1999; Lesure and Blake 2002), including Mound 6, interpreted by Marcus and Flannery (1996:90) as an "initiates' temple."

Mound 6 represents a series of at least nine large structures, built one directly above the other (Fig. 2.4). Traces of the latest buildings have been found only on the edges of the mound because modern plowing has decapitated Mound 6 by more than a meter and a half, according to the testimony of Alberto Sanchez, its first ejido farmer. All sequential buildings in Mound 6 repeat the same general orienta-tion and size. Structure 4, the most elaborate recovered, measured 21.7 × 12.1 m. The Mound 6 platform was clearly the foundation for a special residence at Paso de la Amada that began about 1650 cal. B.C. at ground level and which was ele-vated by subsequent remodeling through time until 1350 cal. B.C. (see Blake 1991;

Blake et al. n.d.; Lesure and Blake 2002). As a rather blunt metaphor, later rein-carnations of the founding structure as a towering dwelling represented a salient marker of elevated status that dominated the local skyline for over three centuries, or about ten generations. This number of major rebuilding episodes could well accord with the number of primary occupants or inheritors of this house. I inter-pret the continuity of residence and privileged status as evidence of hereditary inequality (Clark 1994; Clark and Blake 1994). All that can really be presently demonstrated, however, is the continuity of valuable real estate and associated facil-ities. I assume a continuity of occupation by direct descendants from the founder. This special residence, as well as the ballcourt at Mound 7, fell into disuse at the end of the Ocos phase (ca. 1350 cal. B.C.), a century before the site was finally abandoned. The construction and use of these and other buildings appear to have been tied to fluctuating political fortunes, but these may have transcended individ-ual households and have concerned the community as a whole.

Evidence of Barra occupation at Paso de la Amada is still too sparse to make a case for or against site planning. The wide distribution of Barra ceramics suggests a dispersed village. During the early Locona phase, this dispersed village became consolidated into one entity or community. In the following Ocos phase, the com-munity contracted further but may have increased in residential density. Commu-nity collapse came at the end of the Cherla phase, the time of maximum foreign contact in the Mazatan zone (Clark 1997). Site consolidation and evidence of com-munity integration coincided with the construction of the southern plaza and its flanking buildings, including the ballcourt at Mound 7 and large residence at Mound 6. (San Jose Mogote experienced a similar consolidation of nine village seg-ments and transformation into a compact community, an event coeval with the appearance of "common" space and true public buildings.)

My current understanding of early Paso de la Amada is illustrated in Figure 2.5. After long disbelieving Lowe's (1977) characterization of this site as an early cere-monial center, I have come full circle and now agree with him. The advantage of having tried for a decade to champion an alternative view is that my colleagues and I have now compiled concrete evidence for the date and use of individual build-ings, their sizes, and orientations. I arrived at Lowe's claim reluctantly and with considerable resistance. When Michael Blake and I began thinking about research opportunities in the Mazatan zone in the early 1980s, we were very much caught up in the excitement of the "Early Mesoamerican Village" (Flannery 1976), and most of our guiding assumptions privileged simplicity and adaptation over any alter-natives. We are still in the process of remapping Paso de la Amada with greater pre-cision to detect plowed mounds, but the available map made with a transit and checked against aerial photographs adequately shows the formality of this early site. Note the regularity in orientation along a major axis and its perpendicular, minor axis and the repetition of large modular lengths, as shown schematically in Figure 2.5(b). The southern third of this northeast–southwest-trending center is a large plaza defined by the ballcourt on the west (Mound 7), the elite residence on the south (Mound 6), and a long platform of unknown function on the east (Mound 14). The plaza is shown as a gray square. In 1995, I excavated a 215 m-long trench

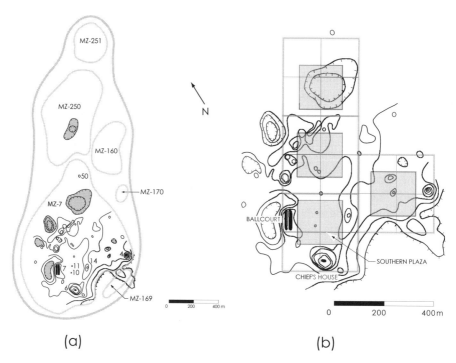

(a)   (b)

Figure 2.5. Paso de la Amada, Chiapas, Mexico: (a) map of greater Paso de la Amada showing 50 cm contours and Locona phase mounds for the southern sector of Paso de la Amada (Mz-7) proper, or the analytical site; bajos are shown in gray; (b) hypothetical alignments and southern plaza (gray squares). I have repeated the southern plaza icon and superimposed it over the other three segments of the site to show relative size rather than the presence of other verified plazas. Note the size correspondence of the northern bajo and the south plaza

that traversed the western edge of the possible plaza and linked up to Mound 6. I found this area to be devoid of Locona phase houses, unlike other areas of the site (see Hill and Clark 2001: fig. 2). The open area appears to have been empty, clean, and flat, ideal conditions for a plaza. I did not detect any especially prepared surface, however, beyond the north courtyard of Structure 4, Mound 6 (Fig. 2.4). This same gray square icon is repeated in Figure 2.5(b) to show the spacing for the rest of the central area.

Northeast of the south plaza is an elevated area, equal to it in size and orientation, and northeast of this is a large *bajo* or low spot that we previously interpreted as a natural water hole. But this low, circular depression is aligned with the other two segments of Paso de la Amada, and at 200 m in diameter it is roughly equivalent in size to the southern plaza. There is too much coincidence here to be natural. This low area could have been a borrow pit or sunken court. Absent features for controlled drainage, it would have filled seasonally with rainwater, so it may have served as a water hole and/or reflecting pool for early Paso de la Amada. It remains to be tested adequately, but a recent coring of the center of this bajo for clay samples revealed Locona ceramics 3 m beneath its modern surface, or 4 m below the present field surface. These artifacts indicate a buried occupation and/or very unusual patterns of refuse disposal. Rather than a natural feature, the bajo appears to be cultural – at least in part. Another bajo is spaced on the same orientation line, and the same distance northeast (Fig. 2.5(a), in MZ-250).

Paso de la Amada was planned using a measurement system based on a 1.666 m unit, and larger measurement modules of 43.32 and 86.63 m (Clark forthcoming). The ballcourt at Paso de la Amada is 86.63 m long, or 52 units of 1.666 m, and it is 20 units wide; the chiefly residence is one-fourth the length of the ballcourt, or 13 indigenous units. The enclosed southern plaza is 173 m² (104 units, twice the length of the ballcourt) and in outside dimensions is about 304 m² (182.5 units). There is clear use of standard measurements and simple multiples and fractions of them. Early Paso de la Amada was carefully laid out, with buildings spaced in modular units that corresponded to numbers significant in later Mesoamerican calendar counts (13, 20, 52, 260, and 365). For example, the perpendicular minor axis is two large squares of 182.5 units each, equal to a solar count of 365 units. The diagonal of each square is 430 m, or 258 units (within 1.0 percent measurement error of 260). Ritual numbers were clearly designed into this space.

These features of alignments, orientations of buildings, size, spacing, measured and multiple intervals, and numbered space reveal detailed site planning and construction. That the space anticipates features of later ceremonial centers is added evidence. Constructing Paso de la Amada would have involved a collective enterprise an order of magnitude beyond any of our previous calculations for collective earth-moving activities at this site (see Blake et al. n.d.; Clark 1994; Hill 1999; Hill and Clark 2001; Rosenswig 2000). If, for example, the northern bajo was a man-made feature, then it would represent about 60,000–120,000 m³ of fill, many more times the earth and clay moved in constructing Mounds 6, 7, and 14. If the southern plaza framed by these structures was leveled and smoothed, then this calculation would go up significantly, also. These possibilities have not been verified or falsified through excavation because they only occurred to us after the last field season, once we stopped privileging naturalistic assumptions. The elevated square between the depression to the north and the plaza to the south could have been built up from fill taken in creating a sunken court and the south plaza. Three bajos parallel the westerly edge of the formal complex, and they may also have been borrow pits and/or circular courts or pools.

Even without these possibilities for an ordered northeastern portion of the formal layout, the southern plaza demonstrates that a portion of the site was planned and built according to a quadripartite plan that foreshadowed later Mesoamerican notions of four quarters and a center point, or *axis mundi*. I believe cosmological notions of world directions and centering were built into early Paso de la Amada by 1650 cal. B.C. The scheme was incredibly ambitious in scale, and it required a significant collective labor project to execute. Late Tierras Largas phase San Jose Mogote, for example, would rattle around in just one of the square, 9 ha segments, and Structure 4 and its courtyard at Mound 6, Paso de la Amada, would smother the 300 m² public area of San Jose Mogote. Clearly, substantial social surpluses had to have been accumulated and deployed over a period of years to construct Paso de la Amada, but by whom, or for what purposes is not clear.

The leaders at Paso de la Amada would have had an ample labor pool. This community extended about 2 km in length and over half a km in maximum width. The formal core or ceremonial center of the site was 37 ha, with an immediately surrounding area of 103 ha. Even with a maximal estimate of three open plazas or waterholes as uninhabited space, this would leave 27 ha of residential space for the center, with 130 ha total for greater Paso de la Amada. This would have represented a ratio of residential space of about 4:1, of outskirts to center. At conservative constants of 15–20 persons/ha, Paso de la Amada during the Locona phase would have had 1,950–2,600 inhabitants, 20 percent of whom were privileged to reside near the formal core. At least this many people occupied the smaller villages, hamlets, and farmsteads within a 2 km radius of Paso de la Amada (Fig. 2.3).

Warren Hill and I (Hill and Clark 2001) discuss the relative building histories for Mounds 6 and 7 and their possible implications for the origins of community identity, social inequality, and rudimentary government or ascribed leadership. Given the evidence for site planning at Paso de la Amada, we may have drastically understated the case for cooperative labor projects, managerial imperatives, and the impact of these work opportunities in bringing people of a dispersed village together as a cohesive, self-perceived community – of *communitas*. The buildings defining the south plaza were clearly constructed as a preconceived set, and at the same time (Hill and Clark 2001). At least two were functionally differentiated and complementary (Mounds 6 and 7), and unexplored others may have been as well. We believe the ballcourt to have been a "public" building in the sense of "common access" for viewing sporting contests and for participating in related activities such as feasting and gambling. We also consider the possibility that the ballcourt was privately owned and sponsored. Mound 6 was a domestic residence, but it may also have served some "public" functions, especially in the patio area north of the house (see Lesure and Blake 2002). More private activities such as cooking took place in the secluded area south of the structure.

The south plaza at Paso de la Amada was large enough to have accommodated over 10,000 spectators on special occasions but probably saw use by much smaller crowds. What the occasions may have been is something to ponder in future investigations. One activity would have involved ballgame matches and related activities on the western edge of the plaza. Others may have involved music and dance. Figurines of fat males, that I have interpreted as shamanic leaders (Clark 1991, 1994), show them wearing animal masks and simple coverings. Lesure (1997b:240) argues that there was a stereotypic set of animal and grotesque masks that varied independently of two clothing formats, thereby indicating that the masked male figurines more likely represented ritual roles rather than leaders portrayed with the badges of office. The rituals for which these males dressed up may have taken place in the plaza. Male and female figurines, themselves, are thought to have been used in household rituals (see Marcus 1998, 1999b), and their fragments are well represented in domestic middens, especially those for Mound 6 (Lesure and Blake 2002).

The construction of Mounds 6, 7, and 14 (and, by definition, the southern plaza) preceded the emergence of hereditary inequality and centralized leadership at this village. We have attributed both building projects to the aggrandizer who built the first house on the locus of the future Mound 6 (Hill and Clark 2001) and who we supposed sponsored these labor projects out of his own household surplus. Given the magnitude of site planning and earthmoving evident at Paso de la Amada, our simplistic explanation is likely wrong. A project this size would probably have required many heads and hands, and it may have been a "communal" endeavor directed and promoted by a coalition of lineage leaders. At the moment, the data provide tantalizing possibilities of events and consequences but no clear answers. Some of the events involved planning and constructing special buildings and plazas. One consequence was that, of all households occupying large Locona platforms scattered throughout Paso de la Amada, only one continued in the same place over many generations (Clark 1994; Lesure and Blake 2002). Paso de la Amada went from being a large dispersed village with segmental organization to an aggregated community and ceremonial center. In the terminology of cultural evolution, this was a transition from tribal to chiefdom society.

Creation of the southern plaza and ballcourt preceded this transformation and may have aided and abetted it. By definition, the transformation to chiefly society involved a fundamental change in personhood as it related to ascribed leadership (Clark 2000; Paynter 1989:383), from an egalitarian ethos to notions of natural superiority of some over others. Rank became institutionalized when villagers began to believe that designated offspring of leaders merited the same deference paid to their powerful uncles or fathers. The flipside of this process of changing subjectivities and identities was that villagers loyal to the same leader came to think of themselves as a natural, non-kinship group – as a community (Hill and Clark 2001).

Forging community identity and feeling among a loose aggregate of lineage groups in a dispersed village may have been related to the construction of public space in at least three ways. First, mutual participation in inter-lineage activities carried out in public plazas and associated buildings may have fostered camaraderie that cross-cut lineage lines. We have proposed that ball games and related activities may have had this effect (Hill and Clark 2001). Second, and perhaps of greater importance, mutual participation in the construction of the formal plaza and buildings could have fostered the same esprit de corps as well as instilling a sense of pride, workmanship, and shared ownership in the results of one's labor (Clark 1997, forthcoming). Third, the construction projects probably had special significance for all involved. This was no mere neighborhood barn-raising. The construction of the plaza most likely was done to create a model of the cosmos – not just "public" space. Bringing the heavens down to earth and giving them form and substance would have gone a long way in motivating laborers, and it would have been hugely significant in forging a strong community identity. The person or persons who conceived and sponsored this grand endeavor would have been held in high esteem and have been accorded founder status. On another level, the whole project could have been couched in terms of a public good and a collective project in which each participant had a stake, and all of whom benefited from the heightened sense of community pride in their special center. Of course, these are only speculative possibilities. But if they are close to the mark, they represent a very different historic trajectory than that proposed for highland Oaxaca.

Centers in Oaxaca and Mazatan

Considered in real time, the Mazatan and Oaxaca sequences differ markedly. Similarities between the two concern different eras and need to be considered analogously rather than aligned historically. Paso de la Amada had a large plaza by at least 1650 cal. B.C., while the common space at San Jose Mogote was not built until about 1250 cal. B.C. Late San Jose phase public constructions at San Jose Mogote appear to have been influenced by peoples of other regions, most notably the San Lorenzo Olmec. I believe the emergence of rank and of ceremonial centers in highland Oaxaca was a secondary development while that in the Mazatan zone was pristine. These differences in genesis may have had a significant impact on the viability of these institutions in each region.

The Paso de la Amada story takes us back to about 1650 cal. B.C., at which time it became an integrated community and center housing about 2,000 people, with at least that many in the immediate sustaining area. San Jose Mogote was barely getting started at this time and would have been a small village of less than 3 ha, with about 100 people. The separate histories of these places converged about 1300 cal. B.C., when both were disrupted by Olmecs. Much controversy swirls around possible Olmec impact in various parts of Mesoamerica (see Clark 1997; Flannery and Marcus 2000), but it is clear that Early Formative peoples were in contact and that the effects of external contacts in individual communities differed. In Mazatan, Paso de la Amada was abandoned, never again to be reoccupied. In the Valley of Oaxaca, San Jose Mogote was transformed and more than quadrupled in size and became the seat of a chiefdom society. I suspect that the reorganization of San Jose Mogote itself around large public buildings and space dates to this time. Prior to this transformation, the site was about 7 ha in extent and inhabited by an estimated 170–350 people. After the transformation, San Jose Mogote increased tenfold to 70 ha and about 1,000–1,400 inhabitants. Of particular interest, the one-room, "public" buildings were replaced by larger, more open, and more centrally situated platforms, and eventually a plaza (Marcus 1999a; Marcus and Flannery 1996).

Considered as parallel cases separated in time as well as space, there is some remarkable congruence between the sequence of changes at San Jose Mogote and Paso de la Amada – taking the emergence of rank and the construction of open, "common" space and facilities as the linking point for aligning their histories. Prior to the creation of "open-to-public" space on a large scale, both sites were dispersed villages on the same order of magnitude (7–10 ha). Both were significantly larger than other settlements within their regions, and both experienced consolidation of formerly dispersed village segments with the creation of public spaces and the emergence of institutions of hereditary leadership. After this occurred, both villages expanded tenfold and housed about half the population in their immediate sustaining areas. Within archaeological precision for ascertaining such things, both chiefdom societies were the same order of magnitude of 3,000–6,000 people.

The nucleation of population, redesign of public space, and increases in size corresponded to the emergence of "communities" from village societies. I use "community" to refer to perceptions of social relationships and identities, of common interests, and of "belonging," as well as the spatial locus housing the bulk of the community (see Cohen 1985; Yaeger and Canuto 2000). The same changes just described also represent scalar changes in social integration. Given social interactions in egalitarian societies, and self-perceptions of agency and personhood, it is likely that there was a practical limit for the number of people who could get along in a single village under the headmanship of a single leader. If the data from Mazatan and Oaxaca are indicative, then that limit would have been roughly ten lineage groups, loosely aggregated, or about 200–400 people. If people in the immediate sustaining area were also included, it would have been an upper limit of about 800. This is well below the threshold of 2,000–3,000 people, calculated cross-culturally and discussed by Feinman (1995:259–261), but the principle is the same. With the organizational and institutional changes described above, both communities grew rapidly to their maximum sizes. Creation of public space appears to have been critical in moving to an increased scale of social integration.

Population nucleation and growth in both instances signal the emergence of true communities and a high level of integration. It should come as no surprise that these changes co-occurred with evidence for large public spaces that could accommodate all the people of the community as well as those immediately outside it. Large formal spaces, such as plazas and their platforms, may have been necessary for successful social integration at this scale (Feinman's 2,000–3,000 estimate). It remains to be determined what public performances and group activities were involved or how they could have been effective, but minimally, a sense of co-participation in critical events would have required that all community members enjoy an entitlement and physical possibility of viewing or participating in these public spectacles. Clear delimitation of public space with architecture was not a sufficient condition related to the emergence of rank society, but it may well have been one of numerous necessary conditions. Viewed in this light, continuity of the secretive "public" buildings at San Jose Mogote served to maintain egalitarianism through rituals closed to public gaze. Group commitment to these facilities and their associated practices was an obstacle for adopting rank society and its institutions of integration. Strong outside force and motivating circumstances were required to effect a change. The change in public buildings, spaces, and related institutions at San Jose Mogote represented a *replacement* rather than a local evolution. Replacement likely also occurred in Mazatan, perhaps under more forceful circumstances (Clark 1997; Clark and Pye 2000), and in a different location; the only consequence currently documented there is that Paso de la Amada was shut down. Its replacement center, Canton Corralito, has been identified and is now being investigated (Clark and Pye 2000).

Paso de la Amada, as formal, constructed space, exhibits the features for "built landscapes" that Earle (2001:107–108) identifies as critical for the evolution of chiefdom societies. The formal plaza and buildings at Paso de la Amada exhibited a large scale, exposure, permanence, and message simplicity. Earle's (2001:111) interpretation of landscapes parallels that presented here for the construction of this formal center: "To the degree that the evolution of human societies involves expanded scales of interaction, those interactions must be channelled. Institutionalization thus must involve physical constructions in the landscape organizing humans in such a way that radical increase in scale and complexity of social groups are practical." The rigid layout of Paso de la Amada can be viewed as a channelling device as well as an "aggregating device" (see Cohen 1985:20).

In terms of long-term viability, the precocious developments at Paso de la Amada proved rather fleeting. Over the long haul, the community at San Jose Mogote remained viable and primary in the Valley of Oaxaca a millennium longer than did Paso de la Amada in Mazatan. In Mazatan, Canton Corralito is deeply buried beneath river sand, so details of any formal plazas or public buildings there are not available for assessing the aftermath of Paso de la Amada's abandonment. The very fact that public plazas, space, or buildings could be so easily interred, however, suggests that public space was still horizontal, with low platforms, as it was at Paso de la Amada, and that pyramids were still not part of the public package. With the rise of La Venta in the Olmec Gulf Coast (González 1996; Reilly 1999), and La Blanca on the Pacific Coast of Guatemala (Love 1991, 2002), Mesoamerica witnessed the emergence of a different kind of ceremonial center. These early Middle Formative centers (ca. 900 cal. b.c.) each had a tall pyramid in the north, a long, rectangular plaza to the south, with elite residences on the east (Fig. 2.6; Clark 2001; Clark and Hansen 2001). One view of these changes is that early centers focused on facilities for amassing crowds which could have co-mingled with the public performers, or at least been at their level. The addition of pyramids, among other things, represented an elevated stage on which activities could be viewed by crowds, but this suggests more passive participation by Middle Formative spectators than in earlier centers, and greater spatial, vertical, and social distance between performers and spectators.

Comparison of Paso de la Amada to La Venta demonstrates that fundamental changes had occurred by the Middle Formative, and these pinpoint features of interest for earlier times. Comparable in size during their beginning phases, both early centers were linear, oriented north–south or roughly so, with major and minor axes of orientation (Fig. 2.6). Principal platforms flanked a large plaza that was quadripartite. At La Venta, north was the direction of ritual emphasis, with its pyramid or cosmic mountain, a marked contrast with the southern position of Mound 6 at Paso de la Amada. The La Venta pattern appears as a symbolic inversion of that of Paso de la Amada, with its reversed directions and accentuation of the vertical. At La Venta, a ballcourt was not associated with the principal plaza, although they may have been at other Middle Formative centers (Clark and Hansen 2001). Some features evident at Paso de la Amada did persist, as evident in the similarities in size and formal layouts among Paso de la Amada, La Venta, and Monte Alban (Fig. 2.6), an inherently improbable group of sites among which to find any similarities.

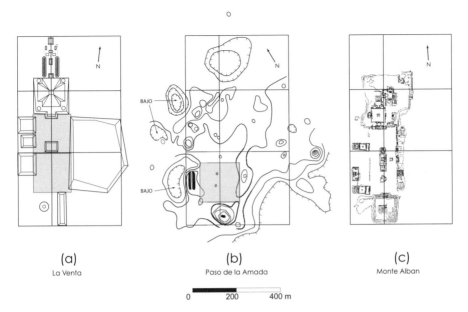

(a)   (b)   (c)
La Venta   Paso de la Amada   Monte Alban

0   200   400 m

Figure 2.6. Comparison of three early centers: (a) reconstruction of early La Venta, Tabasco, Mexico, about 800 cal. B.C. (redrawn from González L. 1988); (b) Paso de la Amada, Chiapas, Mexico, about 1600 cal. B.C. (c) Monte Alban, Oaxaca (redrawn from Winter 1994)

Comparing Paso de la Amada to later Middle Formative centers, the key difference is the disposition of the principal elite residences (Fig. 2.6). Mound 6 is the balancing point at the southwestern terminus of the central spine organizing Paso de la Amada. The only other buildings identified at the site are the ballcourt and some smaller residences. The plaza is sufficiently clear as a public space, but at the moment there is no independent evidence for it having been "ceremonial" space. What was this space used for? Beyond making claims for playing ball, all options are open, from trade fairs, markets, and feasting to ritual dances. All these plausible activities look rather secular. It is harder to imagine sacred or ceremonial activities in this space because we have no evidence for this time period of full-time ritual specialists or kings. These are first evident at San Lorenzo 300 years later.

At Paso de la Amada we see a plaza without a shrine, and at San Jose Mogote we see a shrine without a plaza. Both arrangements proved to be developmental dead ends. One site was abandoned and the other experienced a makeover. Younger Middle Formative centers such as La Venta combined the secular and the sacred, and added a few flourishes such as the cosmic mountain. In their mature manifestations, beginning in the Middle Formative, Mesoamerican "ceremonial centers" had plazas, temple pyramids, and royal residences. The early step-down shrines at San Jose Mogote appear to have been forerunners of summit temples, and the elite residence at Paso de la Amada was a possible forerunner of royal courts and palaces. In Mazatan, aggrandizers attempted to tap into the sacred by creating a cosmological layout at Paso de la Amada, an effort that was successful for about seven generations. In Oaxaca, transcendental rites served to integrate small coteries of committed egalitarians through an emphasis on exclusionary rituals, perhaps associated with ingestion of drugs and induced hallucinatory trances. In contrast, the political lubricant of choice in Mazatan, associated with feasting and collective labor projects, was probably alcohol (Clark and Blake 1994; Clark and Gosser 1995). Compared to later centers, Paso de la Amada appears to have been more secular than sacred, and this may have been part of its undoing.

Constructing Community

I have pursued twin objectives of narrating facts and possible histories in this chapter as they relate to the earliest communities in Mesoamerica, with particular accord to public buildings and ceremonial spaces that may have been integral in the development of first communities in Oaxaca and Mazatan. Throughout, I have been lax in distinguishing *community as a place* from *community as self-perceived membership in a bounded group*, with shared symbols and interests vis-à-vis those of neighboring communities. The subheading of this concluding section extends this ambiguity deliberately to include both the construction of a physical container, a ceremonial center, and the construction of identity through social interaction and inter-subjective understandings. If my recitation of significant facts for Mazatan and Oaxaca is sufficiently accurate, the dual constructions of community were faces of the same coin. Creation of the formal center of Paso de la Amada became an index of changed social relations and identity, both to its occupants and to outsiders, while the actual physical construction of this marker of group identity helped effect the change in self-identification. Paso de la Amada was the public face and per-during symbol of its resident community. Of course, the community need not have been limited strictly to the rearranged soil of the center itself. Given the small size of the Paso de la Amada chiefdom at the time, its community probably included the whole polity and might even have spilled over its edges. I have presumed that the Paso de la Amada community came into being during the early Locona period (1650 cal. B.C.). A more cautious claim would be that it was in place by *at least* this time; it could be earlier but not later. I consider communities to be supra-kin groups and to subsume and cross-cut lineages. Because the transformation at Paso de la Amada at 1650 cal. B.C. involved the coalescence of dispersed resident clusters, possibly lineage groups, into a single aggregate, I believe its community emerged at this time.

At least two shifts in identity from prevailing Archaic notions of achieved statuses would necessarily have been involved in creating communities in Mazatan. At the individual level, persons of like lineage, gender, and age-grade came to perceive themselves as privileged, or not, in a symbolic interactional process of mutual self-definition. Both statuses were necessary for the other's self-concept. At the group level, novel differences in birth entitlements melded in the ecumenical notion of community. Community did not signal social homogeneity or equality, quite the opposite. As relational phenomena, distentions of achieved and kin statuses into ascribed and community ones garnered force as the same distinctions were being made concurrently and in tandem in neighboring polities within the same regional network (Clark and Blake 1994).

Traditional archaeological approaches to architecture and site construction take a "reflective" stance and consider artifacts as mirrors to past realities and processes. Architecture, ceremonial centers, and settlement patterns are consequences, either of blind evolutionary or historical forces or of premeditated actions of agents, or something in between. In this mode, I interpret the settlement patterns, site construction, and building histories at Paso de la Amada as indicative of early rank society there by 1650 cal. B.C. and analogous and contemporaneous evidence from Oaxaca as manifestations of egalitarian society.

A practice theory perspective extends views of architectural consequences. Public works can be viewed as concrete evidence of planned and anticipated projects, of cognitive maps of an ordered cosmos, of motives for the project, of realization of the project, of its scale and energetic requirements, of mobilization, sponsorship, motivation, and direction of a labor force, of social relations of construction between overseers and workers, of accumulation and allocation of social surpluses, of technical and organizational imperatives needed to accomplish projects within specific time frames given finite resources of labor, materials, and food, and of imbuing locations with power and meaning, thereby creating a powerful social landscape. In this last sense, Paso de la Amada was a device for capturing and centering cosmic and social power, as were later Mesoamerican centers. Once completed, this formal center would have become an exceptional recruiting device for attracting others to the community – its expansive architecture and plazas being the best advertisement of community resources, organization, and well-being.

Community can be called into being, but it requires a reason for being, or it ceases to be. A serious challenge for Mesoamerican rulers was to keep their subjects engaged in matters of *communitas* or *civitas*, without overburdening them with frivolous projects of work for its own sake. For later Mesoamerica, possible alternative enterprises to city-building for promoting community may have involved warfare, craft specialization, and commerce. At its birth, however, the primary path to community in Mesoamerica appears to have been construction of public and/or sacred locales. Monumental construction of ceremonial centers continued to elicit this effect in later times, but in the beginning it may well have been midwife to the first communities, hereditary inequality, and chieftainship.

ACKNOWLEDGMENTS

I thank Michael Blake and Warren Hill for permissions to use drawings from Paso de la Amada and Michelle Knoll for preparing the line drawings. I am particularly grateful for Rosemary Joyce's editorial aid in halving my original version of this chapter.

REFERENCES

Blake, M., 1991 An emerging Early Formative chiefdom at Paso de la Amada, Chiapas, Mexico. In *The Formation of Complex Society in Southeastern Mesoamerica*. W. R. Fowler, ed. Pp. 27–46. Boca Raton: CRC Press.

Blake, M., B. S. Chisholm, J. E. Clark, B. Voorhies, and M. W. Love, 1992 Prehistoric subsistence in the Soconusco region. *Current Anthropology* 33, 83–94.

Blake, M., J. E. Clark, B. Voorhies, G. Michaels, M. W. Love, M. E. Pye, A. A. Demarest, and B. Arroyo, 1995 A revised chronology for the Late Archaic and Formative periods along the Pacific Coast of southeastern Mesoamerica. *Ancient Mesoamerica* 6, 161–183.

Blake, M., R. G. Lesure, J. E. Clark, W. D. Hill, and P. L. Barba, n.d. The residence of power at Paso de la Amada, Mexico. Paper prepared for *Ancient American Elite Residences*. J. Christie and P. Sarro, eds. Under review.

Blanton, R. E., 1998 Beyond centralization: Steps towards a theory of egalitarian behavior in Archaic states. In *Archaic States*. G. M. Feinman and J. Marcus, eds. Pp. 135–172. Santa Fe: School of American Research Press.

Blanton, R. E., G. M. Feinman, S. A. Kowalewski, and P. N. Peregrine, 1996 A dual-processual theory for the evolution of Mesoamerican civilization. *Current Anthropology* 37, 1–14, 65–68.

Ceja, J. F., 1985 *Paso de la Amada: An Early Preclassic Site in the Soconusco, Chiapas, Mexico*. Papers of the New World Archaeological Foundation 49. Provo, Utah: New World Archaeological Foundation.

Clark, J. E., 1991 The beginnings of Mesoamerica: Apologia for the Soconusco Early Formative. In *The Formation of Complex Society in Southeastern Mesoamerica*. W. R. Fowler, ed. Pp. 13–26. Boca Raton: CRC Press.

——1994 The development of early formative rank societies in the Soconusco, Chiapas, Mexico. Ph.D. dissertation, Ann Arbor: Department of Anthropology, University of Michigan.

——1997 The arts of government in early Mesoamerica. *Annual Review of Anthropology* 26, 211–234.

——2000 Towards a better explanation of hereditary inequality: A critical assessment of natural and historic agents. In *Agency in Archaeology*. M.-A. Dobres and J. Robb, eds. Pp. 92–112. London: Routledge.

——2001 Ciudades tempranas Olmecas. In *Reconstruyendo la Ciudad Maya: El urbanismo en las sociedades antiguas* [Reconstructing the Maya City: Urbanism in Ancient Societies]. A. Ciudad Real, M. J. I. Ponce de León, and M. d. C. Martínez Martínez, eds. Pp. 183–210. Madrid: Sociedad Española de Estudios Mayas.

——forthcoming Surrounding the sacred: Geometry and design of early mound groups as meaning and function. In *Big Mound Power: Faces of Southeastern Archaic Sociality*. J. L. Gibson and P. J. Carr, eds. Tuscaloosa: Alabama Press.

Clark, J. E., and M. Blake, 1994 The power of prestige: Competitive generosity and the emergence of rank societies in Lowland Mesoamerica. In *Factional Competition in the New World*. E. M. Brumfiel and J. W. Fox, eds. Pp. 17–30. Cambridge: Cambridge University Press.

Clark, J. E., and D. Cheetham, 2002 Mesoamerica's tribal foundations. In *The Archaeology of Tribal Societies*. W. Parkinson, ed. Pp. 278–339. Ann Arbor: International Monographs in Prehistory.

Clark, J. E., and D. Gosser, 1995 Reinventing Mesoamerica's first pottery. In *The Emergence of Pottery*. W. K. Barnett and J. W. Hoopes, eds. Pp. 209–221. Washington, DC: Smithsonian Press.

Clark, J. E., and R. D. Hansen, 2001 The architecture of early kingship: Comparative perspectives on the origins of the Maya royal court. In *Royal Courts of the Ancient Maya.* T. Inomata and S. D. Houston, eds. Pp. 1–45. Boulder: Westview Press.

Clark, J. E., and M. E. Pye, 2000 The Pacific Coast and the Olmec question. In *Olmec Art and Archaeology in Mesoamerica.* J. E. Clark and M. Pye, eds. Pp. 217–251. Washington, DC: National Gallery of Art.

Coe, M. D., and R. A. Diehl, 1980 *In the Land of the Olmec.* Austin: University of Texas Press.

Coe, M. D., and K. V. Flannery, 1964 Microenvironments and Mesoamerican prehistory. *Science* 143, 650–654.

Cohen, A. P., 1985 *The Symbolic Construction of Community.* London: Routledge.

Cyphers, A., 1996 Reconstructing Olmec life at San Lorenzo. In *Olmec Art of Ancient Mexico.* E. P. Benson and B. de la Fuente, eds. Pp. 60–71. Washington, DC: National Gallery of Art.

Drennan, R. D., 1983 Ritual and ceremonial development at the early village level. In *The Cloud People: Divergent Evolution of the Zapotec and Mixtec Civilizations.* K. V. Flannery and J. Marcus, eds. Pp. 46–50. New York: Academic Press.

Earle, T. K., 2001 Institutionalization of chiefdoms: Why landscapes are built. In *From Leaders to Rulers.* J. Haas, ed. Pp. 105–124. New York: Kluwer Academic/Plenum Publishers.

Feinman, G. M., 1991 Demography, surplus, and inequality: Early political formations in Highland Mesoamerica. In *Chiefdoms: Power, Economy, and Ideology.* T. Earle, ed. Pp. 229–262. Cambridge: Cambridge University Press.

——1995 The emergence of inequality: A focus on strategies and processes. In *Foundations of Social Inequality.* T. D. Price and G. M. Feinman, eds. Pp. 255–279. New York: Plenum.

——2000a Corporate/Network: A new perspective on leadership in the American Southwest. In *Hierarchies in Action: Cui Bono?* M. A. Diehl, ed. Pp. 152–180. Carbondale: Center for Archaeological Investigations, Southern Illinois University.

——2000b Corporate/Network: New perspectives on models of political action and the Puebloan Southwest. In *Social Theory in Archaeology.* M. Schiffer, ed. Pp. 31–51. Salt Lake City: University of Utah Press.

——2000c Dual-processual theory and social formations in the Southwest. In *Alternative Leadership Strategies in the Prehispanic Southwest.* B. J. Mills, ed. Pp. 207–224. Tucson: University of Arizona Press.

——2001 Mesoamerican political complexity: The corporate-network dimension. In *From Leaders to Rulers.* J. Haas, ed. Pp. 151–175. New York: Kluwer Academic/Plenum Publishers.

Feinman, G. M., K. G. Lightfoot, and S. Upham, 2000 Political hierarchies and organizational strategies in the Puebloan southwest. *American Antiquity* 65, 449–470.

Feinman, G. M., and L. M. Nicholas, 1987 Labor, surplus, and production: A regional analysis of Formative Oaxacan socio-economic change. In *Coasts, Plains and Deserts: Essays in Honor of Reynold J. Ruppé.* S. Gaines, ed. Pp. 27–50. Anthropological Research Papers 38. Tempe: Arizona State University.

Flannery, K. V., 1968 The Olmec and the Valley of Oaxaca: A model for inter-regional interaction in Formative times. In *Dumbarton Oaks Conference on the Olmec.* E. P. Benson, ed. Pp. 79–117. Washington, DC: Dumbarton Oaks.

——ed., 1976 *The Early Mesoamerican Village.* New York: Academic Press.

——1999 Process and agency in early state formation. *Cambridge Archaeological Journal* 9, 3–21.

Flannery, K. V., and J. Marcus, 1976a Evolution of public buildings in Formative Oaxaca. In *Culture Change and Continuity: Essays in Honor of James Bennett Griffin*. C. E. Cleland, ed. Pp. 205–221. New York: Academic Press.

————1976b Formative Oaxaca and the Zapotec Cosmos. *American Scientist* 64, 374–383.

————eds. 1983 *The Cloud People: Divergent Evolution of he Zapotec and Mixtec Civilizations*. New York: Academic Press.

————1990 Borrón, y Cuenta Nueva: Setting Oaxaca's archaeological record straight. In *Debating Oaxaca Archaeology*. J. Marcus, ed. Pp. 17–69. Anthropological Papers 84. Ann Arbor: Museum of Anthropology, University of Michigan.

————1994 *Early Formative Pottery of the Valley of Oaxaca, Mexico*. Memoirs 27. Ann Arbor: Museum of Anthropology, University of Michigan.

————2000 Formative Mexican chiefdoms and the myth of the Mother Culture. *Journal of Anthropological Archaeology* 19, 1–37.

Flannery, K. V., J. Marcus, and S. A. Kowalewski, 1981 The Preceramic and Formative of the Valley of Oaxaca. In *Handbook of Middle American Indians*, supplement 1: *Archaeology*. J. A. Sabloff, ed. Pp. 48–93. Austin: University of Texas.

González Lauck, R., 1988 Proyecto Arqueológico La Venta. *Arqueología* 4, 121–165.

————1996 La Venta: An Olmec capital. In *Olmec Art of Ancient Mexico*. E. P. Benson and B. de la Fuente, eds. Pp. 73–81. Washington, DC: National Gallery of Art.

Hill, W. D., 1999 Ballcourts, competitive games and the emergence of complex society. Ph.D. dissertation, Vancouver: Department of Anthropology and Sociology, University of British Columbia.

Hill, W. D., M. Blake, and J. E. Clark, 1998 Ballcourt design dates back 3,400 years. *Nature* 392, 878–879.

Hill, W. D., and J. E. Clark, 2001 Sports, gambling, and government: America's first social compact? *American Anthropologist* 103, 1–15.

Lesure, R. G., 1997a Early Formative platforms at Paso de la Amada, Chiapas, Mexico. *Latin American Antiquity* 8, 217–235.

————1997b Figurines and social identities in early sedentary societies of coastal Chiapas, Mexico, 1550–800 B.C. In *Women in Prehistory: North America and Mesoamerica*. C. Claassen and R. A. Joyce, eds. Pp. 225–248. Philadelphia: University of Pennsylvania Press.

————1999 Platform architecture and activity patterns in an early Mesoamerican village in Chiapas, Mexico. *Journal of Field Archaeology* 26, 391–406.

Lesure, R. G., and M. Blake, 2002 Interpretive challenges in the study of early complexity: Economy, ritual, and architecture at Paso de la Amada, Mexico. *Journal of Anthropological Archaeology* 21, 1–24.

Love, M. W., 1991 Style and social complexity in Formative Mesoamerica. In *The Formation of Complex Society in Southeastern Mesoamerica*. W. R. Fowler, ed. Pp. 47–76. Boca Raton: CRC Press.

————2002 *Early Settlements and Chronology of the Río Naranjo, Guatemala*. Papers of the New World Archaeological Foundation 66. Provo, Utah: New World Archaeological Foundation.

Lowe, G. W., 1977 The Mixe-Zoque as competing neighbors of the early Lowland Maya. In *The Origins of Maya Civilization*. R. E. W. Adams, ed. Pp. 197–248. Albuquerque: University of New Mexico Press.

————1989 The heartland Olmec: Evolution of material culture. In *Regional Perspectives on the Olmec*. R. J. Sharer and D. C. Grove, eds. Pp. 33–67. Cambridge: Cambridge University Press.

——— 1998 *Mesoamérica Olmeca: Diez Preguntas* [Olmec Mesoamerica: Ten Questions]. Colección Científica 370. Mexico City: Instituto Nacional de Antropología e Historia.

Marcus, J., 1989 Zapotec chiefdoms and the nature of Formative religions. In *Regional Perspectives on the Olmec*. R. J. Sharer and D. C. Grove, eds. Pp. 148–197. Cambridge: Cambridge University Press.

——— 1998 *Women's Ritual in Formative Oaxaca: Figurine Making, Divination, Death and the Ancestors*. Memoirs 33. Ann Arbor: Museum of Anthropology, University of Michigan.

——— 1999a Early architecture in the Valley of Oaxaca. In *Mesoamerican Architecture as a Cultural Symbol*. J. K. Kowalski, ed. Pp. 58–75. Oxford: Oxford University Press.

——— 1999b Men's and women's ritual in Formative Oaxaca. In *Social Patterns in Pre-classic Mesoamerica*. D. C. Grove and R. A. Joyce, eds. Pp. 67–96. Washington, DC: Dumbarton Oaks.

Marcus, J., and K. V. Flannery, 1994 Ancient Zapotec ritual and religion: An application of the direct historical approach. In *The Ancient Mind: Elements of Cognitive Archaeology*. C. Renfrew and E. B. W. Zubrow, eds. Pp. 55–74. Cambridge: Cambridge University Press.

——— 1996 *Zapotec Civilization: How Urban Society Evolved in Mexico's Oaxaca Valley*. London: Thames & Hudson.

——— 2000 Cultural evolution in Oaxaca: The origins of the Zapotec and Mixtec civilizations. In *The Cambridge History of the Native Peoples of the Americas*, vol. 2: *Mesoamerica*, part 1. R. W. Adams and M. J. Macleod, eds. Pp. 358–406. Cambridge: Cambridge University Press.

Nelson, F. W., and B. Voorhies, 1980 Trace element analysis of obsidian artifacts from three shell middens in the littoral zone, Chiapas, Mexico. *American Antiquity* 45, 540–550.

Paynter, R., 1989 The archaeology of equality and inequality. *Annual Review of Anthropology* 18, 369–399.

Peregrine, P., 2001 Matrilocality, corporate strategy, and the organization of production in the Chacoan world. *American Antiquity* 66, 36–46.

Reilly, F. K. III, 1999 Mountains of creation and underworld portals: The ritual function of Olmec architecture at La Venta, Tabasco. In *Mesoamerican Architecture as a Cultural Symbol*. J. K. Kowalski, ed. Pp. 14–39. Oxford: Oxford University Press.

Rosenswig, R. M., 2000 Some political processes of ranked societies. *Journal of Anthropological Archaeology* 19, 413–460.

Saitta, D. J., 1994a Agency, class, and archaeological interpretation. *Journal of Anthropological Archaeology* 13, 201–227.

——— 1994b Class and community in the Prehistoric southwest. In *The Ancient Southwestern Community: Models and Methods for the Study of Prehistoric Social Organization*. W. Wills and R. Leonard, eds. Pp. 25–43. Albuquerque: University of New Mexico Press.

——— 1994c The political economy and ideology of early population aggregation in Togeye Canyon, A.D. 1150–1250. In *Exploring Social, Political, and Economic Organization in the Zuni Region*. R. Howell and T. Stone, eds. Pp. 47–60. Anthropological Research Papers 46. Tucson: Arizona State University.

——— 1997 Power, labor, and the dynamics of change in Chacoan political economy. *American Antiquity* 62, 7–26.

——— 2001 Marxist theory and tribal political economy. Paper presented at the American Anthropological Association meetings, Washington, DC.

Symonds, S., A. Cyphers, and R. Lunagómez, 2002 *Asentamiento Prehispánico en San Lorenzo Tenochtitlán* [Prehispanic Settlement in San Lorenzo Tenochtitlan]. Mexico City: Universidad Nacional Autónoma de México.

Voorhies, B., 1976 *The Chantuto People: An Archaic Period Society of the Chiapas, Littoral, Mexico*. Papers of the New World Archaeological Foundation 41. Provo, Utah: New World Archaeological Foundation.

——1996 The transformation from foraging to farming in lowland Mesoamerica. In *The Managed Mosaic: Ancient Maya Agriculture and Resource Use*. S. L. Fedick, ed. Pp. 17–29. Salt Lake City: University of Utah Press.

Winter, M., 1994 *Monte Albán: Estudios Recientes* [Monte Alban: Recent Studies]. Contribución No. 2 del Proyecto Especial Monte Albán 1992–1994. Oaxaca: Proyecto Especial Monte Albán.

Yaeger, Jason, and M.-A. Canuto, 2000 Introducing an archaeology of communities. In *The Archaeology of Communities: A New World Perspective*. M. A. Canuto and J. Yaeger, eds. Pp. 1–15. London: Routledge.

Zeitlin, R. N., and J. F. Zeitlin, 2000 The Paleoindian and Archaic cultures of Mesoamerica. In *The Cambridge History of the Native Peoples of the Americas*, vol. 2: *Mesoamerica*, part 1. R. W. Adams and M. J. Macleod, eds. Pp. 45–121. Cambridge: Cambridge University Press.

3

Shared Art Styles and Long-Distance Contact in Early Mesoamerica

Richard G. Lesure

The new theoretical interest in *agents* embedded in *structures* is prompting archae-ologists to rethink the first 1,200 years of settled life in Mesoamerica, from approx-imately 1600 B.C. to 400 B.C. A particular concern involves the relationships that linked communities together across quite large distances. This topic has been explored for over 50 years, ever since it became clear that one Mesoamerican art style was remarkably early compared to other widespread style horizons and in fact dated to the epoch of interest here. The art style has been called "Olmec," a label chosen rather arbitrarily by archaeologists.

Use of a common art style in communities separated by hundreds of kilometers implies significant connections between them, but what was the nature of those connections? One answer has set the tone for successive generations of debates on this issue. The proposal was that people living in one part of Mesoamerica – speci-fically, the southern Gulf Coast, comprising parts of the modern states of Veracruz and Tabasco, Mexico – created the Olmec art style and that from there it spread to other areas. The peoples of the southern Gulf Coast during the period 1200–400 B.C. became known as "the Olmecs," leading to a confusing dual usage for this term. Their culture was identified as the "mother culture" of Mesoamerica, a complex of beliefs from which all subsequent Mesoamerican cultures descended. Over the years, scholars have proposed a variety of models detailing just how the culture of a set of Gulf Coast peoples might have become the progenitor for subsequent Mesoamerican civilizations (Diehl and Coe 1996). Critiques of mother culture per-spectives have been synthesized as "sister cultures" models.

That the anthropological notion of a "mother" culture is so outdated as to seem ridiculous has been recognized for some time. One response has been to ignore the claim and the issues of cultural history it raises, to turn instead to general anthro-pological theory concerning the origins of socio-political complexity. That response aligns itself with a wider movement, prominent in North American archaeology since the 1960s, in which a particular ancient culture is studied not as an end in itself but rather as a test case for general theories applicable world-wide. It is possible to make some headway toward an agency perspective by following that path. Attention focuses on seemingly universal dimensions of agency, such as the ways people manipulate social relationships to gain power and prestige. But this approach necessarily views people as autonomous agents only minimally constrained by structures. To investigate the structures in which agency was embedded in ancient Mesoamerica, archaeologists have to leave the ramparts of general theory and plunge into cultural history. Ancient art provides a particularly important body of evidence. But when we turn to art from early Mesoamerica, we are immediately confronted once again with the long-standing debate over the source of the Olmec style. If we are to successfully inject contemporary theoretical interests into the study of early Mesoamerica, we need to confront (not ignore) this debate, identify its important contributions, and redirect its future course.

The Olmec Style

The term Olmec is problematic because its dual usage – for both a people living in one part of Mesoamerica and an art style characteristic of a wider region – actually privileges the claim that people in the Gulf Coast created the style and spread it across the rest of Mesoamerica. If, however, that claim is actually the subject of debate, then we really should not use the term in this dual fashion (Flannery and Marcus 1994:385–390; Grove 1989). Here I will use *Olmec* as a descriptive label for the widely shared art style; in my usage, there were no people called "Olmecs." (Other authors cited here make different choices with regard to this term.) I will speak of *Olmec style* and *Olmec iconography* interchangeably. For this early period, we do not know what different groups of people called themselves; I will use labels from modern geography to refer to the people of different regions (Fig. 3.1).

From 1200 to 400 B.C., Olmec iconography was widely but unevenly distributed across Mesoamerica. In some periods and places it seems very pure; in others, it is mixed with more localized themes and styles. The artistic media used are also diverse. They include monumental stone sculptures, portable stone objects, modeled ceramic artifacts, and pottery vessels.

Four points concerning the Olmec style deserve emphasis here. First, it comprises a cluster of *readily identifiable motifs and themes*. Some of these are illustrated in Figure 3.2 (see also Joralemon 1971). Second, the limited set of themes suggests a *coherent subject matter*. Pohorilenko (1996) identifies three distinct subjects: a creature with the face of a human baby but supernaturally transformed (Fig. 3.2(a)); a reptilian creature, also with plenty of imaginary elements (Fig. 3.2(c)); and a human form with supernatural and animal modifications of the face (Fig. 3.2(f)). Other analysts reconstruct subject matter in very different ways, but common threads in these accounts are an identification of subjects as imaginary creatures and a sense that people in different areas were depicting the same creatures (Joralemon 1976; Marcus 1989; Taube 1996). Third, there are *both naturalistic and stylized* ways of

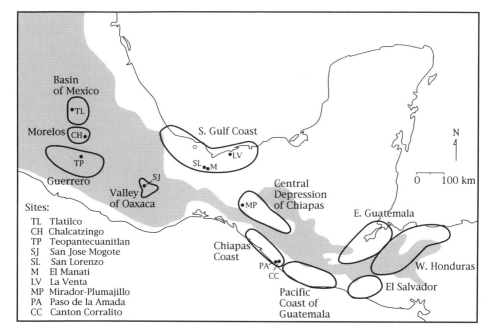

Figure 3.1. Map of Mesoamerica with locations of regions discussed in the text. Archaeological sites to be mentioned are also located and labeled with letter codes. Highland regions are shown in gray

representing these subjects. In particular, on pottery vessels images can be so stylized that only detailed comparative analysis reveals them to be representations rather than simply abstract designs (Fig. 3.3).

Fourth and finally, all lines of evidence point to Olmec art as being *an indigenous creation* of the Native American inhabitants of Mesoamerica, without any influences from Old World regions such as Africa or China. Claims of such contacts are not based on serious scholarship. They ignore context; they often also make grave anthropological errors, by, for instance, using stereotypical concepts of what African facial features should look like and simplistically attempting to identify such features in Olmec art. Haslip-Viera et al. (1997) provide a good review and critique of claims concerning an African source for Olmec art.

Chronology

In the study of early Mesoamerica, it is useful to divide the span of time from 8000 B.C. through A.D. 100 into five successive periods. The *Archaic period* (8000–1600 B.C.) is the epoch of hunter-gatherer life preceding the appearance of settled villages. The domestication of important Mesoamerican crops, including maize, beans, and squash, occurred during this time and led, after 1600 B.C., to the rapid

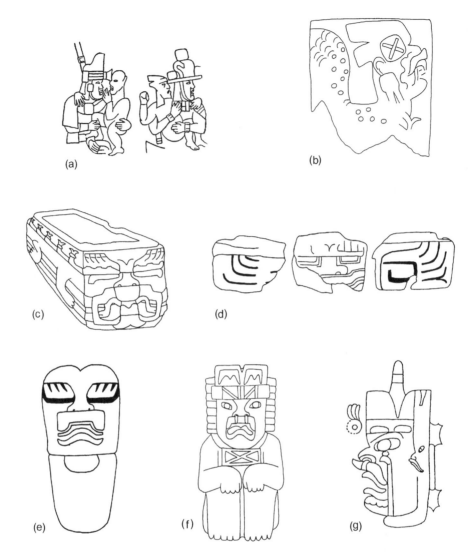

Figure 3.2. Some important themes and motifs in Olmec iconography. Note the supernaturally transformed *babies* (a); the *snarling mouths* with flaring upper lips (b, c, e, f); the *clefts* at the tops of many heads (esp. a, b, e, f, g); the *maize sprouting* from the cleft in one case (g); the *flame eyebrows* (c, e); and the *crossed bands*, a motif shaped like an X in the eye of (b) and on the chest of (f)

The images are of: (a) La Venta Altar 5 side panel; (b) San Lorenzo Monument 30; (c) La Venta Monument 6; (d) La Venta Altar 1; (e) celt from a La Venta offering; (f) San Lorenzo Monument 52; (g) incised design on celt from a La Venta offering. Redrawn by R. Lesure (modified and not to scale) from: (a) Drucker 1952: fig. 52; (b–g) Joralemon 1971: figs 8, 145, 99, 164, 211, respectively; (g) Drucker et al. 1959: fig. 35

Figure 3.3. Naturalistic and stylized representations of supernatural creatures on pottery from the Basin of Mexico. Top: "naturalistic" rendering of what appears to be the same monster depicted in Fig. 3.2(d). Compare the *paw-wing* motif on left part of top image with the side panels in 3.2(d). The face on the right seems to be a profile view of the face we see frontally in the center panel of 3.2(d). Middle and bottom: these are stylized representations of the same image as appears in Fig. 3.2(a). Redrawn by R. Lesure from Covarrubias 1957: fig. 9

appearance of sedentary communities committed to an agricultural lifestyle. The period 1600–1200 B.C. is the *initial Early Formative*. It was a time of settled village life prior to the appearance of the Olmec style and is known for the first appearance of pottery. Unfortunately, in most areas this period is poorly understood.

The Olmec style appeared during the *late Early Formative*, 1200–900 B.C. During this time, there was a rather striking difference in the distribution of media incorporating Olmec iconography. Olmec pottery and molded ceramic artifacts were widespread, but monumental stone sculptures with Olmec themes were carved only on the southern Gulf Coast, notably at San Lorenzo and a few other sites immediately surrounding it. During the *Middle Formative*, 900–400 B.C., monumental sculpture was more widely distributed and in numerous cases conforms to the Olmec style. Particularly prominent among artifacts with Olmec themes from this time are portable objects in jade and other materials. By this period designs on pottery tended to be very abstract, and in many regions it no longer seems useful to refer to them as Olmec. By the *Late Formative*, 400 B.C.–A.D. 100, Mesoamerican art styles in all media had changed so much that Olmec ceases to be a helpful term.

Debate over the Source of the Style

The late Early Formative is the time in which Olmec iconography on ceramics was widespread, but significant numbers of monumental Olmec sculptures were carved only in the Gulf Coast region. That rather simple observation forms the basis for claims that people on the Gulf Coast created Olmec art, which was then adopted by neighboring groups. Different authors have suggested various mechanisms for the spread of the style, including conquest, migrations of elite groups, religious pros-elytization, or simply a process of *emulation* in which people chose to adopt what they saw as desirable ideas and practices (Clark 1997; Diehl and Coe 1996). A common thread among these arguments is the idea that Gulf Coast societies were ahead of their neighbors in institutionalizing social stratification and political com-plexity. For the late Early Formative, such claims are based fundamentally on the sculpture from San Lorenzo, which seems to concern the glorification of rulers and which required a degree of organization and centralization of decision-making to achieve. According to this argument, other Mesoamerican societies did not produce much or any sculpture at this time because they were not yet so complexly organized.

As evidence has accumulated in areas outside the Gulf Coast, scholars have increasingly voiced objections to the idea that the Gulf Coast was the source of Olmec style. They show how self-fulfilling many versions are: everything deemed artistically interesting across Mesoamerica is labeled "Olmec" and then ascribed to the "Olmecs" of the Gulf Coast. Numerous elements of Mesoamerican material culture were instead probably invented in highland Mesoamerica, and some impor-tant themes in the ceramic art are part of regional styles that should not be labeled Olmec. Even when Olmec iconography is defined more carefully, it is clear that people in different regions chose different vessel forms on which to inscribe Olmec motifs, and the sets of motifs used in different areas overlapped only partially (Grove 1989). The most abundant ceramic expressions of the style were in the highlands of Central Mexico rather than the Gulf Coast lowlands (Flannery and Marcus 2000). Finally, no one has yet been able to prove that the Olmec style was invented in the Gulf Coast before it appeared in other areas.

The claim that social and political complexity had a head start in places like San Lorenzo is likewise debated. Large communities with public architecture (but little in the way of sculpture) did appear outside the Gulf Coast during the late Early Formative in places like the Basin of Mexico and the Valley of Oaxaca. In many ways, the crucial question is what was going on at Gulf Coast centers from 1600 to 1200 B.C., before the widespread occurrence of the Olmec style. Unfortunately, evidence from that early period remains elusive.

Scholars objecting to the notion that cultural innovations in early Mesoamerica came from the Gulf Coast have proposed two alternative "sister cultures" explana-tions for the sharing of Olmec iconography. First, the style and the beliefs behind it might already have been shared across Mesoamerica during Archaic times (8000–1600 B.C.). We find them archaeologically only after the invention of pottery, when at long last they were placed on durable media. Second, the sharing might have been the result of interactions during the late Early Formative; groups from all over Mesoamerica could have contributed to the creation of the style. According to such arguments, late Early Formative peoples outside the Gulf Coast were perfectly capable of producing Olmec sculptures had they so wished. Instead, each region gave its own inventive spin to the expression of the shared iconography. Sculptures in places like San Lorenzo reflect different choices rather than greater complexity.

It's Time to Shelve That Debate

An important realization in recent years has been that it is not only the "mother culture" concept that is flawed, but, in addition, much of the debate concerning it. The underlying problem was that the options being debated were impressionistic, overly general, and not actually mutually exclusive. For one thing, it seems impossible that the sister cultures notion could be completely wrong. Wherever or however the Olmec style arose, there were surely lots of influences, interactions, and inventions in early Mesoamerica that did not involve the Gulf Coast. On the other hand, renewed work by Ann Cyphers at the Gulf Coast site of San Lorenzo has re-emphasized the spectacular character of its late Early Formative settlement.

Debate continues, but the implication of recent research is that political complexity likely did begin earliest on the Gulf Coast. Formative developments in the region therefore affected the rest of Mesoamerica, but the effects varied greatly from place to place and were quite ephemeral in some areas. Mesoamerican art of the Early and Middle Formative is a complex combination of borrowings and local inventions, significantly impacted by certain syntheses of ideas that emerged first on the Gulf Coast.

In a loose sense, then, both sides in the previous debates were right. Whether or not that compromise view holds up to critical scrutiny, an additional recent realization is that the source of innovations should not be the question that organizes all others. Archaeologists need to reject the rhetorical urge to collapse everything together in an either/or debate with its familial vocabulary of mothers and sisters. Instead, they should identify the good ideas and intriguing questions raised over the last several decades and start investigating each one separately. Why might an iconographic complex such as Olmec be shared so widely? What kinds of connections between people did that sharing involve? How stable were these connections? Could it be that a variety of different kinds of connections operated simultaneously? What did use of shared symbols mean to people in different regions? To what extent was the subject matter of Olmec art shared along with the motifs and styles of representation? Did shared symbols acquire unique local meanings? Were they associated with elites? What role did Olmec symbols play in ideologies of hierarchy and inequality? Did that role vary across Mesoamerica? For some inspiring recent examples of such work see Clark and Pye (2000a), Grove and Joyce (1999), and Marcus and Flannery (1996).

Toward an Agency-Structure Perspective

Archaeologists today thus seek to answer a whole variety of questions about early Mesoamerica. For the topic of concern in this chapter – the implications of the sharing of Olmec art across Formative Mesoamerica – two general areas of investigation are particularly significant. The first, emphasizing *agency*, comprises research seeking to document actual contacts between people and to explore the ways that objects and symbols associated with those contacts were used, manipulated, and interpreted in local settings. In other words, the studies concern the *social contexts* of shared symbols. "Art" is seen as a medium through which people interpret, manipulate, and transform their worlds. People *use* art, and we are led to ask: Why? How? Under what circumstances?

The second area of investigation emphasizes the importance of *structures*. People grow up within frameworks of beliefs and practices that help to create different kinds of agents and to distribute powers and constraints among them. Children, wives, husbands, mothers-in-law, chiefs, and farmers are all both constrained and empowered by structures of belief and routine. Was Olmec iconography part of such structures? Did art "use" people? In the sections that follow, I consider each of these areas of investigation separately before finishing with an attempt to put the two together.

Social Contexts of Exotic Goods and Olmec Iconography

An investigation emphasizing agency and the social contexts of Olmec imagery needs to be anthropological in the sense of being informed by a comparative understanding of contemporary societies. That realization derives from some of the earliest expressions of dissatisfaction with those mother culture models that fancifully ascribed the spread of the Olmec style to Gulf Coast religious missionaries or armies of invaders. An early article by Kent Flannery (1968) was particularly influential, though it now should only be read alongside his more recent views (Flannery and Marcus 1994, 2000).

Flannery and other archaeologists imagined the late Early Formative as the time in which elite groups first formed in Mesoamerica – when inequalities among people became institutionalized and hereditary. If this claim was correct, they pointed out, then we might be able to predict some very general features of Early Formative societies based on comparisons with other small-scale societies where elites were emerging. A variety of insights followed. If inequalities began to be perpetuated across generations, then ideologies must have appeared that justified that perpetuation by reinforcing the distinctiveness of the elite. Often, for instance, high-status people claim a special relationship with supernatural forces. They mediate between the human and supernatural worlds, overseeing ritual activities that maintain balance in the universe.

Flannery noted such widespread patterns, and went on to link them to the objects archaeologists find in their excavations. Particularly intriguing is the importance to early elites of exotic materials and the objects made from such materials. Such high-status paraphernalia include items of economic value, costume components, and special ritual objects used in ceremonies. At Formative Mesoamerican sites, archaeologists consistently found things imported from great distances: iron ore polished to form mirrors, shells fashioned into ornaments, jade worked into jewelry or ritual implements. Flannery argued that these were status paraphernalia essential to the legitimation of Formative elites. Because the sources of such objects were rare and widely scattered across Mesoamerica, the rise of elites would have created incentives for people to engage in trade over long distances. Comparative anthropology suggested that this trade probably had a significant social dimension involving long-term relations between elite trading partners and the exchange of women or men in arranged marriages between distant groups.

Whatever the specifics of how trade was conducted, Flannery suggested, it was through such far-flung contacts motivated by the exchange of luxury items that Olmec iconography came to be spread across Mesoamerica. Using this basic framework, scholars have pursued a variety of specific lines of inquiry. I consider two. First is the problem of documenting the contact of people from different regions. Second is that of ascertaining the uses of objects bearing Olmec imagery. The relation of Olmec art with status competition forms a backdrop to both those issues.

It may eventually be possible to consider movements of people in Mesoamerica based on specialized analyses of skeletal remains, but thus far most studies focus on the movements of objects that can be traced to their source. For instance, seashells appearing in highland sites must have been carried there, and modern species distributions can be used to assess whether they derive from the Gulf of Mexico or the Pacific. Rocks and minerals can in some cases be traced more precisely by matching the chemical composition of archaeological discoveries to materials from known sources. The success of such studies varies by material. Obsidian – a volcanic glass used for tools and thus primarily of economic importance – has been most amenable to source identification, but researchers have had success also with iron ore. Unfortunately, the sources of jade have proven more difficult to pinpoint, though the usual suspects are eastern Guatemala and Guerrero (see Fig 3.1).

With information about where items originated and where they ended up, it is possible to make significant headway in reconstructing networks of interaction in early Mesoamerica. It is clear that certain goods did indeed move from distant areas to the Gulf Coast; however, status paraphernalia moved among other regions as well. In Christine Niederberger's (2000:187) reconstruction, the full range of imports to the Basin of Mexico included pottery and special clays, pigments, rock crystal, mica, iron ore, jade, serpentine, cotton, sea turtle carapaces, seashells of various kinds, and possibly exotic lowland birds. Primary links beyond Central Mexico may have been to Oaxaca, Guerrero, and the Pacific coast, rather than to the Gulf Coast.

Analyses of such interactions become more interesting when they involve detailed consideration of everything from the collection of raw materials to the arrival of finished products at their destinations. The production of iron ore objects provides two examples. At the large site of San Jose Mogote in Oaxaca, survey and excavations revealed that, during the late Early Formative, people living in one part of the site collected lumps of iron ore from local sources and polished them into small, flat mirrors (Flannery 1968). Mirrors produced in San Jose Mogote made their way to the Gulf Coast, the Basin of Mexico, and probably other places as well, where they were used in jewelry, clothing, or headdresses.

Exchange of a second, rather bizarre, type of iron ore object seems to have been more restricted, focused on the Gulf Coast (Di Castro Stringher 1997). The objects are small, roughly shaped rectangular blocks with multiple holes drilled through them. No one has been able to show conclusively what these were used for; one possibility is that they were important in stoneworking. Debris from the production of these artifacts has been found at the late Early Formative site of Mirador-Plumajillo, near iron ore sources in the Central Depression of Chiapas. Although a scattering of these objects has long been known from the Gulf Coast, those findings in no way prepared investigators for the discovery at San Lorenzo of 6 metric tons of these small blocks. The ancient inhabitants had dumped thousands of them into pits; the drilled blocks in two of these pits were still whole, while in a third they had been broken in half. Whatever the actual use of these strange artifacts, current evidence suggests that the production and distribution system for drilled iron ore blocks was distinctly different from that for iron ore mirrors. The blocks did not make their way across all of Mesoamerica. Instead, they were produced in central Chiapas specifically for export to the Gulf Coast.

Of the exchange patterns found for mirrors and drilled blocks, the first appears to fit a sister cultures model for contacts in early Mesoamerica, while the second seems appropriate for a mother culture model. These two examples thus reinforce my claim that it is time to move beyond that oversimplified debate. What scholars are trying to do now is collect as much information as possible on production and exchange to build a detailed picture of trade in Formative Mesoamerica. Some are attempting also to move further to consider the social relationships involved in transactions. Did those include barter or reciprocity? Or were unequal relations such as that of patron and client involved? These issues were raised by Flannery back in 1968 but have proved extremely difficult to resolve.

My second line of inquiry concerns the ways different peoples across Mesoamerica actually used Olmec art. An obvious question to ask here is whether Olmec iconography itself might have been a symbolic expression of the elite, directly associated with status paraphernalia. The answer turns out to be complex since the relation of Olmec iconography to status shifted over time. From 1200 to 900 B.C., the imagery appeared most abundantly on ceramics, which were widely available to many people. By the Middle Formative, clear Olmec iconography typically disappeared from ceramics and became most common on objects with much more restricted distributions. It thus seems possible that Olmec iconography became more exclusively associated with status paraphernalia and the elite during the Middle Formative (Grove and Gillespie 1992).

Pottery vessels bearing Olmec iconography in the late Early Formative were used to serve food and beverages. Now, when people get together to share food, they are doing more than simply filling their stomachs. Some meals are formal events in which social rules concerning how people should interact with each other can be reinforced or, occasionally, subverted. Imagine, for instance, our stereotypes of dad carving the turkey or parents telling the kids to sit still in front of guests. When actual events mirror those stereotypes, they tend to reinforce traditional notions of the relations between men and women, or adults and children. The sharing of food can also build bonds of community far beyond the family – one doesn't break bread with one's enemy. Finally, because food can be expensive in terms of resources or labor, sharing food on an ambitious scale – sponsoring community feasts, for instance – can be a route to political power open only to a few. Comparative anthropology is again enlightening: elites often seem to establish their authority over others through their ability to be generous with food.

Thus a variety of important social interactions may take place at meals. Relations of both equality and inequality are involved, and those relations can be strengthened, reproduced, or subverted based on actions people take. Anthropologists sometimes sum up all those possibilities by saying that the sharing of meals is an important context for the *negotiation* of social relations. It is thus of anthropological interest that, when people shared food in the late Early Formative, they regularly displayed dishes that were prominently – even spectacularly – emblazoned with Olmec iconography. Was the decorated pottery linked to the social dimensions of meals, in which people negotiated divisions of power and prestige?

One approach to this question is to look carefully at the distribution of decorated ceramics within or between communities to see if their use marked out differences among people. It is clear that, from 1200 to 900 B.C., many people had access to ceramics bearing Olmec iconography. Did elite families use more decorated pottery than others? We might have grounds for making such an argument if we found that decorated ceramics clustered around the remains of larger, fancier houses and/or houses with high frequencies of imported exotics (iron ore, jade, shell, etc.).

For most regions, archaeologists working on the late Early Formative have not been able to demonstrate such a pattern convincingly. One interesting recent discovery on the Chiapas Coast concerns the distribution of decorated ceramics between communities rather than houses. In most communities, 4 to 7 percent of the bowls in late Early Formative trash deposits bear Olmec iconography. But at Canton Corralito, which John Clark (1997) identifies as a local political center and possibly the home of some immigrants from the Gulf Coast, a stunning 24 percent of bowls were decorated. At first glance, this is the kind of pattern we might expect to see if elites had more decorated ceramics than others, but Tomás Pérez's recent excavations indicate that high frequencies of decorated ceramics may have characterized the whole Corralito community rather than just a few (elite) households. It is as if the inhabitants of Corralito collectively held a special status in their region. If so, what was special about this community? Could a special link to the Gulf Coast explain the ceramic patterns? Much more work will be necessary to answer that question with any assurance.

Some of the most detailed evidence of house-to-house variation during the late Early Formative is available from the Valley of Oaxaca. At the large site of San Jose

Mogote – the most populous village in the valley at that time – Flannery and Marcus (1994) identify a continuum of status differences between houses, based on criteria such as the care and effort expended in construction and the presence of imported exotics. They find that there is a tendency for higher-status houses to have more decorated ceramics or a greater variety in decoration.

Marcus (1989) argues that underlying the decorative variation are two basic designs that depict distinct imaginary creatures. She further argues that, to ancient Oaxacans, those imaginary creatures stood for important supernatural forces that we might label Earth and Sky. A rather interesting pattern appears when the distributions of these two designs within the valley are analyzed. At small communities, one or another of the motifs predominates, while at the large village of San Jose Mogote, the frequencies of motifs differ significantly by neighborhood. It thus seems possible that the two motifs marked membership in social groups of some sort: some people were members of a group associated with Earth, others of a group related to Sky.

Marcus and Flannery (1996) elaborate on this idea by turning to another important context in which archaeologists find pottery: as offerings accompanying human burials. Careful analyses of such mortuary remains have proven important to archaeologists since the treatment of people at death often reflects the social positions they held in life. In late Early Formative Oaxaca, pottery bearing Olmec iconography appears predominantly with burials of men, or with infants and children whose sex is unknown. It seems possible that these children were males, too, and that the "Earth" and "Sky" motifs marked membership in one of two patrilineal descent groups. Men passed their group membership on to their children, while women tended to move between the groups at marriage.

In the Basin of Mexico, hundreds of graves dating to the late Early Formative and the beginning of the Middle Formative appeared at the site of Tlatilco. Tolstoy (1989a) found evidence of significant status differences among the graves. Iron ore mirrors appeared in the graves of only the most prominent individuals, but Olmec-style objects were not strongly clustered in the richest graves. Instead, the display of Olmec imagery may have marked other kinds of social differences. That would be generally similar to what has been found in Oaxaca, but the details here differ significantly. Among the graves, Tolstoy identified two sets distinguished by orientation of the body. He tentatively suggests that these were intermarrying groups based on matrilineal descent (distinct from the patrilineal pattern suggested for Oaxaca). Interestingly, objects with Olmec iconography appear mainly in graves of just one group (the richer of the two) and are more common among females than males. Tolstoy suggests that if descent groups at Tlatilco competed for wealth and prestige in the community, one group might have established marriage relations with peoples on the Gulf Coast and claimed these foreign contacts as a source of prestige. Display of Olmec symbols on pottery serving vessels could have advertised that link within the community.

In communities across Mesoamerica, pottery bearing Olmec iconography was important in the negotiation of differences among people. Status differences may in some cases have been involved, but Olmec iconography was not strongly associated with emerging elites during this period, at least in Oaxaca and Central Mexico. Places like San Lorenzo on the Gulf Coast, however, with large bodies of sculpture in Olmec style, had probably already moved toward the Middle Formative pattern at this time.

Instead of status differences, it seems possible that, in the central and southern highlands, Olmec imagery marked membership in lineages or other kin groups. Display of the imagery was probably more inclusive than exclusive, symbolizing bonds of community within the group. It also legitimized the existence of the groups themselves by linking them to mythological creatures or supernatural forces. Perhaps that is why in Oaxaca we find a tendency for higher-status households to have more serving vessels with Olmec imagery: high-status people were more interested in emphasizing the bonds that linked them to others than in dwelling on their own privileges. Such a claim is admittedly quite speculative; something that seems rather more certain is that the details of how people used Olmec iconography as they negotiated social relations differed quite a bit from region to region during the Early Formative.

During the Middle Formative (900–400 B.C.), Olmec iconography was more likely to appear in public ritual contexts or exclusively associated with elite individuals. The organization of many Mesoamerican communities had been significantly altered by this time, establishing patterns of public ceremonial life that would persist until the Spanish Conquest, some 2,000 years later. Special ceremonial areas were established in communities, formed by arranging large, rectangular platforms around open plazas. Atop the platforms, raised high above any onlookers, stood temples or administrative buildings – and sometimes residences of the elite. Particularly important platforms were built high enough to become pyramids. On top of or beside the platforms, elaborately carved stone monuments were displayed, including, most characteristically, vertical stone slabs called *stelae*. The monuments depicted rulers, supernatural or mythological creatures, and important historical events.

The appearance of these features during the Middle Formative marks the emergence of well-developed elites whose hereditary privileges were legitimized through association with supernatural forces. Rulers quite literally portrayed themselves as the center of the universe (Reilly 1996). Archaeologists have made a number of observations linking Mesoamerican elites to ceremonial areas with platforms and plazas. For one thing, building all this required significant resources, including the recruitment and organization of vast amounts of labor. The impressive constructions that rose in the downtown areas of Mesoamerican communities would have been impossible without the existence of powerful decision-makers who could force people to work and direct their activities. Thus, to the extent that a broad consensus favored elaborate downtown areas, the mere construction of such places would have considerably reinforced the position of the elite.

But that wasn't all. There is evidence for all sorts of special activities in site cores, including public ceremonies – in which a few officiants stood high atop temples while the insignificant masses looked on – as well as more esoteric rituals that took place out of public view. Love (1999) charts the development of formally arranged spaces in communities on the Pacific Coast of Guatemala and Chiapas from the initial Early Formative to the end of the Middle Formative. He finds a progressive trend toward more rigid organization of regional capitals and points out that people's activities became steadily less flexible. Perhaps, he suggests, the very spatial organization of communities helped subjugate the emerging class of commoners in these increasingly unequal societies.

At many important Middle Formative sites, a few people, apparently rulers or others at the very summit of society, were buried in the ceremonial platforms. Joyce (1999) compares costume elements from such burials to those of more common graves in residences. She suggests that, during life, people used costume in a variety of ways. In their daily lives, or on special occasions, most people wore individual-ized combinations of jewelry or other ornaments. Perhaps this was because the unique ways individuals presented themselves to others were important in the daily give and take of social relations. But the costumes of people buried away from their homes, in ceremonial platforms and plazas, are different. While they are often more elaborate and costly than those of people buried elsewhere, they are also more stan-dardized. For these people, costume did not mark them as unique individuals, but as holders of offices that transcended the individual.

An important Middle Formative site that exhibits all these patterns is La Venta. Located on the Gulf Coast, La Venta rose to prominence after 900 B.C., as the site of San Lorenzo went into decline. La Venta was, by 600–400 B.C., a *city* (see González Lauck 1996; also Drucker 1952; Drucker et al. 1959). The whole settlement covered 200 hectares and included a carefully planned ceremonial and administrative core with a great variety of platforms, buildings, and monuments, including an earthen pyramid that soared more than 30 m above adjacent plazas. Stone monuments in a central area included gigantic stone heads (generally thought to depict rulers), flat-topped rectangular blocks with carvings around the sides (probably thrones), upright stelae, and a variety of other sculptures. A few elite burials have been excavated. In one funerary chamber constructed of basalt columns, the poorly preserved remains of two or three young individuals were asso-ciated with a rich array of imported jade objects. Numerous isolated offerings were also found in the central part of the site. These included axe blades or *celts* made of jade or other hard stones, deliberately arranged in patterns, and buried. In some cases, the buried celts were associated with other objects, such as large iron ore mirrors. The most astounding offerings were massive pits in which hundreds of roughly shaped blocks of *serpentine* – a greenstone not of the hardness or quality of jade but still quite highly prized – had been stacked together and buried. That these features had a symbolic, offertory character is indicated by the fact that in several cases the uppermost layer of blocks was arranged to form a mosaic design appar-ently related to Olmec iconography. These offerings become doubly impressive when one considers that all of the stones were imported at significant expense, then permanently removed from use through ceremonial burial.

Clearly, at Middle Formative La Venta we can point to the existence of a well-established elite, able to command significant amounts of local labor and linked to other Mesoamerican groups by exchange networks through which flowed large amounts of exotic materials. How did Olmec iconography fit into this picture? We need to be careful here, since many scholars would simply label everything at La Venta "Olmec," whereas I am using the term in a much more restricted sense to refer to elements of a *shared* art style not unique to the Gulf Coast.

Even when the term is used in this restricted sense, the patterns at La Venta seem very clear: Olmec iconography was closely associated with an elite class and it was the style chosen for illustrating deities or supernatural forces worshiped in the ceremonial areas. A few examples will suffice to make these points. The iconography of the thrones, in which a human figure emerges from a cave or the mouth of a monster, sometimes holding a supernaturally transformed baby, is shared with quite distant regions at this time. Excavations at the base of La Venta's massive pyramid revealed stone slabs, several still set where they had been placed in late Middle Formative times, depicting supernatural creatures in unmistakable Olmec style. Were these supernaturals worshiped at the pyramid? Finally, a large stone sarcophagus, found in a more cloistered precinct north of the pyramid, was sculpted to represent the body of an Olmec monster (Fig. 3.2(c)); inside were jade and serpentine objects that had apparently accompanied the remains of an elite person buried in the coffin.

Numerous other sites across Mesoamerica show evidence of a similar complex of elite and ceremonial activity. The distribution of Middle Formative sites with Olmec-style monumental carvings seems actually to be patterned rather than random and may reflect ancient trade routes (Grove 1996). One corridor extends from the Gulf Coast into Morelos and Guerrero (Fig. 3.1) and includes two sites with significant numbers of monuments in the Olmec style: Chalcatzingo and the intimidatingly named Teopantecuanitlan. Another corridor extended from the Gulf Coast to Chiapas and the Pacific Coast of Guatemala, then from there to El Salvador, eastern Guatemala and western Honduras (see, for instance, Clark and Pye 2000b). Portable objects in Olmec style were more widely distributed than sculpture; unfortunately, our understanding of exactly how they were used is poor because so few have been found in context.

We have perhaps more information concerning the use of larger sculptures, though context is often a problem with these as well. Nevertheless, it is clear that Formative period sculptures were in no way like the neglected, pigeon-fouled statues of our own city parks. Instead, many Olmec sculptures appear to have been continuously involved in activity (Cyphers 1999; Grove 1981). They were carved, placed with other statues, moved around, worshiped through the burial of small offerings, defaced, mutilated, broken, and, in at least the case of late Early Formative San Lorenzo, taken to a walled yard where, awaiting recarving into new sculptures, they were nevertheless still treated with reverence. It is possible that there were regular sequences to the recarving: close scrutiny has revealed that some of the monumental heads were recarved from thrones.

So what did people actually do with Olmec imagery? First and foremost, the Olmec style gave shape to a world beyond everyday experience: people used it to represent mythological creatures, supernatural beings, and the interaction (or even fusion) of humans with such entities. It seems quite likely that display of objects in

Olmec style occasioned reverence, respect, and dignity. But people also used these things strategically, to make claims concerning their relations with other people. In other words, display of Olmec objects was not simply a two-way relation between an individual and his or her gods, but a three-way relation between an individual, the gods, and other people. During the late Early Formative, display of Olmec iconography on pottery vessels involved claims about membership in groups. With the major exception of San Lorenzo, differences in status seem to have been a secondary factor at that time, although exactly what these "groups" were seems to have differed from region to region and it seems possible that the imagery could have been used by one kin group to support claims of superiority over another. By the Middle Formative, the social messages of Olmec iconography were everywhere more emphatically ones of difference and status. Exclusion surpassed inclusion as a principal theme. The imagery was inscribed on precious objects available only to a few people. It appeared in architectural settings that controlled and divided people, raising elite officiants high above the commoners who attended public ceremonies.

Structural Implications of the Sharing of Olmec Iconography

Thus far I have emphasized agency by exploring the social uses of Olmec art from 1200 to 400 B.C., with particular attention to the way art was related to the activities of an emerging elite. Such accounts, emphasizing the social strategies people pursue rather than the ways culture shapes those strategies, can give the impression that social and political changes were the result of conspiracies by elites who manipulated the masses with cynical propaganda. Comparative anthropology strongly cautions us against any such idea. Except perhaps in some very centralized state societies, ideologies are never purely the cynical creations of those in charge. Rulers, like everyone else, are enmeshed in cultural contexts that both constrain and enable their actions. The investigation of structures seeks to address such issues. How, it asks, did structures of belief and habit help determine what it meant to be an agent in ancient Mesoamerica? Was Olmec iconography part of such structures?

To claim that an art style was part of a structure is a rather complicated proposition, much more than an assertion that people carried around a set of designs in their heads. Minimally, it is useful to distinguish between a *representational system* (a set of designs, forms, and strategies of illustration) and its *subject matter* (what the representations depict). Particular subjects may also have had further connotations – people would have associated all sorts of complex thoughts and feelings with images of dragons or corn deities. We can refer to such thoughts and feelings as the *symbolism* associated with the subject matter.

Archaeologists are still wrestling with the challenges of reconstructing the subject matter and symbolism of Olmec art. The representational system itself is intricate and complex, and the peoples of this time did not leave any written texts that would help explain it to us. We instead rely on detailed analyses of the representations, careful attention to archaeological contexts, and attempts to link themes in Olmec art to those of later, better-known periods – even to the time of the Spanish Conquest over 2,000 years later. This last approach seems to hold particular promise when done with care. Some Formative concepts of the cosmos do persist through to the conquest, but there is ongoing discussion about whether the supernaturals of Olmec iconography can be linked to specific conquest-era deities (Joralemon 1976; Marcus 1989; Reilly 1996). Taube (1996, 2000) has developed a fascinating argument linking a Middle Formative corn deity to symbolism in later Mesoamerica and even to groups as far away as the Pueblo societies of the American Southwest.

An important question concerns what should be included in these kinds of analyses. A disturbing number of Olmec artifacts have been ripped from their original contexts and sold on the international art market, creating analytical and ethical dilemmas for archaeologists. Should we reject any consideration of a fabulous Olmec-style jade that, smuggled illegally into the U.S., now graces the mantelpiece of some Beverly Hills mansion? Or do we swallow our distaste and consider all objects potentially relevant to understanding ancient Mesoamerica, no matter their lack of context and tainted history in the present? There is no general agreement on such issues, and they do affect investigators' results.

Once we decide that Olmec iconography involved both a representational system and a specific subject matter consisting of supernatural creatures, then my claim that it helped structure human agency in Formative Mesoamerica should seem reasonable. For example, if an Olmec motif illustrated the supernatural Sky, patron of the Sky kin group, it is easy to imagine someone displaying the motif in pursuit of practical social goals – for instance, appealing to group solidarity in convincing relatives to contribute to a village feast. However, people would not have been able to do anything they wanted with Olmec imagery. Their options were constrained by conventions of action, beliefs concerning humans' relations to the supernatural, and so forth.

Now, there are many different directions we could take to investigate the role of Olmec imagery in structures of belief, but most relevant for this chapter are implications of the *sharing* of Olmec imagery among different regions. When people used Olmec-style artifacts did they somehow refer to the fact that people in distant places were using similar objects? It is important to use caution here, because it would be easy to fall back into the mother culture/sister cultures debate. The solution, as I have argued, is to explore specific questions in detail. I consider two questions here: (1) To what extent were the ideas expressed in Olmec art shared already across Mesoamerica before 1200 B.C.? (2) Can we specify the kinds of relationships that existed between people from distant regions between 1200 and 400 B.C.?

Grove (1993) suggests that the subject matter of Olmec imagery, or even the representational system itself, might have been shared across Mesoamerica long before 1200 B.C. If so, then by the late Early Formative the *sharing* of Olmec imagery was probably not very important to its meaning in any one area, since the people there would have gotten it from their own forbears rather than other peoples. This question turns our interests back to the initial Early Formative (1600–1200 B.C.), or even the Archaic period (8000–1600 B.C.), and we immediately face the obstacle of few excavated sites and scarce evidence.

Investigators have experimented with a variety of solutions to this problem. One intriguing example is the holistic approach taken by Marcus (1989; see also Flannery and Marcus 1983: topics 2, 9, 97). She proposes that archaeologists should take greater advantage of historical linguistics, especially in places like Oaxaca, where there is evidence of long-term continuity of neighboring populations speaking related languages. Such languages have gradually diverged from a shared *protolanguage*, in much the way that Spanish, French, and Italian have diverged from Latin. Linguists can reconstruct elements of such protolanguages based on similarities between the modern languages; sometimes they can even estimate the timing of linguistic divergence. Marcus draws on such work to argue that a belief in Sky and Earth as two important supernatural forces is very ancient in Oaxaca, and probably characterized Archaic peoples of the region. If during the late Early Formative of Oaxaca Olmec motifs designated Earth and Sky, then the subject matter of the art was not a recently adopted set of ideas, but rather one that had a long history in the region.

Grove (1999) proposes that the placement of stone sculpture and important buildings helped create a sacred landscape at Formative sites. He compares the sacred landscape of Chalcatzingo in Morelos to sites in the Gulf Coast, and finds that, while Chalcatzingo was strongly influenced by Gulf Coast canons, it was no simple copy. Numerous details were of local origin, and there are hints that the basic organizational plan of the site – and thus, potentially, some local concepts of sacred landscapes – pre-dated any identifiable contact with the Gulf Coast.

Excavations in the southern Chiapas Coast have revealed that Olmec imagery was preceded by a very different representational system in the initial Early Formative. The earlier imagery appeared on ceramic serving dishes and involved the modeling of a diverse array of animals from the local environment, including dogs, peccaries, deer, toads, fish and a variety of birds. This earlier representational system disappeared around the time of the appearance of Olmec imagery, and I argue that the one replaced the other (Lesure 2000). If that is true, then in this case we have evidence that, at the very least, the Olmec *representational system* was something foreign, adopted by the peoples of coastal Chiapas during the late Early Formative.

The results of this last study contrast with those of the first two, and it certainly seems possible that the adoption of Olmec style followed distinct courses in different regions. Remember, however, that the Olmec style comprised a representational system, a specific subject matter, and the further connotations people associated with those subjects. When we investigate to what degree Olmec art expressed beliefs already shared across Mesoamerica before 1200 B.C., we need to consider each of these topics in turn. It seems likely that some of the subject matter and symbolism of Olmec art was widely shared before the late Early Formative, or else that people linked adopted ideas to long-standing local beliefs. Nevertheless, in places like coastal Chiapas and the Basin of Mexico (Tolstoy 1989b) the designs that depicted supernaturals and the custom of placing those designs on pottery do appear to have been adopted by local peoples as a result of their contact with groups in other areas.

Now, obviously someone can adopt something and then eventually forget that he or she hasn't always had it; however, it seems likely that when people displayed pots with Olmec imagery during the late Early Formative, they referred, either implicitly or explicitly, to the network of exchange contacts that was growing up at this time. The *shared* nature of the Olmec style was thus part of its symbolism. Already during the Early Formative a set of associations was bundled together: important supernaturals, precious objects derived from exchange, the conviviality of shared meals, and the ability to be generous to others by giving them food or status paraphernalia. The sharing of the Olmec style was, then, part of a structure, both a resource for people as they negotiated relations with others and a factor in shaping those relations. Symbolic links between the supernatural, exotic goods, and social values such as generosity were surely an important backdrop to the emergence of elites, but Olmec iconography was not a self-serving instrument of the privileged. Indeed, if, as I suggested in the last section, the imagery also signaled group membership of some kind, it may actually have helped keep the ambitions of high-status people in check.

Perhaps it would be more accurate to think of Olmec iconography not as part of "a" structure, but as a component of *structures*, since its symbolism and use seem to have differed quite a bit from place to place during the late Early Formative. I have already discussed the different ways it may have been used to express group identities in Chiapas, Oaxaca, and the Basin of Mexico. Were regional differences in use widely perceived? When people in coastal Chiapas brought out a decorated dish laden with local foods, was some sort of symbolic link to the impressive sculptures of San Lorenzo implied?

In other words, how much did the people of one region know about other parts of Mesoamerica during the late Early Formative, and how did such knowledge affect daily life? One promising approach is to take a careful look at the trade contacts that linked people from different regions, since those were the circumstances in which they gained knowledge of each other. Were these relations of reciprocity or were they unequal in some way? I raised this issue briefly in the last section, noting only that it is still very much unresolved. Nevertheless, some interesting work on the exchange of obsidian deserves mention. Four aspects of obsidian make it a very attractive item for analysis: it was widely distributed across Mesoamerica, it can be accurately sourced, it is quite abundant at Formative sites, and the techniques through which it was broken down into tools can actually be replicated and studied by archaeologists.

During the Middle Formative, an important technological innovation appeared in many parts of Mesoamerica. This was the manufacture of prismatic obsidian blades, an extremely efficient and effective use of the resource, but one that required specialized skills. Clark (1987) argued that the economics and organization of blade manufacture meant that it was typically associated with well-developed elites, or perhaps with *networks* of elites in places like the Central Depression of Chiapas. Since 1987, Clark has continued work on the idea that trade in obsidian was closely related to politics and that by monitoring changes in different areas, including raw material sources, amounts of obsidian traded, and manufacturing techniques, it might be possible to reconstruct political relations between people from different societies. On the Chiapas Coast, the appearance of Olmec iconography coincides with a sharp drop in the amount of obsidian used by local villagers, leading Clark to suggest that exchange relations between Chiapas and Gulf Coast peoples were profoundly unequal. Thus, there would have been political connotations to any display of Olmec imagery in Chiapas, a recognition of unequal relations between leaders in the respective regions. Much more detailed comparative work is necessary, but these sorts of analyses are quite promising.

In sum, to fully understand the Olmec style, we need to recognize that it was not limited to a set of designs, but included, as well, a specific supernatural subject matter and much complex symbolism associated with those subjects. It therefore seems likely that this art style was part of the structures that shaped human agency in Early and Middle Formative Mesoamerica. Further, the *sharing* of the imagery was part of such structures. Between 1200 and 900 B.C., when someone displayed a decorated dish, its Olmec imagery elicited a variety of thoughts and feelings among people present. One strand of that symbolism linked the conviviality of the meal to supernatural forces as well as to the long-distance contacts through which precious objects entered the community. Those kinds of symbolic links, in turn, legitimized growing differences in social status within Mesoamerican villages by tying social values such as generosity and the benevolence of supernaturals to the kinds of access to foreign exchange partners that not everyone could afford to maintain.

An issue of ongoing debate is the specific role that elites of the Gulf Coast played in the sharing of Olmec iconography. At the moment, it seems likely that much of the Olmec representational system, including its complicated approach to representing supernatural subjects (see Figs. 3.2, 3.3), specific customs for using the representations in social interactions, and even potentially the supernatural subjects themselves, were synthesized during the Early Formative in rapidly developing societies of the Gulf Coast. If so, then for people in other parts of Mesoamerica, the exchange relations they entered into with peoples of the Gulf Coast would have been part of the connotations of Olmec iconography. The appearance of Olmec art might in this view be rather crudely compared to a McDonald's in Paris or a Coke bottle in Bangkok, which always to some degree refer to the economic clout and world-wide prestige of the United States. Unfortunately, there has been far too much wild speculation about the specific content of long-distance relations in early Mesoamerica. Careful analyses of things like obsidian may eventually provide some more reliable answers. Nevertheless, whatever specific role the Gulf played in the symbolism of Olmec art, it is important to emphasize that the art did not form part of a single unified structure across all of Mesoamerica. In each region, the sharing of iconography was part of a *local* structure in which ideas borrowed from long-distance contacts were reworked and integrated with local traditions.

Putting the Two Together

Researchers studying Formative Mesoamerica are increasingly trying to locate the causes of social and political change in history. This involves searching for evidence of the strategies different sorts of people pursued in their relations with others (i.e. agency), but it also involves examining the way people's possibilities for strategic action were shaped by their place in culture and society (structure). Putting the two of these together is my obvious final task here. The fundamental challenge is to use the concepts of agency and structure to trace changes over time in early Mesoamerica. As an example of such work, consider the emergence of greenstone – including jade, but also serpentine and other green, metamorphic stones – as a key valuable and symbol.

Greenstone objects have not yet been found in Archaic sites, but it seems likely that the first stirrings of long-distance trade began at that time, since already by 1400 B.C. an offering of greenstone is known from Paso de la Amada on the Chiapas Coast. During the initial Early Formative in that region, greenstone acquired some symbolic importance (Lesure 1999). Used for both tiny, personal ornaments and celts to work wood, greenstone was apparently only moderately valuable. Certainly people regularly lost greenstone beads, suggesting that they treated such items with a certain carelessness. Greenstone was probably of only limited strategic use to people seeking to enhance their social status.

Exactly what was going on in other areas is not clear, but important finds at the ceremonial site of El Manati on the Gulf Coast indicate that the emergence of greenstone as a key valuable was further advanced in that area. Ortiz and Rodríguez (1999) found three phases of ritual use of the site from initial to late Early Formative. Offerings of jade and other items included, by late in the sequence, astounding wooden sculptures in Olmec style, ceremonial staffs, and burials of children – all placed in and around a spring. In the earliest phase of ritual, greenstone celts were tossed into the pool surrounding the spring; later, groupings of celts were ranged in patterns and buried; later still, complex and elaborate sets of objects were deposited, just at the time when sculptures were being carved in abundance just 10 km away at San Lorenzo. We can trace here the gradual elaboration of a set of ceremonial activities linked to the growing network of long-distance trade, but we don't yet have much information on the strategic uses of jade by people living at San Lorenzo.

During the late Early Formative and Middle Formative, small greenstone objects continued to be used as personal ornaments, but there was also an ever-expanding variety of other uses. Ornaments varied from single beads and pendants to elaborate necklaces or belts. The color and quality of stone became important in distinguishing objects. One implication is that greenstone provided increasing scope for making distinctions among *people*. It was becoming a key element in the legitimation of elite power and authority.

That legitimation was lodged in the great variety of uses of greenstone, from the practical and personal to the esoteric and ceremonial. By the Middle Formative, when an ordinary person wore a greenstone pendant with the very simple goal of being attractive and persuasive to others (Joyce 1999), the object would have had a whole variety of connotations over which he or she had no control. It was part of structures that made high-ranking people stewards of the universe. People across a wide social spectrum used greenstone in ways that reflected their own interests. For instance, in some places they buried family members with a jade bead in their mouth (Marcus and Flannery 1996:97), presumably to ensure a loved one's well-being in the afterlife. Activities such as these, however, perpetuated structures that legitimized social inequality, since they accepted the profound religious significance of a material that was scarce and thus subject to control by a small segment of the population.

The structural importance of jade was simultaneously economic and symbolic. Taube (1996, 2000) explores the symbolic ramifications of greenstone and celts during the Middle Formative and traces their legacy in later Mesoamerican societies. Wealth items such as jade and the green feathers of the quetzal bird were linked to maize, a staple of subsistence. Greenstone celts were ceremonially equated with maize cobs. Officiants in some ceremonies strapped celts to their limbs, thereby becoming the axis of the world, "a vital conduit of divine power" (Taube 1996:50). Thus, wealth, power, maize, and agricultural fertility were all bound up in a complex religious and ceremonial system. By this time, greenstone was deeply lodged in structures of belief and routine; it helped shape what it meant to be a member of society and provided a wide scope for the strategic activities of human agents. But the possibilities for activity were unequally distributed in society, and small personal acts – wearing a necklace, making an offering, placing a bead in the mouth of a deceased loved one – helped perpetuate the larger system of beliefs and social stratification.

I have dwelt here on just one example – greenstone – and have been brief and schematic. Nevertheless, this illustrates the kinds of accounts of social and political development that scholars at work on agency perspectives hope to achieve as they both build on and move beyond older debates concerning Olmec art and long-distance contacts in early Mesoamerica.

REFERENCES

Clark, J. E., 1987 Politics, prismatic blades, and Mesoamerican civilization. In *The Organization of Core Technology*. J. K. Johnson and C. A. Morrow, eds. Pp. 259–284. Boulder: Westview Press.
——1997 The arts of government in early Mesoamerica. *Annual Review of Anthropology* 26, 211–234.
Clark, J. E., and M. E. Pye, eds., 2000a *Olmec Art and Archaeology in Mesoamerica*. Studies in the History of Art 58. Washington, DC: National Gallery of Art.
——2000b The Pacific coast and the Olmec question. In *Olmec Art and Archaeology in Mesoamerica*. John E. Clark and Mary E. Pye, eds. Pp. 217–251. Studies in the History of Art 58. Washington, DC: National Gallery of Art.

Covarrubias, M., 1957 *Indian Art of Mexico and Central America*. New York: Alfred A. Knopf.

Cyphers, A., 1999 From stone to symbols: Olmec art in social context at San Lorenzo Tenochtitlán. In *Social Patterns in Pre-Classic Mesoamerica*. D. C. Grove and R. A. Joyce, eds. Pp. 155–181. Washington, DC: Dumbarton Oaks Research Library and Collection.

Di Castro Stringher, A., 1997 Los bloques de ilmenita de San Lorenzo. In *Población, Subsistencia, y Medio Ambiente en San Lorenzo Tenochtitlán* [Population, Subsistence, and Environment at San Lorenzo Tenochtitlan]. A. Cyphers, ed. Pp. 153–160. Mexico City: Instituto de Investigaciones Antropológicas, UNAM.

Diehl, R. A., and M. D. Coe, 1996 Olmec archaeology. In *The Olmec World: Ritual and Rulership*. Pp. 11–25. Princeton: The Art Museum, Princeton University.

Drucker, P., 1952 *La Venta, Tabasco: A Study of Olmec Ceramics and Art*. Bureau of American Ethnology Bulletin 153. Washington, DC: United States Government Printing Office.

Drucker, P., R. F. Heizer, and R. J. Squier, 1959 *Excavations at La Venta, Tabasco, 1955*. Bureau of American Ethnology Bulletin 170. Washington, DC: United States Government Printing Office.

Flannery, K. V., 1968 The Olmec and the Valley of Oaxaca: A model for inter-regional interaction in Formative times. In *Dumbarton Oaks Conference on the Olmec*. E. P. Benson, ed. Pp. 79–110. Washington, DC: Dumbarton Oaks.

Flannery, K. V., and J. Marcus, eds., 1983 *The Cloud People: Divergent Evolution of the Zapotec and Mixtec Civilizations*. New York: Academic Press.

——1994 *Early Formative Pottery of the Valley of Oaxaca, Mexico*. Memoirs 27. Ann Arbor: Museum of Anthropology, University of Michigan.

——2000 Formative Mexican chiefdoms and the myth of the Mother Culture. *Journal of Anthropological Archaeology* 19, 1–37.

González Lauck, R., 1996 La Venta: An Olmec capital. In *Olmec Art of Ancient Mexico*. E. P. Benson and B. de la Fuente, eds. Pp. 73–81. Washington, DC: National Gallery of Art.

Grove, D. C., 1981 Olmec monuments: Mutilation as a clue to meaning. In *The Olmec and their Neighbors: Essays in Memory of Matthew W. Stirling*. E. P. Benson, ed. Pp. 49–68. Washington, DC: Dumbarton Oaks Research Library and Collections.

——1989 Olmec: What's in a name? In *Regional Perspectives on the Olmec*. R. J. Sharer and D. C. Grove, eds. Pp. 8–14. Cambridge: Cambridge University Press.

——1993 "Olmec" horizons in Formative period Mesoamerica: Diffusion or social evolution? In *Latin American Horizons: a Symposium at Dumbarton Oaks, 11th and 12th October 1986*. D. S. Rice, ed. Pp. 83–111. Washington, DC: Dumbarton Oaks Research Library and Collection.

——1996 Archaeological context of Olmec art outside of the Gulf Coast. In *Olmec Art of Ancient Mexico*. E. P. Benson and Beatriz de la Fuente, eds. Pp. 105–117. Washington, DC: National Gallery of Art.

——1999 Public monuments and sacred mountains: Observations on three Formative period sacred landscapes. In *Social Patterns in Pre-Classic Mesoamerica*. D. C. Grove and R. A. Joyce, eds. Pp. 255–299. Washington, DC: Dumbarton Oaks Research Library and Collection.

Grove, D. C., and S. D. Gillespie, 1992 Ideology and evolution at the pre-state level: Formative period Mesoamerica. In *Ideology and Pre-Columbian Civilizations*. A. A. Demarest and G. W. Conrad, eds. Pp. 15–36. Santa Fe, NM: School of American Research Press.

Grove, D. C., and R. A. Joyce, eds., 1999 *Social Patterns in Pre-Classic Mesoamerica*. Washington, DC: Dumbarton Oaks Research Library and Collection.

Haslip-Viera, G., B. Ortiz de Montellano, and W. Barbour, 1997 Robbing Native American cultures: Van Sertima's Afrocentricity and the Olmecs. *Current Anthropology* 38, 419–441.

Joralemon, P. D., 1971 *A Study of Olmec Iconography*. Studies in Pre-Colombian Art and Archaeology 7. Washington, DC: Dumbarton Oaks Research Library and Collection.

——1976 The Olmec dragon: A study in Pre-Columbian iconography. In *Origins of Religious Art and Iconography in Preclassic Mesoamerica*. H. B. Nicholson, ed. Pp. 29–71. UCLA Latin American Studies 31. Los Angeles: UCLA Lation American Center.

Joyce, R. A., 1999 Social dimensions of Pre-Classic burials. In *Social Patterns in Pre-Classic Mesoamerica*. D. C. Grove and R. A. Joyce, eds. Pp. 15–48. Washington, DC: Dumbarton Oaks Research Library and Collection.

Lesure, R. G., 1999 On the genesis of value in early hierarchical societies. In *Material Symbols: Culture and Economy in Prehistory*. J. Robb, ed. Pp. 23–54. Southern Illinois University at Carbondale, Occasional Papers 26. Carbondale: Center for Archaeological Investigations.

——2000 Animal imagery, cultural unities, and ideologies of inequality in early formative Mesoamerica. In *Olmec Art and Archaeology in Mesoamerica*. J. E. Clark and M. E. Pye, eds. Pp. 193–215. Studies in the History of Art 58. Washington, DC: National Gallery of Art.

Love, M. W., 1999 Ideology, material culture, and daily practice in Pre-Classic Mesoamerica: A Pacific Coast perspective. In *Social Patterns in Pre-Classic Mesoamerica*. D. C. Grove and R. A. Joyce, eds. Pp. 127–153. Washington, DC: Dumbarton Oaks Research Library and Collection.

Marcus, J., 1989 Zapotec chiefdoms and the nature of Formative religions. In *Regional Perspectives on the Olmec*. R. J. Sharer and D. C. Grove, eds. Pp. 148–197. Cambridge: Cambridge University Press.

Marcus, J., and K. V. Flannery, 1996 *Zapotec Civilization: How Urban Society Evolved in Mexico's Oaxaca Valley*. London: Thames & Hudson.

Niederberger, C., 2000 Ranked societies, iconographic complexity, and economic wealth in the Basin of Mexico toward 1200 B.C. In *Olmec Art and Archaeology in Mesoamerica*. J. E. Clark and M. E. Pye, eds. Pp. 169–191. Studies in the History of Art 58. Washington, DC: National Gallery of Art.

Ortiz C. P., and M. del C. Rodríguez, 1999 Olmec ritual behavior at El Manatí: A sacred space. In *Social Patterns in Pre-Classic Mesoamerica*. D. C. Grove and R. A. Joyce, eds. Pp. 225–254. Washington, DC: Dumbarton Oaks Research Library and Collection.

Pohorilenko, A., 1996 Portable carvings in the Olmec style. In *Olmec Art of Ancient Mexico*. E. P. Benson and B. de la Fuente, eds. Pp. 119–131. Washington: National Gallery of Art.

Reilly, F. K. III, 1996 Art, ritual, and rulership in the Olmec world. In *The Olmec World: Ritual and Rulership*. Pp. 27–45. Princeton: The Art Museum, Princeton University.

Taube, K., 1996 The Olmec maize god: The face of corn in formative Mesoamerica, *Res* 29/30, 39–81.

——2000 Lightning celts and corn fetishes: The formative Olmec and the development of maize symbolism in Mesoamerica and the American Southwest. In *Olmec Art and Archaeology in Mesoamerica*. J. E. Clark and M. E. Pye, eds. Pp. 297–337. Studies in the History of Art 58. Washington, DC: National Gallery of Art.

Tolstoy, P., 1989a Coapexco and Tlatilco: Sites with Olmec materials in the Basin of Mexico. In *Regional Perspectives on the Olmec*. R. J. Sharer and D. C. Grove, eds. Pp. 85–121. Cambridge: Cambridge University Press.

——1989b Western Mesoamerica and the Olmec. In *Regional Perspectives on the Olmec*. R. J. Sharer and D. C. Grove, eds. Pp. 275–302. Cambridge: Cambridge University Press.

4

Governance and Polity at Classic Teotihuacan

Saburo Sugiyama

Teotihuacan lies 40 km (25 miles) northeast of modern Mexico City in the Central Mexican highlands at an altitude of around 2,280 m (about 7,500 ft). This ancient city is well known for its monumental constructions, such as the Sun Pyramid, the Moon Pyramid, and the Ciudadela (Citadel), with its main temple called the "Feathered Serpent Pyramid." These massive constructions are even more impressive, however, when one realizes that they were complementary elements of a planned city that harmoniously integrated other public buildings, numerous residential complexes, and the surrounding topography, along the "Avenue of the Dead" (Fig. 4.1). The monumentality was so conspicuous and impressive that the Aztecs, who visited the ruins eight centuries after its collapse, considered them as deeds of the gods and named the site in their language "Teotihuacan," meaning the place where the gods lived. Since then, Teotihuacan had been labeled as a legendary place for centuries, until scientific research began to recover its history early last century.

Our current view of Teotihuacan results from many archaeological projects carried out with varied objectives and strategies (Berlo 1992). Numerous public buildings and residences in the central area were excavated, consolidated, and partially reconstructed, mainly by Mexican institutions, to demonstrate national cultural heritage. The grand scale and complexity of Teotihuacan's urbanism were substantiated conclusively with the systematic mapping with aerial photos and extensive data collection that has been undertaken by the Teotihuacan Mapping Project since the 1960s (Millon et al. 1973). Based on crew members' continuous work, many aspects of the urban life and its changing boundaries have been reconstructed scientifically over time. We now know that, at its height, Teotihuacan was one of the largest Pre-Columbian urban centers in the Americas in terms of the metropolitan area it covered (about 20 km^2) and its estimated population (100,000–150,000).

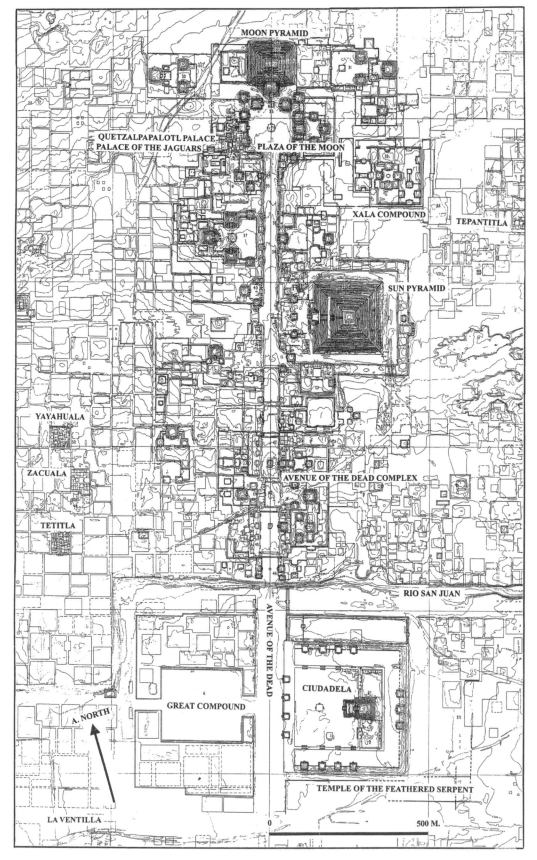

Figure 4.1. General map of the central area of Teotihuacan (after Millon et al. 1973)

Ample data obtained in residential areas indicate that this religious center was also a stratified urban complex from its early years (Sempowski and Spence 1994). Craft specialization and social differentiation were well established, as discussed in Chapter 5 below. A powerful political organization, which we may call the state, was evidently responsible for the creation of the sacred space and regulated the diversified socio-economic activities in the city. Strong political and ideological control over the inhabitants is connoted, for example, by the city's cohesive layout, consistent orientation, standardized architectural style, residential complexes designed for multiple families, and conventional art forms. In fact, no independent single-family house breaking these architectural rules has been discovered in Classic period Teotihuacan.

Powerful rulership of the Teotihuacan state was also translated abroad. During its heyday (the third to sixth centuries A.D.) Teotihuacan materials, and ideas symbolizing rulership, were exported widely. Teotihuacan's influence seems to have reached up to Alta Vista in the current state of Zacatecas to the northwest (Aveni 1980:226–229), and at least as far as the Maya polity of Copan in Honduras to the southeast (Fash and Fash 2000). In particular, ritual items from the metropolis were acquired by the rulers and other elite members of these foreign states as status symbols that were used to reinforce their political power (see Chapter 7). The data suggest that the Teotihuacan state seems to have controlled large areas well beyond the Basin of Mexico, and probably affiliated with distant centers or actually took over certain Mesoamerican regions (Marcus 1983). Teotihuacan was evidently a dominant locus of such socio-political developments in Mesoamerica during the Late Formative to Early Classic periods.

Although increasing information from recent excavations enables us to reconstruct more precisely such expanding urban life in Teotihuacan (Manzanilla 1993; Storey 1992; see Chapter 5), certain aspects of the state polity still remain unclear. In particular, we lack the kind of specific historical information available to scholars of the Classic period Maya, Zapotec, or Postclassic Aztec and Mixtec. This lack is due, in great part, to the nature of Teotihuacan's writing system, which is highly pictorial and apparently not designed to record dynasties or individual achievements. Since writing has not been identified as a tool for historical records, the anthropomorphic figures depicted in the art of the city remain anonymous. This anonymity has often led viewers to call Teotihuacan's art mythological, animalistic, or ahistorical. Also, royal graves have not been found at Teotihuacan to date, and a palace where the leading group lived has not been definitely identified archaeologically, although many palace "candidates" have been excavated at various spots in the city. Thus, we have not yet documented even a single ruler's remains or image at Teotihuacan, in spite of the fact that the state lasted for more than 500 years, under powerful rulership so influential in the city and abroad. Consequently, the lack of these particular data has obstructed our view of the political structure. The limited information has even driven some researchers to propose that royal histories were de-emphasized in Teotihuacan (Pasztory 1997), or that the state was not organized individually by powerful rulers but collectively by several political entities (DeMarrais et al. 1996).

Recent research and methodological and interpretive developments, however, can still give us a good understanding of the power and interests of the Teotihuacan state. We must also realize that the view of the society and the political organization described above has been limited and distorted by what has been excavated and preserved. For instance, much of our data comes mainly from excavated residences and public buildings that had been cleaned, modified, or destroyed intentionally, often for political takeover or looting. Meanwhile, the symbols of the state, that is to say the major monuments, had been explored only partially and superficially before new excavations began in the late 1980s. This chapter mainly discusses the results of new intensive explorations at Teotihuacan's major monuments, particularly at the Feathered Serpent Pyramid and the Moon Pyramid, to reconsider the religious underpinnings of state control and how the state changed over time.

The chapter deals first with the city planning in which the government invested much of its resources. It then focuses on the manifestation of political rulership at the city's three major monuments and connects the evidence from them with iconography. We now think that monuments were not merely "reflections" of the state religion in passive form, but were deliberate manifestations of innovative ideological messages manipulated by rulers to broadcast socio-political statements. We know that most literate Mesoamerican states, characterized by dynastic rule and military institutions, proclaimed their rulership explicitly in religious terms in their central precincts. The texts and images engraved at Maya or Aztec temples suggest that rituals taking place at monuments were among the most important state events for the establishment of political authority. Through this chapter, it is demonstrated that individualistic powerful rulership of the Teotihuacan state was also symbolized at the major monuments. A traditional foundation ritual in Mesoamerica, human sacrifices with militaristic metaphors, often took place at the monuments from the city's early years.

Foundation of the City

Ceramic analyses suggest the sacred center may have had its origin around the time of Christ (Fig. 4.2). At that time, the Basin of Mexico included lakes and fertile lands with a relatively mild and cool climate. Several religious centers had already been flourishing, mainly in the southern basin, including Cuicuilco, a large ceremonial center with a population numbering in the thousands. Agricultural technologies, such as irrigation and terracing, may have been well developed and practiced by the time of Teotihuacan's founding (McClung de Tapia 1992). Sanders et al. (1979) systematically carried out an extensive survey of the Valley of Mexico in order to understand the social transformation processes from perspectives of ecology and social evolution (see Chapter 11). They demonstrated that a drastic depopulation in the southern basin occurred approximately when Teotihuacan's urbanization began in the northern basin. This seems to indicate a massive movement of people from southern villages and centers to Teotihuacan. The eruption of

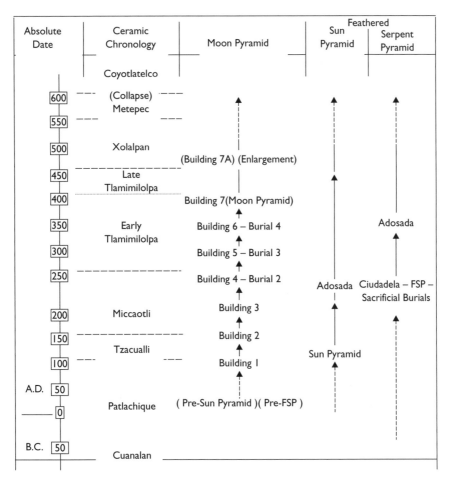

Figure 4.2. Teotihuacan chronology and construction history. Sugiyama and Cabrera 2002, modified from Millon 1992

the volcano Xitle, located in the southwestern edge of the basin, may have caused this population movement, as the lava gradually and widely covered the southern lands, including ceremonial centers (Pasztory 1997:77). Thus, the foundation of Teotihuacan as an urban center may have been related to the abandonment of Cuicuilco and its surrounding areas. However, the timing of the eruption has not yet been dated precisely enough to confirm this causal relationship. Moreover, the eruption cannot explain why Teotihuacan developed as a planned city on such a grand scale in that particular location. In order to understand what created so large and cohesive a population, we must examine more closely the urbanization process from the inside of the city.

According to the spatial distribution of early ceramics found on the surface, the Teotihuacan Valley had only small villages during the Cuanalan phase (500– 100 B.C.). They were located mainly in swampy lands near springs, ideal for highly

productive cultivation. Cowgill (1992) believes that the shift to the following
Patlachique phase (100 B.C.– A.D. 100) was a time of abrupt social change and significant increases in population. The area of highest ceramic concentrations shifted
to less-watered areas: the slopes of Cerro Colorado and Malinalco, the northern
section of the city, and the southern central area where the Ciudadela was later
constructed. However, only a few structures from these phases have been excavated,
and the city's foundation still remains in need of further excavation.

The following Tzacualli (A.D.100–150) and Miccaotli (A.D. 150–250) phases are
well represented by early monumental constructions discussed later in detail. The
urban area possibly expanded to approximately 20 km^2, with about 60,000 to
80,000 inhabitants by the end of the Tzacualli phase (Millon 1981:221). Teotihuacan city planning, best exemplified by the grid layout still seen today, was probably established during the Miccaotli phase. The city grew continuously as a political,
religious, and economic center through the following centuries, corresponding to
the Tlamimilolpa phase (A.D. 250–450) and the Xolalpan phase (A.D. 450–550),
until its rather sudden collapse around A.D. 600 (Metepec phase: A.D. 550–600).
We will now discuss details of the city planning and monuments erected during the
height of the state's development, which materialized the underlying state ideology
and political organization.

City Planning by the State

The rigorous regularity and harmonious spatial distribution of the buildings
strongly argue that the city did not develop as an aggregation of independently built
constructions, but that a master plan existed to create a meaningful urban space.
Although the enlargement and modification of buildings later took place many
times, the spatial structure, established early on, persisted throughout the city's
history. Analogous instances exist around the world; for example, in Inca Cuzco
and in ancient Chinese cities where monuments and important official buildings
were spatially arranged according to cosmological significance to situate governors
and their associates symbolically at the center of the universe (Wheatley 1971;
Zuidema 1983).

In Teotihuacan, all major monuments were fundamentally religious in function,
suggesting that the political realm was undifferentiated from the religious one. We
can assume that state governance sacralized this grand-scale city plan, with specific
areas of significance along the "Avenue of the Dead." Although written records have
not been deciphered, we can still suggest possible meanings of this spatial distribution on the basis of material remains. The following is an interpretation suggested by studies of the orientation of the city, the use of a measurement unit in
Teotihuacan, and spatial analyses of the city layout.

The Teotihuacan grid system was rigorously established to 15.5 degrees east of
astronomical north. Archaeo-astronomical studies by Aveni (1980), Dow (1967),
Drucker (1977), Malmstrom (1978), and others indicate that the Teotihuacan west
orientation coincided with a sightline from the major monuments to the setting of

certain planets and stars on special days. Among them, the most important was the sightline from the Sun Pyramid to the sunset on the western horizon on August 12 and April 29. The interval between these dates is 260 days, which comprised a complete cycle in the most significant ritual calendar widely used in Mesoamerica. The setting sun on August 12 would also have commemorated the legendary date for the beginning of the present era; the date coincides with the initial day of the Maya Long Count calendar, the creation day of time and space. These data indicate that the original planning of the Teotihuacan grid system had profound cosmogonic significance, and that the builders of the city were substantially concerned with the motions of heavenly bodies and related them to Mesoamerican cycles of time. The argument is further supported by "bench marks" found carved on Teotihuacan floors at many spots of the city: these were evidently used as devices for the orientation and calculation of calendar cycles.

Analysis of the measurement unit used for Teotihuacan constructions also indicates the concerns of Teotihuacan leaders relating to celestial bodies and the calendar. Based on the study of the precise measurements of the constructions, it is argued that Teotihuacan people apparently used a basic measuring unit of 83 cm to plan the city layout, and that dimensions of monumental structures and distances between them measure specific multiples of this unit, in numbers significant in Mesoamerican worldview and calendar cycles (Sugiyama 1993). Many coincidences of absolute distances, only some of which are mentioned below, suggest that deliberate ritual meanings, related to possible functions of different precincts, were involved in the city's spatial distribution.

Millon (1973) and others have suggested, applying the model of the later Aztec capital, Tenochtitlan, that Teotihuacan was divided equally into four sections by the Avenue of the Dead and the two east–west-running streets labeled the East and West Avenues. This interpretation, however, has yet to be verified by excavations. It is much clearer that the central ceremonial zone was composed of two distinct sections along the Avenue of the Dead, divided by the canalized "Rio San Juan," with the north section having dense high structures and the south one having scattered, rather flat structures. The naturally higher elevation of the northern section, when compared to the southern area, further emphasizes this distinction in height; this division was obviously intentionally planned. In addition, the Moon Pyramid was perfectly located at the northern end of the avenue exactly against the silhouette of Cerro Gordo, a large mountain range to the north (Fig. 4.3). This would have allowed people standing on the Avenue of the Dead to see the close cosmological relationship of the Moon Pyramid with the mountain and the sky represented by the North Star. In fact, the notion of the sacred city as a hierarchical microcosm like this can be found in other Mesoamerican centers as a shared cultural tradition (Ashmore 1991; see Chapter 7).

The length of the northern section on the Avenue of the Dead (about 1,662 m) is approximately the same as that of the southern section (about 1,654 m), if we consider the Moon Pyramid, "Rio San Juan," and the "Rio San Lorenzo" as the northern, central, and southern boundaries respectively. These distances correspond approximately to 2,000 Teotihuacan measurement units (83 cm × 2,000 =

Figure 4.3. Aerial view of the city's central area, from the south to the north. The Avenue of the Dead is exactly oriented toward the top of the mountain, Cerro Gordo

1,660 m). The northern section was evidently the core of the city, and the Sun Pyramid stands exactly at the mid-point of this northern section. The Sun Pyramid's centrality is also underscored by its exceptional and very purposeful dimensions. The original size of the Sun Pyramid (216 m² at its base), when considered in terms of the basic Teotihuacan measurement unit, symbolized the pan-Mesoamerican ritual calendar of the 260-day cycle (83 cm × 260 = 215.8 m).

The southern section was represented by the Ciudadela (Citadel) complex and its main structure, the Feathered Serpent Pyramid. The vast space of the main plaza indicates its function as a public ritual place. Its surrounding water management programs, like the canal system and a large and deep well found near the center of the Ciudadela Plaza, and the depiction of water-related iconography, support the idea that the Ciudadela represented a connection with the watery underworld. Limited access to its interior and defensive architecture may have symbolized its linkage with warfare; these interpretations are also supported by the excavation data described below.

The integrity of the northern and southern sections is also suggested by the dimensions of the Sun Pyramid and Ciudadela complexes. The distances between the axis of the Avenue of the Dead and the eastern limits of both complexes coincide with each other (431 m and 432 m respectively). This evidence of a deliberate plan is further confirmed by the fact that they are exactly double the original size of the Sun Pyramid. These distances are also very close to the Teotihuacan measurement unit multiplied by 520 (83 cm × 520 = 431.6 m), which is two times 260, the number of days in the ritual calendar, three times a 173.3-day eclipse cycle, and 10 times the important calendric number of 52 (see Chapter 1). These coincidences support the notion that the major monuments were constructed following a master plan with cosmological and calendric significance.

Although precise calculation is often difficult because later constructions cover the original ones, these and many other correlations do not appear accidental. Thus, the study of the measurement unit suggests that the Teotihuacanos were concerned with known Mesoamerican time-reckoning systems, such as the 260-day ritual calendar, the 365-day solar calendar, and the 520-day bundle related to the 173.3-day eclipse cycles, all of which seem to have been encoded into the city's ceremonial core and monumental constructions. In other words, the state government created an earthly microcosm where heavenly space and divine time were fused. Each monument probably represented specific meanings and functions which were integrated into this microcosm. We do not know how many generations labored to complete this project. It is also possible that the city plan we see today was the final sequence of an expanding plan of buildings that was not foreseen at the beginning of the city's existence. In order to reconstruct the process of the actual integration of the major monuments, we need to examine chronological data from each monument, as described below.

Rulership Materialized at Major Monuments

The major monuments have been excavated and consolidated since the beginning of the twentieth century by Mexican national institutions, most recently by the National Institute of Anthropology and History (INAH). Although a significant amount of information was provided by these governmental projects, the question of how these monuments were specifically involved in state politics remained poorly understood until the re-exploration of three major pyramids began in the 1980s. The Ciudadela and Feathered Serpent Pyramid were re-explored by an INAH project in 1982 (Cabrera et al. 1982; Sugiyama 1989). The Feathered Serpent Pyramid was intensively and systematically excavated further in 1988–1989 by a joint project of INAH and Arizona State University (ASU) (Cabrera, Sugiyama, and Cowgill 1991). The Sun Pyramid complex was re-explored by INAH in the early 1990s (Matos 1995). The Moon Pyramid Project developed by Aichi Prefectural University (Japan), ASU, and INAH began extensive excavations in 1998 to further pursue the issues of ancient state formation and transformation. This project is currently in progress. I have summarized below what our excavations had provided by 2001 (Sugiyama and Cabrera 2000; http://archaeology.asu.edu/teo/moon).

The Sun Pyramid

This was the second-largest prehispanic monument ever constructed in the Americas, after the Great Pyramid in Cholula, Puebla. The pyramid was first excavated extensively and partially reconstructed by Leopoldo Batres in 1906 (Matos 1995). It was built in multiple stages. The current reconstructed form (the last construction level) is about 224 m² at the base and a little over 64 m in height. The volume of the entire structure is approximately 1 million m³ (more than 30 million ft³). The upper portion, where a temple was supposedly located, had already been destroyed completely before excavation; therefore no information on the temple itself is available. Burials of children were discovered at the corners of the pyramid, suggesting that sacrificial rituals took place in the dedication of the monument.

Three tunnels were excavated inside, and test excavations took place around the pyramid (Millon et al. 1965; Smith 1987). Surrounding platforms were recently excavated extensively. According to these excavations, the interior of the pyramid is solid, filled mainly with earth and adobe bricks, and the exterior, currently faced with stones, was originally covered with white lime plaster, which probably did not have any painting on it. The ceramic and C14 analyses indicate that the Sun Pyramid was constructed sometime during the Tzacualli phase, making it one of the earliest monuments in Teotihuacan. It was also revealed that the pyramid seems to have covered a smaller, earlier construction, buried inside, although we know almost nothing about it. During the Miccaotli phase, the principal (western) façade was partially covered by the Adosada platform. The pyramid itself was enlarged once later during the Xolalpan phase. The remains of this enlargement can be observed at the lowest tier of the current pyramid. The latest excavations further revealed that the Sun Pyramid complex comprised a long platform, a wide canal system, and a series of functional rooms constructed inside the precinct.

One of the most significant discoveries came in the early 1970s. The entrance to a cave or man-made tunnel was accidentally found at the foot of the main staircase of the Adosada platform. It was revealed that the "cave" goes down 6 m underneath the plaza floor and then continues horizontally toward the center of the pyramid, where six chamber-like "rooms" were uncovered. No mortuary materials were found inside. The "cave" has been interpreted as Chicomoztoc, the legendary place of human origin, recorded in Aztec mythologies (Heyden 1975). Originally the "cave" was believed to be natural and only partially modified by human action (Millon 1981). Manzanilla et al. (1994) recently demonstrated that it was completely human-made and proposed that it was excavated to create ritual space and obtain construction materials. If the "cave" was a human creation, its fundamental function also could have been for a royal tomb, as suggested by the form of the "cave" with chambers and antechamber-like artificial space, and evidence of substantial looting activities which seriously hampered us from determining its real function. At any rate, it is clear that the "cave" was a fundamental reason why the Sun Pyramid was erected where it is now and must have been related to the main function of the pyramid.

Images associated with the Sun Pyramid are not abundant. The façades of the Adosada platform were covered with sculptures of (jaguar) heads, paws, star signs, and serpent rattles, among other images. We also know that murals with checker-like geometric designs once adorned the lateral walls of the Adosada. These representations, predominantly of jaguar symbolism, would have formed conspicuous visual messages at the Adosada of the Sun Pyramid. Only a few offerings or caches have been found inside the pyramid, which include obsidian projectile points and human figures of obsidian, whose forms are very similar to those found at the Moon Pyramid and the Feathered Serpent Pyramid. As described later, they may have represented sacrificial victims, who were often included in the nuclei of major monuments at Teotihuacan. Unfortunately, we do not know what kind of deity or religious attributes were associated with the temple atop the Sun Pyramid, since this was the place where the most serious natural and deliberate destruction took place.

The Moon Pyramid

The Moon Pyramid, the second-largest pyramid of the city, is located at the northern end of the Avenue of the Dead. It is the only major monument located on the central axis of the city. It is about 149 m wide by 168 m long at its base, including the Adosada platform attached on the front façade of the main body. The pyramid is about 45 m in height in its current reconstructed form. A Mexican national project in 1962–64 extensively excavated, consolidated, and partially reconstructed major structures in the central area of the metropolis, including the Moon Plaza and the Moon Pyramid (Acosta 1964; Bernal 1963). However, the excavations were limited and superficial; therefore, the pyramid remained one of the least understood monuments in Teotihuacan before our excavations began in 1998.

After the exploration of the Feathered Serpent Pyramid was concluded, we chose the Moon Pyramid for intensive exploration to better understand state ideology and politics. The search for earlier structures within its interior was undertaken by means of extensive tunnel excavations. Trenches and pits were also excavated around the perimeter of the pyramid in order to locate temporally and spatially the Moon Pyramid in its city-wide context. As a result, the long modification process of the monument is now fully understood: seven overlapping pyramidal platforms were detected at this central location. Each new building was constructed larger and covered earlier constructions. We called the smallest pyramidal structure found under the Adosada platform Building 1, and the last and largest structure, known today as the Moon Pyramid, was named Building 7 (Fig. 4.4). In addition, we discovered inside the pyramid three sacrificial burial complexes, called Burials 2, 3, and 4, with exceptionally rich offerings that were associated with Buildings 4, 5, and 6, respectively. This modification process appears to have reflected changing state politics, and the contents of the burials would have represented the state ideology and characteristics of its government as well.

Building 1 was a square pyramidal platform measuring 23.5 m at its base; its height is unknown. C14 dates indicate that Building 1 was erected early in the second century A.D. The building deviated about 4 degrees from the city's standard orientation and would not have fit the city's grid system. Therefore, it probably predates the currently seen city layout. Although the size of the building was modest, we can point out that public religious ceremonies, as suggested by this pyramidal platform, were already important aspects of the society.

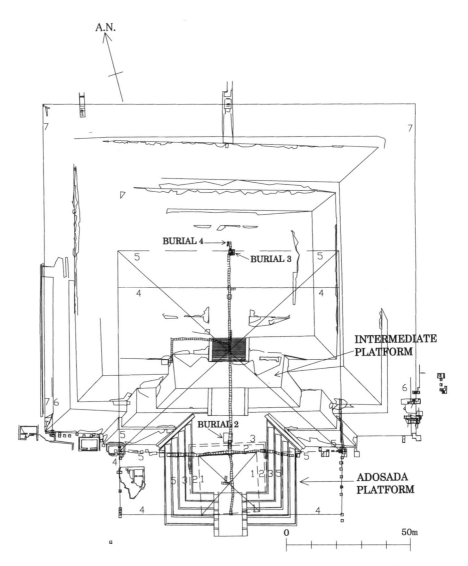

Figure 4.4. General plan of the Moon Pyramid, showing the location of earlier structures (Buildings 1 to 7)

    Buildings 2 and 3 completely covered Building 1, and expanded the east–west width to 29.3 m at its base. The façades consisted of stepped *taluds*, just as Building 1 would have had. The east–west orientation of the platform was moved slightly clockwise from that of Building 1, making it closer to the standard Teotihuacan orientation. C14 dates suggest that Building 2 was constructed around A.D. 150. Building 3 represented a small enlargement of Building 2, expanding the east–west width to 31.3 m. C14 analysis suggests that Building 3 dated around A.D. 200. These first three construction phases, then, corresponded to a gradual enlargement period of the pyramid, as well as of the city itself.

Building 4, in turn, represented a substantial enlargement of the monument; the structure became almost nine times larger than the previous one. The east–west width was expanded to 89.2 m and the north–south width to approximately 88.9 m. The city's spatial structure had been established probably by the time of the Building 4 construction. This would imply that the expanding state had become powerful enough to carry out such an enormous construction program. In addition, a sacrificial grave complex (Burial 2) was integrated into the construction of Building 4. As I describe below, the burial evidently represented the state ideology of that time, including symbols of sacred warfare. We conclude that Building 4 may represent the moment of state establishment. As the results of C14 analyses significantly vary, we tentatively date the building to the first half of the third century A.D.

Burial 2 was found in 1998 in the nucleus of Building 4. The grave, measuring 3.5 m², was bordered on four sides by roughly made stone walls with no outside access or roof. The inside space was filled completely with a homogeneous earth layer after a single body and a large number of offerings were set carefully and symmetrically on the floor (Fig. 4.5). Careful excavation revealed that the person was buried in a seated position near the eastern edge with his hands crossed behind his back as if they were tied together. Therefore we believe that this person, a male of 40–50 years at the time of death, wearing relatively modest ornaments, was a sacrificial victim buried alongside offerings in dedication to the monument.

The associated material comprises the richest offerings in quality excavated to date in Teotihuacan and includes two greenstone anthropomorphic sculptures; several obsidian human figures (probably representing sacrificed victims), knives of exceptionally large size, projectile points and prismatic blades of the same material; many shells, both unworked and worked in the form of ear spools, pendants, and beads; slate disks; and ceramics called Tlaloc vessels, among other items. Most impressive were skeletons of sacrificed animals: two pumas and one wolf (each found in individual wooden cages), nine eagles, one falcon, one owl, and three small rattlesnakes. These animals were most probably buried alive during a mortuary ritual (excrement was found in a cage), and evidently represented military institutions, as iconographic data from later periods suggest. Many militaristic objects included in the burial confirm this association of the Building 4 erection with sacralized warfare.

Building 5 was a further enlargement of the earlier monument but with a substantial change in the architectural style, which implies a shift in state ideology. The form of the building changed from a simple square pyramid to an architectural complex composed of the main body of the pyramid with an Adosada platform attached to its frontal façade. The east–west width of Building 5 remained the same (89 m), while the north–south dimension of the building extended to the north, reaching approximately 104 m. The *talud-tablero* form was used for both the main body and the Adosada platform. Another sacrificial grave (Burial 3), corresponding to Building 5, was discovered under its back (or north) façade; the contents again suggest themes of warfare and ritual sacrifice. We tentatively date Building 5 to the late third century A.D.

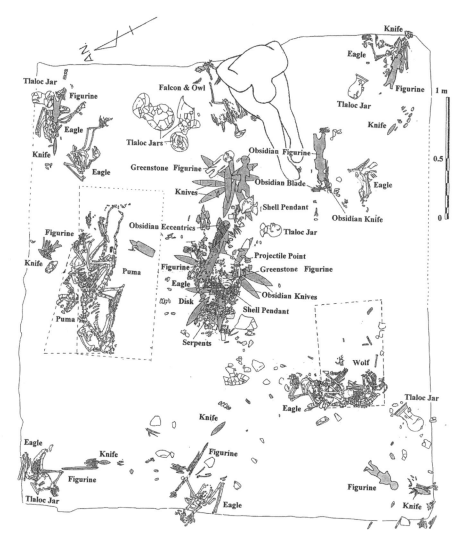

Figure 4.5. Plan of Burial 2 found in the Moon Pyramid

Burial 3 also constitutes a unique dedicatory burial complex, although its contents are significantly different from those of Burial 2. Four individuals, possibly all males, of about 14, 19, 22, and 42 years, evidently tied with their hands crossed behind their backs, were laid down carefully with offerings in a large pit. They were probably buried alive with stones, rocks, and earth, to form the nucleus of Building 5. Quite different types of ornaments have been associated directly with each of them, as if each person represented a different origin or social category. General offerings scattered around them include so-called shell trumpets, several clusters of obsidian projectile points, a large disk, and an organic sheet from something like a mat, which may have symbolized authority. Two clusters of offerings composed of many symbolic items were found in the central area. The most intriguing offerings were 14 wolf skulls, four puma skulls, and one incomplete young owl skull. According to iconographic studies, representations of the heads of wolves or coyotes were symbols used to identify individuals or social groups related to sacrifice and warfare.

Building 6 represented another substantial enlargement of the monument. Outside excavations uncovered evidence of talud walls with plaster, about 2.5 m inside the final walls of the Moon Pyramid (Building 7). Although the data on the southern and northern façades are very scanty, it is obvious that Building 6 had almost the same form and size (east–west width: 144 m) as the final Moon Pyramid. This monument was also dedicated with a sacrificial burial, which contrasted strongly with the previous rich burial complexes. The builders apparently put or threw in 17 severed human heads, without care, along with rocks, while constructing the north wall of Building 6; no offering was associated with them. Based on a few C14 dates and ceramics we tentatively date Building 6 to around A.D. 350.

Building 7 is the latest construction, known today as the Moon Pyramid. Although it was composed of the main body, the intermediate platform, and the Adosada platform, excavation reveals that they comprised a single unit made at once. The pyramid was part of a much larger complex called the Moon Plaza. Ample evidence of later modifications indicates that the Moon Pyramid had been used until the end of the city. However, C14 analysis could not well define the time of the pyramid's construction; only ceramics indicate that it would have been sometime during the Early Tlamimilolpa phase.

These data clearly indicate that the Moon Pyramid sits at a location where state-sponsored construction and dedicatory programs had occurred since the beginning of the city. This implies that religion was a prime variable in social change toward state complexity. In particular, the construction of Building 4, built in the third century A.D. and nine times bigger than the previous Building 3, seems to have represented a substantial enlargement of the political institutions as well. The currently visible city layout was evidently established by that time at the latest. In addition, the contents of Burial 2 confirm that the powerful rulership responsible for this grand construction plan was closely tied to a strong military institution, as indicated by commemorative sacrificial graves. This tradition of human sacrifice seems to have continued at least until the moment of Building 6's erection, as evidenced by the 17 decapitated heads (Burial 4). During the heyday of Teotihuacan, represented by Buildings 6 and 7, the city seems to have functioned actively as a ceremonial center, as suggested by the complicated modification process found in the Moon Plaza. The Moon pyramid apparently was a symbol of state religion until the collapse of the city.

Ciudadela and the Feathered Serpent Pyramid

The Ciudadela (Citadel) was the largest ceremonial precinct in the southern section of the city. It was a huge, nearly rectangular, compound measuring 405 m (north–south) by 397 m (east–west) at its base; it features the largest plaza in the

Figure 4.6. Front façade of the Feathered Serpent Pyramid located as the main monument in the Ciudadela

city, surrounded by four long and wide platforms on each side. Independent platforms, altars, a large and deep well, and a long canal that could have brought water from the "Rio San Juan" were excavated in the plaza. Cowgill (1983) believes that the entire adult population of the city (approximately 100,000 people) could have fit in the main plaza. The most important structure in this precinct was evidently the Feathered Serpent Pyramid, located in its central position (Fig. 4.6). This was a unique monument in Mesoamerica, because its façades were covered completely by sculptures of the Feathered Serpent and an enigmatic sacred entity that I will discuss later. Because the Feathered Serpent was a symbol of political authority until Aztec times, the monument and associated structures can be assumed to have been a politico-religious headquarters of the state (Carrasco et al. 2000). Some researchers further believe that rulers lived in the twin residential complexes, called "Palaces," located at both sides of the main pyramid (R. Millon 1973).

The Ciudadela was extensively excavated by the Mexican archaeologist Manuel Gamio (1922) in 1917–22. Since then, small-scale excavations have occasionally taken place. In 1980–82 INAH re-explored the complex, uncovering the degree to which the state invested resources in it (Cabrera et al. 1982, 1991). Four large platforms with pyramids sitting upon them and all residential complexes located inside were also excavated completely. The remains of previous buildings were detected at the pre-Ciudadela level, confirming there had been construction before the

Ciudadela. Certain ritual objects and utilitarian items, as well as evidence of burning corresponding to the fall of the city, were recovered in rooms and patios of the "Palaces." However, the data were not sufficient to indicate the function of the "Palaces" and the state politics involved, because the removal of items and destruction were extensive. Rather, most evidence pertaining to the governance of the city was recovered from the main pyramid itself.

Motivated by a discovery of multiple sacrificial burials on the southern side of the pyramid in 1983, the interior and exterior of the Feathered Serpent Pyramid were extensively and systematically explored in 1988–89. The remains of an earlier construction prior to the Feathered Serpent Pyramid were uncovered, with a corresponding sacrificial burial. The second level, corresponding to the Ciudadela and the Feathered Serpent Pyramid, was one of the most monumental construction programs in the city, dated to the early third century. The Adosada platform was the third construction level at this location. It covered the front façade of the main Feathered Serpent Pyramid sometime in the fourth century (Sugiyama 1998). One of the most significant discoveries was the more than 137 individuals found with abundant symbolic offerings of exceptional quality in and around the pyramid (Fig. 4.7). Although we intentionally left some burials unexcavated, we believe that more than 200 individuals were buried during the construction of the pyramid.

The distribution pattern of the graves clearly indicates a materialization of the Teotihuacan worldview. The skeletons were located in long rectangular pits excavated into the subsoil and were covered with stones and earth. The pits were symmetrically distributed outside and inside, along the east–west and north–south axes of the pyramid. Excavations showed that all were part of a burial complex dedicated to the erection of the pyramid. Curious regularities in the numbers of individuals the burial complex contained were noted; significant numbers in Mesoamerican cosmology and calendric systems, such as 4, 8, 9, 13, 18, and 20, were evidently used in organizing the burials of people. These would have symbolized the Mesoamerican cosmos, which consists of nine layers of underworld, four directions on earth, 13 layers of upperworld, and/or a ritual calendar of 260 days (20 day signs × 13 prefix numbers), as well as a solar cycle of 365 days (20 days × 18 months + 5 days).

The burial complex was mainly composed of several sets of 18 men in a long pit, and eight women in a shorter one located parallel to it. Their ages varied significantly (from 14 to 43 years old), but there were certain regularities in position, orientation, and other mortuary variables. Nearly 80 percent of the people buried at the pyramid again had their arms crossed behind their backs, as if they had been tied. These data indicate that they were all sacrificial victims buried together. We do not know who they were nor what functions this mortuary program had exactly. However, the formal studies of the bones and ongoing bone isotope and DNA analyses preliminarily suggest that they were probably brought together from different regions in Mesoamerica.

The abundant offerings associated with the sacrificial victims further provide information about the government and the ritual meanings involved. The quality and quantity of the offerings can be contrasted strikingly to those found in resi-

Figure 4.7. Two of 137 individuals found in and around the Feathered Serpent Pyramid. Projectile points and shell ornaments with real human maxilla pendants were also found in association with them

dences. No ceramics were found at the monument, except for Tlaloc vessels that represented the water-related deity. Most of the materials were symbolic items, tools, or ornaments for warriors or priest-warriors. Virtually all the male skeletons were associated with abundant obsidian projectile points, slate disks attached to their hip bones, and shell imitations of human teeth forming pendants representing human upper jaws (maxilla). All of these items can be identified as insignia of warriors. Some individuals carried pendants of real human maxilla or coyote maxilla, which also symbolized Teotihuacan warriors. Female skeletons were also associated with projectile points, although the quantity was much smaller. The burial complex represented a mass sacrifice of people attired as Teotihuacan warriors, who might have been brought to the city as captives.

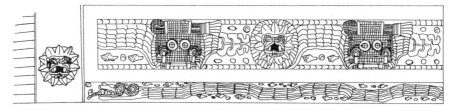

Figure 4.8. The feathered serpent and the primordial crocodilian monster represented on the façades of the Feathered Serpent Pyramid

Skeletons found in graves near the center of the pyramid, especially the central one containing 20 sacrifices, had much more varied offerings of higher quality. The offerings were found dispersed on or around the skeletons in certain patterns, as if a scattering ritual took place just before burying the individuals. Offerings included greenstone ornaments, such as nose pendants symbolizing authority, figurines, and enigmatic conical objects; shell pieces, both unworked and worked as ornaments; slate disks; and organic materials; as well as obsidian figures of humans and feathered serpents, blades, knives, and "needles." Many of these objects were apparently symbols or tools for rulership and human sacrifice or auto-sacrifice. It is well known in Mesoamerica that blood-letting rituals were among the most important events executed by rulers or royal family members, frequently depicted in public space for the proclamation of rulership. Unique objects further include a complete wood baton or scepter, with its curved end depicting a Feathered Serpent head. It was found in one of the two looted pits inside the pyramid, which might have originally contained a ruler's body. The baton may have symbolized individualistic political authority, as it did in other states. The burial complex represented sacrificial rituals of hierarchically varied people for the proclamation of rulership. As they were found together in an anonymous fashion, they would have formed a unified assemblage dedicated to the supreme deity worshipped at the monument. However, they still could also have been retainers for a ruler, who may have been buried at an unidentified spot in Teotihuacan, for several sites of possible royal graves have been completely destroyed, seriously looted, or are still to be explored in the future.

After covering the burials, the leading group directing the building finished the monumental construction with a sculptural program, which was a much more explicit and permanent manifestation of the state religion for the public (Fig. 4.8). The scene carved on the four façades conveyed a specific cosmogonic significance (López et al. 1991; Sugiyama 2003; Taube 1992). A rather simple, repeated scene once covered each stepped platform; two different high-relief sculptural entities jutted out from the talud-tablero panels, where images of shells are scattered as water symbols around them. The Feathered Serpent was obviously the central entity whose entire body was depicted. This deity was believed in the Postclassic period to have been the great initiator of the calendar, who brought the present world out from the watery underworld. The scene can fit well into this cosmogonic meaning, with the Ciudadela possibly serving as the setting representing the underworld. Identification of another entity is more controversial; iconographic studies suggest that it represented a headdress in the form of a primordial crocodilian monster, or what the Aztecs called Cipactli, which represented the first day of the ritual calendar, therefore symbolizing the beginning of time. A nose pendant, similar to those found inside the grave, was carved under this headdress. As a whole, the entire scene apparently represented the creation of a new era brought by the Feathered Serpent bearing on its body the headdress symbolizing the genesis of the present world.

We do not know exactly what this commemoration of a new era implied. If we take into account the leadership needed to execute this grand-scale construction program, we can further consider its significance from a socio-political perspective. The ruler would not have commissioned the erection of this monument simply as a passive reflection of the periodic passage of time. The recreation of the cosmos must have been a fundamental issue for the state. Accordingly, it is more likely that the ruler established his divine status by constructing the monument that depicted the creation of the world by the Feathered Serpent. This deity was shown carrying the headdress and nose pendant symbolizing the divine rulership that were to be granted to him (or her).

Through the dramatization of mass sacrifice and the visualization of a new era, the Teotihuacan ruler may have orchestrated the succession-to-rulership ceremony authorized by a supreme creator. We know that headdresses symbolizing time-beginning were used traditionally by many Mesoamerican elites, especially contemporaneous Maya rulers, as emblems of political authority in depictions of succession to high office (Schele and Miller 1986:114–115). In Teotihuacan, the headdress and nose-pendant set was often depicted alone as insignia without the face of the person who used it. The mass-sacrifice ritual would have been a fundamental factor in this dramatization of rulership, through which warfare was deliberately proclaimed and justified with reference to religious metaphor. The implication is that military institutions would have been functioning centrally for the state apparatus and consolidated supreme rulership during the third century.

Teotihuacan Governance in Social Contexts

The explorations at the major monuments complement each other by providing information about the political actions of leading groups; it can be stressed that warfare and sacrificial rituals were among the most significant events for the state. It was also confirmed that city layout was expanded by enlarging major monuments as cohesively integrated parts of a plan. In particular, a major construction stage in the early third century, represented by the Ciudadela and its main temple the Feathered Serpent Pyramid, the Adosada platform at the Sun Pyramid, and Building 4 of the Moon Pyramid, took place at the most prosperous time of the state, celebrated with sacrificial ceremonies on a grand scale.

However, many questions still remain unanswered. For example, we have not physically identified any rulers in either burials or pictorial representations. We do

Figure 4.9. Representation of a warrior carrying spears and sacrificial knife that sticks in a bleeding heart

not know how and where the ruling entities actually exercised their proclaimed rulership in the city, or how sacrificial rituals or warfare were involved in the social life of its residents. To answer these questions we have to continue archaeological research, especially in living spaces. In this section we will briefly examine the degree to which such characteristic governance is materialized in social contexts through visual representations and symbolic items.

Teotihuacan imagery in murals, ceramics, or sculptures found in residences varies significantly; it comprises god-like creatures, human figures, animals, symbolic objects, and abstract geometric designs. Human-like figures without text or identification codes are often repeated in the same scene without physical characteristics distinctive of individuals. They had therefore been interpreted as being mythological or ahistorical entities or gods. After Clara Millon's (1973) pioneering work, the social contexts in which the images were composed were increasingly taken into account in the interpretation of their identity. Historical perspectives were further pursued after a large number of Teotihuacan murals, which included new data about symbols and signs, were donated to a public museum by a private collector (Berrin 1988; Berrin and Pasztory 1993). New archaeological discoveries at the monuments also provided complementary insights for iconographic reinterpretation. As a consequence, we now commonly share the notion that Teotihuacan imagery was strongly and dominantly associated with the themes of warfare, sacrifice, and rulership (Langley 1986), and that certain "anonymous" figures had attached identification codes (Taube 2001).

Although we cannot find any clear scenes of actual battle, it is evident that warrior-like human (or animal) figures are depicted executing bloody rituals that would have followed war (Fig 4.9). They carry a cluster of spears, atlatls (spear-throwers), shields, or sacrificial knives, often with bleeding hearts. They are sometimes adorned with disks attached to their backs, which are believed to be a diagnostic element for warriors. Our discovery of slate disks attached to the hip-

Figure 4.10. Representation of Tlaloc carrying his own headdress on his left hand. The image can be interpreted as a succession scene of this title

bones of the warriors at the Feathered Serpent Pyramid confirmed this interpretation. Images of certain animals such as jaguar, puma, coyote, wolf, bird (eagle), and butterfly had also been linked strongly with military institutions. Most of them were actually found with other militaristic objects at the monuments, as described above.

Use of political titles has also become clearer, although the specific meanings involved remained ambiguous. In art, warriors' or priests' bodies are often depicted with other kinds of ornaments like greenstone beads, ear spools, or nose pendants of certain types, some of which are similar to those materials attached to individuals found at the Feathered Serpent Pyramid and the Moon Pyramid. Headdresses in special forms may have been status insignia; for example, Clara Millon (1973) identified a tassel headdress as the Teotihuacan emblem for "ambassador," as it appeared in foreign political contexts. Headdresses with calendar signs, like those of the Feathered Serpent Pyramid discussed above, were particularly important, as they represented political offices that controlled the measurement of time, just as they did among the Zapotecs, Mayas, or Aztecs. Most significant for political authority were, however, the Teotihuacan deities. The Storm God, the Feathered Serpent, and the Great Goddess were the most distinguished deities, who were often depicted as title bearers granting rulership (Fig. 4.10). They were also associated with warfare and human sacrifice.

Another fundamental step forward in the study of Teotihuacan iconography in recent decades has been the recognition of "named" or "designated" individuals, although signs or "primitive" words associated with human figures have still not been read phonetically. We still cannot know who these represented individuals were, nor how they were actually involved in state politics. However, we can safely assume that they once constituted political entities such as warriors, priests, or leading elites of the Teotihuacan government. We now suspect that ritual sacrifice and warfare were not mythological or ahistorical, but were central events in urban life. The discovery of sacrificed individuals, discussed earlier, with certain ornaments and symbols once only depicted in art, now confirms this reality.

Certain kinds of ritual items may have been involved fundamentally in state activities. Some of the symbolic offerings associated with sacrificial burials described above have been found exclusively at the monuments. This indicates strong control of their production and distribution by the state. The offerings found in residences include more ceramics and other utilitarian items (see Chapter 5). However, some obsidian, shell, and greenstone objects have been excavated in differentiated mortuary contexts in apartment compounds. The most characteristic ritual objects in living spaces were elaborated ceramics, often painted, and theater-type censers, that would have conveyed specific representational messages. Theater-type censers were also fundamentally associated with military symbolism, as their imagery includes many militaristic representations such as spears and shields. Teotihuacan censers have also been discovered in abundance in distant regions where a strong connection with Teotihuacan has been recognized (Berlo 1984). The archaeological discovery of a ceramic workshop mainly for censer production in the Ciudadela, the architectural complex that represented state militarism and rulership as described above, indicates that ruling entities may have been actively engaged in this censer production or controlled the manufacture. The production of these censers and certain other ritual items abruptly stopped once the state collapsed. This also supports the idea that the state governed the manufacturing of the symbols expressing state ideology and military institutions.

The Collapse of the State

After the major structures and the city layout we see today were established, the modification or renewal programs of the minor public buildings and residences still continued. We now know that the enlargement of the the Moon Pyramid (Building 7A) and the last stage of the Sun Pyramid continued as a state event during the fifth century at least. This may imply that politico-religious activities, such as sacrificial rituals that may have taken place after the construction, would have further stimulated pilgrimages and inter-social and economic transactions at Teotihuacan. In fact, there is abundant evidence of foreigners from distant areas living in the city; some of them established their own ethnic barrios (Millon 1988; Spence 1992; see Chapter 5). The city became a truly metropolitan cultural center attractive to people from many Mesoamerican societies. Very probably, inhabitants and gathering outsiders would have conceived the whole city as a central microcosm.

At the same time, the government may have suffered from internal and/or external threats of certain kinds. Some of the data suggest that ideological or political conflicts existed while the city was fully functioning. Much evidence of deliberate destruction, supposedly for architectural modification, might have been the result of such conflicts. For example, deliberate destruction of the Feathered Serpent Pyramid, which occurred about two centuries prior to the final collapse of the city, suggests that more than a simple modification program took place (Sugiyama 1998). The Adosada platform was constructed around A.D. 350, covering the Feathered Serpent image once celebrated on the main pyramid façade. At the same time, some of the sacrificial burials mentioned above were seriously looted, and sculptures were deliberately torn down or cut off. This suggests that a radical ideological shift, perhaps with political implications, occurred.

The evidence of possible threats to Teotihuacan's government can also be recovered from the city's residential construction. Sometime during the expansion project of the city, thick and high walls were integrated into some of the architectural complexes, perhaps to divide the area into "districts" or barrios. These and other independent walls, a wide and deep canal system, and high platforms like those of the Ciudadela, may have functioned as defensive facilities. In addition, recent excavations revealed that many roughly made stone walls without plaster blocked access to many residential complexes. The latest ones correspond to the final architectural stage just before the city's abandonment. The way in which the walls were constructed gives the impression that the inhabitants suddenly needed to strictly control access to the masonry residences.

The evidence of Teotihuacan's final destruction is unmistakable. Evidence of burning on the floors and walls in residences is conspicuous, and the amount of data is increasing as new excavations progress. Particularly, temples and pyramids seem to have been the targets of burning (Millon 1988). It was a long-standing tradition in Mesoamerica that the burning of an enemy's temple was a symbolic action of conquest. We do not know yet exactly when this happened in absolute years, or who did it. However, we know that the disintegration of the state took place essentially as a consequence of political conflict and very probably involved the military forces that Teotihuacan elites once used to establish their own political hegemonies. It is well documented that after the collapse of the metropolis, regional centers rose with powerful rulership conspicuously proclaimed with military institutions. Recent development of archaeological research described above indicates that such polities, metaphorically expressed with traditional Mesoamerican religious ideology, may be traced back to Teotihuacan itself.

References

Acosta, J. R., 1964 *El Palacio de Quetzalpapalotl* [The Quetzalpapalotl Palace]. Memorias del Instituto Nacional de Antropología e Historia 10. Mexico, DF: Instituto Nacional de Antropología e Historia.

Ashmore, W., 1991 Site-planning principles and concepts of directionality among the ancient Maya. *Latin American Antiquity* 2, 199–226.

Aveni, A. F., 1980 *Skywatchers of Ancient Mexico*. Austin: University of Texas Press.

Berlo, J. C., 1984 *Teotihuacan Art Abroad: A Study of Metropolitan Style and Provincial Transformation in Incensario Workshops*, 2 vols. British Archaeological Reports International Series 199, parts 1 and 2. Oxford: B.A.R.

———ed., 1992 *Art, Ideology and the City of Teotihuacan.* Washington, DC: Dumbarton Oaks.

Bernal, I., 1963 *Teotihuacán: Descubrimientos, reconstrucciones* [Teotihuacan: Discoveries, Reconstructions]. Mexico, DF: Instituto Nacional de Antropología e Historia.

Berrin, K., ed., 1988 *Feathered Serpents and Flowering Trees: Reconstructing the Murals of Teotihuacan.* Seattle: Fine Arts Museums of San Francisco/University of Washington Press.

Berrin, K., and E. Pasztory, eds., 1993 *Teotihuacan: Art from the City of the Gods.* New York: Thames & Hudson/Fine Arts Museums of San Francisco.

Cabrera C., R., I. Rodríguez G., and N. Morelos G., eds., 1982 *Memoria del Proyecto Arqueológico Teotihuacán 1980–1982,* vol. 1 [Report of the 1980–1982 Teotihuacan Archaeological Project]. Mexico, DF: Instituto Nacional de Antropología e Historia.

———————1991 *Teotihuacán 1980–1982: Nuevas interpretaciones* [Teotihuacan 1980–1982: New Interpretations]. Mexico, DF: Instituto Nacional de Antropología e Historia.

Cabrera C., R., S. Sugiyama, and G. Cowgill, 1991 The Temple of Quetzalcoatl Project at Teotihuacan: A preliminary report. *Ancient Mesoamerica* 2, 77–92.

Carrasco, D., L. Jones, and S. Sessions, eds., 2000 *Mesoamerica's Classic Heritage from Teotihuacan to the Aztecs.* Boulder: University of Colorado Press.

Cowgill, G. L., 1983 Rulership and the Ciudadela: Political inferences from Teotihuacan architecture. In *Civilization in the Ancient Americas: Essays in Honor of Gordon R. Willey.* R. M. Leventhal and A. L. Kolata, eds. Pp. 313–343. Albuquerque: University of New Mexico Press; Cambridge, MA: Peabody Museum of Harvard University.

———1992 Toward a political history of Teotihuacan. In *Ideology and Pre-Columbian Civilizations.* A. A. Demarest and G. W. Conrad, eds. Pp. 87–114. Santa Fe: School of American Research Press.

DeMarrais, E., L. J. Castillo, and T. K. Earle, 1996 Ideology, materialization, and power strategies. *Current Anthropology* 37, 15–31.

Dow, J. W., 1967 Astronomical orientations at Teotihuacan, a case study in astro-archaeology. *American Antiquity* 32, 326–334.

Drucker, R. D., 1977 A Solar orientation framework for Teotihuacan. Paper presented at the XV Mesa Redonda of the Sociedad Mexicana de Antropología, Guanajuato.

Fash, W. L., and B. W. Fash, 2000 Teotihuacan and the Maya: A Classic heritage. In *Mesoamerica's Classic Heritage from Teotihuacan to the Aztecs.* D. Carrasco, L. Jones, and S. Sessions, eds. Pp. 433–463. Boulder: University of Colorado Press.

Gamio, M., 1979 [1922] *La población del Valle de Teotihuacán* [The Population of the Teotihuacan Valley]. Mexico, DF: Instituto Nacional Indigenista.

Heyden, D., 1975 An interpretation of the cave underneath the Pyramid of the Sun in Teotihuacán, Mexico. *American Antiquity* 40, 131–147.

Langley, J. C., 1986 *Symbolic Notation of Teotihuacan: Elements of Writing in a Mesoamerican Culture of the Classic Period.* British Archaeological Reports, International Series 313. Oxford: B.A.R.

López A., A., L. López L., and S. Sugiyama, 1991 The Feathered Serpent Pyramid at Teotihuacan: Its possible ideological significance. *Ancient Mesoamerica* 2, 93–106.

Malmstrom, V. H., 1978 A reconstruction of the chronology of Mesoamerican calendrical systems. *Journal of the History of Astronomy* 9, 105–116.

Manzanilla, L., ed., 1993 *Anatomía de un conjunto residencial teotihuacano en Oztoyahualco* [Anatomy of a Teotihuacan Residential Compound in Oztoyahualco]. Mexico, DF: Universidad Nacional Autónoma de México.

Manzanilla, L., L. Barba, R. Chávez, A. Tejero, G. Cifuentes, and N. Peralta, 1994 Caves and geophysics: An approximation to the underworld of Teotihuacan, Mexico. *Archaeometry* 36, 141–157.

Marcus, J., 1983 Stone monuments and tomb murals of Monte Albán IIIa. In *The Cloud People: Divergent Evolution of the Zapotec and Mixtec Civilizations*. K. Flannery and J. Marcus, eds. Pp. 137–143. New York: Academic Press.

Matos, M. E., 1995 *La pirámide del Sol, Teotihuacan* [The Pyramid of the Sun, Teotihuacan]. Mexico, DF: Artes de México, Instituto Cultural Domecq, AC.

McClung de Tapia, E., 1992 The origins of agriculture in Mesoamerica and Central America. In *The Origins of Agriculture: An International Perspective*. C. W. Cowan and P. J. Watson, eds. Pp. 143–171. Washington, DC: Smithsonian Institution Press.

Millon, C., 1973 Painting, writing, and polity in Teotihuacan, Mexico. *American Antiquity* 38, 294–313.

Millon, R., 1973 *Urbanization at Teotihuacan, Mexico*, vol. 1: *The Teotihuacan Map*, part 1: *Text*. Austin: University of Texas Press.

——1981 Teotihuacan: City, state, and civilization. In *Supplement to the Handbook of Middle American Indians*, vol. 1: *Archaeology*. V. Bricker and J. Sabloff Austin, eds. Pp. 198–243. Austin: University of Texas Press.

——1988 The last years of Teotihuacan dominance. In *The Collapse of Ancient States and Civilizations*. N. Yoffee and G. Cowgill, eds. Pp. 102–164. Tucson: University of Arizona Press.

——1992 Teotihuacan studies: From 1950 to 1990 and beyond. In *Art, Ideology and the City of Teotihuacan*. J. C. Berlo, ed. Pp. 339–429. Washington, DC: Dumbarton Oaks.

Millon, R., B. Drewitt, and J. A. Bennyhoff, 1965 *The Pyramid of the Sun at Teotihuacán: 1959 Investigations*. Transactions of the American Philosophical Society, NS 55, part 6. Philadelphia: American Philosophical Society.

Millon, R., B. Drewitt, and G. L. Cowgill, 1973 *Urbanization at Teotihuacan, Mexico*, vol. 1: *The Teotihuacan Map*, part 2: *Maps*. Austin: University of Texas Press.

Pasztory, E., 1997 *Teotihuacan: An Experiment in Living*. Norman: University of Oklahoma Press.

Sanders, W. T., J. R. Parsons, and R. S. Santley, 1979 *The Basin of Mexico: Ecological Processes in the Evolution of a Civilization*. New York: Academic Press.

Schele, L., and M. E. Miller, 1986 *The Blood of Kings: Dynasty and Ritual in Maya Art*. New York: G. Braziller.

Sempowski, M. L., and M. W. Spence, 1994 *Mortuary Practices and Skeletal Remains at Teotihuacan*. Salt Lake City: University of Utah Press.

Smith, R. E., 1987 *A Ceramic Sequence from the Pyramid of the Sun, Teotihuacan, Mexico*. Cambridge, MA: Peabody Museum of Archaeology and Ethnology, Harvard University.

Spence, M. W., 1992 Tlailotlacan: A Zapotec enclave in Teotihuacan. In *Art, Ideology, and the City of Teotihuacan*. J. C. Berlo, ed. Pp. 59–88. Washington, DC: Dumbarton Oaks.

Storey, R., 1992 *Life and Death in the Ancient City of Teotihuacan: A Modern Paleodemographic Synthesis*. Tuscaloosa: University of Alabama Press.

Sugiyama, S., 1989 Burials dedicated to the Old Temple of Quetzalcoatl at Teotihuacan, Mexico. *American Antiquity* 54, 85–106.

——1993 Worldview materialized in Teotihuacan, Mexico. *Latin American Antiquity* 4, 103–129.

——1998 Termination programs and prehispanic looting at the Feathered Serpent Pyramid in Teotihuacan, Mexico. In *The Sowing and the Dawning: Dedication and Transformation in the Archaeological and Ethnographic Record of Mesoamerica*. S. Mock, ed. Pp. 147–164. Albuquerque: University of New Mexico Press.

——2003 *Human Sacrifice, Warfare, and Rulership at Teotihuacan, Mexico: Materialization of State Ideology in the Feathered Serpent Pyramid*. Cambridge: Cambridge University Press. In press.

Sugiyama, S., and R. Cabrera, 2000 Proyecto Pirámide de la Luna: Algunos resultados de la segunda temporada 1999. *Arqueología* 2nd ser., 23, 161–172.

————2002 El Proyecto Pirámide de la Luna: Avances en 2000 y 2001. *Arqueología*, in press.

Taube, K., 1992 The Temple of Quetzalcoatl and the cult of sacred war at Teotihuacan. *Res: Anthropology and Aesthetics* 21, 53–87.

——2001 La escritura Teotihuacana. *Arqueología Mexicana* 8(48), 58–63.

Wheatley, P., 1971 *The Pivot of the Four Quarters: A Preliminary Inquiry into the Origins and Character of the Ancient Chinese City.* Chicago: Aldine.

Zuidema, R. T., 1983 Hierarchy and space in Incaic social organization. *Ethnohistory* 30, 49–75.

5

Social Identity and Daily Life at Classic Teotihuacan

Linda Manzanilla

The expansion of urban life in well-planned cities is one of the main hallmarks of the Classic horizon in Mesoamerica. These first urban centers show internal social differentiation based mainly on occupation. Teotihuacan (Fig. 5.1) was the first vast urban development in the central highlands. Its degree of urban planning and its population density were among the highest in prehispanic times.

Teotihuacan is a 20 km² city, built in the bottom of the Teotihuacan Valley. It has a civic, administrative, and ceremonial core with the Moon Plaza to the north and the Ciudadela to the center. At A.D. 200–350 (following Rattray 1991), five elements of urban planning at the site are already clearly defined (R. Millon 1973):

1   *Existence of axes and streets.* The Street of the Dead (north–south) and the East–West Avenue intersect to the north of the Ciudadela. This last can be followed for more than 3 km to the east, and 2 km to the west of the Great Compound. They would divide the city in four quadrants, in which the Ciudadela, situated in the intersection, would have a special importance. The division of important sites in four quarters can be related to Mesoamerican cosmovision. Nearly all the constructions were distributed along the streets; all run parallel or perpendicular to the main axes, and are traced at regular intervals. In the neighboring mountain slopes, some kilometers from the center of the city, other constructions are aligned to the city's grid (Millon 1967:41).

2   *Water and drainage system.* There seems to have been a drinking water supply and a complex drainage system that derived from a reservoir 200 m to the northwest of the Moon Pyramid. Water from the Piedras Negras stream descended between the Cerro Gordo and Cerro Coronillas. Another element in the water system was the canalization of the San Juan river to follow the city's grid. Also, the San Lorenzo river, originally meandering, was restricted to a straight line, controlling its potential for sudden flooding. The internal drainage system

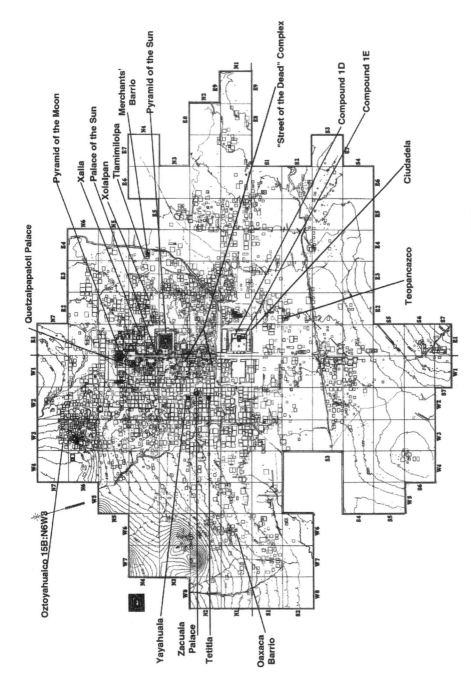

Figure 5.1. The city of Teotihuacan and the different compounds cited (after R. Millon 1973)

Table 5.1. Location, area, and function of some apartment compounds at Teotihuacan

Name	Location l	Area	Paintings	Comments
Tetitla	N2W2	ca. 3600 m²	XXX	9 autonomous sectors small temples
Zacuala	N2W2	ca. 3600 m²	XXX	large temple (16 × 16 m.)
Atetelco	N2W3	ca. 3600 m²	XX	small temples
Yayahuala	N3W2	ca. 3600 m²	XX	medium-large temple
Teopancazco	S2E2	>60 × 60?	X	medium size temple
Xolalpan	N4E2	<30 × 40	–	medium size temple
Tlamimilolpa	N4E4	>3500 m²	–	no temples
La Ventilla B	S1W3	>50 × 50	–	no temples
Oztoyahualco	N6W3	>550 m²	–	portable altars
Tlajinga 33	S3W1	>50 × 50	–	no temples

included a vast network of underground canals that converged into a central canal, that flowed parallel to the Street of the Dead, and discharged into the San Juan river (Sanders 1964:124).

3   *Public and administrative constructions.* These were placed along the Street of the Dead, although the particular functions of these spaces is not known (see Chapter 4). The so-called Great Compound in front of the Ciudadela is the largest structure of the site, larger even than the Ciudadela. It consists of two U-shaped wings (one to the north and the other to the south), with entrances from the Street of the Dead; the wings surround a huge open space. Millon (1967:83) states that the plaza could have housed the main market of the city, due to its central position in the city. This hypothesis has not been tested. Further on we will offer a different interpretation.

4   *Residential compounds.* A series of multifamily residential structures, discussed further below, surround the core of the site: Tlamimilolpa, Xolalpan, Atetelco, Tepantitla, Tetitla, Zacuala, etc. (Fig 5.1). The existence of a construction module of 57 m, with multiples and submultiples, as well as apartment compounds housing 100, 50, and 20 people (corporate groups, mainly devoted to crafts) has been proposed by Millon (1968, 1970:1080; see also Spence 1966). Apartment compounds are isolated from the streets by high external walls deprived of windows, thus allowing privacy. Internal open spaces provided light, air, rainwater (Millon 1967:43), and means for small refuse disposal (Manzanilla 1993b).

5   *Wards and sectors for craft production.* More than 500 concentrations of raw materials and debris (many of which are obsidian) have been considered as evidence of workshops by Millon's project, although some may have been refuse dumps. Specialization to the level of the type of artifact manufactured was observed: some workshops made prismatic blades, others bifacial tools (Millon 1968:116). The greatest obsidian concentration lies to the west of the Pyramid of the Moon, perhaps suggesting state control of craft production (Spence 1987). Other work-

shops were devoted to the production of pottery, figurines, lapidary, polished stone, and slate objects. Only a few have been excavated; some are discussed further below.

Even though the direct catchment area of Teotihuacan was limited to the Basin of Mexico (and probably the Valley of Toluca), in other aspects, such as exchange and ritual relations, the sphere provisioning Teotihuacan included the regions of Puebla-Tlaxcala, Morelos and Guerrero, and the Valley of Tula. Teotihuacan established alliances with Monte Alban in the Oaxaca Valley, and various kinds of intervention in the Maya area. Enclaves of the Teotihuacan state have been proposed for the Guatemalan highlands, the Gulf Coast of Mexico, and probably Michoacan, in Western Mexico. In reciprocity, in the city there are foreign wards: the Oaxaca barrio (Tlailotlacan) to the southwest (Spence 1989, 1992; Rattray 1993); the Merchants' Barrio to the east (Rattray 1987, 1988), where circular adobe domestic structures with Maya polychrome pottery were found; and perhaps a small enclave from Michoacan to the western fringe of the city (Gómez Chávez 1998). Identity was reinforced in these wards through particular culinary and funerary practices, as well as the use of circular adobe domestic constructions in the Merchants' Barrio, which are clearly different from the Teotihuacan patterns.

Two different spatial scales may be used to address the problem of social identity: after studying different activity areas in particular rooms and considering household apartments, the apartment compound as a whole is one of the scales where social identity is recreated through the determination of: (1) access to subsistence resources; (2) occupational specialization; (3) distribution of imported/exotic materials; and (4) religious ritual and funerary practices. In such a complex scenario, social identity was emphasized in the domestic domain, where related families and associated people lived together as corporate groups sharing the domestic walled territory, some activities, common ritual, and perhaps patron deities, attire, and, in part, kinship. In a hierarchical structure, one of the families in each compound was at the head of the corporate group, as we will see further on.

The second scale where social identity may be analyzed is the ward or barrio. At Teotihuacan, different apartment compounds which have complementary activities are arranged around three temple plazas or cult cores. Till now, only the La Ventilla barrio has been excavated at such a scale as to allow a glimpse into the barrio structure: apartment compounds of different social statuses are placed around the ward's religious structures (Cabrera 1996; Gómez Chávez 2000).

Models of Stratification

Stratification in Teotihuacan society has been seen through two models: one proposed by Millon (1976, 1981), Sempowski (1987, 1994), Sload (1987), and Cowgill (1992), with many levels, and clear-cut social distinctions between them. Another

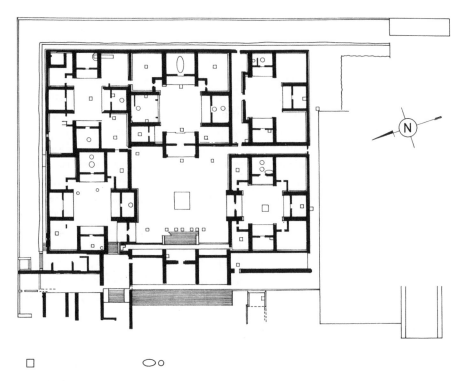

Figure 5.2. Structure ID at La Ciudadela (after Jarquín Pacheco and Martínez Vargas 1982: 102)

model sees a whole range of slight socioeconomic differences between social groups, that may reflect a continuum of statuses within compounds, with multiple opportunities of achievement, and thus a more complex panorama than stated before (Manzanilla 1996). This perception of Teotihuacan society has also been stressed by Pasztory (1988).

From variables such as room size, use of space, decoration, construction techniques, burials, offerings, etc., Millon (1976:227) states that Teotihuacan society comprised six distinct social, economic, and cultural levels.

First, he suggested that the apex of Teotihuacan society may have dwelled in the Quetzalpapalotl Palace, the Palace of the Sun, the so-called "palaces" to the north and south of the Temple of the Feathered Serpent (Fig. 5.2) (Millon 1976:236).

The second level was represented by thousands of very high status people of second rank, including priests of the city's great pyramids and pyramid complexes; they may have lived in the apartment compounds of the Great Compound (Millon 1981:214).

After a major gap we find the third, fourth, and fifth levels of intermediate status. From highest to lowest, such people lived in the Zacuala Palace (Fig. 5.3), at Teopancazco, and at Xolalpan (Fig. 5.4).

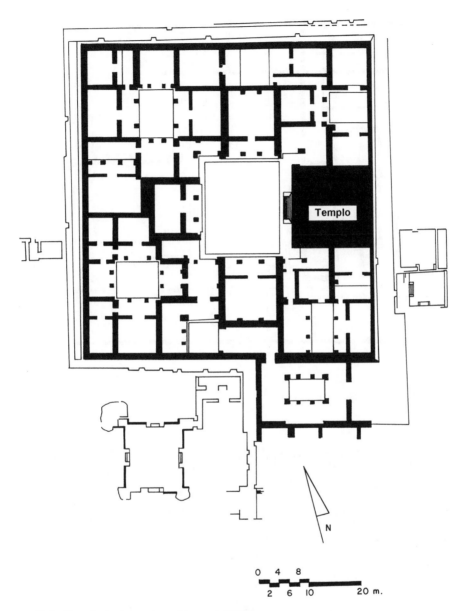

Figure 5.3. Zacuala (redrawn from Séjourné 1966b)

The sixth level comprised low-status compounds, such as Tlamimilolpa and La Ventilla B (Millon 1976:227). Small apartment compounds, such as the one we excavated in the 1980s at Oztoyahualco 15B:N6W3 (Fig. 5.5) (Manzanilla 1993b), could not be taken into consideration in Millon's earlier categories, so I suggest a seventh level be created.

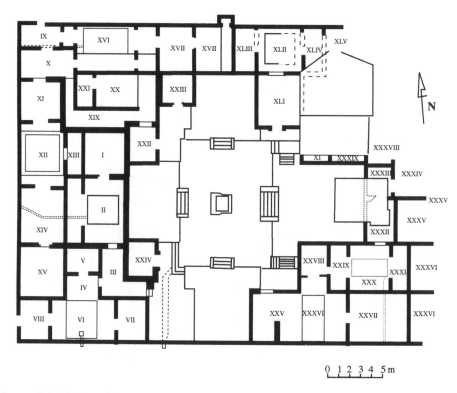

Figure 5.4. Xolalpan (after Linné 1934)

Figure 5.5. Oztoyahualco 15B:N6W3 (after Manzanilla 1993)

Teotihuacan society displayed a diversity of elite and non-elite social groups where ethnic, social, and professional differences were woven in a complex fabric, without sharply defined classes. At Oztoyahualco 15B:N6W3, Teopancazco, and Xalla we have chosen the following methodology to explore this: through extensive excavations, interdisciplinary work, and distributional maps of all types of artifacts and ecofacts – pottery, obsidian, polished stone, bone, antler, shell, as well as chemical compounds, pollen, phytoliths, seeds and faunal macrofossils – we have been trying to differentiate domestic areas, activities, and choices of each household or social group. Although Millon's model, based primarily on surface survey, is suggestive, a more complex scenario has appeared when analyzing data from these extensive excavations.

Apartment Compounds: What They Share and What They Do Not Share

One of the most distinctive characteristics of Teotihuacan society was domestic life in multifamily constructions. Apartment compounds vary considerably in total area. From the extensive excavation of several of them, we now know that some are very large (ca. 3,600 m²: Linné 1942; Séjourné 1966b); others are medium-sized (1,300–2,300 m²: Linné 1934; Sanders 1966, 1994; Sánchez Alaniz 1989; Storey 1992); others are much smaller (280–550 m²: Manzanilla 1993b; Monzón 1989; Sanders 1966).

Investigation of apartment compounds has a long history. Leopoldo Batres was the first archaeologist to excavate a part of an apartment compound, Teopancazco, in 1884 (Gamio 1922: first part, 156–157); we know practically nothing of the findings in this project, except for the extraordinary mural paintings at the site. Afterwards, Sigvald Linné excavated Xolalpan and Tlamimilolpa (Linné 1934, 1942); we have the apartment compound plans, as well as the artifact and object analyses, and some locations of burials and offerings. Then there is a major gap in apartment compound research until Laurette Séjourné directed the excavations at Tetitla, Yayahuala, and Zacuala (Séjourné 1959, 1966b) in the 1950s; nevertheless, we only have the architectural, mural painting, and artifact and object descriptions, and we know nothing about what was found inside each room.

Fully documented excavations of apartment compounds are a more recent development. Leaving aside the foreign wards, in the 1980s there are examples of interdisciplinary research at apartment compounds such as Tlajinga 33 (Storey and Widmer 1989; Widmer 1991) and Oztoyahualco 15B:N6W3 (Manzanilla 1993b, 1996), which have been followed in the 1990s at Teopancazco (Manzanilla 2000) and Xalla (Manzanilla and López Luján 2001). They provide evidence for construction of distributional maps of all types of artifacts and ecofacts, as well as chemical compounds, pollen, phytoliths, seeds and faunal macrofossils, that enable us to differentiate domestic areas, activities, and choices of residents of each compound.

Subsistence and resource procurement

Even when there is variation in size (due to their proximity to the Street of the Dead), when we take into consideration the presence/absence of botanical and faunal resources, as well as exogenous raw materials, we have found that the differences in access are very slight between the excavated compounds; all had similar access to plant resources including maize (Nal-Tel Chapalote, Palomero Toluqueño, and Conical varieties), amaranth, beans, squash, hot peppers, tomato, *huauhzontle*, *Portulaca*, cactus, maguey, Mexican hawthorn, and Mexican cherries (González 1993; Manzanilla 1985, 1993b; McClung de Tapia 1979, 1980:162–163; Storey 1992:64). A greater abundance of tobacco at San Antonio Las Palmas (Monzón 1989), avocado at Teopancazco (McClung de Tapia 1979) and of cotton at Tlamimilolpa (Linné 1942), Teopancazco (McClung de Tapia 1979), Tetitla (McClung de Tapia 1979) and Tlajinga 33 (Storey and Widmer 1989), suggest differential access to imported botanical resources associated with manufacturing and ritual consumption. Cacao trees, another non-local plant, are depicted in mural art.

Important faunal resources included cottontail rabbits and jackrabbits, deer, supplemented by duck and fish, and, in lesser amounts, armadillo, squirrel, goose, quail, dove, turtle, and lizard (Sanders 1994:31; Starbuck 1975; Valadez Azúa 1993). Particularly when dealing with deer, we may see that even small compounds such as Oztoyahualco 15B:N6W3, and foreign wards such as Xocotitla and Mezquititla have remains of several deer in their dumps (Valadez Azúa 1993:2, 795–796). Some slight differences can be cited. For example, Tetitla (Fig. 5.6) showed an unprecedented diversity of birds (as well as a particular richness in botanical species). Yayahuala (Fig. 5.7) had a wide variety of marine mollusks (as well as a high proportion of *Chenopodium* and amaranth plants). At Tlajinga 33, the consumption of small birds and freshwater fish was higher, and at Oztoyahualco 15B:N6W3, the reliance on several species of rabbit. At present, the degree to which these data reflect differential access to faunal and floral resources cannot be determined, because many other alternatives have to be considered: the differences may be related to group preferences and ideology, as well as differential preservation and discard practices.

Yet one difference between compounds that should be pointed out is the presence of different hunting techniques represented in the technological repertoire. For example, Tetitla displays projectile points of various sizes to cope with small, medium, and big animals (Séjourné 1966b: fig. 117). Even though Linné only published offerings from burials, the projectile points at Xolalpan (Linné 1934: figs. 258, 259, 263, 264, 293–297, 298–311) and Tlamimilolpa (Linné 1942: figs. 247, 252, 263–271) show similar size ranges. On the contrary, Oztoyahualco 15B:N6W3 provided projectile points of medium and large size, together with many examples of blow-gun projectiles, perhaps for hunting small animals (Hernández 1993). Linné (1942:187) also found blow-gun projectiles at Tlamimilolpa.

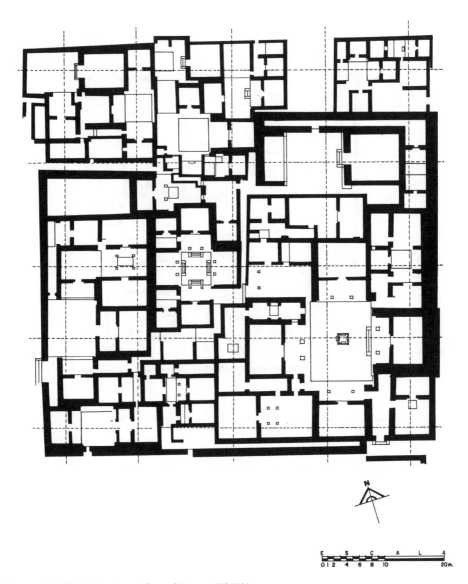

Figure 5.6. Tetitla (redrawn from Séjourné 1966b)

In ritual contexts at Tetitla and Yayahuala there were bones of eagle and hawk; at Oztoyahualco 15B:N6W3 we found bear and a jaguar's fang, this last a non-local animal. Exotic raw materials such as mica, slate, and marine shells were present in many burials not only of intermediate levels in Millon's (1976) hierarchy, but also at Xolalpan, Tlamimilolpa, and Oztoyahualco 15B:N6W3. The difference lies in their quantity, and in the proportion of Pacific versus Atlantic shell species.

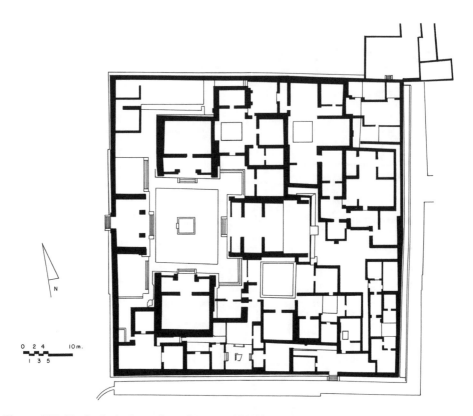

Figure 5.7. Yayahuala (redrawn from Séjourné 1966b)

In this exercise we have concluded that there may be a whole range of socioeconomic possibilities in the excavated apartment compounds. Detecting differences
that are clear-cut would be very difficult; the more examples we have, the more it
looks like a continuum (Manzanilla 1996).

Specialized activities

We have observed differences in specialized activities between household groups of
different compounds, but also in dominant activities of households, which suggest
group and family specializations (Manzanilla 1993b). Differences in the number of
high-status products, particularly decorated ceramic tripod vessels or mural paintings, and variability in the quality of the construction itself have been noted, but
still no sharp distinctions are made.

Edge rejuvenation and prismatic blade extraction from obsidian cores were
carried out in many compounds. Prismatic blade cores have been found at
Maquixco Bajo (Sanders 1994, 1995), Oztoyahualco 15B:N6W3 (Hernández
1993) and Xolalpan (Linné 1934: figs. 325, 327). But core-to-blade ratios were

variable. For example, at Maquixco Bajo 37 prismatic cores (Sanders 1994:66) and 304 prismatic blades were recovered (Santley et al. 1995:483). In contrast, at Oztoyahualco 15B:N6W3, only nine prismatic cores were found for 349 prismatic macroblades and 342 prismatic blades (Hernández 1993:461).

Plaster polishing also was well represented at Oztoyahualco 15B:N6W3. This activity was detected in the northern sector of the compound, where some graves that cut into the plaster floor were intended to be re-covered again with stucco. Yet the compound was abandoned before this task was concluded. The calcium carbonate mixture was already prepared, with a basalt polisher on top of it. There were 42 polishers and 16 fragments in our compound (a total of 58), an abundance that indicates a probable group occupation. A lower figure (40) was obtained for the three compounds in Maquixco Bajo (Sanders 1994:66).

Crespo Oviedo and Mastache de E. (1981) proposed that, in the Tula region, there were two sites that could be considered Zapotec settlements to obtain lime for the plastering of Teotihuacan: El Tesoro and Acoculco. Spence (1992) supported this idea by proposing that this ethnic group controlled the mining, processing, and importation of lime to the city. Our research at Oztoyahualco 15B:N6W3 does not support this interpretation, though this compound is only 3 km to the north of Tlailotlacan, the Oaxaca barrio. Thus, we have concluded that parts of the north-western district of the ancient city had direct links with settlements in the Tula region, and that our compound was perhaps more related to Chingu (Díaz O. 1980), a Teotihuacan settlement in the Tula area, also located in the limestone area. The number of plaster "polishers" made of volcanic scoria (*tezontle*) per square meter could be used to differentiate the relevance of this activity in apartment compounds, assuming that Linné and Séjourné saved all the specimens they found. Tetitla had 0.19 polishers per square meter; the Oztoyahualco compound, 0.10; Xolalpan, 0.04; and Tlamimilolpa, 0.01.

Other craft activities also varied by compound. Lapidary work involving green-stone, marine shells, slate, and onyx, and ceramic manufacture, particularly San Martin Orange Ware, were clearly represented at Tlajinga 33 (Krotser and Rattray 1980; Storey 1991; Widmer 1991). Several figurine molds were found at Xolalpan (Linné 1934: figs. 199–208); and stone celts for cutting wood were particularly abundant in Grave 1 (Linné 1934: figs. 246–256). These objects are not common at Teotihuacan in general. Different kinds of pigments for painting walls, pottery, and probably codices, as well as spindle-whorls and needles, were recorded at Xolalpan. Tlamimilolpa (Linné 1942) also had evidence of textile manufacture, as well as basket-making and fiber-work. Tetitla (Séjourné 1966b) is represented by bone instruments for working hides and polishing pottery.

With respect to figurine production, the Oztoyahualco compound only had 132 figurines and figurine fragments from Teotihuacan times (Manzanilla 1993b:358–369), very few in comparison, for example, to Maquixco Bajo, where Kolb (1995) mentions 2,150 figurines from Teotihuacan times in all the compound and neighboring areas. Regarding the consumption of pottery within the Oztoy-ahualco compound there seems to be a differentiation of wares of diverse colors with respect to each household or family unit. Matte and Red Hematite Wares are associated with Household 1. Household 2 used Black, Brown, Copa, Granular, and San Martin Wares. Household 3 – the poorest in pottery diversity and the richest in burials and foreign fauna – has a concentration of Orange and Thin Orange Wares. This may reflect differential access to pottery production in the urban setting for each nuclear household within a single apartment compound.

Ritual activities

It has been proposed that a superimposition of deities on two levels occurred for the first time at Teotihuacan. Lineage gods were patrons of lines of descent, and above them was the deity Tlaloc as god of place, protector of the territory, and patron of the city and the caves (López Austin 1989). In domestic contexts, the state god Tlaloc was represented in figurines with goggles and elaborate headdresses, as well as on Tlaloc vases and on a "handled cover." However, at Oztoyahualco 15B:N6W3, we also had evidence of patron gods related to particular families. A stucco rabbit sculpture was found on a miniature Teotihuacan temple-shaped shrine (made of basalt) in one of the ritual patios.

Among the deities widely present at Teotihuacan, the Fire God (Huehueteotl), who was known from the Formative period, always appears associated with the eastern portions of apartment compounds. Another deity present in domestic contexts is the Fat God, generally represented in figurines or appliquéd on tripod vessels. The Butterfly Deity is depicted on incense burners and is probably linked to death and fertility; in particular, an impressive theater-type censer (see below) that we found accompanying the burial of an adult male, had butterfly wings in the chest of the main figure, and displayed a wide array of food and economically important plants (Manzanilla and Carreón 1991).

In the Oztoyahualco compound, there were three ritual courtyards, each corresponding to a household; one of them – C41, the largest – probably also served the compound group as a whole and is called the Red Courtyard, because of its mural paintings. It was the only one with a central altar in its early construction level. The second one – Courtyard 25 – had evidence of theater-type censers (see below), and many Aztec pits that probably disturbed offerings or burials. The third one – Courtyard 33 – had the portable model basalt temple with the rabbit sculpture.

Some activity areas related to ritual preparation were detected around these courtyards. At Oztoyahualco 15B:N6W3, in the corner of C9 (near the main shrine), a concentration of 58 obsidian prismatic blade fragments, a basalt percussor, and a limestone half-sphere (with radial cutting marks probably caused by the continuous cutting up of rabbit and hare) were found (Hernández 1993; Manzanilla 1993b). There were also numerous funerary and offering pits, particularly in the eastern half of the compound. The northeastern household had the most burials, and also the greatest quantities of foreign fauna: bear, jaguar, mother-of-pearl and other marine shells (*Spondylys calcifer*).

Religion should be seen as a sphere of sociopolitical integration organized into a hierarchy in which the patron gods of household groups and barrios, occupational deities, the gods of specific priestly groups, and state deities such as Tlaloc are super-imposed (Manzanilla 1993a). Teotihuacan society was integrated mainly through religion. The conception of the four directions of sacred space permeated the domestic domain of Teotihuacan (Manzanilla 1993b). Spatial patterning seems to have been established for the disposition of functional sectors, which extended beyond the framework of the nuclear household. Thus, in general, storage zones were found to the west; those for refuse to the south; funerary areas were concen-trated in the middle of the eastern sector (although exceptions exist); and neonate burials were located primarily on a north–south band, in the eastern third of the compound. The affinity for order so patently manifest in the grid system of the city finds its correspondence on the domestic level as well.

Funerary practices

Burials are common in domestic contexts. However, with the exception of Tlajinga 33 and probably La Ventilla, the number of adults recovered interred in each com-pound is too low, relative to the area of the compound, to account for most of its inhabitants. For example, only seven burials are recorded for Xolalpan, 13 for Tlamimilolpa, and 18 for the compound at Oztoyahualco 15B:N6W3. Perhaps other adults, particularly women, were buried elsewhere.

Although Oztoyahualco 15B:N6W3 has only 18 burials, fewer than found at Tlajinga 33 (Storey 1983, 1987, 1992) or La Ventilla B (Serrano and Lagunas 1974), there are important conclusions to be drawn from these data. We hypothe-size that there were three nuclear households at Oztoyahualco. The first household, in the southeastern section, is represented only by three burials. The second, in the western portion of the compound, also has three burials, all adults. The third, in the northeastern section, has 11 burials, of which six represent newborn babies and children (see Storey 1986). Such over-representation of burials belonging to par-ticular sectors of the apartment compounds is also noted for Xolalpan, where nearly all the burials are concentrated in the southwestern section; at Tlamimilolpa, nearly all are grouped in the central-southern section; at Tetitla, they are concentrated in the northeastern section. It seems that in each compound there is one family that is well represented with respect to funerary practices, and all the rest seem to be under-represented.

Certain burials in each compound had very rich offerings. At Oztoyahualco, Burial 8 was exceptional, for it contained a male adult, 22 years of age, with an intentionally deformed skull, in association with an impressive theater-type incense burner (Manzanilla and Carreón 1991). Teotihuacan's theater-type censers are made by attaching individual ceramic appliqués to a framework surrounding a central figure on one side of the chimney, through which smoke would rise from the censer body. In what seems to represent a funerary ritual, the incense burner appliqués were removed from the lid, and all were placed around the deceased. The chimney was deposited toward the west, with the lid and the figure to the east of the skull. Representations of plants and sustenance (ears of corn, squash, squash flowers, cotton, tamales, tortillas, and perhaps amaranth bread) were placed to the south; the four-petaled flowers, roundels representing feathers, and mica disks to the east and west.

Theater-type censers were used profusely at Xolalpan (where they are found in the altar and in a western courtyard) and Tlamimilolpa (where they are grouped around Burial 4 and kept in caches, ready for ritual use). Decorated tripod vessels also are common at Xolalpan and Tlamimilolpa, but are very rare – though present – at Oztoyahualco 15B:N6W3. Probably one difference in the consumption of decorated tripod vessels lies in the presence of Maya fine wares in the western portion of Xolalpan and in the central part of Tlamimilolpa, possibly due to their proximity to the Merchants' Barrio.

Other imported ceramic wares, such as Thin Orange and Granular Ware, are present in all compounds. Exotic raw materials such as mica, slate, and marine shells were present in burials at Xolalpan, Tlamimilolpa, and Oztoyahualco. The difference among these burials lies in the quantity present, and in the proportion of Pacific versus Atlantic shell species.

Hierarchy and sector differentiation

Thus, we find that the six social levels originally proposed have been expanded to such a degree that a particular compound could house people belonging to different statuses. One household in each compound seems to have been the most active in bonding the household group to the urban hierarchy. At Oztoyahualco 15B:N6W3 this is Household 3, linked to the Tlaloc cult (represented by Tlaloc vases, Tlaloc figurines, and Tlaloc representations in "handled covers"), with the richest burials, and foreign fauna (Manzanilla 1993b, 1996).

At Oztoyahualco 15B:N6W3 there was, in general, a clear differentiation among the various sectors of the structure. The southern sector was associated with refuse; areas for food preparation and consumption, as well as the sleeping quarters, were set around the central portion of the compound; the eastern sector was rich in funerary and ritual components; the western sector was devoted to storage; and finally, the northwestern sector had the largest courtyard, probably the compound's meeting place. As mentioned before, there seems to be a differential distribution of activities for each household within Oztoyahualco 15B:N6W3. The compound was transformed by closing circulation alleys and accesses when the family structure changed.

Distributional maps of all types of archaeological materials – ceramic types, obsidian, polished stone, bone, antler, and shell, as well as chemical compounds, pollen, phytoliths, seeds and faunal macrofossils – help differentiate some activities and choices particular to each nuclear household:

1   Matte and Red Hematite Wares are associated with Household 1 situated to the south, together with the largest concentration of prismatic blades, ritual butchering of rabbits, and the presence of the Butterfly God.

2   Household 2, to the west, used Black, Brown, Copa, Granular, and San Martin Wares, and it was characterized by the holding in captivity of rabbits and hares, the butchering of animals for consumption, activities where side- and end-scrapers were used, the largest presence of foreign wares and minerals, and symbols of fire.

3   Household 3 to the northeast – the poorest in pottery diversity and the richest in burials and foreign fauna – had a concentration of Orange and Thin Orange Wares, together with Tlaloc symbols. This could reflect differential access to pottery production in the urban setting for each nuclear household, as well as activity and ritual differentiation.

One of the great problems of comparing the Oztoyahualco 15B:N6W3 apartment compound with the others excavated at Teotihuacan is the fact that, in the latter cases, a high percentage of the data comes from small-scale intensive excavations, with no context control; these data should be used cautiously, and can only be compared in terms of presence/absence to data coming from large-scale extensive excavations. One may think that there are differences in quantities, but the problem is the comparability of the samples. When we take into consideration the presence/absence of botanical and faunal resources, as well as exotic raw materials, we conclude that the differences in access between compounds are very slight.

There also are differences in specialized activities between household groups of different compounds, but also in dominant activities of households, which suggest group and family specializations. Differences in the number of high-status products, particularly the decorated ceramic tripods or the mural paintings, and variability in the quality of the construction itself have also been noted. There may be a whole range of socioeconomic possibilities, with no clear-cut distinctions between groups in the urban setting.

Beyond the Apartment Compound

Apartment and residential compounds should not be analyzed without taking into consideration the relations to their neighboring structures. We know very little about the barrio settlement unit at Teotihuacan. Different types of apartment compounds may cluster around a barrio ritual center. Many of the three-temple complexes found throughout the northern part of the ancient city could be the centers of barrio groups, where cult and exchange activities took place for a number of specialized corporate groups living in apartment compounds around them. Other types of wards, not involving three-temple complexes, may be distinguished in the southern part of the city. Recently, Cabrera (1996) has excavated a large area of the La Ventilla barrio, with its ceremonial core, and the different apartment compounds around it, some rich, with a large display of mural paintings, and some poor, more domestic in character, with evidence of lapidary work (Gómez Chávez 2000). Barbour (1993) has proposed that host figurines (large hollow pottery human representations, with small painted figurines inside their bodies and related to head,

limbs, and chest) may be a symbolic representation of Teotihuacan's social structure, particularly the group consecrating the offering.

If Millon (1981:209) is right in proposing that the apartment compounds are a
by-product of state decisions to control efficiently the population of the city, then
a further subject of interest would be the articulation of these social units with the
barrio and urban organization as a whole. It is also possible that the inefficiency of
the state bureaucracy and its inflexibility caused its fall (Millon 1988), and was, in
part, provoked by the difficulty in harmonizing the interests of such a vast array of
ethnic, occupational, and social groups.

With respect to coercive elements within Teotihuacan society, Millon (1993:31)
states that there is evidence of two military wards at Teotihuacan: one centered in
Atetelco, in the southwestern part of the city, and the other – Techinantitla – in the
northeastern section. His conclusion derived from the mural paintings in these sites.
Yet we should also emphasize that evidence for large militaristic displays is limited,
not often seen within the city. Evidence for temple dedications with human sacrifices (López Austin et al. 1991) seem to be limited to particular events and times.

A fact that strikes me when comparing Teotihuacan to other Classic sites in
Mesoamerica is the lack of dynastic iconography and propaganda, as Pasztory
(1988) has noted: no individual rulers are depicted. The most common human
depiction in mural art is the procession of anonymous human figures in priestly
attire. This may mean two things: either the rulers are most commonly depicted in
their priestly function, and not in their secular aspect, or there is a collective agency
in charge of the government, so no particular individual is represented.

Paulinyi (1981) suggests that Teotihuacan and Tula inaugurated a new type of
government characterized by the co-regency of three to seven lords. López Austin
(1989) proposes that Teotihuacan was the first place where the transformation from
lineage to state took place, a process in which the old lineage heads separated from
the common people to form an autonomous group of bureaucrats, redistributers,
and nobles. The birth of the state would be derived from the presence of groups of
diverse origin and from the use of power over a territory. C. Millon (1973) and
Pasztory (1978) have interpreted certain human representations with tassel headdresses as emissaries of the state in foreign lands. This stately function could have
guaranteed the adequate flow of foreign raw materials from Teotihuacan enclaves
to the capital.

In our model (Manzanilla 1993a), the Great Compound, more than a market,
would be an administrative and storage place for the different sectors of the city,
and also the main redistributive center. The regional interests that Sload (1987)
invokes for the Great Compound's domestic structures may be closely related to
the storage of specialized products from different sectors of the city.

The Elite and the City

Nobody can contest that Teotihuacan was the capital of an impressive state
that established enclaves in remote provinces of Mesoamerica. Yet there are

different opinions about its type of government. There are some who believe that Teotihuacan was headed by a single lord or maybe two (Cabrera, Cowgill, and Sugiyama 1990). There are others who propose a collective government (Manzanilla 1993a; Pasztory 1988). Paulinyi (1981) proposes the existence of seven district groups within Teotihuacan which may have had a part in co-rulership: one is located to the west of the Great Compound; the second in the northwestern part of the valley; the third to the east of the Street of the Dead; the fourth on the eastern fringe of the city; the fifth to the south of the San Lorenzo river. Following a similar line of thought, through cluster analysis of 16 artifact types, Sload (1987) proposed that each of the apartment compounds on top of the Great Compound was affiliated with a particular region of the city.

Three sites have been mentioned as the possible residence of the rulers of the city. Armillas (1964:307) argued that the rulers of Teotihuacan probably lived in the Ciudadela, by analogy with the *tecpan* of Aztec times. Millon advanced the possibility of dual rulers, each residing in one of the so-called "palaces" to the north and to the south of the Temple of the Feathered Serpent in the Ciudadela (Millon 1976:237). From the limited published evidence of these buildings (Jarquín Pacheco and Martínez Vargas 1982; Romero Noguerón 1982), we know that each of these buildings has five almost identical apartments around a central courtyard, covering an area of $4800\,m^2$. In Structure 1D (north of the Temple of the Feathered Serpent), burials under the floors were found in some of the rooms, the richest of which, found in Compound A (northwest) had jade ear spools, mica disks, a theater-type censer with marine elements, and tripod vessels and plates (Jarquín Pacheco and Martínez Vargas 1982:103). These elements parallel those from other residential compounds, and are not unusual. In Structure 1E (to the south of the temple) stone mortars and grinding tools were found on top of the floor, emphasizing food preparation activity areas, as in other domestic compounds (Romero Noguerón 1982:160). Domestic deities such as Huehueteotl, as well as Tlaloc vases, are found in these two huge structures, as well as in small domestic compounds, such as the one we excavated in Oztoyahualco 15B:N6W3 (Manzanilla 1993b).

The second candidate for the residence of the ruler is the Street of the Dead Complex, which has been cited by Cowgill (1992) as the seat of the political authority of the city. This group of buildings stands between the Pyramid of the Sun and the Ciudadela, and it is a macro-complex of temples and residential structures surrounded by walls (R. Millon 1973:35), comprising the Western Plaza Compound, the *Edificios Superpuestos*, and the Viking Group. Morelos García (1993) excavated extensively in the Western Plaza Compound, a large plaza surrounded by three structures around which different rooms and courtyards are located. In some of the rooms and courtyards, many grinding tools were found (Morelos García 1993:62–63), as well as sculptures, merlons, domestic pottery, etc. Morelos García (1993:66) states that there was a difference between the archaeological materials found on temples and altars, and those found in adjacent rooms and courtyards, with the latter being more domestic in nature. No burials were found, as in other residential compounds at Teotihuacan, so the author assigns an administrative function to the compound, even though the ceremonial function of the main structures is not discussed. Nevertheless, the alignment of small rooms adjacent to the Street of the Dead seem more like offices or warehouses that domestic structures.

Third, the Great Compound has also been cited as a possibility for the city's main marketplace and bureaucratic center (R. Millon 1973; Sload 1987), but we know very little about this area, which seems to be more administrative in nature.

I would contend that it is difficult to designate a particular structure as the seat of the rulers of the city. Many sites have special characteristics because of their privileged location and nearness to the Street of the Dead. I could add to the former three the Quetzalpapalotl Palace in the Moon Plaza (Acosta 1964); and the Xalla Complex between the Pyramids of the Sun and Moon, which we (Manzanilla and López Luján 2001) began excavating in 2000. The Quetzalpapalotl Palace seems to be a huge residential sector attached to one of the temples (Building 5) that border the Moon Plaza, and as such it is exceptional (Acosta 1964:59).

One of the main problems we have to face at Teotihuacan is the analysis of these big buildings; we have not been able to differentiate among rooms that were administrative in function, those that were audience rooms, or those that were domestic quarters. With respect to centralized storage, Cowgill (1987) has shown that there were large concentrations of San Martin amphorae in a 300 m band west and north of the Street of the Dead. Thus, we could suggest that there was some kind of centralized storage near or on the main avenue.

Collective rulership does not require a particular residence for the ruling group; perhaps the residences are located in the different sectors, and the "palace" is only a seat of government affairs and administration. Future research in the Xalla Compound, where the main plaza has four stepped buildings, one to each cardinal point, with a temple in the center of the plaza, can test this hypothesis; perhaps each structure is the seat of a sector lord, and the plaza reflects the ritual component of this corporate rulership.

ACKNOWLEDGMENTS

I thank the reviewers' and editors' enriching comments on the article. I also thank the following people for their participation in particular studies in my projects: Luis Barba, Agustín Ortiz and Alessandra Pecci for the geophysical and geochemical prospection, as well as for the chemical studies of stucco floors; Raúl Valadez and Bernardo Rodríguez for the paleofaunal analysis; Emily McClung de Tapia, Diana Martínez and Cristina Adriano for the paleobotanical data; Beatriz Ludlow, Emilio Ibarra and Margarito Casales for the pollen information; Judith Zurita and Concepción Herrera for the phytolith analysis; Magalí Civera, Mario Millones, Liliana Torres and Rocío Vargas for the osteological, as well as the DNA, analyses; Cynthia Hernández and Beatriz Maldonado for the lithic analysis; Miguel Angel Jiménez and Claudia López for the ceramic distributional maps; Johanna Padró for the bone industry analysis; Miguel Angel Baez for the lapidary study, and the Graphic Department of the Institute of Anthropological Research of the National

Autonomous University of Mexico (particularly Fernando Botas, César Fernández, Rubén Gómez, Rafael Reyes and José Saldaña) for invaluable their help. This inter-disciplinary research was funded by the Institute of Anthropological Research of the National Autonomous University of Mexico (UNAM) and the Consejo Nacional de Ciencia y Tecnología, and carried on thanks to a permit from the Consejo de Arqueología of the Instituto Nacional de Antropología e Historia (INAH).

REFERENCES

Acosta, J. R., 1964 *El Palacio de Quetzalpapálotl*. Memorias del Instituto Nacional de Antropología e Historia 10. Mexico, DF: Instituto Nacional de Antropología e Historia.

Armillas, P., 1964 Northern Mesoamerica. In *Prehistoric Man in the New World*. J. D. Jennings and E. Norbeck, eds. Pp. 291–329. Chicago: University of Chicago Press.

Barbour, W., 1993 Host figurines. In *Teotihuacan: Art from the City of the Gods*. K. Berrin and E. Pasztory, eds. P. 210. San Francisco: Fine Arts Museums of San Francisco.

Cabrera, C. R., G. L. Cowgill, and S. Sugiyama, 1990 El Proyecto Templo de Quetzalcóatl y la práctica a gran escala del sacrificio humano. In *La Epoca Clásica: Nuevos Hallazgos, Nuevas Ideas*. A. Cardós de Méndez, ed. Pp. 123–146. Mexico, DF: Instituto Nacional de Antropología e Historia.

Cabrera, R., 1996 Las excavaciones en La Ventilla: Un barrio teotihuacano. *Revista Mexicana de Estudios Antropológicos* 42, 5–30.

Cowgill, G. L., 1987 Métodos para el estudio de relaciones espaciales en los datos de la superficie de Teotihuacan. In *Teotihuacan: Nuevos datos, nuevas síntesis y nuevos problemas*. E. McClung de Tapia and E. C. Rattray, eds. Pp. 161–189. Mexico, DF: Universidad Nacional Autónoma de México.

——1992 Social differentiation at Teotihuacan. In *Mesoamerican Elites: An Archaeological Assessment*. D. Z. Chase and A. F. Chase, eds. Pp. 206–220. Norman: University of Oklahoma Press.

Crespo Oviedo, A. M., and A. G. Mastache de E., 1981 La presencia en el área de Tula, Hidalgo, de grupos relacionados con el Barrio de Oaxaca en Teotihuacan. In *Interacción cultural en México central*. E. C. Rattray, J. Litvak, and C. Díaz O., eds. Pp. 99–104. Mexico, DF: Universidad Nacional Autónoma de México.

Díaz O., C. L., 1980 *Chingú: Un sitio clásico del área de Tula, Hgo*. Colección Científica 90. Mexico, DF: Instituto Nacional de Antropología e Historia.

Gamio, M., 1922 *La población del Valle de Teotihuacan*. Mexico, DF: Secretaría de Agricultura y Fomento.

Gómez Chávez, S., 1998 Nuevos datos sobre la relación de Teotihuacan y el Occidente de México. In *Antropología e historia del occidente de México*. Pp. 1461–1493. XXIV Mesa Redonda de la Sociedad Mexicana de Antropología, vol. 3. Mexico, DF: Universidad Nacional Autónoma de México y Sociedad Mexicana de Antropología.

——2000 La Ventilla: Un barrio de la antigua ciudad de Teotihuacan. Dissertation. Mexico, DF: Escuela Nacional de Antropología e Historia.

González, J., 1993 Estudio del material arqueobotánico de Oztoyahualco: Macrofósiles botánicos, fitolitos y polen. In *Anatomía de un conjunto residencial teotihuacano en Oztoy-*

ahualco. L. Manzanilla, ed. Pp. 661–673. Mexico, DF: Universidad Nacional Autónoma de México.

Hernández, C., 1993 La lítica. In *Anatomía de un conjunto residencial teotihuacano en Oztoyahualco.* L. Manzanilla, ed. Vol. 1, pp. 388–467. Mexico, DF: Universidad Nacional Autónoma de México.

Jarquín Pacheco, A. M., and E. Martínez Vargas, 1982 Las excavaciones en el Conjunto 1D. In *Memoria del Proyecto Arqueológico Teotihuacan 80–82.* R. Cabrera Castro, I. Rodríguez G., and N. Morelos G., eds. Pp. 89–126. Colección Científica, Arqueología 132. Mexico, DF: Instituto Nacional de Antropología e Historia.

Kolb, C. C., 1995 Teotihuacan period figurines: A typological classification, their spatial and temporal distribution in the Teotihuacan Valley. In *The Teotihuacan Valley Project: Final Report,* vol. 3: *The Teotihuacan Occupation of the Valley,* part 2: *Artifact Analyses.* W. T. Sanders, ed. Pp. 275–465. Occasional Papers in Anthropology 20. University Park: Matson Museum of Anthropology, Pennsylvania State University.

Krotser, P., and E. Rattray, 1980 Manufactura y distribución de tres grupos cerámicos de Teotihuacan. *Anales de Antropología* 17, 91–104.

Linné, S., 1934 *Archaeological Researches at Teotihuacan, Mexico.* Publication 1. Stockholm: Ethnographical Museum of Sweden.

——1942 *Mexican Highland Cultures: Archaeological Researches at Teotihuacan, Calpulalpan and Chalchicomula in 1934–35.* New series, Publication 7. Stockholm: Ethnographical Museum of Sweden.

López Austin, A., 1989 La historia de Teotihuacan. In *Teotihuacan.* Pp. 13–35. Mexico, DF: El Equilibrista, Citicorp/Citibank.

López Austin, A., L. López Luján, and S. Sugiyama, 1991 The Feathered Serpent Pyramid at Teotihuacan: Its possible ideological significance. *Ancient Mesoamerica* 2, 93–106.

Manzanilla, L., 1985 El sitio de Cuanalan en el marco de las comunidades pre-urbanas del Valle de Teotihuacan. In *Mesoamérica y el Centro de México.* J. Monjarás-Ruiz, E. Pérez Rocha, and R. Brambila, eds. Pp. 133–178. Mexico, DF: Instituto Nacional de Antropología e Historia.

——1993a The economic organization of the Teotihuacan priesthood: Hypotheses and considerations. In *Art, Ideology, and the City of Teotihuacan.* Janet C. Berlo, ed. Pp. 321–338. Washington, DC: Dumbarton Oaks Research Library and Collections.

——ed., 1993b *Anatomía de un conjunto residencial teotihuacano en Oztoyahualco.* Mexico, DF: Universidad Nacional Autónoma de México.

——1996 Corporate groups and domestic activities at Teotihuacan. *Latin American Antiquity* 7, 228–246.

——2000 Hallazgo de dos vasijas policromas en Teopancazco, Teotihuacan. *Arqueología Mexicana* 8, 80.

Manzanilla, L., and E. Carreón, 1991 A Teotihuacan censer in a residential context: An interpretation. *Ancient Mesoamerica* 22, 299–307.

Manzanilla, L., and L. López Luján, 2001 Exploraciones en un posible palacio de Teotihuacan: el Proyecto Xalla 2000–2001. *Mexicon* 13(3), 58–61.

McClung de Tapia, E., 1979 Plants and subsistence in the Teotihuacan Valley A.D. 100–750. Ph.D. dissertation. Brandeis University, Ann Arbor: University Microfilms.

——1980 Interpretación de restos botánicos procedentes de sitios arqueológicos. *Anales de Antropología* 17, 149–165.

Millon, C., 1973 Painting, writing, and polity in Teotihuacan, Mexico. *American Antiquity* 38, 294–313.

Millon, R., 1967 Teotihuacan. *Scientific American* 216, 38–48.

——1968 Urbanization at Teotihuacan: The Teotihuacan Mapping Project. In *Actas y Memorias del 37 Congreso Internacional de Americanistas I*. Pp. 105–120. Buenos Aires: Departamento de Publicaciones Científicas Argentinas.

——1970 Teotihuacan: Completion of map of giant city in the Valley of Mexico. *Science* 170, 1077–1082.

——1973 *Urbanization at Teotihuacan, Mexico*, vol. 1: *The Teotihuacan Map*, part 1: *Text*. Austin: University of Texas Press.

——1976 Social relations in ancient Teotihuacan. In *The Valley of Mexico: Studies in Pre-Hispanic Ecology and Society*. E. R. Wolf, ed. Pp. 205–248. Albuquerque: University of New Mexico Press.

——1981 Teotihuacan: City, state, and civilization. In *Supplement to the Handbook of Middle American Indians*, vol. 1: *Archaeology*. V. Bricker and J. Sabloff, eds. Pp. 198–243. Austin: University of Texas Press.

——1988 The last years of Teotihuacan dominance. In *The Collapse of Ancient States and Civilizations*. N. Yoffee and G. Cowgill, eds. Pp. 102–164. Tucson: University of Arizona Press.

——1993 The place where time began: An archaeologist's interpretation of what happened in Teotihuacan history. In *Teotihuacan: Art from the City of the Gods*. K. Berrin and E. Pasztory, eds. Pp. 16–43. San Francisco: Fine Arts Museums of San Francisco.

Monzón, M., 1989 *Casas prehispánicas en Teotihuacan*. Toluca: Instituto Mexiquense de Cultura.

Morelos García, N., 1993 *Proceso de producción de espacios y estructuras en Teotihuacán*. Colección Científica 274. Mexico, DF: Instituto Nacional de Antropología e Historia.

Pasztory, E., 1978 Artistic traditions of the Middle Classic period. In *Middle Classic Mesoamerica: A.D. 400–700*. E. Pasztory, ed. Pp. 108–142. New York: Columbia University Press.

——1988 A reinterpretation of Teotihuacan and its mural painting tradition, and catalogue of the Wagner murals collections. In *Feathered Serpents and Flowering Trees: Reconstructing the Murals of Teotihuacan*. K. Berrin, ed. Pp. 45–77, 135–193. San Francisco: Fine Arts Museums of San Francisco.

Paulinyi, Z., 1981 Capitals in Pre-Aztec Central Mexico. *Acta Orientalia Academiae Scientiarum Hung*. 35, 2–3, 315–350.

Rattray, E. C., 1987 Los barrios foráneos de Teotihuacan. In *Teotihuacan: Nuevos datos, nuevas síntesis y nuevos problemas*. E. McClung de Tapia and E. C. Rattray, eds. Pp. 243–273. Mexico, DF: Universidad Nacional Autónoma de México.

——1988 Nuevas interpretaciones en torno al Barrio de los Comerciantes. *Anales de Antropología* 25, 165–182.

——1991 Fechamientos por radiocarbono en Teotihuacan. *Arqueología* 6, 3–18.

——1993 *The Oaxaca Barrio at Teotihuacan*. Monografías Mesoamericanas 1. Puebla: Universidad de las Américas, Instituto de Estudios Avanzados.

Romero Noguerón, M., 1982 *Conjunto 1E: Memoria del Proyecto Arqueológico Teotihuacan 80–82*. R. Cabrera Castro, I. Rodríguez G., and N. Morelos G., eds. Pp. 157–162. Colección Científica, Arqueología 132. Mexico, DF: Instituto Nacional de Antropología e Historia.

Sánchez Alaniz, J. I., 1989 Las unidades habitacionales en Teotihuacan: El caso de Bidasoa. Dissertation. Mexico, DF: Escuela Nacional de Antropología e Historia.

Sanders, W. T., 1964 The Central Mexico symbiotic region: A study in prehistoric settlement patterns. In *Prehistoric Settlement Patterns in the New World*. G. R. Willey, ed. Pp. 115–127. Viking Fund Publications in Anthropology 23. New York: Johnson Reprint Co.

—— 1966 Life in a Classic village. In *Teotihuacan, Onceava Mesa Redonda*. Pp. 123–147. Mexico, DF: Sociedad Mexicana de Antropología.

—— 1994 *The Teotihuacan Valley Project: Final Report*, vol. 3: *The Teotihuacan Occupation of the Valley*, part 1: *The Excavations*. Occasional Papers in Anthropology 19. University Park: Matson Museum of Anthropology, Pennsylvania State University.

Santley, R. S., J. M. Kerley, and T. P. Barrett, 1995 Teotihuacan Period obsidian assemblages from the Teotihuacan Valley. In *The Teotihuacan Valley Project: The Teotihuacan Occupation of the Valley*, part 2: *Artifact Analyses*. W. T. Sanders, ed. Pp. 466–483. Occasional Papers in Anthropology 20. University Park: Matson Museum of Anthropology, Pennsylvania State University.

Séjourné, L., 1959 *Un palacio en la ciudad de los dioses*. Mexico, DF: Instituto Nacional de Antropología e Historia.

—— 1966a *Arqueología de Teotihuacán: La cerámica*. Mexico, DF: Fondo de Cultura Económica.

—— 1966b *Arquitectura y pintura en Teotihuacán*. Mexico, DF: Siglo XXI.

Sempowski, M. L., 1987 Differential mortuary treatment: Its implication for social status at three residential compounds in Teotihuacan, Mexico. In *Teotihuacan: Nuevos datos, nuevas síntesis y nuevos problemas*. E. McClung de Tapia and E. C. Rattray, eds. Pp. 115–131. Mexico, DF: Universidad Nacional Autónoma de México.

—— 1994 Mortuary practices at Teotihuacan. In *Mortuary Practices and Skeletal Remains at Teotihuacan*. M. L. Sempowski and M. W. Spence, eds. Pp. 1–314. Salt Lake City: University of Utah Press.

Serrano, C., and Z. Lagunas, 1974 Sistema de enterramiento y notas sobre el material osteológico de La Ventilla, Teotihuacan, México. *Anales del Instituto Nacional de Antropología e Historia* 7, 105–144.

Sload, R., 1987 The Great Compound: A forum for regional activities. In *Teotihuacan: Nuevos datos, nuevas síntesis y nuevos problemas*. E. McClung de Tapia and E. C. Rattray, eds. Pp. 219–241. Mexico, DF: Universidad Nacional Autónoma de México.

Spence, M. W., 1966 Los talleres de obsidiana de Teotihuacan. In *XI Mesa Redonda: Teotihuacan. El Valle de Teotihuacan y su entorno*. Pp. 213–218. Mexico, DF: Sociedad Mexicana de Antropología.

—— 1987 The scale and structure of obsidian production. In *Teotihuacan: Nuevos datos, nuevas síntesis, nuevos problemas*. E. McClung de Tapia and E. C. Rattray, eds. Pp. 429–450. Mexico, DF: Universidad Nacional Autónoma de México.

—— 1989 Excavaciones recientes en Tlailotlacan, el Barrio Oaxaqueño de Teotihuacan. *Arqueología* 5, 81–104.

—— 1992 A comparative analysis of ethnic enclaves. Paper presented at the 57th Annual Meeting of the Society for American Archaeology Pittsburgh, April 8–12.

Starbuck, D. R., 1975 Man–animal relationships in Pre-Columbian Central Mexico. Ph.D. dissertation. New Haven: Department of Anthropology, Yale University.

Storey, R., 1983 The paleodemography of Tlajinga 33: An apartment compound of the Pre-Columbian city of Teotihuacan. Ph.D. dissertation. Pennsylvania State University, University Park. Ann Arbor: University Microfilms.

—— 1986 Perinatal mortality at Pre-Columbian Teotihuacan. *American Journal of Physical Anthropology* 69, 541–548.

—— 1987 A first look at the paleodemography of the ancient city of Teotihuacan. In *Teotihuacan: Nuevos datos, nuevas síntesis, nuevos problemas*. E. McClung de Tapia and E. C. Rattray, eds. Pp. 91–114. Mexico, DF: Universidad Nacional Autónoma de México.

—— 1991 Residential compound organization and the evolution of the Teotihuacan state. *Ancient Mesoamerica* 2, 107–118.

—— 1992 *Life and Death in the Ancient City of Teotihuacan: A Modern Paleodemographic Synthesis.* Tuscaloosa: University of Alabama Press.

Storey, R., and R. J. Widmer, 1989 Household and community structure of a Teotihuacan apartment compound: S3W1:33 of the Tlajinga Barrio. In *Households and Communities.* S. MacEachern, D. J. W. Archer, and R. D. Garvin, eds. Pp. 407–415. Calgary: Archaeological Association of the University of Calgary.

Valadez Azúa, R., 1993 Macrofósiles faunísticos. In *Anatomía de un conjunto residencial teotihuacano en Oztoyahualco.* L. Manzanilla, ed. Vol. 2, pp. 729–825. Mexico, DF: Universidad Nacional Autónoma de México.

Widmer, R. J., 1991 Lapidary craft specialization at Teotihuacan: Implications for community structure at 33:S3W1 and economic organization in the city. *Ancient Mesoamerica* 2, 131–147.

6

Social Diversity and Everyday Life within Classic Maya Settlements

Cynthia Robin

What was life like for people in the past? As a discipline archaeology has always sought to answer questions about the diversity of human life in past societies. With 150 years of archaeological research in the Maya area now complete, Maya archaeologists have uncovered the evidence to document that Classic Maya society was large, diverse, and complicated. Given this complexity how are we to understand the myriad peoples that inhabited and constructed the ancient Maya world? What roles did different people play in society? How did they live their lives? What can we learn about the inner workings of ancient Maya society by examining the lives of its diverse constituency?

The social world is constructed by and for people. By accessing archaeological evidence on ancient social life we can document the diverse lives and roles of people in the past. Two classes of evidence – *representations of people* and *people's living spaces* – can provide particularly rich information on ancient social life. By studying Classic period representations of people we can learn how the creators of these representations depicted social differences in their society (e.g., Joyce 2000; Reents-Budet 2001). By studying Classic period living spaces we can learn how the various members of Classic Maya society actually lived their lives (e.g., Ashmore 1991; Folan 1969; Gonlin 1994; Hendon 1991; Marcus 1995; Robin 2001a, 2002a).

As philosopher of science and archaeologist Alison Wylie (1985, 1992) has cogently noted, the more lines of evidence that a researcher can bring together on a given topic, the more richly textured their understanding of that topic will be. In this regard, Maya archaeology is particularly well suited to the study of ancient social life because we have access to a plethora of human representations and the remains of living spaces. Ancient Maya people represented themselves in both *words* (the Maya *hieroglyphic texts*) and *images*. Rosemary Joyce (1993, 1996, 2000) has compared two groups of Classic Maya imagery: *small-scale ceramic figurines* and *monumental images*. Small-scale figurines are largely found in noble Maya residential contexts (Hammond 1975; Hendon 1991; Willey 1972, 1990). Monumental images carved in stone are usually commissioned by Maya royalty. These images typically adorn *stelae* – two-sided, freestanding stone monuments located in the open, public plazas of Maya cities or the less accessible doorway *lintels* of royal residences. Images and hieroglyphic texts are often found together on the same monuments.

The archaeological evidence for people's living space encompasses an even more diverse range of evidence including *buildings, artifacts, human burials, plant and food remains*, and even other "invisible" data sets such as the *soil chemical remains* of a garden or field (e.g., Ashmore 1991; Gonlin 1994; Hendon 1991; Middleton and Price 1996; Robin 2001a, 2002a). By studying the remains of living spaces, archaeologists can learn about ancient *everyday life* – the ordinary, and often routine, daily practices of people's social, economic, and ritual lives. By bringing together these "multiple lines of evidence" (in the sense defined by Wylie 1985, 1992) we can piece together a picture of the diverse roles and lives of ancient Maya people.

I argue that in the history of Maya archaeology there have been three critical turning points which have enabled Maya archaeologists to gain detailed insights into the diverse lives of ancient Maya people: *the decipherment of Maya hieroglyphs, the development of household archaeology*, and *the development of feminist archaeology*. In the 1950s and 1960s, after a century of debate over whether the Maya hiero-glyphs recorded historical information about people or ahistorical information about celestial bodies and deities, scholars such as Tatiana Proskouriakoff (1963, 1964) explicitly demonstrated that Maya hieroglyphs included historical informa-tion about actual royal individuals and their lives. Research such as this led the way to an explosion of new work on Maya hieroglyphs which has enabled us to under-stand what Maya royalty wrote about their history, worldviews, family relations, and political agendas (e.g., Houston 1993; Martin and Grube 2000; Schele and Freidel 1990). But beyond this upper royal echelon of Maya society the vast majority of people in the Classic period were non-royal nobles or commoners. The terms *royal* and *royal court* refer to the ruling families and group of people who surround rulers and perform courtly activities (as defined by Inomata and Houston 2001). The term *noble* (following Joyce 2000) refers to the asserted high status of non-royal families, and the term *commoner* refers to the vast and diverse bulk of ancient Maya society (farmers, laborers, craftspeople, etc.) who were never discussed in Classic Maya writing and presumably had lower status than other members of Maya society (as discussed by Valdez and Lohse n.d.).

Developments in the fields of household archaeology in the 1980s and feminist archaeology in the 1990s have been critical for increasing our understanding of the lives of all people in Classic Maya society. Initially, and perhaps unsurprisingly, much of the archaeological work in the Maya area focused on the impressive Maya temples and the monumental remains of Maya city centers. Household archaeol-ogy brought to the Maya area a research focus on the places where Maya people lived – the households of both the rich and the poor (e.g., Ashmore and Wilk 1988). The study of ancient households developed alongside the fields of settlement and landscape archaeology (Chapter 7). Feminist scholars working with household archaeology and other data sets drew further attention to the diversity of ancient experiences based on gender as well as other lines of difference such as age, status, and occupation (e.g., Joyce 1993, 2000). Given the complementary focus of household and feminist archaeologists on understanding the diversity of people's lives, we can integrate the questions these researchers ask to more successfully demonstrate the dynamics and meanings of people's varied actions and experiences in the past (Hendon 1996). Information from hieroglyphic texts and images complements household data – particularly for Maya royalty and nobility – by allowing us to assess the purposeful representations (both textual and iconographic) that certain segments of Maya society created and used to represent themselves and others. It is important to be aware of both representational and household evidence when trying to understand ancient Maya social life, because:

1   these data sets provide windows into different segments of Maya society (representational data largely relate to royal and noble lives and household data to all people's lives depending on the household that was excavated);
2   these data sets provide different types of information about ancient social life from purposeful representation of people (located in either the public plazas of cities or the intimate confines of households) to the often unintentionally discarded or left-behind ordinary remains of people's everyday lives.

Given the wealth of archaeological evidence on ancient Maya social life, Maya archaeologists are in a good position to answer a key question of contemporary social theory: what is the relationship between representations of social life and people's experiences of living in a social world (e.g., Bourdieu 1979; Butler 1990; de Certeau 1984)? As Classic period representations of social life are largely authored by royal and noble (and often male) individuals, we must question the relationship between the highly conventionalized human representations and the everyday practices and experiences of people's lives (e.g., Hendon 1997; Joyce 1993, 2000, 2001). By comparing representations and everyday living spaces we can assess the intersections and disjunctions between the ways people represented their world and they ways they lived in their world. As historian James Scott (1985, 1990) has suggested, *the public transcripts* – the overt and public representations in writing, art, and architecture of society's dominant groups – which historians (and archaeologists) have traditionally studied, may not "represent" the living experiences of all members of that society. Stated this succinctly, Scott's assertion seems quite obvious. To what extent did ancient Maya representations of social life, which were largely created by royalty and nobility, represent or pervade the everyday lives of the different people in Maya society – commoners, nobles, or royals? To answer this question and understand social diversity in the Classic Maya past I will first discuss research on royal and noble representations of Classic Maya social life and then compare and contrast analyses of everyday life within three strata of Maya society: the royal court at the city of Calakmul, noble residential complexes at the city of

Copan, and common farmers in the village of Chan outside of the city of Xunantunich.

Royal and Noble Representations of Classic Maya Social Life

Classic Maya rulers manipulated monumental images, art, and architecture in public settings within their cities to express their power. Rulers, who were mostly men, but occasionally women (e.g., Hewitt 1999; Marcus 2001) commissioned the majority of the hieroglyphic texts and visual representations that adorn the building interiors and façades within Classic Maya cities. Some other royal and noble men and women did commission texts and images (e.g., Hendon 1991; Tate 1992), but the perspective on Maya society that we can ascertain from these media is largely that of the male ruler at the top of the social hierarchy. As Wendy Ashmore has demonstrated through her own work (e.g., 1991, 1998) and discusses in Chapter 7, Classic Maya rulers arranged and manipulated monumental architecture in meaningful ways throughout Maya cities which represented their worldviews and position in society. Royal residences were often located in central, elevated, and/or northern positions within cities, plausibly to represent the ruler and royal family's power as a zenith of power, as these cardinal (north) and relative (central, elevated) locations are associated with power in Classic Maya cosmology.

Of the wide array of people who comprised Maya society, a very few were mentioned in hieroglyphic texts: rulers (*ajaw*), secondary rulers (*sajal*), royal women, scribes, singers, musicians, and dancers (e.g., Houston and Stuart 2001; Inomata 2001). Completely omitted from the hieroglyphic texts were most nobles and all commoners. Where lower-status people were documented in hieroglyphic texts they were usually captives who literally and figuratively represented the ruler's power over others (as rulers were often depicted standing on top of captives: Marcus 1974). Spatial conventions (such as up/down, right/left, front/back, and cardinal directionality) in the arrangement of Classic Maya monuments and the arrangement of images within compositions also emphasized the separate but complementary roles of men and women in Maya political ideologies (e.g., Joyce 1996, 2000; Robin 2001b; Stone 1988).

Rosemary Joyce's (1992, 1993, 1996, 2000, 2001) comparisons of royal monumental images of people and small-scale human figurines have illustrated differences and similarities in royal and noble Maya portraits of social diversity – particularly gender, age, and occupational differences. In monumental images royal men and women were typically depicted in regal ritual rather than productive roles. In these rituals royal women often presented cloth bundles and ceramic bowls (Fig. 6.1). Cloth and food are the two products most associated with women's productive activities in small-scale figurines. Rosemary Joyce suggests that the absence of productive activities in monumental images and the presence of images of royal women using and offering the products of other women's labor may represent

Figure 6.1. Paired male and female figures, Yaxchilan Lintel 1. Ian Graham and Eric von Euw, *Corpus of Maya Hieroglyphic Inscriptions*, vol. 3, part 1: *Yaxchilan*. Peabody Museum of Archaeology and Ethnology. Copyright 1977 by the President and Fellows of Harvard College. Used with permission

royalty's interests in controlling and thus de-emphasizing the economic production and potential economic importance of other households' production.

Royal men were typically portrayed in a wider range of regal roles than royal women, including engaging in political events, warfare, and dancing. Where images of royal males and females are paired, these images relate the interdependence or complementarity of separate male and female actions in completing ritual perfor- mances and military and marriage alliances (Fig. 6.1). In monumental images, royal persons – be they a young male heir coming of age or an aged royal female – were all depicted at a single youthful age in the life cycle. The dress of royal individuals (both males and females) often combined elements of typical male and female wardrobes. By encompassing male and female identities through dress, de- emphasizing age differences, and co-opting the production of other people, royal Maya persons (both male and female) seem to have been depicting themselves as the pinnacle and unification of the differences within their society.

In contrast with monumental representations of people, small-scale figurines por- trayed men and women across their life course. Although the roles of men in small- scale figurines were consistent with those of men in monumental depictions, female roles were quite different. Small-scale figurines of women portrayed them in pro- ductive roles as food preparers, weavers, caretakers of animals, and caretakers of children (Fig. 6.2). As Rosemary Joyce suggests, these images appear to celebrate

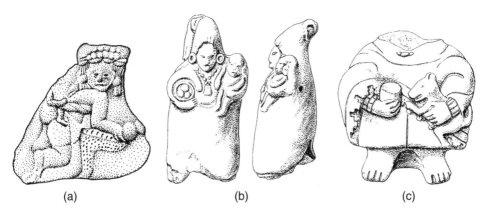

(a)   (b)   (c)

Figure 6.2. Ceramic figurines from Maya lowlands: (a) woman grinding corn, Lubaantun, Belize (courtesy of Norman Hammond); (b) woman holding child and pot of tamales, Altar de Sacrificios, Guatemala (Willey 1972: fig. 34b); (c) woman holding dog and ceramic vessel, Altar de Sacrificios, Guatemala (Willey 1972: fig. 34f). Used with permission

the role of women as producers, the very productive activities that royal individuals sought to control to promote a unified and totalizing royal identity.

Everyday Life within Classic Maya Settlements

By comparing representations of people in monumental art and small-scale figurines we are able to document both similarities and differences in royal and noble representations of social difference in Classic Maya society. There was no unified notion of social life in Classic Maya society and no singular means of representing social differences. But how do these representations of social diversity relate to the lived experiences of people in Classic Maya society? To what extent did these representations constrain the variability in people's practices (Joyce 2000, 2001)? To answer these questions I turn to household archaeology and studies of the places where Classic Maya people lived and worked.

Living in the royal court in the city of Calakmul

The place
The city of Calakmul is located in Campeche, Mexico immediately west of a large 34 × 8 km *bajo* (a natural depression that is a major chert and water source). Calakmul was founded in the Middle Formative period and became one of the largest urban centers in Mesoamerica. With at least 117 stelae, Calakmul's rulers may have erected the most carved stone monuments of any Maya royal group. Calakmul reached its political peak during the Late Formative to Late Classic periods. During the Late Classic period its population rose to 50,000 people. The

1.75 km^2 monumental center of the city (called the Central Plaza) consists of an elevated plaza surrounded by temple-pyramids, royal palaces, and other public and ritual buildings. The largest building in the Central Plaza is Str. II, a 55 m high temple-pyramid. There are seven *sacbeob* (raised plastered roads) at Calakmul. Five lead from the Central Plaza to other nearby cities and two are internal to the city leading to nearby noble residential complexes. Like many Maya cities, including Copan and Xunantunich, Calakmul is laid out in roughly concentric zones with the royal court at the center of the city, surrounded by noble complexes with commoner residences further beyond these. The archaeological research discussed here is drawn from the Calakmul Project directed by William Folan between 1982 and 1994. Ceramic specialist María del Rosario Domínguez Carrasco and lithic specialist Joel Gunn analyzed the artifacts from the excavations at Calakmul (e.g., Folan 1992; Folan et al. 1995, 2001a, 2001b). Joyce Marcus (1987; see also Folan et al. 1995) undertook the epigraphic study of Calakmul's inscriptions.

To understand the everyday lives of Calakmul's royal court we can draw on the interpretations of archaeologist William Folan and his colleagues, based on detailed excavations of the final Terminal Classic phase occupation of Calakmul's 86-room temple-pyramid, Str. II, and the 12-room royal palace, Str. III. Three monumental stairways lead from the plaza area to the summit of the Str. II temple-pyramid. The multiroom buildings that line the lower terraces of the Str. II pyramid were constructed with cut-stone walls and vaulted stone or thatch roofs. Two building complexes surmount the summit of the pyramid. The upper and southernmost complex is a triadic temple complex. The lower and northernmost complex is dominated by a nine-room palace. Northeast of Str. II, the 12-room freestanding royal palace Str. III stood on a 5 m high platform. Palace Str. II had cut stone walls and a vaulted stone roof with painted stucco bas-relief roof combs. The larger and more elaborate Str. III palace had two large stucco masks on its façade.

The people

Project epigrapher Joyce Marcus has interpreted the texts and images on monuments that were commissioned on stelae throughout the city between at least A.D. 435 and A.D. 830. Many of the hieroglyphic texts on these monuments are now quite eroded, but their narratives told of political and ritual events in the lives of at least 15 male rulers and five royal women. The prevalent paired or single stelae depicting royal men and women highlight the complementary roles of men and women and the importance of royal marriage at Calakmul. Spatial conventions were employed to represent the separate but complementary roles of men and women, as images of women were placed on the left stela of a stela pair or the back of a single stela, and vice versa for men. Like other Classic period inscriptions, the names, positions, and productive actions of lower-status members of the Calakmul royal court went unnoted. Calakmul's royalty portrayed themselves engaged in political and ritual actions. They showed themselves as the consumers of the goods produced by the faceless people absent from the texts. The people of lower standing mentioned or depicted on Calakmul's monuments were captives upon which royal men and women stood.

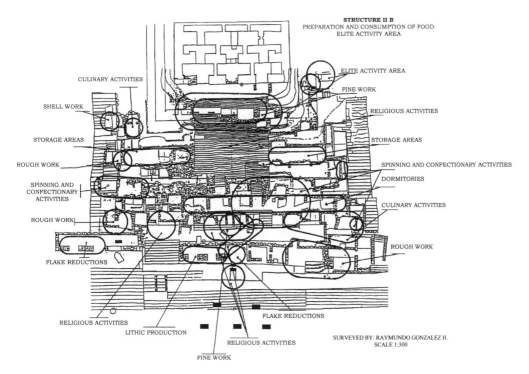

Figure 6.3. Plan of Str. II, showing activity areas. Used by permission of William Folan

Even though the social diversity within Calakmul's royal court was omitted from its inscriptions it was quite well marked by the activities, material possessions, and architecture of the different residents of Str. II and III. Based on their excavations, the archaeologists document that the unadorned buildings on the lower terraces of the Str. II pyramid contained residential and production areas. Each room within these multiroom buildings tended to be used for a single function – sleeping, preparing food, cooking, eating, flake reduction, stone tool and jewelry production, storage, cloth production, bone object production, or shell working (Fig. 6.3). At the base of the pyramid people produced utilitarian items such as stone tools. Higher up on the terraces people produced higher-status items such as shell ornaments and cloth.

The various artisans of Calakmul's royal court lived and worked along the lower terraces of Str. II. The close spatial association of their places of residence and places of production contrasts with the relative absence of productive activities beyond food preparation and cooking in the royal palace on the summit of Str. II. Individual rooms within the royal palace were used largely unfunctionally for sleeping, or ritual activities, or eating, preparing food and cooking. Unlike the artisans living below them, palace residents had access to a wide range of imported items including chert, ceramics, obsidian, marine shell, jade, manta ray spines, and jasper.

The residents of the Str. II palace were likely high-status members of the royal court involved with overseeing the production ongoing below their residence. They seem to have had a lower social status than the royal family residing in the larger and more elaborate palace Str. III, which contained the burial of the ruler nicknamed Long-Lipped Jawbone, who Joyce Marcus has suggested is possibly Calakmul's dynastic founder, and who died around A.D. 350. In addition to the types of rooms found in the Str. II palace, the Str. III palace had a sweat bath and tool production room. Perhaps unsurprisingly, the royal family had access to greater quantities of imported goods than the residents of the Str. II palace.

Experiencing life at Calakmul's royal court
The pomp and circumstance of royal ceremonies, political negotiations, military and administrative affairs are the aspects of life in the "public" monumental center of a Maya city that are most apparent from its imposing temple-pyramids and open plazas. Indeed these are the types of events that the royalty inscribed in their "public transcripts," the hieroglyphic texts and images that they commissioned in their cities. The central open plazas of Maya cities are often likened to stages because the texts describing these areas emphasize ritual activities (also see Ashmore's discussion in Chapter 7 of the ritual nature of cities). The archaeological record at Calakmul provides a window into another side of life around the Central Plaza – a secular life of day-to-day domestic and productive living.

The domestic and productive socio-spatial world constructed by Calakmul's architects replicated the political-ideological order represented in monumental images. As William Folan and colleagues have shown, at the base of the temple-pyramid Str. II labored the most common of artisans in the royal court, the producers of utilitarian stone tools from local chert. As one proceeded up the pyramid, higher-status artisans produced items such as cloth and imported shell objects. At the pinnacle of the pyramid was a palace and temple complex, where some of the most important families of the royal court oversaw other people's production, consumed the products of their labor, and expended these goods in the name of politics and ritual for the gods.

The Central Plaza architecture is far from a passive remnant of the past, but was actively constructed and used to structure and circumscribe the lives of the diverse members of the royal court. By largely excluding productive activities from their palaces, Calakmul's royalty set their homes (their palaces) apart from other people's homes in a quite vivid way – a royal home consumed a distinctive lifestyle enabled by the labor undertaken in other people's homes. Although the royal palace-dwellers lived in quite close proximity to lower-status members of the royal court, Folan and colleagues note that palace residents built their world to keep their exclusive lifestyles quite separate from the daily lives of those around them. Their palaces were elevated on high platforms and had restricted inner access to guard their privacy. The various artisans who lived and worked on Str. II, also did so in quite close proximity to each other. While Folan and colleagues did document some artisan work occurring on exterior terraces and stairways of Str. II, most production took place inside its many buildings. As each daily task was segregated into its own interior room bounded by stone walls, people would have spent their days working alongside others whose status, occupational skills, and possibly gender (particularly in the case of gender-specific crafts, such as cloth production) were most similar to their own. While the ultimate outcome of the work of the royal court combined the work of all these different individuals, the everyday lives of the diverse members of the royal court was quite segregated by status, occupation, and gender along spatial divisions that replicated the royal political-ideological ordering of the world.

Living in a noble complex in the Sepulturas area of the city of Copan

The place

The city of Copan is located in the Copan river valley of western Honduras. During the Classic period Copan reached its political and population peak and was a major city in the southeastern Maya region. The $1 \, km^2$ monumental center of the city (called the Main Group) consists of elevated plazas surrounded by temple-pyramids, a ball court, royal palaces, and other public and ritual buildings. The largest building in the Main Group is Str. 10L-26, a temple-pyramid which has a central hieroglyphic stairway that records the history of Copan's rulers. A *sacbe* leads from the Main Group to nearby areas of noble residential complexes called Sepulturas. Further beyond the noble complexes were commoner residences.

Archaeologist Julia Hendon (1987, 1989, 1991, 1992, 1997, 2000) investigated three noble complexes in the Sepulturas group as part of the larger Proyecto Arqueológico Copan, phase 2, directed by archaeologist William Sanders (1986) which investigated the relationship between Sepulturas and the Main Group at Copan. The Sepulturas noble complexes 9M-22, 9M-24, and 9N-8 were occupied during the Late Classic from A.D. 600 to A.D. 1000. Typical of Classic period noble complexes, each complex consists of one or more residential courtyards (groups of buildings surrounding an elevated courtyard: Fig. 6.4). 9N-8 is one of the largest noble complexes in the Copan valley, with 15 residential courtyards; 9M-22 has 3 courtyards, and 9M-24 has one.

Three different types of buildings surround each courtyard: (1) residences (which were used for sleeping as well as most other daily activities); (2) ancillary buildings (which were multifunctional as well, but only used for food preparation and storage); and (3) ritual buildings. These buildings were elevated on stone plat-forms that varied in height from 30 cm to 4.75 m. Most residences had cut stone walls and one of three types of roofs: (1) a vaulted stone roof; (2) a beam and mortar roof; or (3) a thatch roof. The interiors of each residence had from one to ten rooms per building. Some of the rooms had stone "benches" for sleeping and sitting, and others were used multifunctionally for preparing food, storage, and producing util-itarian and status items (cloth, shell ornaments, bone objects, and/or obsidian tools). Ancillary and ritual buildings differed from residences as they consisted of simpler, usually one-room, buildings with wattle and daub walls.

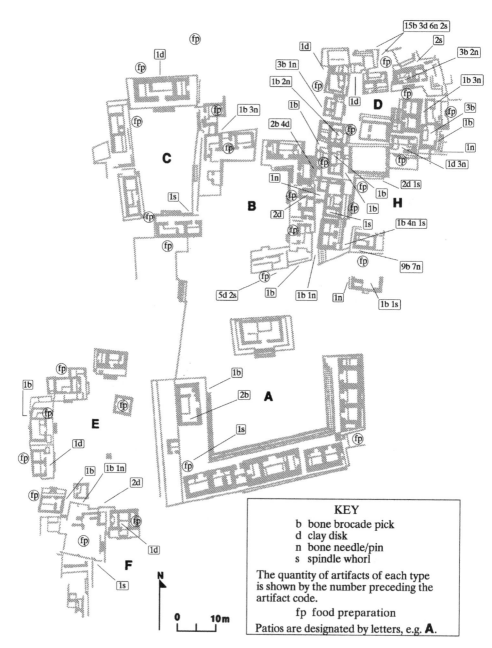

Figure 6.4. Distribution of evidence for women's labor in Group 9N-8, Sepulturas, Copan (figure by Julia A. Hendon). Used with permission

The people

Within each courtyard at Sepulturas noble families prepared food, cooked, ate, stored their possessions, produced utilitarian and status items, observed rituals, and slept. Given the redundancy of domestic activities within each courtyard, Julia Hendon concludes that each courtyard housed a large extended family household and possibly other non-related persons or families working for the noble household. These noble families performed their day-to-day activities within Sepulturas' enclosed buildings, but food preparation, cloth production, and rituals also occurred outside of buildings. Hendon notes a particularly high frequency of outdoor food preparation activities.

Beyond the basic similarities of everyday domestic life in Sepulturas there were wide differences in the production activities, wealth, and status of the families that lived around a courtyard. Each courtyard typically had one more elaborate residence. These elaborate residences resembled smaller versions of royal places described above for Calakmul. They tended to be the largest, on the highest platform, constructed entirely with stone, and decorated with relief sculpture and hieroglyphic texts. Their hieroglyphic texts discussed the same themes that royalty discussed in their texts, but focused on noble male Sepulturas residents. The elaborate residences tended to have a central room with a larger open floor space which could accommodate a meeting of important dignitaries. Hendon suggests that noble extended family households seem to have been internally ranked around a senior family that had greater access to resources, cultural symbols, and political opportunities.

Beyond these inter-courtyard differences, there were also clear socio-economic distinctions between the three noble courtyard complexes. Noble families at Sepulturas had access to a wide variety of local and imported material possessions. The imported items included greenstone ornaments, obsidian, marine shell, and some figurines and ceramic vessels. Ceramic vessels were the most common possession, and overall 30 percent of the ceramics used in day-to-day life at Sepulturas were "fancy" polychrome vessels. Most of these were locally made, but most extended families (except for the group living around courtyard B at 9M-22) had some imported polychrome vessels. While most families in the Copan area had access to local polychrome vessels, noble families residing at the largest and most elaborate complex 9N-8 had greater quantities of imported polychrome vessels and other imported items than other noble families living elsewhere. Through these non-local objects the residents of complex 9N-8 created a distinctive world of material objects that contributed to their creation of a distinctive social identity for themselves at Sepulturas.

Along with these differences in architecture and material possessions, noble families did not all produce the same quantities of status items. Cloth production, which would have been undertaken largely by women, was the most widespread productive activity at the Sepulturas noble courtyards. Julia Hendon identified a clear correlation between the intensity of cloth production and the highest-status residences at 9N-8 (Fig. 6.4). Here the "mute" archaeological record of spindle whorls and weaving tools seems to be voicing what hieroglyphic texts commissioned by noble men left out – the important role of Maya noble women as weavers in the Classic Maya economy. Weaving archaeological and epigraphic data together, we can see the different yet complementary roles played by noble men and noble women.

Experiencing life at Sepulturas

Day-to-day working and living around Sepulturas occurred both within enclosed buildings and outside of buildings. Working outside of buildings, residents could see or even talk with one another. The people working inside buildings would have been separated and invisible to the people in other buildings and the people outside of buildings. While within the walls of their residences, the families that were living in quite close proximity to other families around a courtyard would have had the privacy to develop the family-oriented practices and identities that we can still see as differences in the archaeological record. As they walked, worked, and relaxed outside each day they would have been constantly aware of, if not actively engaged in, the lives of their neighbors.

Within Sepulturas' buildings the work areas where women prepared food and made cloth were in close proximity and often even within the same room as the work areas where people (men and/or women) produced obsidian tools, shell ornaments, and bone items, and performed rituals. As Julia Hendon concluded, differing from the conventionalized spatial structuring of gender and work represented on royal political monuments, there was no exclusive partitioning of gender and work areas in noble residential complexes.

In terms of architecture, material possessions, certain cultural symbols, and political activities, the Sepulturas noble residences, particularly those of Sepulturas' highest-status residents, resembled smaller versions of royal palaces. But, as Hendon notes, in other ways day-to-day life in a noble complex was quite difference from that of the royal court – there was less spatial separation of noble men's and women's work by gender, production type, or production vs. consumption. Sepulturas' highest-status residents may have lived on the highest platforms, but the spatial ordering of residences of different status around the horizontal space of the courtyard was quite different from the dramatic vertical replication of status hierarchy in lived space across the façade of temple-pyramid Str. II at Calakmul.

Living in the Chan Noohol farmsteads in the environs of the city of Xunantunich

The place

Chan Noohol is just one of many small clusters of farmsteads located in the environs of the mid-sized city of Xunantunich in the Belize river valley of western Belize. Chan Noohol was a southern sector of a farming village called Chan (*nòohol* means south in Yucatec Maya). It was situated 4 km east-southeast of Xunantunich. Xunantunich's 0.6 km^2 monumental center consists of elevated plazas surrounded by temple-pyramids, three ballcourts, royal palaces, and other public and ritual buildings. The 40 m high temple-pyramid nicknamed "El Castillo" located at the

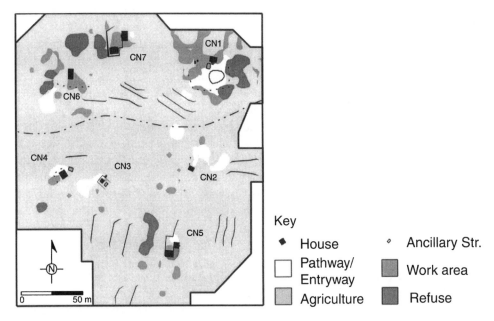

Key

◆ House   ⁰ Ancillary Str.

☐ Pathway/   ▨ Work area
  Entryway

☐ Agriculture   ■ Refuse

Figure 6.5. Plan view showing activity areas at Chan Noohol

center of the city could be seen from far across the countryside. Each day, from their homes and fields, the residents of Chan Noohol could see this monumental temple-pyramid in the distance. Given the proximity of Chan Noohol and Xunan-tunich, Xunantunich was most likely the center of major ceremonial celebrations and other political and administrative activities for the residents of Chan Noohol. As they viewed "El Castillo" each day, Chan Noohol's farmers would have had a constant reminder of the broader society in which they were participants. This distant image of monumental construction, that was unlike any construction at Chan Noohol, may also have reminded Chan Noohol residents of the limits of their social world and of the social differences that existed in their society.

My archaeological research on Chan Noohol (e.g., Robin 1999, 2001a, 2002a, 2002b) was part of the larger Xunantunich Archaeological Project directed by archaeologists Richard Leventhal and Wendy Ashmore which investigated the interrelationships between the city of Xunantunich and the surrounding settlement (e.g., Ashmore 1993, 1998; Ashmore et al. 2003; Leventhal and Ashmore forth-coming). Chan Noohol's seven small farmsteads (CN1–CN7: Fig. 6.5) were occu-pied for only a short period of time, between A.D. 660 and A.D. 790 at the end of the Late Classic period. During this time period many other small clusters of farmstead like Chan Noohol were constructed and occupied throughout the Xunantunich region. This boom in agrarian populations occurred parallel with Xunantunich's rather short-lived regional political apogee. This correlation is not surprising because the scale and intensity of construction at Xunantunich certainly required a large labor force to build. And, possibly even more critical, this part of the Belize river valley had always been an important area of agricultural production for Maya society.

The commoner architecture at Chan Noohol was quite different from the royal and noble architecture just discussed. In contrast with elaborate and elevated masonry residences, residences and ancillary buildings at Chan Noohol were constructed close to the ground surface, on low stone platforms that ranged in height from 10 cm to 1.1 m. Chan Noohol's houses were constructed of perishable materials: pole walls and thatch roof. Only one side of one residence at farmstead CN6 had a wattle and daub wall like those of the lowest-status residences at Sepulturas. Residences and ancillary buildings were encircled by agricultural areas. Each farmstead consisted of only one or two residences. Given the redundancy of domestic and agricultural activities within each farmstead, farmsteads were likely inhabited by one or two related families.

The people

The people of Chan Noohol were farmers. By constructing agricultural terraces and adding nutrients such as phosphorous to the soil, these farmers intensified the majority of the land around Chan Noohol to enhance its agricultural production. Modern soil surveys in Belize have classified Chan Noohol's soils as Vaca suite, Cuxu subsuite soils which have marginal agricultural potential under today's mechanized agricultural practices because of the sloping and rocky nature of these soil formations. But Chan Noohol's farmers were not constrained by the same limitations that constrain modern farmers; they transformed the land to create a productive agricultural landscape that supported centuries of habitation.

At Chan Noohol's farmsteads people prepared food, cooked, ate, stored their possessions, produced stone tools and cloth, observed rituals, slept, and produced foodstuffs. Low frequencies of remains associated with stone tool and cloth-making indicate that these activities were only done for household-level provisioning. The majority of artifacts and activity areas at Chan Noohol were associated with the food production process – from sowing to serving – indicating that farmwork was the primary intra- and extra-household production activity for the entire farm family – men, women, and children. When agricultural production is technologically intensive and situated near the house, as was the case at Chan Noohol, collaborative participation of all family members in agricultural work tends to be high.

Unsurprisingly, people at Chan Noohol had few material possessions. The majority of their possessions were utilitarian ceramic vessels for preparing, serving, and storing food and water. People recycled their possessions at Chan Noohol. If a ceramic pot was broken one of the fragments might be crafted into a spindle whorl. If a stone axe was broken it might be re-used as a pounding implement. Like their residences, their possessions were relatively undecorated. With the exception of hard granite grinding stones and a few sharp obsidian cutting tools, most possessions at Chan Noohol were made of locally available materials. With few exceptions, instead of imported ornaments, Chan Noohol residents wore ornaments made of locally available materials such as gray slate which were shaped to look like simple greenstone ornaments.

Despite the limited possessions of Chan Noohol's farmers and the uniform focus of their production on agriculture, life at Chan Noohol was far from homogeneous. The residences at the two-residence farmsteads (CN5 and CN7) were constructed on the highest platforms and gave onto low courtyard areas – resembling much smaller versions of the Sepulturas courtyards. While roughly 8 percent of the ceramic vessels from farmsteads CN5 and CN6 and a one-residence farmstead (CN1) were volcanic ash-tempered ceramics, a ceramic type that is commonly finished with "fancy" polychrome decoration, none of these ceramics was found at other farmsteads. Only the residents of CN5 and CN7 had access to any imported status items (jade fragments and marine shell beads). Although the residents of CN5 and CN7 neither made grand modifications to residences nor had many imported items, through these non-local items and residential modifications plausibly made in reference to the residences of higher-status members of Maya society, the residents of CN5 and CN7 created materially distinctive living places that contributed to their distinctive social identity at Chan Noohol.

Experiencing Life at Chan Noohol

The natural forest setting of Chan Noohol's residences encircled by fields would have been quite a visually different place from the crowded, bright-red-painted, cut stone buildings, plazas, and courtyards of Classic royal courts and noble complexes such as at nearby Xunantunich. Separated by their fields, different farm families lived dispersed from one another. Despite the openness of their pole-walled buildings and outdoor work areas, this distance between families would have allowed them a certain amount of privacy to develop the family-oriented practices and identities that we can still see as differences in the archaeological record. Beyond Chan Noohol's houses much daily domestic and agricultural work took place out of doors. Agricultural work is of course outside work, but women also prepared food and men and/or women made stone tools on outdoor domestic work surfaces and in ancillary buildings.

Within Chan Noohol farmsteads the people who were making tools and the people who were preparing food were doing these activities in the same space, regardless of whether or not they were the same people or were working there at the same time. Similarly the people who were involved in agriculture were working within seeing, talking, or yelling distance of the people who were preparing food and making stone tools. As domestic and agricultural activities were largely undertaken in outside spaces, this allowed communication between persons working on these activities (even when people were working in "enclosed" buildings, they could peer or talk through the pole walls). Since the majority of people's work took place in spaces that were neither rigidly enclosed nor divided by great distances, people's separate as well as collaborative daily work was organized spatially in such a way that it could facilitate interaction and communication rather than division. The spatial and social commingling of agricultural and domestic work created through people's practices promoted situated experiences where work around the house involved consumption and production and the input of male and female, old and young. In contrast with royal political ideologies and living experiences, the practices and experiences of day-to-day living and working around Chan Noohol emphasized the collaborative rather than segregated efforts of members of farmsteading families.

Conclusion

What was life like for the diverse Maya peoples of the Classic period? How did they represent their social world? How did they live and experience their lives? Classic Maya royalty constructed and conventionalized representations of gender, age, status, and work through texts, images, and city planning. Using spatial conventions they represented social differences as spatially separate. Royal personages (men, women, and children) manipulated these conventions to present themselves as the pinnacle and totality of these differences. Perhaps unsurprisingly, daily life within the Classic Maya royal court at Calakmul was very much structured along similar socio-spatial lines as political-ideological representations. As Pierre Bourdieu (1979) has noted, societies' upper echelons are most invested in and able to emulate and control their social world along the lines that they themselves are promoting as defining their distinction and high culture.

While the Maya nobility, like the residents of Sepulturas, were quite well situated socially and economically and they adopted and acquired many of the materials and symbols of high Classic Maya culture, their daily lives were in many ways quite different from royal lives. In part, this difference may have been created by their ability to control their own production of items of high Maya culture within their households. They seem to have celebrated this control through the creation of representations that portrayed their own productive activities, the very activities that the royalty left out of their representations.

Conversely, the social and economic situation of Chan Noohol's farmers did not allow them to take advantage of the materials and symbols of high Classic Maya culture. Although they produced no representations of themselves, the intensity of their agricultural production has left many traces in the archaeological record. Despite quite dramatic differences in the possession of materials and symbols, some aspects of day-to-day experiences of living and working at Chan Noohol and Sepulturas seem to have had more in common than either had with living experiences within the royal court at Calakmul. Daily living at Chan Noohol and Sepulturas was less marked by a spatial segregation of different people's lives and work along cosmological and political-ideological lines than at Calakmul's royal court. To an even greater extent at Chan Noohol than at Sepulturas, spatial arrangements and living experiences highlighted the complementary and/or collaborative aspects (rather than separate aspects) of people's lives.

With 150 years of archaeological research in the Maya area now behind us, we have the archaeological evidence to people the diverse and complex world of Classic Maya society. Bringing together our multiple lines of evidence we can now see an active and vibrant Maya world, with socially and economically distinct creators and inhabitants. The more Maya archaeologists can learn about the diversity and meaning of social life in Classic Maya society the closer we will come to understanding what it was like to be human in another time and place.

REFERENCES

Ashmore, W., 1991 Site-planning principles and concepts of directionality among the ancient Maya. *Latin American Antiquity* 2, 199–226.

——1998 Monumentos políticos: Sitio, asentamiento, y paisaje alrededor de Xunantunich, Belice. In *Anatomía de una civilización: Aproximaciones interdisciplinarias a la cultura Maya.* A. Ciudad Ruiz, Y. Fernández Marquínez, Ma. J. I. Ponce de León, A. L. García-Gallo, and L. T. Sanz Castro, eds. Pp. 161–183. Madrid: Sociedad Española de Estudios Mayas.

Ashmore, W., and R. R. Wilk, 1988 Household and community in the Mesoamerican past. In *Household and Community in the Mesoamerican Past.* R. R. Wilk and W. Ashmore, eds. Pp. 1–28. Albuquerque: University of New Mexico Press.

Ashmore, W., J. Yaeger, and C. Robin, 2003 Commoner sense: Late and Terminal Classic social strategies in the Xunantunich area. In *The Terminal Classic in the Maya Lowlands: Collapse, Transition, and Transformation.* D. S. Rice, P. M. Rice, and A. A. Demarest, eds. Boulder: University of Colorado Press. In press.

Bourdieu, P., 1979 *Distinction: A Social Critique of the Judgment of Taste.* Cambridge, MA: Harvard University Press.

Butler, J., 1990 *Gender Trouble: Feminism and the Subversion of Identity* London: Routledge.

de Certeau, M., 1984 *The Practice of Everyday Life.* Berkeley: University of California Press.

Folan, W. J., 1969 Dzibilchaltun, Yucatan, Mexico, Structures 384, 385, and 386: A preliminary interpretation. *American Antiquity* 34, 434–461.

——1992 Calakmul, Campeche: A centralized urban administrative center in the northern Peten. *World Archaeology* 24, 58–168.

Folan, W. J., J. D. Gunn, and M. de R. Domínguez Carrasco, 2001 Triadic temples, central plazas and dynastic palaces: A diachronic analysis of the royal court complex, Calakmul, Campeche, Mexico. In *Royal Courts of the Ancient Maya,* vol. 2: *Data and Case Studies.* T. Inomata and S. D. Houston, eds. Pp. 223–265. Boulder: Westview.

Folan, W. J., J. Marcus, S. Pincemin, M. de R. Domínguez Carrasco, L. A. Fletcher, and A. Morales López, 1995 Calakmul, Campeche: New data from an ancient Maya capital in Campeche, Mexico. *Latin American Antiquity* 6, 310–334.

Folan, W. J., J. May Hau, J. Marcus, W. F. Miller, and R. González Heredia, 2001 Los caminos de Calakmul, Campeche. *Ancient Mesoamerica* 12, 293–298

Gonlin, N., 1994 Rural household diversity in Late Classic Copan, Honduras. In *Archaeological Views from the Countryside: Village Communities in Early Complex Societies.* G. M. Schwartz and S. E. Falconer, eds. Pp. 177–197. Washington, DC: Smithsonian Institution Press.

Hammond, N., 1975 Maya settlement hierarchy in northern Belize. *Contributions of the University of California Archaeological Research Facility* 27, 40–55.

Hendon, J. A., 1987 The uses of Maya structures: A study of architecture and artifact distribution at Sepulturas, Copan, Honduras. Ph.D. dissertation. Department of Anthropology, Harvard University. Ann Arbor: University Microfilms.

——1989 Elite household organization at Copan, Honduras: Analysis of activity distribution in the Sepulturas zone. In *Proceedings of the 21st Annual Conference*. S. MacEachern, D. J. W. Archer, and R. D. Garvin, eds. Pp. 371–380. Calgary: Archaeological Association of the University of Calgary.

——1991 Status and power in Classic Maya society: An archaeological study. *American Anthropologist* 93, 894–918.

——1992 The interpretation of survey data: Two case studies from the Maya area. *Latin American Antiquity* 3, 22–42.

——1996 Archaeological approaches to the organization of domestic labor: Household practice and domestic relations. *Annual Review of Anthropology* 25, 45–61.

——1997 Women's work, women's space, and women's status among the Classic-period Maya elite of the Copan valley. In *Women in Prehistory: North America and Mesoamerica*. C. Claassen and R. A. Joyce, eds. Pp. 33–46. Philadelphia: University of Pennsylvania Press.

——2000 Having and holding: Storage, memory, knowledge, and social relations. *American Anthropologist* 102, 42–53.

Hewitt, E. A., 1999 What's in a name? Gender, power, and Classic Maya women rulers. *Ancient Mesoamerica* 10, 251–262.

Houston, S. D., 1993 *Hieroglyphs and History at Dos Pilas: Dynastic Polities of the Classic Maya*. Austin: University of Texas Press.

Houston, S. D., and D. Stuart, 2001 Peopling the Classic Maya court. In *Royal Courts of the Ancient Maya*, vol. 1: *Theory, Comparison, and Synthesis*. T. Inomata and S. D. Houston, eds. Pp. 54–83. Boulder: Westview.

Inomata, T., 2001 King's people: Classic Maya courtiers in a comparative perspective. In *Royal Courts of the Ancient Maya*, vol. 1: *Theory, Comparison, and Synthesis*. T. Inomata and S. D. Houston, eds. Pp. 27–53. Boulder: Westview.

Inomata, T., and S. D. Houston, 2001 Opening the royal Maya court. In *Royal Courts of the Ancient Maya*, vol. 1: *Theory, Comparison, and Synthesis*. T. Inomata and S. D. Houston, eds. Pp. 3–26. Boulder: Westview.

Joyce, R. A., 1992 Images of gender and labor organization in Classic Maya society. In *Exploring Gender through Archaeology: Selected Papers from the 1991 Boone Conference*. C. Claassen, ed. Pp. 63–70. Monographs in World Archaeology. Madison: Prehistory Press.

——1993 Women's work: Images of production and reproduction in pre-hispanic southern Central American. *Current Anthropology* 34, 255–273.

——1996 The construction of gender in Classic Maya monuments. In *Gender in Archaeology: Essays in Research and Practice*. R. P. Wright, ed. Pp. 167–198. Philadelphia: University of Pennsylvania Press.

——2000 *Gender and Power in Prehispanic Mesoamerica*. Austin: University of Texas Press.

——2001 Negotiating sex and gender in Classic Maya society. In *Gender in Pre-Hispanic America*. C. F. Klein, ed. Pp. 109–141. Washington, DC: Dumbarton Oaks.

Leventhal, R. M., and W. A. Ashmore, forthcoming Xunantunich in a Belize Valley context. In *Archaeology of the Belize Valley: Half a Century of Maya Settlement Studies*. J. F. Garber, ed. Gainesville: University Press of Florida.

Marcus, J., 1974 The iconography of power among the Classic Maya. *World Archaeology* 6, 83–94.

——1987 *The Inscriptions of Calakmul: Royal Marriage at a Maya City in Campeche, Mexico.* Museum of Anthropology Technical Report 21. Ann Arbor: University of Michigan.

——1995 Where is lowland Maya archaeology headed? *Journal of Archaeological Research* 3, 3–53.

——2001 Breaking the glass ceiling: The strategies of royal women in ancient states. In *Gender in Pre-Hispanic America.* C. F. Klein, ed. Pp. 305–340. Washington, DC: Dumbarton Oaks.

Martin, S. and N. Grube, 2000 *Chronicle of Maya Kings and Queens: Deciphering the Dynasties of the Ancient Maya.* London: Thames & Hudson.

Middleton, W. D., and T. D. Price, 1996 Chemical analysis of modern and archaeological house floors by means of inductively coupled plasma-atomic emission spectroscopy. *Journal of Archaeological Science* 3, 673–687.

Proskouriakoff, T., 1963 Historical data in the inscriptions of Yaxchilan, part 1. *Estudios de Cultura Maya* 3, 144–167.

——1964 Historical data in the inscriptions of Yaxchilan, part 2. *Estudios de Cultura Maya* 4, 177–201.

Reents-Budet, D., 2001 Classic Maya concepts of the royal court: An analysis of renderings on pictorial ceramics. In *Royal Courts of the Ancient Maya*, vol. 1: *Theory, Comparison, and Synthesis.* T. Inomata and S. D. Houston, eds. Pp. 195–236. Boulder: Westview Press.

Robin, C., 1999 Towards an archaeology of everyday life: Maya farmers of Chan Noohol and Dos Chombitos Cik'in, Belize. Ph.D. dissertation. Department of Anthropology, University of Pennsylvania. Ann Arbor: University Microfilms.

——2001a Peopling the past: New perspectives on the ancient Maya. *Proceedings of the National Academy of Sciences* 98, 18–21.

——2001b Kin and gender in Classic Maya society: A case study from Yaxchilan, Mexico. In *New Directions in Anthropological Kinship.* L. Stone, ed. Pp. 204–228. Lanham: Rowman & Littlefield.

——2002a Outside of houses: The practices of everyday life at Chan Nòohol, Belize. *Journal of Social Archaeology* 2, 245–268.

——2002b Gender and Maya farming. In *Ancient Maya Women.* T. Ardren, ed. Pp. 12–30. Walnut Creek: Alta Mira Press.

Sanders, W., ed., 1986 *Proyecto arquelógico de Copan segunda fase: Excavationes en el área urbana de Copan.* Tegucigalpa: Secretaría de Cultura y Turismo, Instituto Hondureño de Antropología e Historia.

Schele, L., and D. A. Freidel, 1990 *A Forest of Kings.* New York: William Morrow.

Scott, J. C., 1985 *Weapons of the Weak: Everyday Forms of Peasant Resistance.* New Haven: Yale University Press.

——1990 *Domination and the Arts of Resistance: Hidden Transcripts.* New Haven: Yale University Press.

Stone, A., 1988 Sacrifice and sexuality: Some structural relationships in Classic Maya art. In *The Role of Gender in Pre-Columbian Art.* V. Miller, ed. Pp. 75–104. Lanham: University Press of America.

Tate, C. E., 1992 *Yaxchilan: The Design of a Maya Ceremonial City.* Austin: University of Texas Press.

Valdez, F., and J. Lohse, n.d. *Ancient Maya Commoners.* Austin: University of Texas Press.

Willey, G. R., 1972 *The Artifacts of Altar de Sacrificios.* Cambridge, MA: Papers of the Peabody Museum of Archaeology and Ethnology 64:1.

——ed. 1990 *Excavations at Seibal, Department of Peten, Guatemala.* Cambridge, MA: Memoirs of the Peabody Museum of Archaeology and Ethnology 17:1–4.

Wylie, A., 1985 The reaction against analogy. In *Advances in Archaeological Method and Theory.* M. B. Schiffer, ed. Pp. 63–111. New York: Academic Press.

——1992 The interplay of evidential constraints and political interests: Recent archaeological research on gender. *American Antiquity* 57, 15–35.

7

Classic Maya Landscapes and Settlement

Wendy Ashmore

Landscapes in the Maya world engage visitors by their grandeur and often their drama. Their visual impact can awe us, and take our breath away. In some locales, they embrace us with a sense of calm and tranquility. John Lloyd Stephens captured many of these feelings 150 years ago, in his lively accounts of travels in the Maya area (Stephens 1963[1843], 1969[1841]). His traveling companion Frederick Catherwood, and many other artists, captured the visual fascination of Maya landscapes, through paintings, photographs, and poetry (Fig. 7.1).

In many of these portrayals, exotic landscapes are principally backdrops for ancient Maya ruins, whose description and interpretation were the underlying goals of the accounts. Together, landscapes and ruins, in images both verbal and graphic, prompted many questions about ancient Maya life in these locales. How did people apparently thrive in what seems to some outsiders such a forbidding environment – or to other observers, such a lush one? What kinds of places did the Maya establish on the land: were they cities or something else? How did these places and the people in them relate to one another? Why were these places abandoned? Landscapes and settlements provide information crucial to answering these questions, and continue to offer significant new ways of understanding ancient Maya lives.

To address the questions just posed, this chapter focuses on the Classic period in the Maya area (ca. A.D. 250–1000). Geographically, the Maya area extends south to north from the Pacific shores of modern-day Guatemala to Yucatan's coast on the Gulf of Mexico, and west to east, from lowland southern Mexico to western Honduras (Fig. 7.2). Although the Guatemalan and Chiapas highlands and Pacific coast were scenes of important and complex developmental histories, attention here highlights lowland areas.

Two central points underlie and shape the discussion. First, Maya landscapes and the traces of settlement on them are inseparable, and neither can be considered without the other. Second, both landscapes and settlement reveal a great deal about ancient Maya economics, politics, and belief systems.

F. Catherwood.   GENERAL VIEW OF PALENQUE.

Figure 7.1. Landscape at Palenque as depicted by Frederick Catherwood (from Stephens 1969[1841])

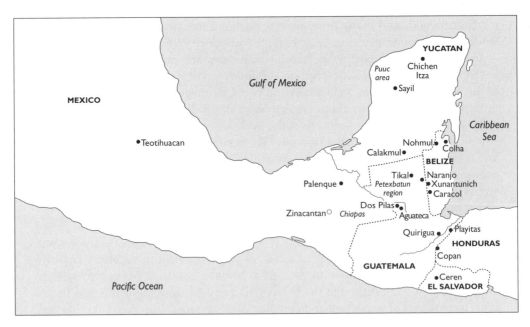

Figure 7.2. Map of the Maya area, showing places mentioned in text (prepared by Chelsea Blackmore)

Landscapes and Settlement: Inseparable Entities

Human *settlement* is frequently defined as the material traces of people's presence on the land. The term is used most commonly to refer to buildings and their distribution, but in its widest sense properly embraces a much wider range of traces, from homes and temples, to roads, walls, fields, and artifact scatters (e.g., Willey 1953). Examining such material evidence of settlement, archaeologists and other scholars infer many aspects of social life, including where individual households are situated, with respect to neighbors, superiors and subordinates, and what activities household members undertook. Settlement evidence also reveals how multiple households are organized in communities and larger social, economic, and political groups. And settlement studies allow such socially diverse inferences as distinguishing rural from urban living conditions, identifying the roads and walls deliberately built to materialize interpersonal relations, and the fields, reservoirs, and other constructions that testify to family and community subsistence strategies. The richly textured social understanding gained through settlement study have made it one of the most productive and widely used approaches in archaeology today (e.g., Sabloff and Ashmore 2001).

Landscape is more difficult to define, precisely because so many scholars have sought to define it in recent years, from quite varied perspectives (e.g., Knapp and Ashmore 1999; Stoddart 2000; Ucko and Layton 1999). Whereas some equate landscape with physical terrain, others hold the opposite view, that human presence is what defines landscape, most especially through the meanings and memories that people attach to their surrounding world (e.g., Ingold 1993; Schama 1995). In this discussion, landscape is considered as the larger concept, as embracing environment and the human activities and settlements supported there. Centrally important are not only the physical characteristics of terrain, but also the multiple ways humans interact with it – economically, politically, and with respect to meaning and belief. As social agents, people conceive and structure the world around them; even as they reshape and reinterpret landscapes, they extend social memory of what constitutes a proper world, and reproduce social and cosmic orders therein (Barrett 1999; Basso 1996; Joyce and Hendon 2000).

Defining specifically Maya landscapes requires some additional remarks. Both now and in antiquity, the world of the Maya has consisted of three domains, all of which are significant landscape components. The earth is the Middle World, characterized as a crocodilian being floating in a primordial sea. That underworld sea is home to supernatural beings, and its presence is manifest in lakes, ocean, *cenotes* (limestone sinkholes), and rivers, which latter may spill across the earth's surface or flow through caves, underground. Above the earth, the celestial domain is also fundamental, and likewise home to supernatural beings. Until recently, archaeologists have tended to focus on the more mundane – and more readily accessible – Middle World. But it is now abundantly clear that positions of the stars and planets forecast the fate of Maya wars, alliances, and other strategic events, in addition to mapping the story of creation for all to see (Aveni 1992; Freidel et al. 1993). And as a growing host of truly intrepid scholars demonstrate, the ancient Maya, like their descendants today, passed as pilgrims into the caverns of the earth, to do homage to the earth lord (e.g., Bassie-Sweet 1996; Brady 1997; Stone 1995). To seek understanding of Maya lives, then, requires expanding effective definition of landscape to include, as well, both celestial and underground spheres.

The inseparability of landscapes and settlement may seem obvious initially, but the full reasons bear closer examination. Certainly the Maya, like other peoples, have situated their homes, fields, and temples on the land, and this is an undeniable physical link. Less immediately obvious, however, the physical and conceptual boundaries between intentionally *built* environment and natural landscape are often blurred, disguised, or even absent. In other words, juxtaposition becomes more like continuity. For example, Maya (and other) constructions often incorporate natural rises in topography to augment building height (e.g., Becquelin and Baudez 1979). Roads and paths may be either obtrusive or subtle in how their courses are traced on the ground (e.g., Trombold 1991). Frequently material marking is inconspicuous, and sometimes actively avoided, at pilgrimage destinations or other customary gathering places, despite their pronounced importance in social life (e.g., Bradley 2000; Eliade 1959). Even when terrain is modified substantially, however, whether by architecture, agricultural fields, or other alterations, the boundaries between constructed and natural can become blurred in many ways. Some ways are conceptual, others physical.

Conceptually, architecture and monuments are commonly described as metaphors for the natural world, mimicking the landscape in constructed forms (e.g., Benson 1985). For example, a Classic Maya plaza set with portrait stelae is a "forest of kings," whose "trees" are the stelae and the rulers they embody (e.g., Schele and Freidel 1990). In a similar manner, a funerary temple with its internal tomb stands metaphorically as mountain and sacred cave. Human-made tunnels were portals to the underworld, equivalent to natural caves where the latter were lacking (e.g., Brady and Veni 1992). And maize grew on the back of the floating crocodilian earth deity (Fig. 7.3), with ancient drained fields signifying the waffle-like patterns of raised "shields" on the crocodile's skin (Puleston 1977).

Insightfully expressive as these metaphors are, the situation grows rather more complex when the metaphors transform back into mountains. This is where physical merging further clouds the distinctions between built and natural environments.

That is, even carefully constructed cultural landscapes also get *naturalized*. Over time, if not immediately, buildings, monuments, fields, and delimited open spaces become accepted as part of the natural landscape. The physical process of naturalization, or ruin formation, is illustrated clearly in archaeological sites everywhere. With regard to landscapes, William Denevan remarks insightfully that what we think of as a "pristine" New World at the time of European arrival is, in fact, a myth:

> There is substantial evidence . . . that the Native American landscape of the early sixteenth century was a humanized landscape almost everywhere. Populations were large. Forest composition had been modified, grasslands had been created, wildlife disrupted, and erosion was severe in places. Earthworks, roads, fields, and settlements were ubiq-

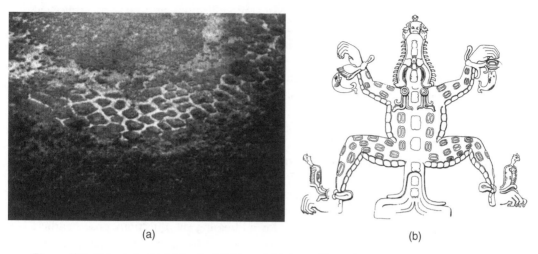

(a) (b)

Figure 7.3. Paired views of (a) raised fields and (b) Annie Hunter's drawing of splayed crocodile body on Copan Altar T. Figure 7.3(a) reprinted, with author and publisher permission, from "Prehistoric raised-field agriculture in the Maya lowlands," by B. L. Turner II and P. D. Harrison, *Science* 213:401, Fig. 3, copyright © 1991 American Association for the Advancement of Science. Figure 7.3(b) after Maudslay 1889–1902: vol. I, plate 95

uitous. With Indian depopulation in the wake of Old World disease, the environment recovered in many areas. A good argument can be made that the human presence was less visible in 1750 than it was in 1492. (Denevan 1992:369)

Ethnographic evidence among the Maya and other peoples indicates that *social* processes of naturalization also pertain: metaphorical, architectural landscapes are thought to have "always been there," and thereby merge with the "natural world" (Barrett 1999; Bradley 1993). Cumulatively, social memory blurs whatever distinctions might once have existed, and reinforces senses of social continuity in place (e.g., Joyce 2000). Similarly, people transform constructed "settlement" into seemingly natural, socially enduring "community" by "repetition, or *citation*, of the practices of others who move through the same spatial locations carrying out the same range of practices" (Joyce and Hendon 2000:143, emphasis in original). As Janet Richards remarks, discussing Edgar Casey's writings:

Part of the power of a place is its dynamism, its encouragement of event and motion in its midst . . . Human bodies, moving within a place or between places, animate and impute meaning to them through experience and perception, and in turn take away seemingly "natural" images of social or cosmological order from the structure of their movement in that place or landscape. An essential trait of these dynamic places is that they *gather* things in their midst: associations, experiences, and histories, becoming repositories of memory, concrete and complex arenas of common engagement over space and time. (Richards 1999:83–84, emphasis in original)

The foregoing factors collectively indicate the impossibility of drawing indisputable distinctions between the built environment and the natural world. In other words, because of frequently subtle physical modification, because of metaphorical equation of artificial and natural features, and because of social and physical transformation of construction into seemingly pristine nature, analysts like us need to consider settlements and settings together. Simply put, for the Maya, as for other peoples, the landscape and settlement on it were effectively inseparable in antiquity, and their study today requires simultaneous attention to both.

Landscapes and Settlement: Economics, Politics, and Belief

As asserted at the outset of this chapter, both landscapes and settlement reveal a great deal about ancient Maya economics, politics, and belief systems. I turn now to landscape and settlement evidence for addressing the questions posed earlier: How did people apparently thrive in what seems to some outsiders such a forbidding environment – or, to other observers, such a lush one? What kinds of places did they establish on the land – were they cities or something else? How did they relate to one another? Why were these places abandoned?

Economics

Rather romanticized depictions of Maya landscapes opened this chapter. Specific accounts cited were published in earlier centuries, but variants continue to appear today. In counterpoint, archaeologists writing in the late twentieth century emphasized Maya landscapes as environments, following approaches linked to cultural ecology – broadly speaking, study of the relation of people to the environment (e.g., Rice 1993). From these well-established perspectives, we continue to learn much about environmental resources and risks, the materially nurturing and constraining aspects of the landscape.

For example, perceived resource deficiencies of the Maya lowlands have sparked multiple and long-standing debates, especially about the role of environment and resources in the rise and "collapse" of Classic society (e.g., Abrams and Rue 1988; Puleston and Puleston 1971; Rathje 1971; Sabloff 1973; Sanders 1973). Depictions of the Maya lowlands as resource-deficient yielded dire characterization of its settlers as limited to small populations and, ultimately, doomed to failure (e.g., Meggers 1954). Not only, however, have Classic populations proven to have been extensive and often dense on the land, the ingenuity of Maya farmers has impressed modern scholars as inventive and – in a word – resourceful. In short, seemingly durable models of ancient slash-and-burn farming have given way to others recognizing a mosaic of quite diverse strategies for food procurement and production (e.g., Fedick 1996; Whitmore and Turner 1992). Whether peasant farmers in their own lands or kings commissioning large-scale communal projects, Maya social agents reshaped repeatedly the potential of their landscapes.

Beyond nurturance, of course, Maya landscapes can actively threaten, in the violence of hurricanes, volcanic eruptions, floods, or earthquakes, as well as in the quieter perils of drought (e.g., Freidel and Shaw 2000; Gunn and Folan 2000; Sheets 2002). The very same traits can both constrain and nurture, of course, as in legacies of long-term soil productivity from initially destructive volcanism, or in stimuli to social integration from local shortages or abundance – prompting exchange, pilgrimage, or other acts to alleviate productive shortfalls, tender tribute, or recognize allies.

In prevailing models of Classic Maya settlement, economic factors play key roles in shaping the sizes, forms, and distribution of resident populations. Where people lived, and in what numbers, certainly depended on availability of food and water. But as already noted, the Maya – like people elsewhere – elaborated means for amplifying quantities and predictability of such critical resources. What appeared to European explorers as exotic settings, alternately forbidding and lush, had often been modified extensively by the ancient Maya to produce stable and productive places to live.

For example, soils are commonly relatively shallow in lowland Guatemala, parts of Belize, and in Yucatan. They are also quite varied in agricultural productivity. Compounding challenges to farmers, the Yucatan peninsula is a porous limestone platform, and as a rule both rainfall and surface water are increasingly scarce as one moves across the peninsula from south to north. Elsewhere in the Maya area, the challenge was "too much" water, in swampy *bajo* locations such as one finds in parts of northeast Guatemala and northern Belize. Archaeological evidence indicates that none of these was an absolute deterrent to settlement.

Well before Classic times, Maya farmers reshaped the land to capture scarce rainwater in reservoirs, called *aguadas*, which were carefully lined to retain the precious water. In some cases, as at eighth-century Sayil, water resources were managed at the level of individual households, where each would create a domestic cistern by lining a *chultun*, or artificial pit in the limestone bedrock (e.g., McAnany 1990). At places like Tikal (Fig. 7.4) and sites of northern Belize, traces remain of sophisticated and often intricate hydraulic features, including drainage channels and dams as well as aguadas (Dunning et al. 1999; Scarborough 1996).

Maya farmers also enhanced agricultural productivity using strategies suited expertly to local terrain (Fedick 1996). In hilly topography like that of Caracol or Xunantunich, terrace construction increased the amount of flat land available, creating pockets of artificially deepened soils and slowing rainwater runoff (e.g., Dunning and Beach 1994). In bajo zones, soils rich in organic nutrients were dredged from swamp bottoms to elevate, dry, and simultaneously enrich the planting surface (e.g., Siemens and Puleston 1972). And in the arid plains of Yucatan, farmers used moist soil pockets in natural depressions to enhance cultivation (e.g., Gómez-Pompa et al. 1990; Kepecs and Boucher 1996), while elsewhere they clustered small stones around trees to maintain soil moisture. Indeed, some analysts suggest that many "*chich* mounds" of the region, low stone piles too small to be house sites, are the extensive remains of arboriculture (Kepecs and Boucher 1996).

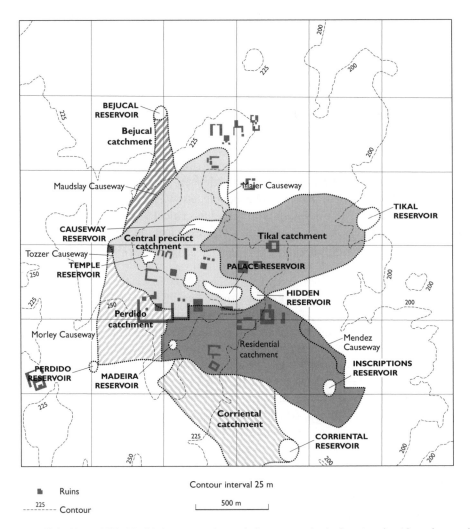

Figure 7.4. Map of Tikal highlighting aguadas and their watersheds. Reprinted, with author and publisher permission, from "A water storage adaptation in the Maya lowlands," by Vernon L. Scarborough and Gary G. Gallopin, *Science* 251:659, Fig. 2, copyright © 1991 American Association for the Advancement of Science

Amid all these local strategies, of course, and especially in areas of lower population density, swidden (slash-and-burn) techniques of milpa farming frequently remained critical (e.g., Drennan 1988). Because milpas require no permanent terrain modification they are seldom preserved archaeologically. Around A.D. 600, however, a catastrophic volcanic eruption in what is now highland El Salvador abruptly buried nearby villages and adjoining fields and gardens under thick ash layers; from the local village site now called Ceren, archaeologists have documented planting rows and furrows preserved in at least one milpa field, and have recovered casts of young maize stalks growing there (Sheets 2002).

Classic Maya farmers lived variously in such scattered village settlements and in closer proximity to the lords who governed them. The settlements where the farmers built temples and palaces for their overlords used to be considered ceremonial centers, relatively empty of permanent residents. We now know that many of these settlements were cities, with permanent occupants numbering in the tens of thousands or more (Culbert and Rice 1990).

Remains of ancient domestic compounds, civic plazas, and other constructed settings point collectively to the presence of diverse social classes, from peasants of varied economic means, through nobles of differing ranks, and the king and his royal court. Robin (Chapter 6) reviews in detail the social orders and daily life within Classic cities and more rural settings. Of most direct relevance for this chapter is the information that buildings and other settlement evidence provide for economic differentiation and integration of people within and among distinct communities (e.g., Canuto and Yaeger 2000; Chase and Chase 1992; Iannone and Connell 2002; Inomata and Houston 2001).

In smaller, village-level communities, differentiation was often marked materially by diverse sizes of house compounds, and their correspondingly varied implications for the labor pool on which the household head drew (e.g., Yaeger 2000). Reciprocally, households with larger networks on which they could draw often evinced material evidence for hosting feasts and other communal events; household grounds themselves, as well as remains of food and its preparation, attest to facilities and residues of such gatherings (e.g., Robin 1999; Yaeger 2000). Repetition of practices like the foregoing, especially their materialization in architecture and other enduring and visible items, served to reinforce a sense of community (Hendon 2000; Joyce and Hendon 2000).

Although comparing these and other categories of evidence across cities and countryside seems initially to suggest that the same kinds of reciprocal obligations bound villages and farmers with kings, the webs were more complex at these larger scales. Not only did farmers create food, they often doubled as artisans who created items for exchange, and more specialized artisans resided in or near royal courts to fashion goods for luxury consumption or ritual display (e.g., McAnany 1993). At these expanded social and economic scales, political economy bound farmer, artisan and king in larger networks of exchange and obligation. Considering political economy illustrates ways in which these networks exceed local forms of differentiation and integration.

Traditionally, for example, we have inferred that the range of settlements materialized a relatively simple hierarchical order of importance. Because such settlements as Tikal, Calakmul, Copan, or Caracol apparently had the largest populations, the largest buildings, and the greatest public displays of royal portrait sculptures, these places were taken as defining the top rungs of a hierarchical ladder. Below them, the far more numerous smaller settlements occupied progressively lower rungs in a single ladder line. All attributes of grandeur and development were thought to differ in the same order between ranks, such that an architecturally more majestic site should have more public sculpture, a larger populace, and all other traits thought to correlate with those – including adjoining evidence for large-scale agricultural production.

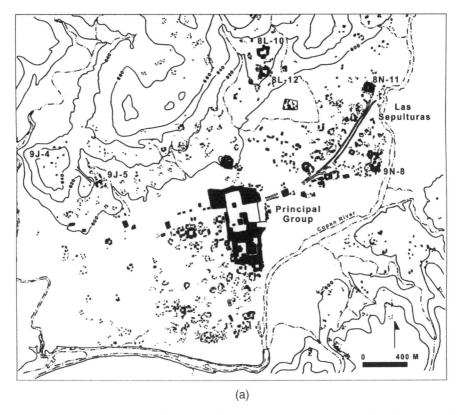

(a)

Figure 7.5. Schematic plans of (a) Copan; (b) Xunantunich; (c) Naranjo; (d) Calakmul (after Ashmore and Sabloff 2002)

A growing number of settlements, however, resisted such neat hierarchical placement. Nohmul and Quirigua, for example, had populations too small for the agricultural fields they appeared to have cultivated. Nohmul also had buildings that seemed overly large relative to population size, and Quirigua had portrait sculptures out of proportion with both civic architecture and population (e.g., Ashmore 1990; Pyburn 1996, 1997). Another architecturally and demographically unassuming settlement, Colha, had *two* community specializations – agricultural production and intensive manufacture of stone tools, made from locally distinctive honey-colored chert (King 2000).

All of these sites resisted ranking in traditional ways relative to other settlements in their regions. They could, however, be understood within a heterarchical framework, in which choosing different criteria can rank elements of a set (in this case, sites of a region) in different orders (e.g., Crumley 1979; Joyce and Hendon 2000; Potter and King 1995). Nohmul, Quirigua, and Colha rank quite differently with respect to their neighbors when the criteria for ranking shift between architecture, public sculpture, population, agricultural holdings, and other economic production.

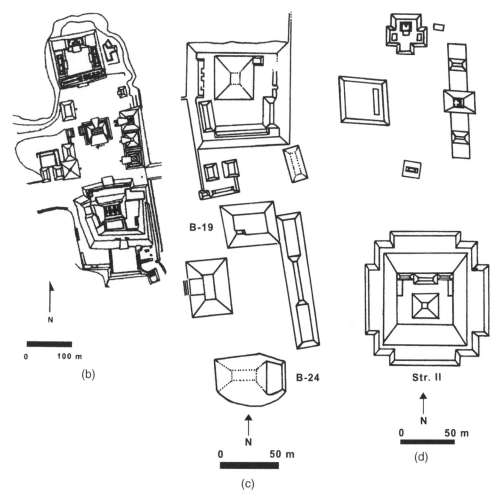

B-19

B-24

Str. II

(b)

0   100 m

N

(c)

(d)

0   50 m

0   50 m

N

N

Figure 7.5. Continued

The Nohmul and Quirigua cases – and one aspect of their heterarchical regional importance – return discussion to the question of settlement and landscape evidence for differentiation and integration within Maya regional economies. Both these settlements were likely "breadbasket" producers of maize and perhaps other foods for a much larger regional populace. At Quirigua, in particular, the food was likely rendered as tribute to nearby Copan (Fig. 7.5(a)). In the seventh century, massive flooding devastated Quirigua, and hieroglyphic text and sculptural imagery document a direct visit from Copan's king. In the same century, and the next, expanding populace at Copan outstripped capacity for adequate food production in the immediate Copan valley (Wingard 1996). Settlement and landscape evidence in both places tells us what texts, images, and artifacts do not, suggesting strongly that Copan's king promised help for his vassals at Quirigua, in exchange for renewed fealty – to be expressed in tribute including desperately needed food.

In a similar way, farmers at Xunantunich likely provided badly needed sustenance to people in the vicinity of distant Tikal, at a time in the eighth and ninth centuries when Tikal's own production and governance capacities were deteriorating (Ashmore et al. 2003). But as regional political conditions declined further, benefits accrued from supporting local lords and distant neighbors grew progressively less compelling, and any threats to farmers' departure apparently evaporated. At Xunantunich, peasants simply moved away. Each of these cases, as well as that of Nohmul and other settlements, indicate reliance on political economies that, in these Terminal Classic times, were beset by fragility in both environmental and political terms.

Indeed, the Terminal Classic of the ninth and tenth centuries is identified with a phenomenon commonly known as the "Classic Maya collapse." Debates about the nature, duration, and sometimes even the existence of such a collapse have highlighted the complex array of localized events and circumstances of the times in the Maya lowlands (Rice et al. 2003). But ecological and political stresses feature prominently in most locations and most accounts. Attempts to feed large populations often led to slope erosion, as in Copan and around Peten lakes Yaxha and Sacnab. Some analysts infer a distinct worsening of the climate, through warming and drying (e.g., Freidel and Shaw 2000; Hodell et al. 1995). Heightened political competition led to sometimes protracted warfare, illustrated most dramatically in the Petexbatun region, at Dos Pilas, Aguateca, and Punto de Chimino (Demarest et al. 1997). For these reasons and more, by the end of this period, the Maya had abandoned much of what had been the core settled landscape of the Maya lowlands.

Localized failures clearly affected kings and peasants differently. As noted, at least some peasant farmers may have simply moved to other lands, in the north or toward the Caribbean coast, where they had heard of opportunities and perhaps knew distant kin. In contrast, royal courts were decimated or destroyed. Their heirs, however, may have been the ones who founded newly arising cities in the hilly Puuc area of northwest Yucatan. And, to many analysts, the rise of Chichen Itza in the central plains of Yucatan may mark a culmination of Classic orders, and perhaps of the environmental and political stresses that affected them, rather than a distinctly different successor to their demise (e.g., Andrews 1990; Sabloff 1985).

Politics

Social agents are readily perceptible in political spheres, and as the foregoing section suggested, decisive actions were not confined to the ruling classes. In Classic times, of course, kings and their courts governed the Maya world (e.g., Chase and Chase 1992; Inomata and Houston 2001; Martin and Grube 2000). Rulers followed one another in dynastic succession at individual cities, waging war on competing lords, while elsewhere cementing alliances by marriage and other means. Sometimes governance was shared, with regents occasionally serving on behalf of child rulers at such places as Palenque (e.g., Schele and Freidel 1990), or dynastic kings consulting with councils of local nobles, as in eighth-century Copan (Fash et al. 1992). The shared rule by brothers identified with Chichen Itza may have had more precedent than we once thought (e.g., Schele and Freidel 1990).

Martin and Grube (2000) have outlined Classic political history – succession, marriage, and war – as currently known, across a wide range of polities and dynasties. Although texts tell a highly textured and important story, evidence from landscape and settlements complements that story significantly. Sometimes the material information is consistent with the texts; at other times, it contradicts hieroglyphic data, and in still other cases it provides insights for subject matter on which the texts are silent.

Three aspects of Classic Maya political history stand out boldly. First, local dynastic succession and political alliances varied in their stability and longevity (e.g., Marcus 1992, 1993). Second, kings of two major centers, Tikal and Calakmul, dominated otherwise shifting networks of local alliance and warfare for the duration of the Classic period (Martin and Grube 2000). Third, beginning in A.D. 378, royal emissaries from the central Mexican city of Teotihuacan intruded directly in Maya affairs, significantly shaping dynastic identities and politics – and other spheres of Maya life – for generations thereafter (Coggins 1979; Stuart 2000). Each of these factors informs the paragraphs that follow.

Settlement and landscape evidence augments appreciably our understanding of deciphered histories. Perhaps most dramatically, it allows political consideration of the enormous number of archaeological sites that lack hieroglyphic inscriptions and about which the texts are therefore silent. As indicated in the preceding section, places like Nohmul and Colha were important in their regional political economies, but have yielded no inscriptions. Even their names are modern labels; not knowing their ancient names, we would not recognize reference to them in inscriptions at other places. Data on settlement and landscapes, however, indicate important roles in wider political and economic spheres.

Two further cases – Quirigua and Xunantunich – illustrate more broadly how settlement and landscape data amplify political interpretations. One political event, the Quirigua visit of Copan's king in A.D. 652, was proposed earlier as linking Copan's assistance in flood recovery to expanded provision of food tribute. A second text-based inference is likewise understood more fully by considering more material kinds of evidence. Specifically, Quirigua's most famous king, K'ak' Tiliw, captured and killed his Copanec lord in A.D. 738. The event is one of the pieces of deciphered Maya history longest known to modern scholars. Matthew Looper (1999) recently identified the overthrow as underwritten by the king of Calakmul. The meddling from afar makes sense for Calakmul as part of the longstanding rivalry with Tikal, inasmuch as Copan (and with it Quirigua) had by then been part of the Tikal alliance network for more than four centuries. K'ak' Tiliw's eagerness to rebel against Copan and Tikal was plausibly heightened by the increase in tribute load that may have marked the early years of his rule. Population kept growing at Copan, even as the capacity of the local landscape to provide adequate food diminished. Perhaps Quirigua's rebellion was a signal that the tribute load had become unacceptably burdensome. Landscape and settlement data from Copan indicate that the need for imported maize reached a maximum in the half-century after the rebellion (Wingard 1996).

Moreover, Quirigua's secession may have prompted similar rebellions at Playitas and more than 14 other locales in adjoining parts of modern Guatemala and Honduras. In these areas, the abrupt rise of settlements with mutually similar and distinctly non-Maya civic plans suggests that a series of local groups took quick advantage of the rupture in regional control by Copan and Quirigua to create alliance networks of their own (e.g., Schortman and Nakamura 1991). People not originally members of ruling classes seized opportunities for autonomy, perhaps for the first time. Texts, however, say nothing of these developments beyond the immediate events of the capture and sacrifice of Copan's ruler and his captor's antecedent encouragement from Calakmul.

To the north, at Xunantunich, texts are few and eroded to near illegibility, but a record of assertive social agency and active political affiliation emerges nonetheless from settlement and the landscape. Specifically, the form of civic settlement at Xunantunich suggests that its abrupt rise in the eighth century was linked to turbulence in the affairs of its overlords at Naranjo, a political capital 15 km to the west (e.g., LeCount et al. 2002). The key civic zone at Xunantunich strongly resembles the layout of a slightly earlier central precinct at Naranjo, and both, in turn, resemble the core of Calakmul (Fig. 7.5(b), (c), (d)). Texts do link the latter two political centers as allies. The single hieroglyphic reference to Naranjo at Xunantunich is ambiguous in its brevity and verbal isolation, but the settlement evidence in architectural arrangements strongly suggests that rulers of the upstart center were expressing ties to the larger network. That is, the specific plan of the civic center was political propaganda, a public declaration of affiliation.

Like the distinctive settlement layouts of non-Maya centers that arose in the wake of Quirigua's rebellion, the plan of Xunantunich suggests a means of mapping political organization in the absence of hieroglyphic evidence. Of further interest, the two most distinctive layouts that occur repeatedly in Classic Maya centers seem to mimic mutually distinct civic plans at the two major centers in Maya history, Tikal and Calakmul. The two distinctive plans share organization along a strongly marked north–south axis, widespread in Classic times, and perhaps emulating, in part, the so-called "Street of the Dead" at Teotihuacan. But Tikal- and Calakmul-model core layouts differed in such key details as the end of the axis where royal residences were placed (south and north, respectively) and where the primary arenas for commemorating royal ancestry lay (north and south, respectively; Ashmore 1989, 1998). Indeed, it may be that civic plans provide clues to Maya politics that expand what the inscriptions relate (Ashmore and Sabloff 2002). One must interpret with caution, however: although Xunantunich, for example, asserted ties to Naranjo and Calakmul in its settlement layout, it arguably negotiated relations with Tikal that yielded Xunantunich-grown food for Tikal people.

Other aspects of settlement and landscapes amplify more directly competitive elements of political history. Walls, moats, and further defensive features attest to warfare, and often dramatically so. In the Petexbatun region of Guatemala, the eighth-century Maya of Punto de Chimino excavated a huge moat and erected defensive walls and parapets on what thereby became a fortified "island." Settlement on one side of a deep natural fissure at Aguateca was similarly fortified. And at nearby Dos Pilas, the same period of endemic warfare witnessed dismantling of core civic buildings, to create a wall encircling hastily built houses for the remaining besieged populace (Demarest et al. 1997).

Of course, evidence of conflict appeared in the archaeological and textual record long before the developments cited for the Petexbatun, and it is clear that warfare played a role in the founding of some of the most enduring dynasties of the Maya Classic period. Siyah K'ak', the fourth-century royal emissary from Teotihuacan, figures prominently as sponsor in these founding events (Martin and Grube 2000; Stuart 2000). From the great distance of the central Mexican highlands, he seems to have orchestrated the rise of intrusive rulers at, for example, Tikal and Copan. Although evidence of these rulers' arrival and rise to power comes prominently from texts, settlement and other material data amplify the circumstances and impacts of their reigns. Within the range of these material data, much hinges on the use of architecture and landscape in political propaganda, and in materializing belief and symbol – topics to which we now turn.

Belief and symbol

As noted earlier, studies of landscapes increasingly emphasize the meaning people attach to the world in which they live. These meanings and the symbolism expressing them can involve anything from events in one's personal life to stories of the creation of humankind. In the undivided continuum of natural, cultural, and naturalized cultural features described at the beginning of the chapter, all elements are subject equally to attachment of meaning.

The three-level structure of the Maya cosmos was described earlier in the chapter. Horizontally, it is a cosmos with four corners, each of them associated with distinctive deities, wildlife, and fates. Like people elsewhere, the Maya related local landscape elements to that structured cosmos through practices of daily life. In short, they joined with other creatures to perform and enact the world, and to imbue it with meaningful social memories.

Among the Maya of modern Zinacantan, for example, Evon Vogt (1992) and others describe ritual circuits, pilgrimages through the landscape, paying respects at primordial places by conducting rituals and repeating proper verbal accounts, and thereby ensuring that the meaning and importance of these mountaintops, caves, and other places continued. In this same vein, ethnographers, archaeologists, and epigraphers write about both ancient and modern Maya as re-enacting creation by repeatedly establishing the four-sided universe in buildings, cloth, and fields; by repeatedly recounting human histories and genealogy; by repeatedly reading the cosmic creation story in the stars and planets; and by fitting historically "unique" events into the overall picture. Through these steps, people reproduce an encompassing landscape that is both orderly and meaningful.

In other ways as well, people's actions contributed to animating individual buildings and other constructions, to completing their creation as living things. For
instance, burials set beneath a house floor – or in a temple's tomb – completed and
"ensouled" the buildings involved (e.g., Gillespie 2000; McAnany et al. 1999). As
Janet Richards's remarks illustrated earlier in this chapter, buildings, fields, sky, settlement, landscape – all become whole and become alive because of the actions
people perform through time and across space.

The Acropolis of Copan embodies allusions to cosmic order, dynastic authority,
and political genealogy. Built above the court buildings of K'inich Yax K'uk' Mo',
its dynasty's Teotihuacan-supported founder, the increasingly monumental accumulation of architecture repeatedly commemorated that king and his reign (Sharer
1999). His burial and that of his queen likely "ensouled" the original buildings.
Over the next four centuries, the sequence of buildings subsequently superimposed
on those burial sites created an *axis mundi*, a place marking the center of the
Copanec world (Sharer et al. 1999). At the same time, the buildings' westward orientation alludes to the place of death, and the horizon where the sun – of whom
the king is earthly counterpart – dies on a daily basis. In this, they may refer further
to Teotihuacan: Not only do very early buildings in the Acropolis incorporate the
distinctive *talud-tablero* profile of Teotihuacan architecture, but the westward orientation of the sequence above the Copan founder's tomb may mimic Teotihuacan's Ciudadela. The latter may be the burial place of an early king there (e.g.,
Cowgill 1992; Sugiyama 1993), perhaps specifically that of Spearthrower Owl,
the sovereign whose emissary, Siyah K'ak', had such impact on the course of
Maya history, including Copan's (Fash and Fash 2000; Martin and Grube 2000;
Stuart 2000). Whether or not the latter inference is true, it is clear that the Copan
Acropolis embodies repeated centering of the local landscape in political and
cosmological terms. It became a mountain whose innermost cave was the
underworld resting-place of K'inich Yax K'uk' Mo', the man credited in antiquity
with setting the city and polity on track. The place became a naturalized pivot for
landscape and settlement, whose important meanings were repeatedly reinscribed
in the buildings by activities held at them.

Bodies of water likewise carried political and ritual meanings in landscape and
settlement. We tend to think of such bodies in the largely static economic terms
used earlier in the chapter. At the same time, Scarborough (1998) describes the
active ritual and political importance held by water features in Classic times. He
observes that the largest aguadas or reservoirs at Tikal were positioned at approximately cardinal points, such that they helped define a landscape structured with
those four appropriate corners. Their creation was likely also a means of reinforcing the authority of the kings under whose governance the features were created
and maintained. Moreover, like cenotes farther north, the Tikal aguadas were
portals to the watery underworld. Rituals were certainly conducted at such water-
places, as we know through archaeological evidence, from Chichen Itza and elsewhere (e.g., Coggins 1992). And the shimmering mirror-like surface of the water
plausibly lent itself to shamanic divination; Taube (1992) describes mirrors as
implements for divination, noting further that in Mesoamerica and the southwest

mirrors were widely equated with supernatural caves. These reservoirs, then, were potent factors inscribing the local landscape with cosmic dimensions, repeatedly installed in social memory both visually and by the various actions performed at them.

In analogous ways, the sounds, smells, and colors experienced in moving through the landscape reinforced the symbolism of local settings – and the sense of a world in order. Taube and others have called attention to the importance of brilliant red in the colors of Classic civic buildings; elsewhere he and Andrea Stone, separately, have spoken of the wildness of the forest beyond the city's edge (Stone 1992; Taube 1998). As Simon Martin recently put this contrast: "Whatever its other cultural resonances, red, as the complementary opposite and antagonist of green – the color of the surrounding farmland and forest – denotes the otherness of royal and sacred space" (Martin 2001:170–171). Creating landscapes and settlement, then, requires enveloping them in appropriate and meaningful colors. Some colors were already in place, in the forest; others were put there by people. In either case, all became part of the natural or natural*ized* landscape, firmly inscribed in social memory with time spent and actions therein.

Attending to a different sensory dimension, that of sound, Brady describes the annual rush of water from the cave beneath the main pyramid at Dos Pilas (Brady 1997; Brady and Ashmore 1999). Still today, the sudden thunderous din signals the arrival of the rainy season, making a dramatic clamor that, in antiquity, doubtless convinced those in inescapable earshot of how much power and authority the king atop that pyramid held over the rains, the seasons, the food supply, and their general well-being. Humans allied with what analysts distinguish today as "nature" to enact this event, to retell its meaning, and thereby to inscribe its memory indelibly on the local landscape. The king's building was set deliberately in this place above the cave; only the endemic warfare that later engulfed Dos Pilas could counteract the vociferous assertion of his authority that the naturalized built landscape had supplied.

Buildings, mountains, and other features of the naturalized landscape doubtless carried meanings under constant recall and reshaping. Some influential places have been identified in now-deciphered texts and on the ground, as in the palace buildings of Palenque (e.g., Schele and Freidel 1990; Schele and Mathews 1998). Others exist in hieroglyphic allusions, with less certainty about their specific location. Still others we will never recognize. We can be sure, however, that the landscapes and settlements of the Classic Maya gave order and meaning to their lives. In general form, these persist in Maya belief and symbols; at most, it is the details of local meaning that were dislodged from social memory with the abandonment at the end of Classic times.

Conclusions

To better understand Classic Maya landscapes and settlement, analysts are broadening the domain of study, recognizing that the Maya created these settings, from the sky to the underworld, by drawing on natural and "naturalized" elements, then by animating the whole through what they saw, heard, and did there. Social agents created these landscapes, and by inhabiting them, in turn, actively reproduced proper conditions for living. Certainly, the places of Classic times have changed since first built and inhabited. But the ruins and landscapes we examine today hold abundant information for addressing questions like the ones that were raised at the outset of the chapter. By critical observation of these landscapes and settlements, we continue to learn much about where the Classic Maya lived, how they thrived, how they related to one another, and why their homes and cities were abandoned. Stephens and Catherwood helped inspire interest in these places 150 years ago; moving the equivalent amount of time into the future, we will surely have learned things about them that we don't yet imagine.

ACKNOWLEDGMENTS

I am grateful to the editors for the invitation to contribute to this volume. Partial antecedents of this paper were presented in 2001 at the Eighth Annual Maya Weekend at UCLA, and the 100th Annual Meeting of the American Anthropological Association. For inspiration, encouragement, and critiques, I thank the editors and Chelsea Blackmore, Scott Fedick, Tom Patterson, Dominique Rissolo, Karl Taube, and Christina Halperin.

REFERENCES

Abrams, E. M., and D. J. Rue, 1988 The causes and consequences of deforestation among the prehistoric Maya. *Human Ecology* 16, 377–396.

Andrews, A. F., 1990 The fall of Chichén Itzá: A preliminary hypothesis. *Latin American Antiquity* 1, 258–267.

Ashmore, W., 1989 Construction and cosmology: Politics and ideology in lowland Maya settlement patterns. In *Word and Image in Maya Culture*. W. Hanks and D. S. Rice, eds. Pp. 272–286. Salt Lake City: University of Utah Press.

——1990 Ode to a dragline: Demographic reconstructions at Classic Quiriguá. In *Prehistoric Population History in the Maya Lowlands*. T. P. Culbert and D. S. Rice, eds. Pp. 63–82. Albuquerque: University of New Mexico Press.

——1998 Monumentos políticos: Sitios, asentamiento, y paisaje por Xunantunich, Belice. In *Anatomia de una civilización: Aproximaciones interdisciplinarias a la cultura Maya*. A. Ciudad Ruiz, Y. Fernández Marquinez, J. M. García Campillo, Ma. J. Iglesias Ponce de León, A. Lacadena García-Gallo, and L. T. Sanz Castro, eds. Pp. 161–183. Madrid: Sociedad Española de Estudios Mayas.

Ashmore, W., and J. A. Sabloff, 2002 Spatial order in Maya civic plans. *Latin American Antiquity* 13, 201–215.

Ashmore, W., J. Yaeger, and C. Robin, 2003 Commoner sense: Late and Terminal Classic social strategies in the Xunantunich area. In *The Terminal Classic in the Maya Lowlands:*

Collapse, Transition, and Transformation. D. S. Rice, P. M. Rice, and A. A. Demarest, eds. Boulder: University of Colorado Press. In press.

Aveni, A. F., ed., 1992 *The Sky in Mayan Literature.* Oxford: Oxford University Press.

Barrett, J., 1999 The mythical landscapes of the British Iron Age. In *Archaeologies of Landscape: Contemporary Perspectives.* In W. Ashmore and A. B. Knapp, eds. Pp. 253–265. Oxford: Blackwell.

Bassie-Sweet, K., 1996 *At the Edge of the World: Caves and Late Classic Maya World View.* Norman: University of Oklahoma Press.

Basso, K. H., 1996 *Wisdom Sits in Places: Landscape and Language among the Western Apache.* Albuquerque: University of New Mexico Press.

Becquelin, P., and C. F. Baudez, 1979 *Toniná: Une cité Maya du Chiapas.* Etudes Mesoamericaines 6(1). Mexico: Mission Archéologique et Ethnologique Française au Mexique.

Benson, E. P., 1985 Architecture as metaphor. In *Fifth Palenque Round Table 1983.* M. Greene Robertson and V. M. Fields, eds. Pp. 183–188. San Francisco: Pre-Columbian Art Research Institute.

Bradley, R., 1993 *Altering the Earth: The Origins of Monuments in Britain and Continental Europe.* Edinburgh: Society of Antiquaries of Scotland.

——2000 *An Archaeology of Natural Places.* London: Routledge.

Brady, J. E., 1997 Settlement configuration and cosmology: The role of caves at Dos Pilas. *American Anthropologist* 99, 602–618.

Brady, J. E., and W. Ashmore, 1999 Mountains, caves, and water: Ideational landscapes of the ancient Maya. In *Archaeologies of Landscape: Contemporary Perspectives.* W. Ashmore and A. B. Knapp, eds. Pp. 124–145. Oxford: Blackwell.

Brady, J. E., and G. Veni, 1992 Man-made and pseudo-karst caves: The implications of subsurface geologic features within Maya centers. *Geoarchaeology* 7, 149–167.

Canuto, M. A., and J. Yaeger, eds., 2000 *The Archaeology of Communities: A New World Perspective.* New York and London: Routledge.

Chase, D. Z., and A. F. Chase, eds., 1992 *Mesoamerican Elites: An Archaeological Assessment.* Norman: University of Oklahoma Press.

Coggins, C. C., 1979 A new order and the role of the calendar: Some characteristics of the Middle Classic period at Tikal. In *Maya Archaeology and Ethnohistory.* N. Hammond and G. R. Willey, eds. Pp. 38–50. Austin: University of Texas Press.

——1992 *Artifacts from the Cenote of Sacrifice, Chichén Itzá, Yucatan.* Memoirs of the Peabody Museum of Archaeology and Ethnology 10(3). Cambridge, MA: Harvard University.

Cowgill, G. F., 1992 Toward a political history of Teotihuacan. In *Ideology and Pre-Columbian Civilizations.* A. A. Demarest and G. W. Conrad, eds. Pp. 87–114. Santa Fe: School of American Research Press.

Crumley, C. L., 1979 Three locational models: An epistemological assessment for anthropology and archaeology. *Advances in Archaeological Method and Theory* 2, 141–173.

Culbert, T. P., and D. S. Rice, eds., 1990 *Prehistoric Population History in the Maya Lowlands.* Albuquerque: University of New Mexico Press.

Demarest, A. A., M. O'Mansky, C. Wolley, D. Van Tuerenhout, T. Inomata, J. Palka, and H. Escobedo, 1997 Classic Maya defensive systems and warfare in the Petexbatún region: Archaeological evidence and interpretations. *Ancient Mesoamerica* 8, 229–253.

Denevan, W., 1992 The pristine myth: The landscape of the Americas in 1492. *Annals of the Association of American Geographers* 82, 369–385.

Drennan, R. D., 1988 Household location and compact versus dispersed settlement in prehispanic Mesoamerica. In *Household and Community in the Mesoamerican Past.* R. R. Wilk and W. Ashmore, eds. Pp. 273–293. Albuquerque: University of New Mexico Press.

Dunning, N. P., and T. Beach, 1994 Soil erosion, slope management, and ancient Maya terracing in the Maya lowlands. *Latin American Antiquity* 5, 51–69.

Dunning, N. P., V. Scarborough, F. Valdez Jr., S. Luzzadder-Beach, T. Beach, and J. G. Jones,
1999 Temple mountains, sacred lakes, and fertile fields: Ancient Maya landscapes in
northwestern Belize. *Antiquity* 73, 650–660.

Eliade, M., 1959 *The Sacred and the Profane*. New York: Harcourt Brace.

Fash, B., W. Fash, S. Lane, R. Larios, L. Schele, J. Stomper, and D. Stuart, 1992 Investigations of a Classic Maya council house at Copán, Honduras. *Journal of Field Archaeology*
19, 419–442.

Fash, W., and B. Fash, 2000 Teotihuacan and the Maya: A Classic heritage. In *Mesoamerica's Classic Heritage: From Teotihuacan to the Aztecs*. D. Carrasco, L. Jones, and S. Sessions,
eds. Pp. 432–463. Boulder: University Press of Colorado.

Fedick, S. L., ed., 1996 *The Managed Mosaic: Ancient Maya Agriculture and Resource Use*.
Salt Lake City: University of Utah Press.

Freidel, D., L. Schele, and J. Parker, 1993 *Maya Cosmos: Three Thousand Years on the Shaman's
Path*. New York: William Morrow.

Freidel, D., and J. Shaw, 2000 The lowland Maya civilization: Historical consciousness and
environment. In *The Way the Wind Blows: Climate, History, and Human Action*. R. J.
McIntosh, J. A. Tainter, and S. Keech McIntosh, eds. Pp. 271–300. New York: Columbia
University Press.

Gillespie, S. D., 2000 Maya "nested houses": The ritual construction of place. In *Beyond
Kinship: Social and Material Reproduction in House Societies*. R. A. Joyce and S. D. Gillespie,
eds. Pp. 135–160. Philadelphia: University of Pennsylvania Press.

Gómez-Pompa, A., J. Salvador Flores, and M. Aliphat Fernández, 1990 The sacred cacao
groves of the Maya. *Latin American Antiquity* 1, 247–257.

Gunn, J. D., and W. J. Folan, 2000 Three rivers: Subregional variations in earth system
impacts in the southwestern Maya lowlands Candelaria, Usumacinta, and Champotón
watersheds. In *The Way the Wind Blows: Climate, History, and Human Action*. R. J.
McIntosh, J. A. Tainter, and S. Keech McIntosh, eds. Pp. 223–270. New York: Columbia
University Press.

Hendon, J. A., 2000 Having and holding: Storage, memory, knowledge, and social relations.
American Anthropologist 102, 42–53.

Hodell, D. A., J. H. Curtis, and M. Brenner, 1995 Possible role of climate in the collapse of
Classic Maya civilization. *Nature* 375, 391–394.

Iannone, G., and S. V. Connell, eds., 2002 *The Social Implications of Ancient Maya Rural Complexity*. Los Angeles: Cotsen Institute of Archaeology.

Ingold, T., 1993 The temporality of the landscape. *World Archaeology* 25, 152–174.

Inomata, T., and S. D. Houston, eds., 2001 *Royal Courts of the Ancient Maya*, 2 vols. Boulder:
Westview Press.

Joyce, R. A., 2000 Heirlooms and houses: Materiality and social memory. In *Beyond Kinship:
Social and Material Reproduction in House Societies*. R. A. Joyce and S. D. Gillespie, eds. Pp.
189–212. Philadelphia: University of Pennsylvania Press.

Joyce, R. A., and J. A. Hendon, 2000 Heterarchy, history, and material reality: "Com-
munities" in Late Classic Honduras. In *The Archaeology of Communities: A New World
Perspective*. M. A. Canuto and J. Yaeger, eds. Pp. 143–160. New York and London:
Routledge.

Kepecs, S., and S. Boucher, 1996 The pre-hispanic cultivation of *rejollada* and stone-lands:
New evidence from northeast Yucatán. In *The Managed Mosaic: Ancient Maya Agriculture
and Resource Use*. S. L. Fedick, ed. Pp. 69–91. Salt Lake City: University of Utah Press.

King, E. M., 2000 *The Organization of Late Classic Lithic Production at the Prehistoric Maya Site of Colha, Belize: A Study in Complexity and Heterarchy.* Ann Arbor: University Microfilms International.

Knapp, A. B., and W. Ashmore, 1999 Archaeological landscapes: Constructed, conceptualized, ideational. In *Archaeologies of Landscape: Contemporary Perspectives.* W. Ashmore and A. B. Knapp, eds. Pp. 1–30. Oxford: Blackwell.

LeCount, L. J., J. Yaeger, R. M. Leventhal, and W. Ashmore, 2002 Dating the rise and fall of Xunantunich: A Late and Terminal Classic Maya center. *Ancient Mesoamerica* 13, 41–63.

Looper, M. G., 1999 New perspectives on the Late Classic political history of Quiriguá, Guatemala. *Ancient Mesoamerica* 9, 263–280.

Marcus, J., 1992 *Mesoamerican Writing Systems: Propaganda, Myth, and History in Four Ancient Civilizations.* Princeton: Princeton University Press.

——1993 Ancient Maya political organization. In *Lowland Maya Civilization in the Eighth Century* A.D. J. A. Sabloff and J. S. Henderson, eds. Pp. 111–183. Washington, DC: Dumbarton Oaks.

Martin, S., 2001 Court and realm: Architectural signatures in the Classic Maya southern lowlands. In *Royal Courts of the Ancient Maya*, vol. 1: *Theory, Comparison, and Synthesis.* T. Inomata and S. D. Houston, eds. Pp. 168–194. Boulder: Westview Press.

Martin, S., and N. Grube, 2000 *Chronicle of the Maya Kings and Queens: Deciphering the Dynasties of the Ancient Maya.* London: Thames & Hudson.

Maudslay, A. P., 1889–1902 *Biologia Centrali-Americana: Archaeology*, 5 vols. London: Porter.

McAnany, P., 1990 Water storage in the Puuc region of the Northern Maya lowlands: A key to population estimates and architectural variability. In *Precolumbian Population History in the Maya Lowlands.* T. P. Culbert and D. S. Rice, eds. Pp. 263–284. Albuquerque: University of New Mexico Press.

——1993 The economics of social power and wealth among eighth-century Maya households. In *Lowland Maya Civilization in the Eighth Century* A.D. J. A. Sabloff and J. S. Henderson, eds. Pp. 65–89. Washington, DC: Dumbarton Oaks.

McAnany, P., R. Storey, and A. K. Lockard, 1999 Mortuary ritual and family politics at Formative and Early Classic K'axob, Belize. *Ancient Mesoamerica* 10, 129–146.

Meggers, B. J., 1954 Environmental limitation on the development of culture. *American Anthropologist* 56, 801–824.

Potter, D. R., and E. M. King, 1995 A heterarchical approach to Lowland Maya socioeconomies. In *Heterarchy and the Analysis of Complex Societies.* R. M. Ehrenreich, C. L. Crumley, and J. E. Levy, eds. Pp. 17–32. Arlington: American Anthropological Association.

Puleston, D. E., 1977 The art and archaeology of hydraulic agriculture in the Maya lowlands. In *Social Process in Maya Prehistory.* N. Hammond, ed. Pp. 449–467. London: Academic Press.

Puleston, D. E., and O. S. Puleston, 1971 An ecological approach to the origins of Maya civilization. *Archaeology* 24(4), 330–337.

Pyburn, K. A., 1996 The political economy of ancient Maya land use: The road to ruin. In *The Managed Mosaic: Ancient Maya Agriculture and Resource Use.* S. L. Fedick, ed. Pp. 236–247. Salt Lake City: University of Utah Press.

——1997 The archaeological signature of complexity in the Maya lowlands. In *The Archaeology of City-States: Cross-Cultural Approaches.* D. L. Nichols and T. H. Charlton, eds. Pp. 155–168. Washington, DC: Smithsonian Institution Press.

Rathje, W. L., 1971 The origin and development of Classic Maya civilization. *American Antiquity* 36, 275–285.

Rice, D. S., 1993 Eighth-century physical geography, environment, and natural resources in the Maya lowlands. In *Lowland Maya Civilization in the Eighth Century* A.D. J. A. Sabloff and J. S. Henderson, eds. Pp. 11–63. Washington, DC: Dumbarton Oaks.

Rice, D. S., P. M. Rice, and A. A. Demarest, eds., 2003 *The Terminal Classic in the Maya Lowlands: Collapse, Transition, and Transformation.* Boulder: University of Colorado Press. In press.

Richards, J. E., 1999 Conceptual landscapes in the Egyptian Nile Valley. In *Archaeologies of Landscape: Contemporary Perspectives.* W. Ashmore and A. B. Knapp, eds. Pp. 83–100. Oxford: Blackwell.

Robin, C., 1999 *Towards an Archaeology of Everyday Life: Maya Farmers of Chan Noohol and Dos Chombitos Cik'in, Belize.* Ann Arbor: University Microfilms International.

Sabloff, J. A., 1973 Major themes in the past hypotheses of the Maya collapse. In *The Classic Maya Collapse.* T. P. Culbert, ed. Pp. 35–40. Albuquerque: University of New Mexico Press.

——1985 Ancient Maya civilization: An overview. In *Maya: Treasures of an Ancient Civilization.* C. Gallenkamp and R. E. Johnson, eds. Pp. 34–46. New York: Harry N. Abrams.

Sabloff, J. A., and W. Ashmore, 2001 An aspect of archaeology's recent past and its relevance in the new millennium. In *Archaeology at the Millennium: A Sourcebook.* G. M. Feinman and T. D. Price, eds. Pp. 11–32. New York: Kluwer/Plenum.

Sanders, W. T., 1973 The cultural ecology of the lowland Maya: A reevaluation. In *The Classic Maya Collapse.* T. P. Culbert, ed. Pp. 325–365. Albuquerque: University of New Mexico Press.

Scarborough, V. L., 1996 Reservoirs and watersheds in the central Maya lowlands. In *The Managed Mosaic: Ancient Maya Agriculture and Resource Use.* S. L. Fedick, ed. Pp. 304–314. Salt Lake City: University of Utah Press.

——1998 Ecology and ritual: Water management and the Maya. *Latin American Antiquity* 9, 135–159.

Scarborough, V. L., and G. G. Gallopin, 1991 A water storage adaptation in the Maya lowlands. *Science* 251, 658–662.

Schama, S., 1995 *Landscape and Memory.* New York: Alfred A. Knopf.

Schele, L., and D. Freidel, 1990 *A Forest of Kings.* New York: William Morrow.

Schele, L., and P. Mathews, 1998 *The Code of Kings: The Language of Seven Sacred Maya Temples and Tombs.* New York: Scribner.

Schortman, E. M., and S. Nakamura, 1991 A crisis of identity: Late Classic competition and interaction on the southeast Maya periphery. *Latin American Antiquity* 2, 311–336.

Sharer, R. J., 1999 Archaeology and history in the royal acropolis, Copán, Honduras. *Expedition* 41(2), 8–15.

Sharer, R. J., W. L. Fash, D. W. Sedat, L. P. Traxler, and R. Williamson, 1999 Continuities and contrasts in Early Classic architecture of central Copán. In *Mesoamerican Architecture as a Cultural Symbol.* J. K. Kowalski, ed. Pp. 220–249. Oxford: Oxford University Press.

Sheets, P., ed., 2002 *Before the Volcano Erupted: The Ancient Ceren Village in Central America.* Austin: University of Texas Press.

Siemens, A. H., and D. E. Puleston, 1972 Ridged fields and associated features in southern Campeche: New perspectives on the lowland Maya. *American Antiquity* 37, 228–239.

Stephens, J. L., 1963[1843] *Incidents of Travel in Yucatan.* New York: Dover Publications.

——1969[1841] *Incidents of Travel in Central America, Chiapas and Yucatan.* New York: Dover Publications.

Stoddart, S., 2000 Introduction. In *Landscapes from Antiquity.* S. Stoddart, ed. Pp. 1–5. Cambridge: Antiquity Publications.

Stone, A., 1992 From ritual in the landscape to capture in the urban center: The recreation of ritual environments in Mesoamerica. *Journal of Ritual Studies* 6, 109–132.

——1995 *Images from the Underworld: Naj Tunich and the Tradition of Maya Cave Painting.* Austin: University of Texas Press.

Stuart, D., 2000 "The arrival of strangers": Teotihuacan and Tollan in Classic Maya history. In *Mesoamerica's Classic Heritage: From Teotihuacan to the Aztecs*. D. Carrasco, L. Jones, and S. Sessions, eds. Pp. 465–513. Boulder: University Press of Colorado.

Sugiyama, S., 1993 Worldview materialized in Teotihuacan, Mexico. *Latin American Antiquity* 4, 103–129.

Taube, K. A., 1992 The iconography of mirrors at Teotihuacan. In *Art, Ideology, and the City of Teotihuacan*. J. C. Berlo, ed. Pp. 169–204. Washington, DC: Dumbarton Oaks.

——1998 The jade hearth: Centrality, rulership, and the Classic Maya temple. In *Function and Meaning in Classic Maya Architecture*. S. D. Houston, ed. Pp. 427–478. Washington, DC: Dumbarton Oaks.

Trombold, C. D., ed., 1991 *Ancient Road Networks and Settlement Hierarchies in the New World.* Cambridge: Cambridge University Press.

Turner, B. L., and P. D. Harrison 1981 Prehistoric raised-field agriculture in the Maya lowlands. *Science* 213, 399–405.

Ucko, P. J., and R. Layton, eds., 1999 *The Anthropology and Archaeology of Landscapes.* London: Routledge.

Vogt, E. Z., 1992 The persistence of Maya tradition in Zinacantan. In *The Ancient Americas: Art from Ancient Landscapes*. R. F. Townsend, ed. Pp. 60–69. Chicago and Munich: Art Institute of Chicago, and Prestel-Verlag.

Whitmore, T. M., and B. L. Turner II, 1992 Landscapes of cultivation in Mesoamerica on the eve of the Conquest. *Annals of the Association of American Geographers* 82, 402–425.

Willey, G. R., 1953 *Prehistoric Settlement Patterns in the Virú Valley, Peru*. Washington, DC: Bureau of American Ethnology, Smithsonian Institution.

Wingard, J. D., 1996 Interactions between demographic processes and soil resources in the Copán Valley, Honduras. In *The Managed Mosaic: Ancient Maya Agriculture and Resource Use*. S. L. Fedick, ed. Pp. 207–235. Salt Lake City: University of Utah Press.

Yaeger, J., 2000 The social construction of communities in the Classic Maya countryside: Strategies of affiliation in western Belize. In *The Archaeology of Communities: A New World Perspective*. M. A. Canuto and J. Yaeger, eds. Pp. 123–142. New York and London: Routledge.

8

Sacred Space and Social Relations in the Valley of Oaxaca

Arthur A. Joyce

During the period from 300 B.C. to A.D. 800 Mesoamerica's political landscape was dominated by numerous complex urban centers. The earliest and largest city in the southern Mexican highlands was Monte Alban in the Valley of Oaxaca (Fig. 8.1). Monte Alban was founded about 500 B.C. and rapidly grew into the largest community in the Oaxaca Valley (Joyce and Winter 1996). The founding of Monte Alban represented a vast increase in polity scale as measured by the area and population that were under the political authority of the ruling elite. Monte Alban was both a political capital and a sacred center reflecting the interconnectedness of political power and religion in ancient Mesoamerica. By the Classic period (A.D. 200–800), the city covered 650 ha with an estimated population reaching perhaps 30,000 people (Blanton 1978). The polity ruled by Monte Alban's nobility had by this time developed into a state. At approximately A.D. 800, the state collapsed and the city declined rapidly in population.

Most studies of Monte Alban have focused on elite relations with other polities, both within and outside of the Oaxaca Valley, to explain its history of sociopolitical development. For example, researchers have argued that interpolity conflict triggered the founding and early growth of Monte Alban (Blanton et al. 1999; Marcus and Flannery 1996; Spencer 1982), while the city's collapse has been linked to the decline of Teotihuacan, viewed as an external threat that maintained social cohesion in the Oaxaca Valley (Blanton 1983). In these models, nobles are seen as directing the course of social change in response to competition or threats from other polities. While interpolity interaction was clearly important, these models undertheorize the complex changes in culture and sociopolitical relations within the Monte Alban polity, which account for historical developments in the Valley of Oaxaca.

The theoretical perspective through which I address social relations in ancient Oaxaca is derived from practice theories (Ortner 1984). Practice theories view social processes as resulting from the ongoing recursive relationship between agency

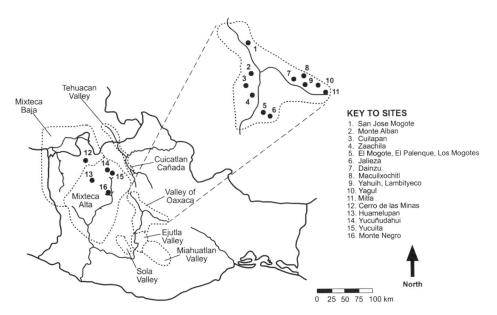

KEY TO SITES

1. San Jose Mogote
2. Monte Alban
3. Cuilapan
4. Zaachila
5. El Mogote, El Palenque, Los Mogotes
6. Jalieza
7. Dainzu
8. Macuilxochitl
9. Yahuih, Lambityeco
10. Yagul
11. Mitla
12. Cerro de las Minas
13. Huamelupan
14. Yucuñudahui
15. Yucuita
16. Monte Negro

Figure 8.1. Map of Oaxaca showing sites and regions mentioned in the text

and structure. The structurally conditioned and situated practices of agents at all levels of society create patterns of social behavior, which in turn reproduce or change structure, thereby creating the setting for future action. Following Giddens (1979:88–94), I define power as the transformative capacity of an agent to achieve an outcome, which can either reproduce or change social systems and structure. Ideology, as an aspect of structure, often justifies or legitimates domination, although subordinates are able to see through and resist dominant ideologies to varying degrees (Joyce et al. 2001).

In this chapter, I consider how the negotiation of power among noble and commoner classes contributed to changes in the scale and complexity of the Monte Alban polity. Since political power in ancient Mesoamerica was created, legitimated, and negotiated largely through religious beliefs and practices (Joyce 2000; Schele and Freidel 1990), I focus on the construction of sacred spaces and the ongoing ritual practices within those spaces. The religious and political center of the Oaxaca Valley was the Main Plaza at Monte Alban, a huge public plaza surrounded by temples and palaces that housed nobles and ruling institutions. In complex societies, constructed landscapes, especially monumental spaces like Monte Alban's Main Plaza, are important aspects of structure that both shape and are shaped by social action (Ashmore and Knapp 1999). I argue that, beginning with the initial construction of the Main Plaza at ca. 500 B.C., the architectural arrangement and symbolism of buildings, plazas, and monumental art created a sacred geography that cosmically sanctified authority by positioning nobles as powerful intermediaries between commoners and the divine forces that created and maintained the cosmos. Monte Alban's Main Plaza, like ceremonial precincts in many ancient cities, served as an *axis mundi* where cosmic planes like earth, sky, and underworld intersected (Ashmore 1991; Wheatley 1971).

The power of the Main Plaza at Monte Alban, however, did not derive just from the ideas that it embodied, but was produced and experienced through the practices that took place there (Ashmore and Knapp 1999). I argue that the creation, use, and alteration of Monte Alban's Main Plaza embodied changes in power and domination in the Valley of Oaxaca. During Monte Alban's first several centuries people participated in emotionally charged ritual performances, often invoking the cosmic creation, through which they came to identify with and incorporate in their dispositions ideological messages about their place in the social and cosmic order. By the Classic period, however, nobles were diverging from earlier principles of sacred geography as the Main Plaza was used less for large public ceremonies that engaged commoners, and more as an elite residential precinct and an area for private ceremonies. The disengagement of commoners from state ceremonies may have weakened their allegiance to rulers and been a factor in the collapse of the Monte Alban state at around A.D. 800. The remainder of this chapter considers the relationship between monumental spaces and the construction and negotiation of politico-religious power in the Oaxaca Valley. The discussion begins with the period immediately preceding the city's founding and considers changes in sacred space and power until the collapse of the polity at ca. A.D. 800.

The Founding of Monte Alban

The Valley of Oaxaca is a semi-arid highland valley that includes the largest area of flat, agriculturally productive land in Mesoamerica south of the Basin of Mexico. At the time of the Spanish Conquest, Zapotecs were the primary inhabitants of the valley. Archaeological and linguistic evidence suggest that Zapotec-speakers have lived in the valley for several thousand years. The Oaxaca Valley is y-shaped, consisting of three connected arms: the Etla Valley to the north, the Valle Grande to the south, and the Tlacolula Valley to the east. Monte Alban is located on several hills in the center of the valley where the three arms meet. The city was founded about 500 B.C. during a period of great political change in Oaxaca and throughout Mesoamerica. Within a few hundred years of its founding, Monte Alban grew into the most powerful political and religious center in southern Mexico. To understand the early development of the site, however, one must consider social developments during the centuries prior to the founding of Monte Alban.

The largest community in the Valley of Oaxaca prior to 500 B.C. was San Jose Mogote in the Etla arm, which reached 70 ha by 700 B.C. Archaeologists have debated precisely when complex societies with hereditary social inequality developed in Oaxaca (Blanton et al. 1999; Marcus and Flannery 1996), although most researchers agree that they had emerged during the Middle Formative (850–300 B.C.); almost certainly by 700 B.C. San Jose Mogote was the dominant center in the valley, controlling a three-tiered settlement hierarchy that included perhaps a dozen subject communities in the Elta arm.

The power of the nobility at San Jose Mogote, as in complex societies throughout Mesoamerica, was based on the belief in their abilities as ritual specialists (Joyce 2000; Marcus and Flannery 1996). While all people could communicate with the divine forces and deities that were believed to control the cosmos, nobles were seen as intermediaries between commoners and the supernatural, leading important religious ceremonies involving shamanism, sacrifice, and ancestor veneration. Mesoamerican cultural principles allowed nobles to have sacred knowledge and objects that were unavailable to commoners. Sacred knowledge and materials therefore gave nobles the ability (power) to affect the cosmos in ways that commoners could not.

Middle Formative elites at San Jose Mogote conducted public rituals on Mound 1, a natural hill architecturally modified into a huge platform 15 m high on which several temples were built. Mound 1 was one of the first monumental ceremonial precincts built in the Oaxaca Valley. One of the most potent means for contacting the sacred realm during the Middle Formative was through the autosacrificial letting of blood by piercing parts of the body such as the lips, tongue, or genitals. Sacrifice was a key theme in Mesoamerican creation myths as recorded in many sixteenth-century indigenous documents, including the Mixtec codices Vienna and Nuttall, the Quiche Maya Popol Vuh, and in Mexican (Aztec) writing and oral literature. These documents recount the story of a sacred covenant whereby people agreed to offer sacrifices to the deities in return for fertility and prosperity, although only nobles could carry out the most potent forms of sacrifice (Joyce 2000; Monaghan 1990). Religious ceremonies were often carried out in the context of ritual feasts sponsored by nobles. In return for the ritual services and generosity of the elite, commoners offered their allegiance and provided goods and labor as tribute. Thus, the structure of Middle Formative Oaxaca included a kind of social contract between elites and commoners: elites used their special ritual abilities to contact the sacred realm on behalf of all people, while commoners provided tribute and allegiance in return. Religious beliefs were ideological in that they legitimated the prestige and power of nobles. Commoners, however, contributed to the social negotiation of power since they had some choice over which nobles they supported. Commoners could also express resistance by contacting the sacred via household rituals without the assistance of elites.

Another source of power for Middle Formative elites was through relationships with nobles from other parts of Mesoamerica. Evidence from San Jose Mogote indicates that nobles exchanged materials, ideas, and perhaps mates with elites from other important Middle Formative sites in Mesoamerica, including San Lorenzo and La Venta on the Gulf Coast, Tlatilco in the Basin of Mexico, and Chalcatzingo in the Valley of Morelos (Blanton et al. 1999:46; Marcus and Flannery 1996:119). Prestige goods acquired through long-distance trade as well as those produced by local craftspeople were used by elites to create alliances with nobles from other communities. Exotic goods obtained through long-distance exchange, such as obsidian and stingray spine bloodletters, shell ornaments, and jade were important objects used in ritual performances. Prestige goods produced locally and traded to nobles from other regions included elaborate pottery vessels probably used in ritual feasting.

The latter part of the Middle Formative, from about 700–300 B.C., was a time of political upheaval throughout much of Mesoamerica that disrupted networks of long-distance interaction. This period witnessed the decline of many of the most important Middle Formative centers of population and political power. In the Gulf Coast, the huge Olmec center of La Venta as well as the smaller center of San Lorenzo were virtually abandoned. In the central Mexican highlands, Chalcatzingo, Teopantecuanitlan, and Tlatilco declined and were largely abandoned. Monumental construction activities at Chiapa de Corzo in the central depression of Chiapas declined for a time and other regional centers such as La Libertad were abandoned. On the Pacific coast, the huge site of La Blanca decreased in size. The factors responsible for the decline of these Middle Formative centers are not clear, although conflict and the disruption of inter-elite interaction networks are indicated in many regions.

In the Valley of Oaxaca, the period from 700 to 500 B.C. was a time of conflict and political instability, especially for the elites of San Jose Mogote (Joyce 2000). Warfare within the Oaxaca Valley is suggested by a high frequency of structures destroyed by fire and by a sparsely occupied buffer zone separating the Etla arm of the valley from the two other arms which were occupied by competing polities (Kowalewski et al. 1989:70–75). At approximately 600 B.C., a temple on Mound 1 at San Jose Mogote was burned to the ground, suggesting that the most restricted and ritually important part of the site was penetrated by a raiding party (Marcus and Flannery 1996:129). Survey data indicate that San Jose Mogote was losing population, with the site decreasing from 70 ha to 34 ha by 500 B.C. (Kowalewski et al. 1989:72–77). These data suggest that many commoners were expressing resistance, withdrawing support from the rulers of San Jose Mogote, and leaving the community. At the same time, competing centers in the Oaxaca valley, especially Yeguih in the Tlacolula arm and El Mogote in the Valle Grande, were increasing in size, with the latter growing to 25 ha (Spencer and Redmond 2001:217). It is not certain why these competing centers were gaining power, although the decline of traditional exchange partners like La Venta and Chalcatzingo may have decreased the ability of San Jose Mogote's nobles to acquire prestige goods used for ritual performances and to cement alliances with other elites. This may have allowed competing elites in the valley to gain power by establishing exchange relationships with new centers that were emerging at this time.

Monte Alban was founded about 500 B.C. in the midst of this political crisis. Similarities in architecture, iconography, and mortuary practices between San Jose Mogote and Monte Alban indicate that people from the former site founded the latter. At the same time, many sites in the Etla arm declined in size or were abandoned indicating that Monte Alban's founding population included people from several communities within the former San Jose Mogote polity (Kowalewski et al. 1989:91).

The founding and early development of Monte Alban represented a dramatic transformation in the Oaxaca Valley's social system. By 300 B.C., 200 years after the founding of the hilltop center, Monte Alban far exceeded any other site in the valley in size, population, and scale of monumental architecture. During the Late Formative (300–100 B.C.) the city grew to cover 442 ha with an estimated population of 17,242 (Blanton 1978:52; Kowalewski et al. 1989:130), and the population of the valley as a whole increased an estimated 27-fold (Kowalewski et al. 1989:123–126). While nobles lived near the Main Plaza on the summit of Monte Alban, commoners lived on residential terraces on the slopes of the hill. The rulers of the city were successful in defeating their Oaxaca Valley rivals, and by the Terminal Formative (100 B.C.–A.D. 200) Monte Alban had developed into a state polity with a bureaucracy able to administer a five-tiered settlement hierarchy that probably encompassed the entire valley. Social inequality increased during this period, with elites living in large, architecturally elaborate houses near the ceremonial precincts of sites. Upon death nobles were interred in tombs, with elaborate offerings, often including dozens of ceramic vessels, jade, and ornamental shell.

The archaeological evidence indicates to me that the founding of Monte Alban was a response to the political crisis facing people in the Etla arm, especially the loss of power experienced by nobles from San Jose Mogote. Defensive concerns were one reason for establishing the site. Its location on a series of hills in the center of the Oaxaca Valley made it a natural fortress. During the Late Formative (300–100 B.C.), a defensive wall was constructed around portions of the site (Blanton 1978:52–54). The wall reached heights of 4–5 m and was up to 20 m thick. Depictions of sacrificial victims, probably war captives, on carved stone monuments at Monte Alban as well as evidence for the military conquest of the El Palenque site in the Valle Grande are more direct indications of warfare (Spencer and Redmond 2001).

Defensive concerns alone, however, cannot explain the dramatic social transformation that occurred with the founding and early development of Monte Alban (Joyce 2000). In addition to hostile neighbors, the nobles who founded Monte Alban were also faced with a major decline in followers and the disruption of trade and alliances with elites from distant regions. The problem wasn't simply defense, but responding to the more general social disruptions and insecurities of the period that were causing the loss of followers. Moving the community to a defensible hilltop would not have led to the growth of the urban center if people continued to express dissatisfaction by "voting with their feet" and shifting their allegiance to other nobles.

Given the dramatic increase in the population of Late Formative Monte Alban relative to Middle Formative San Jose Mogote, commoners as well as nobles must have chosen to move to Monte Alban. Commoners were largely economically self-sufficient, and there is little evidence suggesting that people moved to Monte Alban for material gain. In fact the establishment of Monte Alban probably had a negative effect on the economic circumstances of many people, since data indicate an increase in tribute payments to the nobility (Joyce and Winter 1996) and there is evidence that some communities may have become materially impoverished (Blanton et al. 1999:8). Living on the infertile slopes of Monte Alban probably would have required people to travel a greater distance to work their agricultural fields. It is unlikely that, at 500 B.C., rulers had the military might to force thousands of people to move to the hilltop center. Instead, there must have been some inducement for commoners to support the rulers and institutions of Monte Alban. Given the ideological significance of religious belief for creating and legitimating political power in the Middle Formative, it seems likely that religion played a role in the founding and early development of the city. The loss of followers at San Jose Mogote indicates that the traditional means nobles had used to attract followers and mobilize resources were declining in effectiveness. In the following section, I argue that, in addition to defense, Monte Alban was founded as a ceremonial center designed to communicate with the sacred realm in new and more powerful ways so as to reverse the fortunes of the people, both nobles and commoners, who founded the site.

Monte Alban as an *Axis Mundi*

The first large-scale communal construction project at Monte Alban involved build- ing a monumental ceremonial precinct that housed politico-religious institutions and was a stage for public ceremonies (Acosta 1965). The ceremonial precinct con- sisted of the Main Plaza complex, a huge public plaza measuring roughly 300 m north–south by 150 m east–west. In its final form the Main Plaza was bounded on its north and south ends by high platforms supporting numerous public buildings (Fig. 8.2). The eastern and western sides of the Main Plaza were defined by rows of monumental buildings; a third row of structures ran north-to-south through the center of the plaza. The initial version of the Main Plaza, dating from 500 to 100 B.C., consisted of only the plaza itself, along with the western row of buildings and much of the eastern half of the North Platform. The central and eastern rows of buildings and probably the South Platform do not appear to have been built until the Terminal Formative (100 B.C.–A.D. 200).

The early version of the Main Plaza represents a great increase in the scale of monumental architecture and sacred space relative to San Jose Mogote. Public buildings constructed during Monte Alban's first few centuries included Building L along the southwestern end of the Main Plaza, whose walls were built with huge monoliths many of which were carved with representations of sacrificial victims. Building IV-sub along the northwestern end of the Main Plaza included a 6 m-high sloping wall. The Late Formative version of the North Platform consisted of a huge architectural complex that encompassed much of the eastern half of the platform's final area and included structures that reached heights of 15 m above the Main Plaza. East of the North Platform was Area A3, which consisted of a series of ter- races with platforms on which were built several high-status residences. The effort expended on constructing the Main Plaza complex shows that religion, as well as warfare, were important concerns for the early inhabitants of Monte Alban.

The symbolism and spatial arrangement of architecture and iconography around the Main Plaza, suggest that the site was founded as a cosmogram that symbolized the Zapotec version of the cosmos (Joyce 2000). Like monuments at other ceremonial centers in Mesoamerica and throughout the world, the Main Plaza complex was built as an *axis mundi* creating a point of communication and

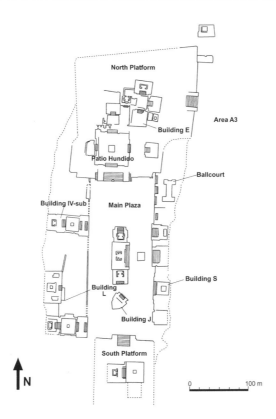

Figure 8.2. Plan of the Main Plaza at Monte Alban

mediation between the human world and the supernatural otherworld. Iconographic, archaeological, ethnographic, and linguistic research has demonstrated that some Mesoamerican pyramids were considered sacred mountains of creation (Schele and Freidel 1990). Since Monte Alban's Main Plaza was built on the top of an imposing mountain that rose over 300 m above the valley floor, it is likely that the entire ceremonial precinct may have been considered a sacred mountain. Several of the early buildings incorporated large portions of the natural hill, thereby crafting a modified cultural version of the original hilltop. From its earliest years, the sacred geography of Monte Alban resembled other Mesoamerican cities where the cosmos was rotated onto the surface of the site's ceremonial center such that north represented the celestial realm and south the earth or underworld (Ashmore 1991; Sugiyama 1993).

The southern end of the Main Plaza contained iconographic references to sacrifice, warfare, and earth or underworld. Building L was the location of a gallery of carved stone monuments that included nearly 400 portraits of sacrificial victims, probably war captives (Fig. 8.3(a)). In Mesoamerican beliefs, sacrificial victims would go into the earth at death. These monuments, known as the *danzantes*, represent the single largest corpus of carved stones for Late Formative Mesoamerica

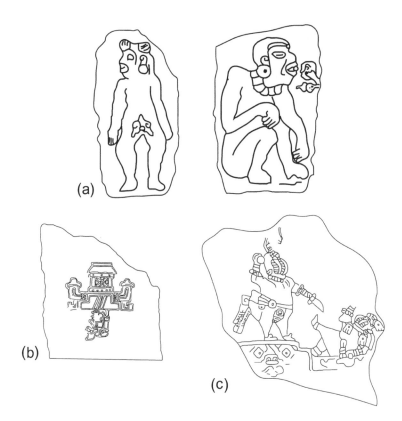

Figure 8.3. Late/Terminal Formative carved stones from Oaxaca: (a) danzante sculptures from Monte Alban Building L (redrawn from Scott 1978); (b) Building J "conquest slab" from Monte Alban (redrawn from Caso 1947: fig. 41); (c) Dainzu ballplayers (redrawn from Orr 1997: fig. 2.26)

and constitute roughly 80 percent of the total monument record from Monte Alban. The danzantes, along with a slightly earlier (ca. 600–500 B.C.) carved stone (Monument 3) from Mound 1 at San Jose Mogote, provide the earliest evidence for human sacrifice in Oaxaca. The danzantes depict men, often in contorted poses, with closed eyes, who are naked except for elaborate headdresses, which suggests that they were captured nobles. Forms of sacrifice that appear to be represented on the danzantes include heart sacrifice, genital mutilation, and decapitation. The genital mutilation apparent on many danzantes suggests a combination of earlier forms of autosacrifice with death sacrifice. Some of the danzantes have short hieroglyphic texts, including dates in the 260-day ritual calendar. The Building-L gallery included one representation of a noble who may have been supervising the sacrifices, although like many of the danzantes, it was later removed and reused in other buildings at the site.

The North Platform included iconographic references to sky, rain, and lightning. The earliest celestial reference is found with the stucco frieze known as the *viborón* (Fig. 8.4) located beneath the southeast corner of the North Platform (Acosta

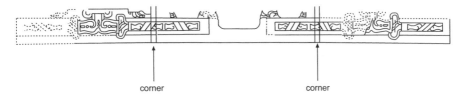

corner   corner

Figure 8.4. *Viborón* frieze from the North Platform at Monte Alban (redrawn from Urcid 1994: fig. 7)

1965:816; Orr 1997). The frieze dates to the Late Formative (300–100 B.C.) and consists of a sky band with scrolls similar to the s-scroll raincloud motif (Reilly 1996:36). The sky band is broken by serpentine figures, similar to Cociyo, the Zapotec lightning (sky) deity. Scrolls that may represent clouds form the mouth and bifid tongue or fangs. Rain issues from the figure's mouth, and its goggle eyes resemble those of Tlaloc, the later Central Mexican rain deity. The *viborón* frieze covers the sides of what appears to have been a sunken court. In Mesoamerica, sunken or enclosed plaza areas and ballcourts often symbolized infraworld inter-faces. It is possible that the sunken court represented a "sky cave" entrance to the otherworld.

The majority of high-status residences and tombs were concentrated in areas around the North Platform, creating an elite-ceremonial precinct that was spatially segregated from the rest of the community (Joyce 2000). The placement of elite residences around the northern end of the Main Plaza symbolically linked nobles and noble ancestors to the celestial realm. Upon death, nobles were buried in formal masonry tombs beneath the patios of elite residences, while commoners were buried in simple graves or stone-lined cysts. The interment of elites in formal tombs, which first occurred at San Jose Mogote in the century prior to the founding of Monte Alban, allowed for noble ancestors to be contacted via tomb re-entry ceremonies (Miller 1995). During the Postclassic period (A.D. 800–1521) the remains of Oaxacan nobles were often kept as mummy bundles in sacred caves and temples, where they were consulted as oracles. Tombs at Monte Alban often contained effigy vessels depicting Cociyo, the Zapotec lightning (sky) deity. These data suggest not only an increasing association of nobles with the celestial realm, but also the deifi-cation of noble ancestors. An increasing association between elite residences and religious symbols and artifacts further indicates that nobles were gaining greater control of politico-religious ideas, practices, and institutions (Joyce and Winter 1996:36).

By 100 B.C. this early version of the Main Plaza was in place with its cosmic symbolism and references to the creation and regeneration of the world through sacrifice. Similarities between the sacred geography of Monte Alban, La Venta, Chalcatzingo, and Chiapa de Corzo (Clark 2001) suggest that Zapotec elites may have appropriated ideas about sacred space from those earlier centers, many of which were in decline when Monte Alban was being founded. For example, Middle Formative Chalcatzingo like Monte Alban is aligned along a north–south axis with references to rulers/ancestors to the north and themes of sacrifice and fertility to the south (Grove 1999). In the northern sector of Chalcatzingo's ceremonial precinct are stelae with iconographic representations of rulers as well as a sunken court containing a tabletop throne. To the south, on Cerro Chalcatzingo, are a series of bas-relief carvings in a processional arrangement with themes of human sacrifice and rain. The uppermost bas-relief in the processional arrangement is Monument 11, which depicts an elite personage seated in a mountain cave with rain falling from clouds. The cave is depicted as a sectioned quatrefoil, which closely resembles the Zapotec hill/place glyph first found at Monte Alban during the Late/Terminal Formative (see below).

Beyond spatial symbolism, Monte Alban's Main Plaza was an arena where thousands of people participated in dramatic public rituals organized and led by the nobility, which probably included sacrifice, bloodletting, processions, shamanism, dance, divination, feasting, and ancestor veneration (Joyce 2000; Orr 1997). People standing on the Main Plaza would have been physically and psychologically engaged in the proceedings. Until the Terminal Formative, the Main Plaza was open on its eastern side, making activities on the plaza both accessible and easily visible to commoners living on the terraces below. The archaeological record indicates both continuity and innovations in ritual beliefs and practices through which people petitioned supernaturals for prosperity. In the structural setting of the time, the Main Plaza ceremonial precinct as well as innovations in ritual practices like human sacrifice would have allowed nobles to communicate with the supernatural realm in powerful new ways to reverse the political crises of the time and defeat their enemies. The evidence for the increasing religious significance of noble ancestors, especially their interment in formal masonry tombs, further suggests that elites were struggling to find new ways to communicate with the sacred. New religious cults are indicated by the first occurrence of effigy vessels depicting deities like Cociyo, the Old God, and the Wide-Billed Bird deity (Blanton et al. 1999:105–107; Winter 2001:286–287). Blanton and his colleagues (1999:105) have suggested that the increasing standardization and perhaps mass production of Gray Ware pottery vessels may have been the result of their use in large-scale ritual feasting.

Human sacrifice in particular would have provided both a ceremonial spectacle and, at least during the first few centuries of Monte Alban, would have been a new and exotic form of ritual practice. Through captive sacrifice, nobles both re-enacted the creation myth and renewed the current world by petitioning supernaturals for fertility and prosperity on behalf of all their followers. Human sacrifice was a more dramatic and potent means to communicate with the supernatural realm than earlier practices of autosacrifice and would have been a means by which nobles demonstrated both their power and generosity to supporters. In this new version of the sacred covenant, warfare was linked to sacrificial practices through which the sacred covenant was enacted. The danzantes gallery, with its nearly 400 depictions of sacrificial victims, was constructed so that the images could be viewed as processions moved past Building L (Orr 1997) and would have continually communicated the significance of human sacrifice and warfare as well as the coercive power of the nobility.

Public ritual performances would have created powerful psychological forces that affected people's dispositions by binding them to the rulers, the symbols, and the new social order at Monte Alban. The choice of an unoccupied hilltop in the center of the valley for this new ceremonial center distanced Monte Alban from traditional centers of settlement and politico-religious power. As argued by Blanton (1978), this "disembededdness" may have made Monte Alban more attractive as a political and religious center to people throughout the valley, enhancing the ability of the site's nobles to gain followers and mobilize labor and resources as tribute. Because Monte Alban is visible from much of the valley floor, its power as a sacred mountain and a political center would have been present in the everyday lived experiences of people throughout the region. The creation of a corporate identity linked to Monte Alban is evident both in evidence for public rituals, but also in the huge volume of monumental building activity. The construction of the Main Plaza complex represents active and uncoerced commoner involvement in the ceremonial center that served to enroll them in the new structural principles embodied in the sacred geography of the site. The creation of shared identities and alliances with people throughout the valley is indicated by the construction of public architecture and high-status residences similar to those from Monte Alban in many valley communities during the Late/Terminal Formative (Marcus and Flannery 1996; Spencer and Redmond 2001). Warfare may also have united people since it was no longer waged just to defeat competing elites and obtain tribute, but was conducted to capture sacrificial victims that in the Zapotec belief system ultimately contributed to human prosperity (Joyce and Winter 1996:38–39). Since commoners were increasingly dependent on nobles for ritual communication with the sacred realm, the possibility of the capture and sacrifice of nobles by competing elites had dire consequences for all people.

Commoners who aligned themselves with Monte Alban would have gained from their association with this powerful political and religious center. The tremendous population explosion in and around Monte Alban after the site's founding suggests that the new beliefs and practices attracted many people from valley communities. The innovative ideas, institutions, and practices of the first several centuries of Monte Alban initially may have been conceived at least partially in corporate terms. Ironically, however, commoners who were contributing their allegiance, resources, and labor to construct and support the ceremonial center and its nobles were also contributing to their own subordination (Joyce 2000). Sacred public spaces, unifying ritual practices, labor appropriations, and centralizing beliefs were increasingly appropriated by the nobility and would soon come to embody and affirm dominant ideologies that constrained the agency of commoners. Many of the innovations in ritual practices and spatial structure communicated the increasing separation of elite and commoner identities. The special role that elites played as shaman and sacrificers dramatically communicated and reinforced their identities as mediators between commoners and the sacred. Sacrificial practices would have been especially important in communicating the power of nobles to contact the sacred realm, since in prehispanic Mesoamerica nobles performed the most potent forms of sacrifice, especially human sacrifice. Monumental buildings around the

Main Plaza would have served as stages elevating and separating nobles from the commoners on the plaza below. This separation would also have been communicated by the visible association of elite residences, tombs, and the North Platform symbolizing the linkage between nobles and the celestial realm. Elite identities were also symbolized by control of exotic artifacts such as urns and incense burners, and knowledge including hieroglyphic writing and calendrics.

Some people and communities, however, chose not to align themselves with Monte Alban. In particular, people living in the Valle Grande and Tlacolula arms of the Valley of Oaxaca were traditional competitors with the Etla nobles who founded Monte Alban. At least some communities in the Oaxaca Valley attempted to remain independent, although as Monte Alban's size and power grew, independence became increasingly risky as shown by the danzantes, which probably depict elites captured in warfare. Spencer and Redmond (2001) have found evidence that the Late Formative Valle Grande center of El Palenque was conquered and a high-status residence and temple were destroyed by fire. Late Formative migrations of people from the Oaxaca Valley to the nearby valleys of Ejutla, Miahuatlan, and Sola, as well as into mountainous regions (Marcus and Flannery 1996:199–203), may also have been expressions of resistance to the authority of Monte Alban.

Overall, human sacrifice and the more general appropriation of religious ideas, spaces, and practices by nobles during the late Middle Formative (500–300 B.C.) and Late Formative (300–100 B.C.) increased their power to attract followers, mobilize resources, defeat competitors, and interact with the sacred. A reason for the dramatic growth in the scale of the Monte Alban polity may have been the popularity of the sacred principles and practices that were a central motivating factor for the early inhabitants of the site. It is doubtful, however, that the founders of Monte Alban could have foreseen the dramatic increase in the scale of the polity as people moved to the hilltop center (Joyce 2000). The huge population concentrating at Monte Alban created provisioning problems that forced elites to mobilize food from commoners in the valley. The provisioning problem may have encouraged nobles to conquer and incorporate independent communities to gain control of agricultural land. The ritual innovation of human sacrifice would have further legitimated military expansion and conquest. Provisioning problems also led to the short-lived piedmont strategy that involved population expansion and agricultural intensification in the piedmont (Kowalewski et al. 1989:123–126). Productive intensification by commoners increased the demand for labor, making it advantageous to have larger families, which further drove population growth. People in some communities began to specialize in certain crafts, such as ceramics and stone tools, taking advantage of the fact that most commoners would have had less time to carry out the full array of productive tasks that they had previously undertaken. People may have developed markets to provide a central location to obtain products manufactured by specialists. These and other unanticipated problems created by the increasing scale of the Monte Alban polity likely contributed to the development of new administrative institutions, leading to the emergence of the state (Kowalewski et al. 1989; Spencer 1982).

Political Consolidation in the Valley of Oaxaca

By the Terminal Formative (100 B.C.–A.D. 200) the rulers of Monte Alban, through social negotiation, religious persuasion, and military conquest, had extended their authority over the entire Valley of Oaxaca and probably also over the contiguous valleys of Ejutla, Miahuatlan, and Sola. A five-tiered settlement hierarchy had developed in the Oaxaca Valley, with lesser nobles at subregional and local centers who were tied to Monte Alban through political obligation and probably kinship. Lower-order centers had their own public administrative precincts where rituals were carried out by the resident nobility. Beginning in the Late Formative, Monte Alban's rulers engaged in warfare with polities in surrounding regions (Joyce and Winter 1996). Some sparsely populated regions such as the Cuicatlan Cañada (Spencer 1982) and mountainous areas around the Oaxaca valley appear to have been conquered by Monte Alban and incorporated into a small empire. Some researchers have argued that Monte Alban's empire eventually encompassed $20,000 \, km^2$ (Marcus and Flannery 1996), although in many areas evidence for conquest is weak or nonexistent (Zeitlin and Joyce 1999). Monte Alban's expansion into other regions was part of a more general pattern of interpolity warfare at this time. Terminal Formative elites throughout the Oaxacan highlands and beyond appear to have been trying to gain control of long-distance trade routes through which they could establish alliances and gain access to prestigious goods and ideas. The political landscape in Late/Terminal Formative Mesoamerica was very dynamic, with new regional powerhouses like Monte Alban, Teotihuacan, El Mirador, Izapa, and Tikal vying with smaller centers for prestige and dominance over long-distance interaction. Another reason to engage in warfare was to obtain sacrificial victims required for important state rituals.

At Monte Alban, elite appropriation of ritual ideas, spaces, and practices continued as nobles increasingly consolidated power. During the Terminal Formative, early versions of the South Platform and the eastern row of buildings were constructed, effectively closing off the Main Plaza (Winter 2001). The central row of structures was also built, which served to further restrict and channel traffic during ritual performances. By closing off the Main Plaza nobles were able to more effectively control access to and the use of the ceremonial precinct. Beyond the Main Plaza, the defensive walls surrounding portions of the site could have been used to control the flow of people. Control of space was reflected on a smaller scale by the Zapotec two-room temple, which was a common form of public architecture from the Terminal Formative until the time of the Spanish Conquest. Two-room temples consisted of a smaller outer room where priests received people and performed ceremonies, and a more private back room restricted to ritual specialists. In addition to the control of space, the development of the ritual calendar, which dates to at least the Middle Formative, allowed nobles to increasingly control time. Important religious ceremonies were often timed according to cycles in the 260-day ritual calendar and certain types of warfare were initiated according to the cycle of Venus (Schele and Freidel 1990).

Terminal Formative additions and alterations to the Main Plaza (Acosta 1965; Winter 2001) reinforced the basic themes of sacred geography. Building J in the southern end of the plaza continued the themes of sacrifice, warfare, and the underworld. Set into the foundations of Building J in a processional arrangement, were over 50 carved stone slabs known as the "conquest slabs" that depicted places conquered by Monte Alban (Fig. 8.3(b)). Many of the slabs depict the severed head of a captured ruler extending down beneath the terrestrial hill glyph with vegetation sprouting from the top of the hill sign. The association of sacrifice, warfare, and agricultural fertility is clearly represented. Since the Zapotec hill glyph may have been derived from the depiction of caves as sectioned quatrefoils, as seen at Middle Formative Chalcatzingo, the "conquest slabs" may also reference the descent of sacrificial victims into the underworld via a cave portal.

In the North Platform, the *viborón* court was built over, but an even larger sunken court, the Patio Hundido, was constructed in the southern end of the platform. Elite residences continued to be concentrated to the north of the Main Plaza and by this time some were being constructed on the North Platform itself. One of the elite residences on the North Platform had a larger number of rooms and a more complex layout than other high-status residences of this period. High-status residences were also located in some areas of Monte Alban beyond the Main Plaza, probably indicating the emergence of the pattern of neighborhoods or barrios that was clearly present by the Late Classic (A.D. 500–800).

A ballcourt was built during the Terminal Formative on the northeastern corner of the Main Plaza. Ballcourts, like sunken courts, were seen as portals to the otherworld and were associated with warfare, sacrifice, and the negotiation of political relations with foreign polities (Gillespie 1991). Ballcourts were often placed on spatial boundaries both between polities and, as in this case, between ceremonial spaces and the outside world. The Main Plaza ballcourt was located at what was probably the primary entrance point to the plaza, since by the Late Classic period, if not before, three roads came together just east of this area (Blanton 1978:63–66). Elsewhere, ballcourts were built both in the ceremonial precincts of political centers and along the edges of the valley.

During the Terminal Formative, public architecture and ceremonial spaces that housed the politico-religious institutions and nobles of the state were also built at smaller centers in the Valley of Oaxaca (Marcus and Flannery 1996:172–191; Spencer and Redmond 2001). Terminal Formative two-room temples, ballcourts, and high-status residences have been identified at several sites in the valley, including San Jose Mogote, Cuilapan, and Los Mogotes. Second-order political centers in each arm of the valley exhibited public architecture and iconography that resembled the capital at Monte Alban. For example, at San Jose Mogote, which had recovered to become a secondary administrative center for the Etla arm, the ceremonial precinct was built as a nearly identical copy of Monte Alban's Main Plaza. At Dainzu in the Tlacolula arm, toward the end of the Terminal Formative, nobles constructed a gallery of carved stones on a monumental building at the base of Cerro Dainzu depicting victorious ballplayers dominating defeated ones (Fig. 8.3(c)). As argued convincingly by Orr (1997), the Dainzu gallery exhibited a similar theme to that of the danzantes since versions of the prehispanic ballgame involved a kind of staged mock-combat ritual leading to the eventual sacrifice of defeated ballplayers, who usually were war captives. Petroglyphs on Cerro Dainzu are similar to the gallery of carved stones at the base of the hill except that defeated ballplayers are depicted as decapitated heads.

The similarities in public art and architecture between Monte Alban and its lower-level political centers indicate the emergence of a state bureaucracy (Kowalewski et al. 1989). State-sponsored rituals at ceremonial precincts in lower-order sites throughout the valley would have been important in connecting people in the peripheries to the capital and its rulers. Kertzer (1988) argues that rituals can provide powerful means for integrating diverse factions within complex societies by reifying politico-religious institutions and creating shared experiences that emotionally connect people to state symbols, institutions, and practices. Orr (1997) has argued that pilgrimages to Monte Alban, as well as processional rituals on the Main Plaza, would have been effective mechanisms for social integration. Since Zapotec nobles had little direct control over the subsistence economy, state integration was achieved largely through ritual practices, although by the Terminal Formative the military could have provided a means of coercion.

By the end of the Terminal Formative Monte Alban had been the dominant center in the Oaxaca Valley for 700 years. The sacred geography of the Main Plaza was a symbol of, as well as a stage for, ritual practices that proved extremely successful in attracting followers and integrating an increasingly larger and more complex polity. By A.D. 200, however, the Main Plaza was becoming spatially segregated and controlled by the nobility. This trend would continue during the Classic period as the rulers of Monte Alban shifted their focus away from rituals that emphasized communal identity and toward self-aggrandizement.

Elite Appropriation of Sacred Space

In the highlands of Oaxaca the Formative to Classic period transition was a time of interpolity conflict and political instability (Joyce and Winter 1996). At about A.D. 200, the urban centers of Yucuita, Monte Negro, and Huamelulpan in the Mixteca Alta region declined, perhaps due to conflict, and Monte Alban's rulers retreated from the Cuicatlan Cañada (Spencer 1982). Archaeologists argue that the huge urban center of Teotihuacan in the Basin of Mexico may have by this time posed a sufficient threat to the people of the Oaxacan highlands to trigger a political retrenchment and the lessening of interpolity hostilities (Spencer 1982:255). While Winter (2001) suggests that Monte Alban was conquered by Teotihuacan, the data at present support the exchange of prestige goods, ideas, and personnel between the two great powers, although competition and conflict cannot be ruled out. At Teotihuacan, a group of Zapotec nobles resided in an apartment compound where they made Oaxaca-style ceramics and buried their dead in a Zapotec-style tomb. Elites from Teotihuacan may also have resided for periods at Monte Alban (Winter 2001). Regardless of the exact relationship between Monte Alban and

Teotihuacan, the Oaxacan highlands were politically stable with centers like Monte Alban, Yucuñudahui, and Cerro de las Minas maintaining their prominence through the Classic period. Perhaps in part because of the political stability of the Classic period, Zapotec nobles increasingly represented their personal power, rather than communal themes of warfare and sacrifice, in monumental art and architecture at Monte Alban.

To some extent, Classic period building projects at Monte Alban maintain earlier patterns of sacred geography (Acosta 1965; Winter 2001). The North Platform continued as a focus for symbolism related to the celestial realm, nobles, and noble ancestors. During the Classic period the North Platform was marked by numerous depictions of the "jaws of the sky" motif on carved stones (Urcid 1992). This motif referred to noble descent and the divine home of elite ancestors in the celestial realm (Miller 1995:11). Elite residences continued to be concentrated on and around the North Platform. On the South Platform, a program of stone monuments carved around A.D. 500–600 depicted a Zapotec ruler presiding over six bound captives presumably destined for sacrifice (Urcid 1992). These carved stones were later reused in the final construction phase of the South Platform so their original location is uncertain, although it was likely on that platform.

Archaeological and iconographic evidence indicates, however, that during the Classic period nobles increasingly diverged from earlier principles of sacred geography, iconographic themes on monumental art, and related aspects of ideology. Prior to the Classic period public art focused on themes of sacrifice and warfare with very few depictions of rulers. Formative period iconography may reflect an ideology that attempted to conceal the relationship between sacrifice, warfare, and elite interests. The role of nobles appears to have been muted in iconography, which perhaps instead symbolically stressed communal involvement in and benefits from warfare and sacrifice. As the Classic period progressed, nobles at Monte Alban and other sites in the Oaxaca Valley increasingly erected portraits of themselves and their ancestors in public art. This pattern can be seen as early as the end of the Terminal Formative with the Dainzu ballgame program, which depicts several victorious nobles in addition to defeated ones destined for sacrifice. Along with the South Platform program and its focus on bound war captives, carved stone monuments from the Early Classic and the early part of the Late Classic at Monte Alban included depictions of processional scenes commemorating living nobles and their ancestors (Urcid 1992), a possible diplomatic meeting between a Zapotec lord and an emissary from Teotihuacan (Marcus and Flannery 1996:233), and a scene of divination by a Zapotec noble (Orr 1997:259). Several Classic period carved stones depicting nobles and noble ancestors have been found on the South Platform. While none of these monuments has been found in their primary context, their distribution suggests that depictions of nobles and noble ancestors were no longer restricted to the northern part of the Main Plaza complex.

The breakdown of the strong association between nobles and the North Platform is seen in the distribution of elite residences. While elite residences continued to be concentrated around the North Platform, during the Early Classic period a high-status residence was also built in the southwestern corner of the plaza just west of the South Platform. By the Late Classic this area included at least ten residences, some with tombs, although no more than five residences were occupied simultaneously. Elaborate palace complexes were built directly facing each other on the southern end of the Main Plaza (Building S and Building L). On the southeastern end of the plaza was Building S, which included three contiguous patio groups and was the largest of the Late Classic palaces. By the end of the Late Classic the number of residences around the Main Plaza was far greater than in earlier periods. In addition, each of Monte Alban's barrios also had resident nobles. The data suggest that by the Late Classic the population of nobles and their retainers had increased considerably.

The construction of noble residences throughout the ceremonial precinct suggests that the Main Plaza was becoming a focus of elite domestic activities and was less frequently used as an arena for large-scale public ceremonies. This hypothesis is supported by Blanton's (1978:63–66) study of the spatial organization of Monte Alban, which indicates that by the Late Classic the Main Plaza was largely closed off. The main access points were probably the northeastern and southeastern corners of the plaza since the other corners were blocked by elite residences. Another major change in the spatial configuration of the Main Plaza during the Late Classic was the construction of several temple–patio–altar (TPA) complexes. The TPA consisted of a temple elevated on a platform that faces a patio with an altar in the center. In most cases, access to the TPA was restricted either by building a wall around the patio, sometimes with a smaller platform on the side opposite the temple, or by constructing a sunken patio. While TPAs like the Patio Hundido on the North Platform date back to the Terminal Formative, they are rare until the Late Classic. During the Late Classic at least ten TPAs were located at Monte Alban, and others occur at administrative centers in the valley such as at Lambityeco. At Monte Alban, two TPAs were built on the west side of the Main Plaza, which effectively segregated portions of the plaza creating restricted ceremonial spaces. This trend toward restricted ceremonial spaces is found in administrative centers throughout the valley (Kowalewski et al. 1989:262–263).

A shift away from large-scale public ceremonies and toward restricted, private ones is indicated by a contextual analysis of monumental art. As the Classic period proceeded, there were fewer carved stones made for placement in public settings. Earlier stone monuments, including many danzantes and "conquest slabs," were taken from their original locations, reset in building foundations, and often plastered over, in most cases probably as parts of building dedication ceremonies (Masson and Orr 1998). After about A.D. 500, however, most newly carved stones at Monte Alban and other sites in the valley were set in highly restricted locations such as on the North Platform, or were carved as lintels and door jambs for tombs. Genealogical registers were the most common type of carved stone monument of the Late Classic. These carved stone slabs are generally smaller than earlier monuments, and the few that have been found *in situ* were mostly in tombs. An exception is Stela MA-VGE-2, which is large relative to typical genealogical registers, measuring $276 \times 100 \times 25$ cm, and was found on the southern side of Building E on the North Platform (Fig. 8.5). Genealogical registers depict several generations

Figure 8.5. Stela MA-VGE-2 from Monte Alban (redrawn from Urcid et al. 1994: fig. 3A)

of nobles, sometimes showing marriage scenes or rituals related to ancestor veneration. Both males and females were depicted as principal figures suggesting that
women as well as men were ruling elites (Urcid et al. 1994), a pattern that continued into the Early Colonial period. Another form of elite art that dates largely
to this period is the painted murals found in the most elaborate tombs in the valley,
which depict scenes of ancestor veneration (Miller 1995). Genealogical registers
and tomb murals have been recovered from sites throughout the valley and not just
at Monte Alban.

The dominant theme in Late Classic elite art was genealogical relations and
ancestor veneration rather than human sacrifice and warfare as it had been in the
Formative. The data on both spatial organization of ceremonial space as well as the
context and iconography of monumental art suggest that, by the Late Classic,
Zapotec nobles were less concerned with large-scale public ceremonies and more
focused on rituals involving restricted audiences of other elites. The concern with
genealogy and ancestors, especially in the context of tomb rituals, suggests that
establishing genealogical linkages to powerful ancestors was crucial in negotiating
and legitimating political power, including claims to land and other resources. The
death of a ruler would have been a time of crisis and struggle over succession,

requiring the establishment of genealogical relations and the renegotiation of alliances. Genealogical sequences indicate that lines of succession were traced back to powerful ancestors through both male and female lines, a pattern seen in the Early Colonial period among Zapotec nobles (Urcid et al. 1994:34).

It is not clear what factors may have caused this shift toward rituals restricted to noble audiences and away from public ceremonies, although several factors can be hypothesized. By the Classic period the Oaxaca Valley was politically stable and the ideological principles of the Zapotec state were well established. Political stability may have lessened the necessity of large-scale ceremonies that engaged people in dealing ritually with insecurities like those of the Middle Formative, and lessened the motivation to communicate ideological principles to commoners. By the Late Classic the nobility had grown in size and the social setting had become highly factionalized with numerous subregional centers led by lesser nobles such as at Lambityeco, Jalieza, Yagul, and Macuilxochitl (Kowalewski et al. 1989). Monte Alban itself was divided into various barrios, each led by an elite family (Blanton 1978). The collapse of Teotihuacan around A.D. 700 would have lessened the role of Monte Alban's nobles in negotiating relations with this powerful neighbor to the north. Without the potential threat of Teotihuacan, local nobles may have increasingly asserted their independence and distanced themselves from Monte Alban. I argue that these factors led to intense competition among noble factions throughout the valley, which was negotiated ritually in highly restricted settings where genealogical relations and alliances could be worked out without undermining elite authority in relation to commoners. Nobles were able to maneuver for power through alliances and by strategic marriages allowing individuals to claim descent from several powerful ancestors through multiple lines of descent.

Ironically, an unintended outcome of competition among the nobility may have been to create conditions that increased commoners' penetration of the dominant ideology. The decrease in public ceremonies would have meant that commoners had less access to the supernatural realm and were less actively engaged in the kinds of dramatic ritual performances and shared experiences that created a sense of belonging and identity with state symbols, rulers, and institutions (Kertzer 1988). If local nobles were actively competing and attempting to undermine the authority of Monte Alban, then central unifying symbols, especially surrounding the rulers of Monte Alban, would have been further confused. The absence of Teotihuacan as a unifying threat may also have contributed to commoners becoming more distanced from the capital and its rulers. Under these circumstances, tribute payments to Monte Alban may have been increasingly resisted and refused both by local nobles and commoners alike. Future research should investigate the possibility that commoners increased household ritual activities that allowed them to contact the sacred and offset their decreasing involvement in public ceremonies.

Increasing factional competition among nobles, along with commoner resistance, may have contributed to the collapse of the Monte Alban state. By A.D. 800 the city was in decline with its people relocating to other parts of the valley and its nobles supplanted by other elites. Political centers that may have been aligned with Monte Alban, such as Lambityeco, also collapsed. Centers like Mitla, Yagul, and Zaachila became major powers in the fragmented political landscape of the Postclassic period (A.D. 800–1521). While Monte Alban would remain a sacred mountain until after the Spanish Conquest, it would never again be an important political center.

Conclusions

The founding and early development of Monte Alban represents one of the most dramatic transformations in social relations and structure in prehispanic Mesoamerica. In the 200 years prior to the founding of the urban center, San Jose Mogote was the largest site in the valley at 34 ha with an estimated population of 564 people (Kowalewski et al. 1989:77). Public buildings along with a high-status residence were concentrated on a single platform (Mound 1) and its rulers were losing power relative to competing polities in the valley. By the Late Formative Monte Alban covered 442 ha with an estimated population of 17,242 (Kowalewski et al. 1989:130). The civic-ceremonial center of the site was the Main Plaza complex with its huge public plaza, numerous temples, high-status residences, and hundreds of carved stone monuments. By the Terminal Formative, the city had defeated its competitors in the valley and was expanding into nearby regions. The rulers of the hilltop center continued to govern the Oaxaca Valley until the polity's collapse at A.D. 800. By this time, Monte Alban had been the dominant center in the southern Mexican highlands for 1,300 years.

Much of the archaeological research on the social history of the Valley of Oaxaca has stressed the role of elite power-building and interregional interaction in the origins and development of the state (Marcus and Flannery 1996; Spencer and Redmond 2001). These scholars argue that Monte Alban was founded and grew into a state as nobles responded to interpolity conflict by developing new institutions to organize a larger social system initially for defense. The construction of plazas, temples, ballcourts, and palaces is viewed simply as a correlate of the administrative institutions of the state. In the process of state formation, elites consolidated power and enhanced their wealth. This perspective tends to view only elites as actors able to affect social systems. While interregional relations and power-building elites are important, these models fail to adequately consider the complexity of social relations within polities. These scholars effectively reify the Monte Alban state as an administrative organization strategically designed by nobles and imposed on commoners to deal with interpolity conflict.

Practice theory forces us to consider all people as social agents and to view history as the outcome of struggle, negotiation, competition, and cooperation among actors. In this chapter, I have argued that the development of the Monte Alban state was a result of the consequences, intended and unintended, of the ongoing actions and interactions of elites and commoners alike. The model developed here is admittedly hypothetical and will no doubt be modified as it articulates with the empirical record. The model, however, provides a more complete and humanistic view of social relations during the history of the Monte Alban polity.

Monte Alban was founded not as a great city and state capital, but as a new community where people hoped to deal more effectively with immediate contingencies in their lives. Problems faced by Etla nobles just before the founding of the hilltop center included the loss of followers, prestige, and long-distance interaction partners, as well as increasing interpolity competition. For commoners who chose to remain loyal to those nobles, there was a decline in the prestige of their community and in its ability to communicate with the sacred, as well as increasing threats from the outside. Nobles and their followers built the Main Plaza complex as an *axis mundi* to more effectively communicate with the otherworld and reverse their fortunes. The monumental spaces and buildings constructed on the Main Plaza symbolized the longstanding Zapotec view of the cosmos, but with a scale and grandeur that far exceeded anything previously in the Oaxaca Valley. Innovations in ritual practices, especially human sacrifice, were also developed to petition the sacred realm for prosperity. The hilltop location and walls provided defense against enemies.

While Monte Alban's nobles undoubtedly hoped to reverse the loss of followers and gain power, it is unlikely that they strategically planned to build a novel administrative organization to dominate the valley. This view leaves unexamined the agency of commoners and how they may have contributed to social process. Political organizations like states are symbolic constructs that are produced and reproduced through the ongoing negotiation and struggle of nobles and commoners. I argue that commoners gave their allegiance to Monte Alban and its rulers and relocated to the hilltop center in large numbers because they found the symbolism of the sacred mountain and the ritual performances on the Main Plaza to be compelling. Emotionally charged rituals linked people's identities to the symbolism of Monte Alban as embodied in its sacred geography, art, and nobility, creating a new corporate identity. The significance of the Main Plaza complex was not just that it reflected a new form of political organization. The plaza was part of the structural setting by which social practices gained their vitality; it was a product of new practices, but in turn shaped the dispositions of people who participated in its ceremonies or looked up at it from the valley floor in awe or fear.

While rulers could not have foreseen the great increase in the scale of the Monte Alban polity, they apparently took advantage of it to defeat competitors and to enhance their wealth and power. Through time, nobles increasingly appropriated religious ideas, spaces, and practices and were able to consolidate and expand their power. Even before the founding of Monte Alban, nobles were seen as having special ritual abilities and were mediators between people and the sacred. The religious innovations of the first several centuries of Monte Alban, especially human sacrifice and the deification of noble ancestors, made commoners increasingly dependent on elites for communication with the supernatural realm. These structural changes were internalized as distinctive elite and commoner identities. As the scale of the polity grew, nobles developed institutions to collect tribute, provide defense, enact state rituals, and organize corvée labor. These administrative institutions were not strategically planned, but were developed *ad hoc* as state rulers, lesser nobles, and commoners negotiated both anticipated and unanticipated social circumstances. The success of the nobility was seen in their increasingly larger and more elaborate residences, ornate tombs, and wealth. The size of the noble class appears to have grown, and by the Classic period powerful elites were found not just at Monte Alban but also at secondary centers in the valley.

As a symbol of the Zapotec cosmos where rituals were performed that invoked the sacred covenant and re-enacted the cosmic creation, elite appropriation of the Main Plaza was perhaps the most significant act in power consolidation. Beginning in the Terminal Formative the plaza was increasingly closed off and controlled by the nobility. By the Classic period, nobles were diverging from the principles of sacred geography that had been so important in the initial layout and ritual use of the precinct. The Main Plaza was used less for large public ceremonies that engaged commoners, and more as an elite residential precinct and an area for private ceremonies. The appropriation of the Main Plaza may have been a response to increasing independence and competition among lesser nobles, especially following the collapse of Teotihuacan. Commoners, however, had built and maintained the Main Plaza as well as other architectural complexes that housed the institutions and rulers of the state. By the Classic period, commoners were increasingly excluded from important ceremonies and sacred spaces, while they continued to provide tribute. Given the political and military power of Classic period nobles, commoners probably had little ability to actively rebel against these structural changes, although they may have resisted them in more subtle ways (Joyce et al. 2001).

The combination of inter-elite conflict and commoner disengagement may have been an important factor in the collapse of Monte Alban. The disengagement of commoners from state ceremonies could have weakened their allegiance, especially to the distant rulers of Monte Alban. When the social and political relations that linked Oaxaca Valley elites began to crumble in factional competition around A.D. 800, commoners may have declined to support nobles. While the initial success of Monte Alban was a result of the engagement of commoners in rituals, labor projects, and military actions that came to be important symbols of the state, the polity's collapse may have been an unintended outcome of their exclusion from these same symbolically, emotionally, and politically laden practices.

ACKNOWLEDGMENTS

I would like to thank Julia Hendon and Rosemary Joyce for inviting me to participate in this volume. I would also like to thank Cathy Cameron, Steve Lekson, Cynthia Robin, Payson Sheets, and Marcus Winter for comments on earlier drafts of this chapter.

REFERENCES

Acosta, J. G., 1965 Preclassic and Classic architecture of Oaxaca. In *Handbook of Middle American Indians*, vol. 3: *Archaeology of Southern Mesoamerica*, part 2. R. Wauchope and G. R. Willey, eds. Pp. 814–836. Austin: University of Texas Press.

Ashmore, W., 1991 Site-planning principles and concepts of directionality among the ancient Maya. *Latin American Antiquity* 2, 199–226.

Ashmore, W., and A. B. Knapp, eds., 1999 *Archaeologies of Landscape*. Oxford: Blackwell.

Blanton, R. E., 1978 *Monte Albán: Settlement Patterns at the Ancient Zapotec Capital*. New York: Academic Press.

—— 1983 The urban decline of Monte Albán. In *The Cloud People: Divergent Evolution of the Zapotec and Mixtec Civilizations*. K. V. Flannery and J. Marcus, eds. P. 186. New York: Academic Press.

Blanton, R. E., G. M. Feinman, S. A. Kowalewski, and L. M. Nicholas, 1999 *Ancient Oaxaca*. Cambridge: Cambridge University Press.

Caso, A., 1947 Calendario y escritura de las antiguas culturas de Monte Albán. In *Obras completas de Miguel Othón de Mendizábal*. 1, 116–143. Mexico: no publisher given.

Clark, J. E., 2001 Ciudades tempranas olmecas. In *Reconstruyendo la ciudad Maya: El urbanismo en las sociedades antiguas*. A. Ciudad Ruiz, M. J. Iglesia Ponce de Léon, and M. del Carmen Martínez Martínez, eds. Pp. 183–210. Madrid: Sociedad Española de Estudios Mayas.

Giddens, A., 1979 *Central Problems in Social Theory*. Berkeley: University of California Press.

Gillespie, S. D., 1991 Ballgames and boundaries. In *The Mesoamerican Ballgame*. V. L. Scarborough and D. R. Wilcox, eds. Pp. 317–345. Tucson: University of Arizona Press.

Grove, D. C., 1999 Public monuments and sacred mountains: Observations on three Formative period sacred landscapes. In *Social Patterns in Pre-Classic Mesoamerica*. D. C. Grove and R. A. Joyce, eds. Pp. 255–300. Washington, DC: Dumbarton Oaks Research Library and Collection.

Joyce, A. A., 2000 The founding of Monte Albán: Sacred propositions and social practices. In *Agency in Archaeology*. M. Dobres and J. Robb, eds. Pp. 71–91. London: Routledge.

Joyce, A. A., L. Arnaud Bustamante, and M. N. Levine, 2001 Commoner power: A case study from the Classic period collapse on the Oaxaca coast. *Journal of Archaeological Method and Theory* 8, 343–385.

Joyce, A. A., and M. Winter, 1996 Ideology, power, and urban society in prehispanic Oaxaca. *Current Anthropology* 37, 33–86.

Kertzer, D., 1988 *Ritual, Politics, and Power*. New Haven: Yale University Press.

Kowalewski, S. A., G. M. Feinman, L. Finsten, R. E. Blanton, and L. M. Nicholas, 1989 *Monte Albán's Hinterland*, part 2: *Prehispanic Settlement Patterns in Tlacolula, Etla, and Ocotlán, the Valley of Oaxaca, Mexico*. Memoirs of the Museum of Anthropology 23. Ann Arbor: University of Michigan.

Marcus, J., and K. V. Flannery, 1996 *Zapotec Civilization*. London: Thames & Hudson.

Masson, M. A., and H. Orr, 1998 The writing on the wall: Political representation and sacred geography at Monte Albán. In *The Sowing and the Dawning*. S. B. Mock, ed. Pp. 165–175. Albuquerque: University of New Mexico Press.

Miller, A. G., 1995 *The Painted Tombs of Oaxaca, Mexico*. Cambridge: Cambridge University Press.

Monaghan, J., 1990 Sacrifice, death, and the origins of agriculture in the Codex Vienna. *American Antiquity* 55, 559–569.

Orr, H. S., 1997 Power games in the Late Formative Valley of Oaxaca: The ballplayer sculptures at Dainzú. Ph.D. dissertation, Department of Art and Art History, University of Texas. Ann Arbor: University Microfilms.

Ortner, S. B., 1984 Theory in anthropology since the sixties. *Comparative Studies in Society and History* 26, 126–166.

Reilly, F. K. III, 1996 The Lazy-S: A Formative period iconographic loan to Maya hieroglyphic writing. In *Eighth Palenque Round Table, 1993*. M. J. Macri and J. McHargue, eds. Pp. 413–424. San Francisco: Pre-Columbian Art Research Institute.

Schele, L., and D. A. Freidel, 1990 *A Forest of Kings: The Untold Story of the Ancient Maya.* New York: William Morrow.

Scott, J. F., 1978 *The Danzantes of Monte Albán*, part 2: *Catalogue.* Studies in Pre-Columbian Art and Archaeology 19. Washington, DC: Dumbarton Oaks.

Spencer, C. S., 1982 *The Cuicatlán Cañada and Monte Albán.* New York: Academic Press.

Spencer, C. S., and E. M. Redmond, 2001 Multilevel selection and political evolution in the Valley of Oaxaca, 500–100 B.C. *Journal of Anthropological Archaeology* 20, 195–229.

Sugiyama, S., 1993 Worldview materialized in Teotihuacán, Mexico. *Latin American Antiquity* 4, 103–129.

Urcid, J., 1992 Zapotec hieroglyphic writing. Ph.D. dissertation, Department of Anthropology, Yale University. Ann Arbor: University Microfilms.

——1994 Un sistema de nomenclatura para los monolitos grabados y los materiales con inscripciones de Monte Albán. In *Escritura Zapoteca prehispánica*. M. Winter, ed. Pp. 53–79. Oaxaca: Contribución 4 del Proyecto Especial Monte Albán 1992–1994.

Urcid, J., M. Winter, and R. Matadamas, 1994 Nuevos monumentos grabados en Monte Albán, Oaxaca. In *Escritura Zapoteca prehispánica*. M. Winter, ed. Pp. 2–52. Oaxaca: Contribución 4 del Proyecto Especial Monte Albán 1992–1994.

Wheatley, P., 1971 *The Pivot of the Four Quarters.* Chicago: Aldine.

Winter, M., 2001 Palacios, templos y 1300 años de vida urbana en Monte Albán. In *Reconstruyendo la ciudad Maya: El urbanismo en las sociedades antiguas*. A. Ciudad Ruiz, M. J. Iglesia Ponce de Léon, and M. del Carmen Martínez Martínez, eds. Pp. 253–301. Madrid: Sociedad Española de Estudios Mayas.

Zeitlin, R. N., and A. A. Joyce, 1999 The Zapotec imperialism argument: Insights from the Oaxaca coast. *Current Anthropology* 40, 383–392.

9

The Archaeology of History in Postclassic Oaxaca

John M. D. Pohl

The historical source in which I specialize is a series of Pre-Columbian-style pictographic manuscripts or "codices" painted by the scribes of Mixtec Indian kings who dominated much of Oaxaca throughout Mesoamerica's Postclassic period from A.D. 950 to 1519. When I first began studying these remarkable books over 25 years ago as a graduate student in an interdisciplinary archaeology program, I was searching for ways to integrate approaches to the study of Pre-Columbian civilizations through archaeology, ethnohistory, and art history. I was absolutely fascinated with the way the codices portrayed a purely indigenous form of history, but I questioned how such a unique database could be employed as a predictive source of cultural behavior and tested archaeologically. The tendency at the time was for Mixtec specialists to tailor their interests according to the composition of their data, in other words the archaeologist might be interested in ceramics for the development of a chronology of culture change, the ethnohistorian might be interested in social structure, and the art historian might be interested in religion. It seemed to me that these varying approaches illuminated cultural complexity but rarely solved a joint problem. Lewis Binford always advocated that any interdisciplinary approach to archaeology would only prove effective as long as investigators were able to ask the same questions of the varying data sets (Binford 1972). I decided to direct my questions to a topic that concerned all three subdisciplines: landscape.

Codices like Nuttall and Vindobonensis contain veritable inventories of hills, plains, rivers, towns, and other landscape features. Remembering what Laura Bohannan (1952) had written about the integral connection between lineage hierarchies and territorial distribution in traditional societies, I began to work out a research design that employed a study of descent among Mixtec royal dynasties together with what appeared to be a pattern of shifting settlement distribution. The results of my study became the nucleus of a settlement pattern survey of the southern Nochixtlan Valley in which I demonstrated that what the Mixtecs celebrated as acts of world creation, cosmic war, and the miraculous deeds by divine ancestors in their codices could be understood as indigenous allegories for the actual social processes that led to the foundation of Postclassic kingdoms (Byland and Pohl 1994; Pohl and Byland 1990). In this chapter I will discuss that project and the issues that it raised among my colleagues, and then illustrate how the techniques I developed can be applied systematically to the northern end of the Nochixtlan Valley.

Dynasties and Place Signs

As I sat atop the ruins of the main pyramid at Tilantongo years ago, I kept replaying the frightening scenario over and over in my mind, trying to determine where the brutal murders might have taken place. Spread out before me were copies of ancient pictographic books called codices. I could identify the figure of Lord Eight Deer brutally assassinating his nephews in a bloody ritual before a temple. I was wondering if that event hadn't actually taken place in the very plaza before me. Lord Eight Deer, known as Yya Nacuaa in his own language, was a great conqueror and legendary hero who lived nearly a thousand years ago between A.D. 1063 and 1115. His biography is portrayed in the Mixtec codices, animal-hide religious books that contain the longest continuous history known for any American Indian civilization. The Mixtec Indian people, over whom Eight Deer ruled, occupied the rugged mountains of what is today the Mexican state of Oaxaca. They were famous for creating astounding masterpieces of art in miniature; not only the codices, but also jewelry of gold, silver, and turquoise, intricate weaving and embroidery of cotton so fine it was compared to silk, mosaics of feathers from rare tropical birds, and ornamental paintings in ceramic and fresco. Using their prowess as both artisans and warlords, the Mixtecs eventually intermarried with the royal families of the Zapotecs to the east and the Nahuas and Popolocas to the north, founding confederacies of city-states that dominated southern Mexico between A.D 1100 and 1521 (Pohl 2003a, 2003b). Fearless in defense of their mountain homeland, some Mixtec kingdoms had waged war against the later Aztec empire nearly continuously for 70 years. Today over 300,000 Mixtec people continue to live in western Oaxaca. Most lead lives as farmers growing maize, beans, and other agricultural products in much the same way as their Pre-Columbian ancestors. They are fascinated with the ruins of ancient palaces and temples and continue to invoke the legends of ancient kings and queens.

Regrettably, the Spaniards recorded little about the codices, aside from noting that they were displayed in the palaces. It was in these noble surroundings that the heroic legends were recounted by a royal poet who used the painted images to inspire his recitation during theatrical re-enactments of the events by costumed performers at royal feasts. The tales of love affairs, marriages, wars, murders, and political intrigue rival the works of Shakespeare, Sophocles, or Homer. By fortunate circumstances, eight outstanding examples of the Pre-Columbian-style codices have survived centuries of neglect following the sixteenth-century Spanish Conquest of Mexico.[1] Today these priceless artifacts are preserved in various libraries and museums around the world. My own interest in them began as a university student in archaeology. Having once worked as a staff artist for the Guthrie Theatre in Minneapolis, I was always searching for novel ways to bring the past to life through dramatic or artistic reconstructions. I was attracted to the potential of motion pictures and thought that the Mixtec pictographs were perfectly adapted to character animation. I made a short film of Eight Deer executing his nephews and showed it to several experts in the field. I was dumbfounded to learn that very little was known about where the actual events took place and decided to pursue a study of the Eight Deer saga for my graduate work.

"You can't take them seriously as real history, they have no basis in archaeological fact. They're simply fables or aristocratic propaganda!" So one professor scolded me when I proposed my dissertation topic. Fellow students could hardly believe that anyone would consider the codices as anything but cartoons. Nevertheless, I was captivated by the painted images and began to work carefully through scholarly writings on the subject by myself. The most convincing evidence that these were not fables but histories was not only the continuous 500-year chronology of events, but also the fact that Eight Deer's direct descendants were known to the Spaniards personally. It was the famous Mexican archaeologist Alfonso Caso who first proved conclusively that the eight codices were even Mixtec. In 1932 Caso had discovered a tomb in the Valley of Oaxaca that contained a Mixtec treasure of gold and other gems (Caso 1969). Most of the jewels were magnificently carved or cast with figures recognizable from the painted books. Many years later, Caso published a landmark study of a Colonial Mixtec painting on linen, the Mapa de Teozacoalco preserved at the University of Texas in Austin (Caso 1949). Caso was the first to note that the map depicted Eight Deer and his descendants up through the time of the conquest. A Spanish text identified the dynasty of the great king as that of Tilantongo, a remote village in the mountains of the Mixteca Alta. The map proved to be a Rosetta Stone for determining the location of not only Eight Deer's kingdom but even the House of Heaven symbolized by a temple with stars ornamenting its roof. Mary Elizabeth Smith, who worked closely with Caso up to his death in 1970, subsequently identified the nearby town of Jaltepec as the kingdom of Lady Six Monkey, the queen who challenged Eight Deer's right to rule (Smith 1983). It was the pioneering work of these two individuals that led me to travel to these remote mountain valleys to investigate the ruins of their ancient palaces.

After years of researching the story, I determined that the saga of Lord Eight Deer and Lady Six Monkey originated with a tragic dynastic conflict that I call the War that Came from Heaven waged over a millennium ago between A.D. 963 and 979 (Pohl 2001). This war began after the lords of two prominent royal families ruling at a place that Caso identified as Hill of the Bee, married princesses from Hill of the Sun. Apparently these alliances upset a balance of power, for shortly thereafter war broke out. There were several participating factions, including a group of people who appear as if they were made of stone. At the outbreak of the war, the Stone Men first attacked Hill of Flints, but they were repelled by the mighty Mixtec god, Lord Nine Wind. Then they attacked the palace of the royal family at Hill of the Bee, where they not only sacrificed one lord and lady, but all the male heirs to the throne as well. Two daughters, children of a second couple, were either spared or escaped the destruction of their kingdom. One princess married the king of Tilantongo while the other married the lord from a neighboring kingdom that I call Red and White Bundle for lack of a more precise identification. The dynasty of the once mighty Hill of the Bee was thereby divided between two rival families. By A.D. 1041, Tilantongo and a third kingdom, Jaltepec, had allied their royal houses through two generations of marriage leading to a period of relative peace in the region. War erupted again, however, when three princes from Jaltepec were mysteriously assassinated. We can only speculate that Tilantongo was to blame, for the Jaltepec king broke the alliance by marrying his daughter, Lady Six Monkey, to the rival king of Red and White Bundle. A young Tilantongo heir was later found dead under mysterious circumstances, either suicide or murder, thus ending the kingdom's first dynasty. Lord Eight Deer, the son of a high priest, usurped the throne of Tilantongo shortly thereafter. He spent four years carefully negotiating new alliances with the Toltec kings to the north and finally prepared to re-establish his kingdom's venerated position. By one account, war was declared in A.D. 1100, when Eight Deer's half-brother was assassinated. This time we surmise that Lady Six Monkey and her husband were to blame, for Lord Eight Deer led an assault on Red and White Bundle assassinating not only Queen Six Monkey but all of the male heirs to that kingdom, including his own nephews. He then forced their sister into marriage. By executing the last heirs to the throne of Red and White Bundle, and fusing their dynasty with his own, Eight Deer had finally destroyed Tilantongo's powerful rival, after nearly a century of regicide that began with the War that Came from Heaven. Lord Eight Deer later took several wives and had many children. By the time of the Spanish Conquest in 1521, the dynasty of Tilantongo kings was the most exalted in Oaxaca.

Aside from the place-sign identifications of Tilantongo and Jaltepec, little was known of the locations of any of the other kingdoms, particularly with regard to the remarkable accounts of the War that Came from Heaven. Caso believed that what he called Hill of the Bee, for example, was a great metropolis, yet no archaeological site as large as that was known for the Mixteca (Caso 1960). The codices had become a map for some real geographical space, yet for the most part I was at a loss to identify where that piece of geography might lie. Tracing the royal families of Tilantongo and Jaltepec back to their roots at Hill of the Bee, Hill of Flints, and Red and White Bundle, I concluded that the War that Came from Heaven and Eight Deer conflicts were for the most part very localized. This in turn meant that the settlements represented by the place signs in the codices must have been relatively small, perhaps simply elite palaces or isolated ceremonial centers and not large communities at all.

Together with Bruce Byland, I began to make settlement maps of the ruins around Tilantongo and Jaltepec (Byland and Pohl 1994; Pohl and Byland 1990). Initially I had wanted to survey the region, if for no other reason than to prove that the place signs in the codices applied to small elite estates and not entire cities as others had proposed. Before long we encountered many farmers who knew actual Mixtec names for the ruins as well as ancient legends. Some scholars think that Eight Deer may have proposed marriage to Lady Six Monkey. Indeed, he appears in the codices as if he were her consort. Others have speculated that they were lovers. One day I was showing my friend Don Crispín a picture of Eight Deer and Six Monkey together and he told me a remarkable story. There was once a Tilantongo prince who wished to be the queen of Jaltepec's lover. The queen was very fond of him as well. Unable to resolve a dispute over who among her suitors to choose, the queen directed them to gather on a mountain to the east of Tilantongo where they made a wager. He who could throw a stone farthest towards the spring where the queen was bathing would become her lover. Each stepped forward and took his turn, and, being semi-divine, many could throw their stones very far. But the king of Tilantongo was very clever. He had concealed a small gray bird in his cape and when it came to be his turn he threw the bird instead of the stone. The bird flew those many miles over the valley to exactly where the queen was bathing. The others were astounded but still fooled by the trick and so the king of Tilantongo won the bet.

The story fascinated me. Obviously the people of Tilantongo and Jaltepec had been passing on an oral tradition of Pre-Columbian legends for over 500 years that was directly related to what I was seeing in the codices. A few weeks later, my survey team encountered ruins on Hill of the Bee and found out that the site was also called Yucu Yuhua or Hill of the Enclosure, but it was the adjoining temple complex located a few hundred yards to the south that really fascinated me. I asked a farmer working nearby what he called the place. "Yucu Yoco . . . Cerro de Avispa!" he said. I looked up *yoco* in my dictionary and was surprised to see that it not only could mean *avispa* or "wasp" but also *abeja* or "bee" (Arana and Swadesh 1965:135). The name matched the place sign in the codices that marked the royal house involved in the War that Came from Heaven first identified by Caso (Fig. 9.1).

Byland and I examined ceramic collections from Hill of the Bee intently. There was nothing later than Classic period material, which meant that the noble families who first built the temple at Yucu Yoco and surrounding sites abandoned the area sometime between A.D. 950 and 1000. Significantly, that was precisely the time of the War that Came from Heaven and the destruction of Hill of the Bee in the codices. I was convinced that I was finding the actual locations portrayed in the codices. After three further field seasons of survey and excavation, Byland and I were able to identify most of the major sites involved in the War of Heaven and Eight Deer periods in the codices, including Eight Deer's palace at Tilantongo. During the Jaltepec survey, we not only discovered the ruins of the palace of Six Monkey but also other sites across from Hill of the Bee that we believe are the ruins of Red and White Bundle and Hill of Flints that were also involved in the war. By correlating our archaeological dates for the abandonment of Hill of the Bee, Hill of Flints, and Red and White Bundle with the dates for the War of Heaven and Eight Deer's conquests in the codices, an interesting conjunction in data emerged. Both the codices and archaeological reconnaissance tell us that, before A.D. 1000, powerful centers like Hill of the Bee had been ruled by multiple royal families who administered their surrounding estates and tributaries jointly. These families bound themselves together and maintained their privileged status through intermarriage. Eventually the aristocracy became quite large and kinship relations became very

(a)

(b)

complex. We know from the War that Came from Heaven story that different families then sought to better their rank by making alliances with kingdoms outside the
normal alliance scheme. Unfortunately, this practice destabilized family corporate
rule, creating internal strife, disunion, and abandonment. Today piles of stones
marking the community borders between Tilantongo and Jaltepec are set upon the
ruins of Hill of the Bee, a testimony to the outcome of the War of Heaven.

Figure 9.1. (a) The author holds an aerial photo used for creating a survey map; (b) aerial detail of the Hill of the Bee-Wasp ridge. The site is contiguous with Yucu Yuhua or Hill of the Enclosure (also known as Hill of the Bee or Hill of Chocolate). The two sites along with Huachino to the southeast and Hill of Flints located across a deep canyon to the south compose the dominant Classic or Las Flores period urban occupation of the southern Nochixtlan Valley with a population in excess of 7,000 people; (c) Hill of the Bee-Wasp as it appears in Bodley 4

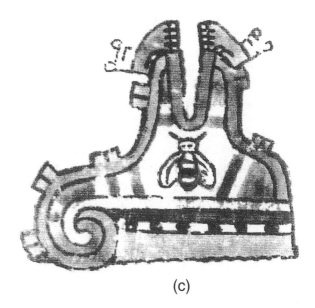

(c)

In the Realm of Eight Deer

My survey method was consistent with that of other scholars working in Mexico at the time (Blanton et al. 1982; Sanders et al. 1979). Byland and I elected to examine 100 percent of the survey area because we believed that to be able to describe adequately the ancient Mixtec social system we needed a map that would show us a complete configuration of human settlement at any one time. Crews of between three and five members systematically traversed the countryside and recorded data concerning the distribution of archaeological material on 1:5,000-scale aerial photographs. Sites were identified by artifacts and outstanding geographical features such as walls, platforms, terraces, etc. The result was a large regional map upon which we could plot settlement patterns through six major periods of cultural activity over a 3,000-year period. Over the course of five field seasons we met hundreds of Mixtec men and women who spent their days living and working in and around the ruins of ancient temples and palaces that we were mapping. Rather than make the recording of their local knowledge of place names and legends a separate task as previous scholars had done, we integrated interviews into the full-coverage survey process. The technique was especially fruitful. By stopping and talking with all the people I encountered, I incorporated every interested person into the survey process. In this way the landscape became a common framework upon which to apply an extraordinary diversity of information from archaeological, ethnohistorical, art-historical, and even ethnographic perspectives that could then be cross-referenced and scrutinized for significant social patterns extending through time.

The results of the southern Nochixtlan Valley survey were published in a book called *In the Realm of Eight Deer: The Archaeology of the Mixtec Codices* (Byland and

Pohl 1994). The reception by most of my colleagues was highly enthusiastic (Berlo 1996; Hamann 1996; Kowalewski 1997). I have responded to critics more reluctant to accept my conclusions on the localized origins of Tilantongo's dynasty in subsequent publications (Jansen 1998; Oudijk 1998a:125–126; Pohl 1999, n.d.). The differences of opinion are rooted in fundamentally different approaches. For example, one colleague expressed the opinion that scholars working in Oaxaca should be extremely cautious about using data from any other discipline but their own, warning that "one does not know all the necessary data and the publications on the particular matter are never exhaustive" (Oudijk 1998b:13). I couldn't disagree more, and argue that as a social scientist it is my responsibility to account for all of the facts that relate to a problem, not simply those which concern any single mode of inquiry, whether it be linguistic, archaeological, art-historical, ethnohistorical, or ethnographic.

A good case in point is the location of the home site of Tilantongo's original dynastic founder Lord Nine Wind Stone Skull. In Codex Bodley 4V, Nine Wind appears marrying one of Hill of the Bee's surviving daughters, Lady Five Reed, at Tilantongo. In an earlier account, however, he appears as the descendant of a marriage couple who are born from River of the Serpent. In Codex Nuttall 23 he appears as the ruler of a hill qualified by a leafy green plant. The apparent contradiction in a single lord being associated with three different place signs was resolved when I realized that the hill with the plant had been identified by Alfonso Caso (1989:91) on a pictographic manuscript from the Coixtlahuaca Valley signifying Yucu Cui or Green Mountain. Relying on a place-sign analysis alone I might have concluded that Nine Wind was from Coixtlahuaca, but then it would be very difficult to explain how he got to be ruler of Tilantongo. I might have also considered that, with a little linguistic fiddling, Yucu Cui could be interpreted as a name for Monte Alban, the ancient Zapotec capital (see Smith 1973b:205). I suppose it is possible that Monte Alban married its princes out to local Mixtec dynasties (see Jansen 1998), but archaeological interpretation depends on a good deal of common sense if nothing else, and it seems silly to resort to pure conjecture of that kind when there's a simpler explanation to be found in data related to the Tilantongo Valley itself. Yucu Cui is actually a very common place name. Given the fact that Nine Wind was living at the same time when I had documented the period of dramatic settlement shifting in the southern Nochixtlan Valley, I began to wonder if there wasn't a Classic period site located in that vicinity named Yucu Cui which would constitute a more logical place for investigation.

In reading through the Relación de Mitlantongo, a document produced by Tilantongo's neighbor to the south, I discovered that the first lord of that kingdom was named Ya Co Ñooy or Lord One Monkey and that he was said to have been born from a mountain called Yucu Cui or Green Hill (Acuña 1984:237–238). Then I remembered that Alfonso Caso had identified Lord One Monkey as Nine Wind's brother in Codex Bodley 3 IV (Caso 1960). A subsequent visit to Mitlantongo confirmed my hypothesis about Nine Wind's original home. I discovered that Yucu Cui is a promontory that marks Tilantongo's boundary with Mitlantongo, and the river running along the mountain's eastern side is called Yute Coo or Serpent River, the

Figure 9.2. (a) Lord Nine Wind appears marrying at Yucu Cui or Green Hill in Nuttall 23. The "green" in the name is symbolized by a large leafy plant; (b) Yucu Cui features a very large Classic or Las Flores period archaeological zone located on a promontory overlooking both the Tilantongo and Mitlatongo valleys. To the west, Yucu Cui descends to the Yute Coo or River of the Serpent from which Nine Wind's ancestors were magically born

(a)

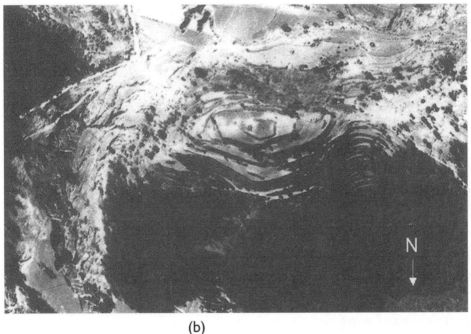

(b)

waters of which gave birth to Nine Wind's ancestors. The site itself was fascinating. Like Yucu Yoco, it featured a major temple–patio–adoratorio complex that typifies religious architecture in Oaxaca throughout the Classic period (Winter 1986) (Fig. 9.2). Here again, we see confirmation that Tilantongo's ancestors did not originate from some distant capital like Monte Alban or even Teotihuacan as some scholars have speculated, but rather they are "home-grown" divinities invoked by their descendants to make a direct connection with the ancient citadels that surrounded their domains.[2] My predictive methodology continues to work for the southern Nochixtlan Valley; can the same approach be applied to other regions as well? I believe it can, and I will now turn my attention to the northern end of the Nochixtlan Valley. Although Mixtec is not as widely spoken and there are few indigenous people who know traditional legends and place names, we have the benefit of a series of remarkable sixteenth-century testimonies in which Mixtec gods and ancestors were named, together with the principal landscape features with which they were associated.

Lord Eight Wind

A significant cycle of legends is portrayed on Codex Nuttall 1–8; these recount the saga of Lord Eight Wind. On the first two pages, Eight Wind is depicted as a patriarch who is magically born from the earth at four different locations. These include River of Plucked Feathers (Apoala), Hill of the Monkey, and Hill of the Rain God.

Eight Wind's narrative is then interrupted on Nuttall 3–4 by another rendition of the War the Came from Heaven. Here Stone Men first attack Hill of the Rain God and capture Lady Nine Monkey (see Hamann 2002 for discussion). The bloody war then rages on at Hill of the Flower where Lady Six Eagle and Lord Seven Serpent defend themselves. Next we see Lord Seven Earthquake sacrificing a Stone Man at Hill of the Jewel-Hill of Feathers followed by a sequence of additional conflicts at Black Hill by Lord Seven Wind and Lady Eight Deer, Town of Blood by Seven Wind Flint Eagle, and Feather Plain by Lord Five Dog and Lord Nine Dog. On page 4 we see three red and white striped men, personifications of stars, descending from the sky before Lady Eleven Serpent at Hill of the Ballcourt. Next Lord Four Serpent and Lord Seven Earthquake appear again, capturing two of the star warriors.

After the war is resolved, the story of Lord Eight Wind continues again on pages 5–7. On page 5, Eight Wind again emerges from the earth at two additional place signs. He is blessed by the rain god Dzahui and takes his rightful place as ruler of Hill of the Monkey–Platform of Flowers. His marriage to Lady Ten Deer produces five children. Two additional wives and seven nobles who attend the marriage are portrayed on page 6. The Eight Wind saga then concludes on pages 7–8, where the great patriarch, now a very old man, advises Prince Two Rain Ocoñaña to form a confederation of allies.

Place Signs

The key to attributing both the Eight Wind saga and an alternative portrayal of the War of Heaven to the northern Nochixtlan Valley are the place signs. M. E. Smith first identified a kingdom with which Eight Wind is associated in Codices Selden and Bodley as Suchixtlan, one of a string of communities located along the northern lower slopes of Cerro Jasmin, the enormous Classic period citadel that domi-

Figure 9.3. Cerro Jasmin rises over the town of Suchixtlan in the distance. The Colonial church of Yanhuitlan appears in the foreground

nated most of the surrounding region (Smith 1973a:79). Elsewhere, I have argued that Hill of the Monkey was connected to Cerro Jasmin (Byland and Pohl 1994:100–103). A Mixtec toponym associated with this general vicinity is Danacodzo (Terraciano 2001:110). *Da* is a corruption of *dza* meaning "place" (see Smith 1973a:42). *Na* has not been interpreted. *Codzo* means "monkey" (Smith 1973a:25; see Byland and Pohl 1994:100–103 for discussion). No other place sign containing a monkey has ever been identified in the codices. Similarly, no other toponym for *codzo* has been identified anywhere else in the Mixteca (Fig. 9.3).

Even more significant is the portrayal of Hill of the Rain God. The hill displays the frontal image of a deity with the blue, disk-shaped eyes and fanged mouth commonly associated with the Aztec rain god Tlaloc, but we know from Colonial documents that the Mixtecs called this god Dzahui (Smith 1973b:60) (Fig. 9.4a). The place sign should be translated as something like Yucu Dzahui. The largest archaeological site in the northern Nochixtlan Valley is in fact named Yucuñudahui. The term is composed of the substantives "hill" or *yucu*, and *ñu* meaning "town." *Dahui* or *dzahui* is usually translated as "mist" today, but it is clearly a dialectical variant of the name of the rain god. The appearance of the place sign with both Eight Wind and the War of Heaven in Codex Nuttall (Fig. 9.4b) is clearly a representation of the toponym for the archaeological zone (Pohl 1994:34, 52; 1995:31–34).

Yucuñudahui is located on a 400 m-high ridge lying 8 km northeast of Cerro Jasmin. The site is composed of a series of plazas, mounds, and patios running along an L-shaped ridge for approximately 1 km from west to east and then nearly 3 km from north to south. Preliminary reconnaissances were made in the 1930s by Eulalia Guzmán, Martin Bazán, and others (Guzmán 1934; Spores 1967, 1972, 1983, 1984). Alfonso Caso briefly investigated several major architectural features at the site in 1937 and recorded significant fragments of paintings and stone carvings with Late Classic Nuiñe-style glyphs (Caso 1938). No further work was done until 1966 when Ronald Spores surveyed the site. Four years later Spores excavated the remains of dwellings on the western and southern peripheries of the central ceremonial complex. Despite its prominence, Yucuñudahui was only the largest of an intensive network of Classic period sites that extended along a series of adjacent ridges from Coyotepec in the north to Yucu Ita in the south. Codex

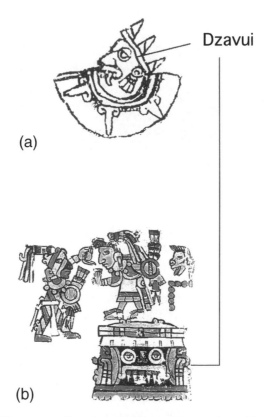

Figure 9.4. (a) The Mixtec term Dzavui as the personal name of a nobleman in Codex Muro. Dzavui is a dialectical variant of Dzahui or Sahui meaning rain god; (b) the place sign of Yucuñudahui appears in Codex Nuttall 4 where Lady Eight Monkey is captured by a Stone Man during the War of Heaven

Vindobonensis 9–10 portrays a large landscape profile that matches such a settlement system. Not only is Yucuñudahui prominently featured, but probably Coyotepec and other nearby promontories as well.

In examining the War of Heaven scenes appearing on Nuttall 2–3, I noted that Hill of the Rain God or Yucuñudahui is followed by a Hill of the Flower. While flowers frequently appear as qualifiers for place signs in the codices, this particular one can be correlated with the Mixtec term *ita* in Codex Muro (Smith 1973b:87) (Fig. 9.5(a), (b)). Hill of the Flower then should be called Yucu Ita. An archaeological site named Yucuita is located 4 km south of Yucuñudahui. Yucuita flourished throughout the Formative as one of the largest occupations in Oaxaca. Later its power was subsumed by Yucuñudahui during the Late Classic. Nevertheless, the site clearly continued to play an integral role as a secondary center within Yucuñudahui's sphere of influence. Following a preliminary reconnaissance by Ronald Spores, the site was more intensively surveyed by Marcus Winter (1982, 1989) and Patricia Plunkett (1983). Characterized by a towering conical hill con-

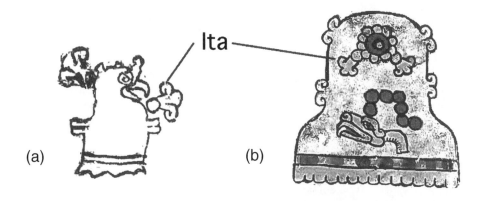

Figure 9.5. (a) The sign for *ita* or "flower" appearing as part of a compound place sign in Codex Muro; (b) Yucuita in Codex Nuttall 4; (c) a photo taken from Nochixtlan looking northwest. Yucuita is the large cone-shaped hill in the foreground. In the distance is Yucuñudahui

nected to a long narrow ridge descending to the valley floor, numerous ceremonial and residential structures were mapped over the promontory's entire extent. Excavations uncovered large fortification walls, some over 5 m high, as well as expansive networks of ceremonial platforms and plazas constructed over an ingenious system of drains and tunnels (Fig. 9.5(c)).

Even more compelling evidence that the first eight pages of Nuttall concern legends associated with the northern end of the Nochixtlan Valley is found in a remarkable series of Colonial testimonies. Between 1544 and 1546 the indigenous noblemen of Yanhuitlan, a community located 2 km north of Cerro Jasmin, were investigated by the Dominican order for practicing rituals dedicated to ancient Mixtec gods. Hoping to take advantage of political rivals, caciques from surrounding communities were quick to give testimony about the idols that they said were kept in a hidden chamber in a Yanhuitlan palace. Among the images that were specifically named were Xacuv, or Seven Earthquake, Sachi, or Seven Wind, Xio, or

Eleven Serpent, Xiq, or Ten Lizard, and Siqui, or Eleven Crocodile (Jansen 1982:283–285; Jiménez-Moreno and Mateos Higuera 1940:48; Pohl 1994:62). All five of these deities are depicted among the principal combatants in the War of Heaven portrayed in Nuttall 3–4. Lord Seven Earthquake was the hero who sacrificed the Stone Man at Hill of the Feathers-Hill of the Jewel, Lord Seven Wind was one of the defenders of Black Mountain, Lady Eleven Serpent appears at Hill of the Ballcourt. Eleven Crocodile appears by name at the same location and according to Codex Vindobonensis 3, Lady Eleven Serpent's husband was known to have been Lord Ten Lizard.

At the time of the Spanish Conquest, Yanhuitlan was regarded as the most powerful of the Postclassic kingdoms that dominated the northern end of the Nochixtlan Valley. Archaeologists have proposed it was a direct inheritor of the venerable traditions of power and authority established in this region at the Classic ceremonial centers of Cerro Jasmin, Yucuñudahui, and Yucuita some 500 years earlier (Spores 1972, 1983, 1984). We can see that this hypothesis is verified by the ethnohistorical record as well.

Having established that the Eight Wind and War of Heaven sagas portrayed in Nuttall 1–8 take place in the northern Nochixtlan Valley, it should be possible to identify other sites with which Cerro Jasmin, Yucuñudahui, and Yucuita are associated in the codices. Codex Vindobonensis features a list of over 200 place signs between pages 47 and 38. The list begins with a scene in which the creator-hero Nine Wind, Ehecatl Quetzalcoatl, stands atop Yucuñudahui and separates the sky and waters from the earth to reveal the Mixtec landscape for the first time. However, it is a second appearance of Yucuñudahui at the end of Vindobonensis 45 that particularly interests me for it is followed on pages 44 and 43 by representations of Hill of the Ballcourt, Yucuita, Hill of the Jewel, Place of Blood, and Black Mountain.

The juxtaposition of Hill of the Ballcourt with Yucuita implies that this site should also be located in the same general vicinity. Since the Vindobonensis foundation rituals can be dated to around the middle of the tenth century we would expect the site to feature a Late Classic component as well. Hill of the Ballcourt appears in the Codex de Yanhuitlan, a pictorial manuscript composed by Mixtec Indian artists of that town in early Colonial times. Jiménez Moreno and Mateos Higuera (1940:61) proposed that this was the place name for Tlachitongo or Yucu Yuhua meaning Hill of the Ballcourt in Mixtec.[3] The community is located 10 km south of Yanhuitlan. Spores identified two major Classic period hilltop sites surrounding the community that featured a series of platforms and plazas of high-quality cut stone masonry (Spores 1972:102–103). Although there were obviously many sites with ballcourts, Tlachitongo is the only place sign I am aware of in where the ballcourt is the primary qualifier for the toponym.[4]

Hill of the Jewel is more difficult to identify. It appears on Vindobonensis 45 as a compound place sign with Hill of the Feathers in much the same way as Nuttall 3. The jewel can represent either the Mixtec word *ndaa* meaning "blue" or *yusi* meaning "turquoise" (Smith 1973a:60–61). Feather, on the other hand, is possibly *yodzo*. There is no known archaeological zone that can be specifically associated with Hill of the Feathers today, but there are several archaeological zones that contain words for jewel in their place signs. Ayuxi (Place of the Jewel?) is located

1.5 km north of Yanhuitlan, but it features a largely Postclassic occupation (Spores 1972:84–85). Cerro de la Joya, on the other hand, is a smaller site occupied during both the Classic and Postclassic 1 km west of Nochixtlan (Spores 1972:129). Sayucunda (At the Foot of the Hill of the Jewel?), on the other hand, was a major Classic period site located on a hilltop 2 km south of Yucuita (Spores 1972:115). Finally, I wouldn't entirely rule out the possibility that Hill of the Jewel represents either Texupan-Ñuu Ndaa, or Teposcolula-Ñuu Yucu Ndaa, but I think Acatlan-Yucu Yusi lies too far outside the sphere of influence of the region under discussion (see Smith 1973a:40, 60–61).[5]

Hill of the Place of Blood and Black Hill have also proven more difficult to identify. No known toponym for Place of Blood has ever been identified in the northern Nochixtlan Valley. Black Hill, on the other hand, may refer to Tliltepec or Yucu Tnoo, a community located 5 km south of Yanhuitlan. A series of sites surrounding the modern community appears to have been densely occupied from Classic through Postclassic times (Spores 1972:94–95). It is worth noting in this regard that the defendants in the Yanhuitlan idolatry trials were accused of making sacrifices and carrying out other rites on hilltops at Tiltepec. Yucu Tnoo is also the name of a significant portion of the archaeological zone of Yucuñudahui. This is a less likely candidate given the obvious separation that is portrayed between the Black Hill under discussion and Yucuñudahui in the place sign lists, however. Vindobonensis 5 illustrates a broad landscape profile that not only includes Yucuñudahui but the associated Yucu Tnoo, Coyotepec, and other locations in the surrounding vicinity of the great capital.

There are other place signs that may refer to significant occupations in the northern Nochixtlan Valley even though they do not play a specific role in the War of Heaven scenes. Some display qualifiers that are compounded with the place signs that we have just examined, suggesting that they are located in the same region. For example, Hill of the Place of Blood is ornamented with an unusual lattice work that appears as part of Hill of the Mosquito in Nuttall 38. Likewise, Hill of the Mosquito appears just to the right of Hill of the Place of Blood in the Vindobonensis 43 place-sign list as well. Hill of the Mosquito probably represents Sayultepec. Its Mixtec name, Yucutiyuq, means Hill of the Fly or Mosquito in Mixtec, but the adjoining community of Tillo should not be ruled out either (Alvarado 1962:152[v]; Bradomín 1992:113). Tillo is a corruption of Tiyoho or "flea," but the insect under discussion here does not appear very flea-like. A major archaeological zone of both Classic and Postclassic period extends across three hills surrounding the present-day community of Sayultepec (Spores 1972:150–152). The densest concentration of Classic period material was found at site N-807 alongside a road that joins Sayultepec to the neighboring community of Chindua lying 2 km to the southwest. Tillo is located 2.5 km to the northwest. Like Sayultepec, both a Classic and Postclassic occupation extends over a series of small hills surrounding the present community.

On both Nuttall 38 and Vindobonensis 42, Hill of the Mosquito appears with a hill or ravine qualified by a spider web. The spider web is an unusual place-sign qualifier and most likely refers to either Andua or Chindua, two communities that border both Sayultepec and Tillo. The question is: Which one? Andua was known as Tocatzahualla or Place of the Spider Web in the Nahua language, while Chindua was known as Tocatzahualtongo or Little Place of the Spider Web (Jiménez Moreno and Mateos Higuera 1940:3, 6, 87). The Mixtec *a* means "place" and *chindu* means mound, but *ndua* can be a contraction of either *nduhua*, meaning "spider web," or *nduvua*, meaning "arrow." We know that Andua is portrayed as Place of the Arrow in Colonial Mixtec documents (Smith 1983:252).[6] A Hill of the Arrow also appears in the Vindobonensis 44–43 place-sign list as well. It seems most likely then that Mixtec artists chose to differentiate Chindua from Andua with spider web and arrow qualifiers respectively.[7] Major occupations are found on ridges surrounding both Andua and Chindua (Spores 1972:102–103, 151). For the most part these are systems of dense Classic to Postclassic occupations that flow into the neighboring zones associated with Tlachitongo to the east and Sayultepec to the west.

There are three other place signs that appear on Vindobonensis 43 which could also represent identifiable locations in the northern end of the Nochixtlan Valley: Place of the Cactus, Ravine of the Conch Shell, and Rock of the Eagle. Place of the Cactus appears in Vindobonensis 43 next to Yucuita. The only known site that features a cactus as a place-sign qualifier is Nochixtlan or Atoco, Place of the Nopal Cactus (see Smith 1973a:42 for discussion). Nochixtlan is located 4 km southeast of Yucuita, but any archaeological site directly associated with this location would be buried under the modern town.

Ravine of the Conch Shell is composed of two hills between which is set a shell of the style used for Pre-Columbian trumpets. It appears on Vindobonensis 44 to the right of Hill of the Arrows. It also appears on another major landscape profile that features Yucuñudahui. Spores identified a major archaeological zone extending between Yanhuitlan and Yucuñudahui called La Concha (the Conch Shell). The place sign for Ravine of the Conch is paired in both appearances with a ritual staff ornamented with a ball of red feathers. The staff may represent a variant of the place sign for Topiltepec, meaning Hill of the Staff. There is a problem, however, in that Topiltepec is located 8 km south of La Concha. Either there is another name for the staff which is now lost but which applied to a part of the La Concha site, or Ravine of the Conch Shell is actually located near Topiltepec. Finally, Vindobonensis 43 portrays Rock of the Eagle in association with several of the place signs that I have discussed above. It is worth noting that Smith (1988:696–710) proposed that a very similar Rock of the Eagle appears in Codex Selden as a location 4 km south of Sayultepec near the town of Etlatongo (Fig. 9.6)

Summary

In this discussion I have demonstrated that the Eight Wind and War of Heaven sagas appearing in Nuttall 1–8 concern people and places associated with the Las Flores or Late Classic period of settlement in the northern Nochixtlan Valley. At the very least Yucuñudahui and Yucuita can be positively identified. Hill of the Monkey still needs some work, but there is little doubt that it is a part of Cerro Jasmin. Other sites are somewhat more tentative.

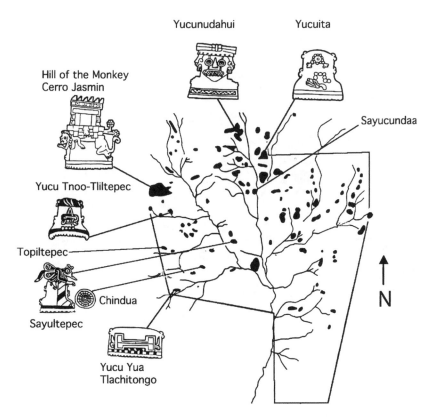

Figure 9.6. Classic or Las Flores occupation of the northern Nochixtlan valley showing the locations of prominent place signs discussed in the text. Map based on survey maps by Ronald Spores

At the risk of over-extending my data and opening myself up to colleagues who might criticize the less secure identifications and thereby throw the baby out with the bathwater, I have made several tentative suggestions for the locations of other place signs with which Yucuñudahui and Yucuita are associated. I argue that these are not based on any single-instance appearances but rather on significant place-sign clusters that closely match both the names and locations of settlements in and around the Yanhuitlan area. Finally, we know that creation heroes associated with these archaeological sites and the place signs with which they are correlated were specifically invoked as the "gods" of Yanhuitlan by that kingdom's Postclassic and Colonial caciques (Fig. 9.7).

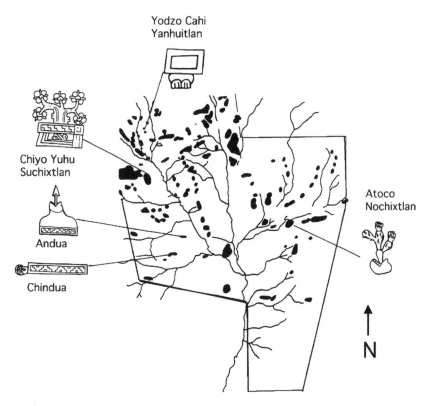

Figure 9.7. Postclassic or Natividad occupation of the northern Nochixtlan Valley showing place-sign shifting consistent with political dynamics in codices and other ethnohistoric sources. Map based on survey maps by Ronald Spores

NOTES

1 Eight principal examples are preserved in various institutions throughout Europe and Mexico: Codices Zouche-Nuttall and Egerton (British Museum, London); Codices Bodley and Selden (Bodleian Library, Oxford); Codex Vindobonensis (National Bibliotek, Vienna); Codex Colombino* (Museo Nacional de Antropología, Mexico City); Codices Becker I* and II (Museum für Völkerkunde, Vienna). *Colombino and Becker I are two parts of the same manuscript.

2 Despite overwhelming archaeological and ethnohistorical evidence to the contrary, some scholars have persisted in attributing creation legends in codices to exotic places and peoples other than the Mixtecs themselves. Their theories are not only conjectural but also counter-intuitive. For example, in a strange reversal of much of his earlier work, Jansen advocates that the codices are not really concerned with local Mixtec history at all, but rather portray a kind of national Mexican history in which leaders like Eight Deer are reduced to serving as minor attendants to larger-than-life heroes like Nacxit of Tula or the Maya Captain Sun of Chichen Itza. Clearly more interested in trying to aggran-

dize Mixtec history by associating place signs with world-renowned archaeological sites rather than actual Mixtec communities, Jansen goes on to proclaim, erroneously, that Monte Alban is the source of Tilantongo's dynastic heritage, with Eight Deer and Lady Six Monkey battling one another at the ancient Zapotec capital for control of the Toltec copper trade (Jansen 1998). Karl Taube (2000:314) proposed that a place sign in Nuttall 17 is a depiction of the Ciudadela at Teotihuacan even though we know that the individuals involved in the ceremony taking place there are the gods and ancestors of local Mixtec dynasties. Anne-Marie Vié-Wohrer (1989, 1999) and Carmen Aguilera (2002) put the kingdom of Red and White Bundle conquered by Eight Deer in Guerrero and Morelos respectively. In fact Colonial manuscripts, maps, and lienzos, the "Rosetta stones" of historical and dynastic research in codex studies, are explicit in emphasizing the local territorial concerns of Mixtec dynastic history (Smith 1973a). Although some neighboring kingdoms such as Cholula and Zaachila might appear occasionally in reference to Mixtec alliances with the Tolteca-Chichimeca or the Zapotecs, the actual scope of events is decidedly focused on the Mixteca itself.

3   Tlachitongo also appears in Mixtec as Yucu Yua, meaning Hill of Ice (see Bradomín 1992:254). However, this is a very common translation for what is more correctly *yuhua* by Mixtec farmers today. I have encountered it in my own survey of the Tilantongo Valley in relation to Yucu Yua as Hill of the Enclosure or Fortification Wall (Byland and Pohl 1994:100).

4   For example, Hill of the Monkey is portrayed with a ballcourt as a place-sign qualifier on Nuttall 1.

5   The fact that some of the place signs might be associated with Teposcolula rather than the Nochixtlan Valley proper doesn't bother me. Teposcolula is an easy stretch over a single mountain ridge. Tlachitongo is actually affiliated with Teposcolula even though it sits on the edge of the Nochixtlan Valley. We also know that the community of Chachoapan contains the Nahuatl term *chalchihuitl* or jewel. However, its Mixtec name is Yuta Ñani, which translates as River of the Brothers (Smith 1983:249). It is possible that Chachoapan had another name in Mixtec that contained a word for jewel at one time. Constructed along the southern slopes of Yucuñudahui, Chachoapan was a Postclassic successor to the power manifested in the great citadel during the Classic (Lind 1979). The 1544–46 Inquisition revealed that the lords of Yanhuitlan held a celebration each year at a hill lying adjacent to Chachoapan, which featured voladors, or fliers, who swung down on ropes from poles planted firmly in the ground, possibly a reference to rituals celebrating the War of Heaven or the descent of the first priests with sacred bundles from the sky (Jiménez Moreno and Mateos Higuera 1940:39).

6   Cobweb also appears as *duva* in Codex Muro (Smith 1973b:78).

7   Taube (1983) has identified a symbolic connection between the spider web and the arrow in Pre-Columbian iconography in general which may underlie the Mixtecs' decision to use the two qualifiers synonymously. A Yanhuitlan lord who reputedly fought against the Aztecs was named Lord Three Monkey (Herrera 1945:170). However, Lord Three Monkey appears as a ruler of Place of the Spider Web in Codex Bodley 17 IV, suggesting that the original location of Yanhuitlan's dynasty was Chindua. A possible variant of the Andua place sign may confirm late Postclassic origins for Yanhuitlan's dynasty as well. Examining a document in the National Archives of Mexico, Caso (1966) noted that the grandparents of the famous Colonial Cacique of Yanhuitlan, Don Gabriel de Guzmán, were named Namahu (or Eight Death) and Cauaco (or One Flower). Lord Eight Death and Lady One Flower appear in Codex Bodley 19 III seated on a place sign consisting of a feather mat or "plain" substantive qualified by a bird beak that ends in arrow points.

236

At least one Colonial land document gives an alternative name for Andua (or Place of the Arrow) as Zandua (Spores and Saldaña 1976:28). We have seen that *ndua* means "arrow." Smith (1973a:42) proposed that *a* meaning "place" is ordinarily symbolized by a human chin in pictographs. *Za*, on the other hand, may be a contraction of *dzaa* meaning "bird", hence the usage of the bird beak with arrow is depicted in the Bodley example to signify Andua's alternative name.

REFERENCES

Acuña, R., ed., 1984 *Relaciones geográficas del siglo XVI: Antequera*, vol. 2. Mexico: Universidad Nacional Autónoma de México.

Aguilera, C., 2002 Descubriendo a un niño sol. *Arqueología Mexicana* 10(55), 58–63.

Alvarado, F. de, 1962 *Vocabulario en lengua Mixteca: Reproducción facsimilar con un estudio de Wigberto Jiménez Moreno*. Mexico: Instituto Nacional Indigenista e Instituto Nacional de Antropología e Historia.

Arana, E., and M. Swadesh, 1965 *Los elementos del Mixteco antiguo*. Mexico: Instituto Nacional Indigenista e Instituto Nacional de Antropología e Historia.

Berlo, J. C., 1996 Review of *In the Realm of Eight Deer: The Archaeology of the Mixtec Codices* by Bruce E. Byland and John M. D. Pohl. *Latin American Research Review* 31, 263–264.

Binford, L., 1972 *An Archaeological Perspective*. New York: Seminar Press.

Blanton, R., S. Kowalewski, G. Feinman, and J. Appel, 1982 *Monte Albán's Hinterland*, part 1: *Prehispanic Settlement Patterns of the Central and Southern Parts of the Valley of Oaxaca, Mexico*. Memoirs of the Museum of Anthropology 15. Ann Arbor: University of Michigan.

Bohannan, L., 1952 A genealogical charter. *Africa* 22, 301–315.

Bradomín, José María, 1992 *Toponimia de Oaxaca*, 3rd edn. Oaxaca, Mexico: no publisher given.

Byland, B. E., and J. M. D. Pohl, 1994 *In the Realm of Eight Deer: The Archaeology of the Mixtec Codices*. Norman: University of Oklahoma Press.

Caso, A. 1938 *Exploraciones en Oaxaca: Quinto y sexta temporadas, 1936–1937*. Publication 34. Mexico: Instituto Panamericano de Geografía e Historia.

Caso, A., 1949 El mapa de Teozacoalco. *Cuadernos Americanos* 8(5), 145–181.

——1960 *Interpretation of the Codex Bodley 2858*. Mexico: Sociedad Mexicana de Antropología.

——1966 The lords of Yanhuitlan. In *Ancient Oaxaca*. J. Paddock, ed. Pp. 313–335. Stanford: Stanford University Press.

——1969 *El tesoro de Monte Albán, México*. Mexico: Instituto Nacional de Antropología.

——1989 *Alfonso Caso: De la arqueología a la antropología*. Mexico: Universidad Nacional Autónoma de México.

Guzmán, E., 1934 Exploración arqueológica en la Mixteca. *Anales del Museo Nacional de Arqueología, Historia, y Etnografía* 5(1), 17–42.

Hamann, B. E., 1996 Review of *In the Realm of Eight Deer: The Archaeology of the Mixtec Codices* by Bruce E. Byland and John M. D. Pohl. *The Nahua Newsletter* 21, 26–30.

——2002 The social life of pre-sunrise things. *Current Anthropology* 43, 351–362.

Herrera, A. de, 1945 *Historia general de los hechos de los Castellanos, en las islas, y tierra-firme de el mar océano*, vol. 4. Buenos Aires: Editorial Guarania.

Jansen, Maarten E. R. G. N., 1982 *Huisi Tacu: estudio interpretativo de un libro mixteco antiguo: Codex Vindobonensis Mexicanus*. Incidentele Publicaties CEDLA 24. Amsterdam: Centrum voor Studie en Documentatie van Latijns Amerika.

——1998 Monte Albán y Zaachila en los códices Mixtecos. In *The Shadow of Monte Albán: Politics and Historiography in Postclassic Oaxaca, México*. M. Jansen, P. Kröfges, and M. R. Oudijk, eds. Pp. 67–122. Leiden: Research School CNWS, School of Asian, African and Amerindian Studies.

Jiménez-Moreno, W., and S. Mateos Higuera, 1940 *Códice de Yanhuitlan*. Mexico: Museo Nacional del Instituto Nacional de Antropología e Historia.

Kowalewski, S. A., 1997 Review of *In the Realm of Eight Deer: The Archaeology of the Mixtec Codices* by Bruce E. Byland and John M. D. Pohl. *Latin American Antiquity* 8, 157–158.

Lind, M., 1979 *Postclassic and Early Colonial Houses in the Nochixtlan Valley, Oaxaca*. Publications in Anthropology 23. Nashville, TN: Vanderbilt University.

Oudjik, M. R., 1998a The genealogy of San Lucas Quiaviní. In *The Shadow of Monte Albán: Politics and Historiography in Postclassic Oaxaca, Mexico*. M. Jansen, P. Kröfges, and M. R. Oudijk, eds. Pp. 123–137. Leiden: Research School CNWS, School of Asian, African and Amerindian Studies.

——1998b The genealogy of Zaachila: Four weddings and a dynastic struggle. In *The Shadow of Monte Albán: Politics and Historiography in Postclassic Oaxaca, Mexico*. M. Jansen, P. Kröfges, and M. R. Oudijk, eds. Pp. 13–35. Leiden: Research School CNWS, School of Asian, African and Amerindian Studies.

Plunkett, P., 1983 An intensive survey in the Yucuita sector of the Nochixtlan Valley, Oaxaca, Mexico. Ph.D. dissertation, Tulane University. Ann Arbor: University Microfilms.

Pohl, J. M. D., 1994 *Codex Zouche-Nuttall: Mixtec Pictographic Writing Workshop Book #1*. Austin: Department of Art, University of Texas.

——1995 *Codex Vindobonensis: Mixtec Pictographic Writing Workshop Book #2*. Austin: Department of Art, University of Texas.

——1999 Review of *The Shadow of Monte Albán: Politics and Historiography in Postclassic Oaxaca* by M. Jansen, P. Krófes and M. R. Oudijk. *Latin American Antiquity* 10, 317–318.

——2001 *The Legend of Lord Eight Deer: An Epic of Ancient Mexico*. Oxford: Oxford University Press.

——2003a Creation stories, hero cults, and alliance building: Postclassic confederacies of central and southern Mexico from A.D. 1150–1458. In *The Postclassic Mesoamerican World System*. M. Smith and F. Berdan, eds. Salt Lake City: University of Utah Press.

——2003b Royal marriage and confederacy building among the eastern Nahuas, Mixtecs, and Zapotecs. In *The Postclassic Mesoamerican World System*. M. Smith and F. Berdan, eds. Salt Lake City: University of Utah Press.

——n.d. The lintel painting of the Arroyo Palace Group at Mitla: The lintel paintings of Mitla, part 2. Prepared for a forthcoming volume dedicated to manuscript studies in honor of M. E. Smith. E. Boone, ed. New Orleans: Middle American Research Institute, Tulane University.

Pohl, J. M. D., and B. E. Byland, 1990 Mixtec landscape perception and archaeological settlement patterns. *Ancient Mesoamerica* 1, 113–131.

Sanders, W. T., J. Parsons, and R. Santley, 1979 *The Basin of Mexico: Ecological Processes in the Evolution of a Civilization*. New York: Academic Press.

Smith, M. E., 1973a *Picture Writing from Ancient Southern Mexico: Mixtec Place Signs and Maps*. Norman: University of Oklahoma Press.

——1973b The relationship between Mixtec manuscript painting and the Mixtec language: A study of some personal names in Codices Muro and Sánchez Solís. In *Dumbarton Oaks*

Conference on Mesoamerican Writing Systems. E. Benson, ed. Pp. 47–98. Washington, DC: Dumbarton Oaks.

—— 1983 Codex Selden: A manuscript from the Valley of Nochixtlan? In *The Cloud People: Divergent Evolution of the Zapotec and Mixtec Civilizations*. K. Flannery and J. Marcus, eds. Pp. 248–255. New York: Academic Press.

—— 1988 It doesn't amount to a hill of beans: The frijol motif in Mixtec place signs. In *Smoke and Mist: Mesoamerican Studies in Memory of Thelma D. Sullivan*. J. Kathryn Josserand and Karen Dakin eds. Pp. 696–710. BAR International Series 402(2). Oxford: British Archaeological Reports.

Spores, R., 1967 *The Mixtec Kings and their People*. Norman: University of Oklahoma Press.

—— 1972 *An Archaeological Settlement Survey of the Nochixtlan Valley, Oaxaca*. Publications in Anthropology 1. Nashville, TN: Vanderbilt University.

—— 1983 Yucuñudahui. In *The Cloud People: Divergent Evolution of the Zapotec and Mixtec Civilizations*. K. Flannery and J. Marcus, eds. Pp. 155–157. New York: Academic Press.

—— 1984 *The Mixtecs in Ancient and Colonial Times*. Norman: University of Oklahoma Press.

Spores, Ronald, and Miguel Saldana, 1976 *Documentos para la etnohistoria del estado de Oaxaca: índice del Ramo de Tributos del Archivo General de la Nación, México*. Vanderbilt Publications in Anthropology 17. Nashville, TN: Vanderbilt University, Department of Sociology and Anthropology.

Taube, K., 1983 The Teotihuacan Spider Woman. *Journal of Latin American Lore* 9, 107–189.

—— 2000 The turquoise hearth: Fire self-sacrifice and the central Mexican cult of war. In *Mesoamerica's Classic Heritage: Teotihuacan to the Aztecs*. D. Carrasco, L. Jones, and S. Sessions, eds. Pp. 269–340. Niwot, CO: University Press of Colorado.

Terraciano, K., 2001 *The Mixtecs of Colonial Oaxaca: Ñudzahui History, Sixteenth through Eighteenth Centuries*. Stanford: Stanford University Press.

Vié-Wohrer, A. M., 1989 Glyphes toponymiques porteurs d'éléments determinatifs de Xipe Totec dans "Codex Nuttall." In *Descifre de las escrituras mesoamericanas: Códices, pinturas, estatuas, cerámic*. J. Galarza, U. de Silvestri, R. Goin-Langevin, J. González Aragón, and M. Thouvenot, eds. Pp. 281–312. British Archaeological Reports, International Series 518. Oxford.

—— 1999 *Xipe Totec, notre seigneur l'Ecorché*. Mexico: Centre français d'études mexicaines et centraméricaines.

Winter, M., 1982 *Guía zona arqueológica de Yucuita*. Oaxaca: Centro Regional de Oaxaca, Instituto Nacional de Antropología e Historia.

—— 1986 Templo–patio–adoratorio: Un conjunto arquitectónico no-residencial en el Oaxaca prehispánico. *Cuadernos de Arquitectura Mesoamericana* 7, 51–59.

—— 1989 *Oaxaca: The Archaeological Record*. Mexico: Editorial Minutiae Mexicana.

10

Meaning by Design: Ceramics, Feasting, and Figured Worlds in Postclassic Mexico

Elizabeth M. Brumfiel

> There was singing. . . . There was the giving of pleasure. . . . And some did nothing else but sit content and rejoicing, laughing and making witty remarks, making others burst into laughter . . . (Sahagún 1950–1982: bk. 4:119)

How did people decide to act in ancient Mexico? What criteria guided their behavior? How were their ideas determined by existing cultural principles and by changes in economic and political structure? In this chapter I will argue that, among other ways, the people of ancient Mesoamerica expressed their understanding of the world around them in the designs painted on ceramic vessels. An analysis of ceramic designs reveals frameworks of meaning that people used to choose their action. Differences in the decorated ceramics of the Early, Middle, and Late Postclassic periods in the Basin of Mexico suggest how these frameworks of meaning varied in response to economic and political change.

Postclassic Mexico

The Postclassic era includes the last six centuries of Mexican prehistory. It began in A.D. 900, a time when the political power of classic Teotihuacan was completely dissipated, and it ended in A.D. 1521 with the Spanish Conquest. During the Postclassic, central Mexico was filled with scores of autonomous petty kingdoms, each with a population of 5,000 to 50,000 people and an area of 80 to 200 km² (Sanders et al. 1979:151–152). Each kingdom centered on a principal town which contained the palace of the local hereditary ruler, a temple complex, a marketplace, and some commoners' residences. The town was surrounded by subject villages and hamlets inhabited by lower-ranking nobles and commoners. Rulers and nobles were supported by the produce of tribute fields, cultivated for them by their commoner sub-

Date A.D.	Phase	Ceramic types	Major sites
1521 1430	Late Postclassic	Aztec III and IV Black-on-Orange Red ware	Tenochtitlan
1300	Middle Postclassic	Aztec II Black-on-Orange Red Ware	Xaltocan (and others)
1200 1100	Early-to-Middle Postclassic transition	Aztec I and II Black-on-Orange Chalco-Cholula Polychrome Cane-incised Red Ware	
1000 900	Early Postclassic	Lake system and S. Basin: Aztec I Black-on-Orange Chalco-Cholula Polychrome Northern Basin: Mazapan Toltec Red-on-Buff	Cholula Culhuacan Tula

Figure 10.1. Dates, phases, ceramic types, and major sites discussed in the text

jects. Commoners supported themselves by farming and craft production. Commoners also performed domestic service in the palaces of the elite and served as soldiers in time of war (Carrasco 1978; Hicks 1982, 1986).

In the Basin of Mexico, the Postclassic era is divided into three periods: the Early, Middle, and Late Postclassic periods (Fig 10.1). The Early Postclassic was a relatively quiet period. The basin contained about a dozen petty states, and population densities were low. Two important urban centers lay just outside the basin: Tula to the northwest and Cholula to the southeast. Apparently, the basin served as a hinterland, or a buffer zone, for these major centers (Sanders et al. 1979:137–149). Culhuacan (whose pottery is discussed below) was one of the most important kingdoms in the Postclassic Basin of Mexico, and it was probably occupied during the Early Postclassic.[1]

The Middle Postclassic was an era of political instability and conflict. According to the native histories of central Mexico, the twelfth through fourteenth centuries were years of intense dynastic competition within petty kingdoms and chronic warfare between them (Brumfiel 1983). The fortunes of the 14 kingdoms in the Basin of Mexico rose and fell, as alliances were forged and broken. Xaltocan (whose pottery is discussed below) was an important regional center from A.D. 1200 to 1400 (Brumfiel in press).

The Late Postclassic coincides with the Aztec empire. The Aztec empire was a military alliance created in 1430 by the rulers of three petty kingdoms: Tenochtitlan, Texcoco, and Tlacopan. In nearly a century of continuous warfare, this alliance established its dominance over all the kingdoms in central Mexico and extended its domain from the Gulf of Mexico to the Pacific Coast and from central Mexico to the Isthmus of Tehuantepec. At its height in 1519, the Aztec empire encompassed 200,000 km^2, with a population of 6 million people (Armillas 1964:324). In fierce battle, the Aztecs were defeated by the Spanish conquistadors and their Indian allies in 1521.

Pottery styles provide very convenient indicators of these time periods. During each period, potters produced vessels using a range of conventional techniques, shapes, and design motifs. These conventions changed over time, making pottery styles or types good indicators of the times when they were manufactured and used. Archaeologists use changing pottery types to identify sites and occupation levels within sites as belonging to the Early, Middle, and Late Postclassic periods (Griffin and Espejo 1947, 1950; Noguera 1932; Parsons 1966; Parsons et al. 1996). Post-classic pottery types will be described in some detail later in this chapter.

In addition to using pottery to date sites, archaeologists have used pottery for many other purposes: to identify archaeological "cultures" or ethnic groups, to plot trade patterns, to study the distribution of wealth in society, and to measure the intensity of political competition (e.g., Brumfiel 1987; Garraty 2000; Hodge and Minc 1990; Nichols et al. 2002; Smith 1984, 1987). Only rarely have archaeologists used ceramics to understand native world views (Vega 1984). And yet, in Postclassic Mesoamerica, this type of analysis is potentially very useful. Ceramic designs can reveal the frameworks of meaning that prehistoric people used to understand the world around them and to define their goals. Ceramics were used in household feasts, and in Postclassic Mexico these feasts were important occasions for learning and shaping cultural meanings and values. It is to feasts and figured worlds that we now turn.

Ceramics, Feasting, and Figured Worlds

In recent years, the economic and political dimensions of feasting have become popular topics of study by archaeologists (Bender 1985; Brumfiel 1987; Clark and Blake 1994; Dietler 1996; Dietler and Hayden 2001; Friedman 1975; Gero 1992; Godelier 1977; Hayden 1990, 1995,1996; Sherratt 1987). But the cultural consequences of feasting have not been extensively explored. This is unfortunate because feasts are an important locus of cultural production. Feasts provide hosts and guests with opportunities to hammer out the common values, norms and understandings that organize their actions. Feasts provide occasions for learning and shaping the frames of meaning and value around which people construct their lives, frames of meaning that Dorothy Holland and her colleagues (1998) call "figured worlds."

At the heart of figured worlds are narratives, stories which are peopled by stereo-typical characters, activities, and artifacts. The plot lines of these stories establish expectations for how particular types of real-world events ought to unfold and how they do unfold. Thus, they establish contexts for interpreting real-world speech and action. These stories also guide people's aspirations and feelings of self-worth.

People assume the roles of characters within these figured worlds, and their desires become tied to the goals of these worlds and their rules. Figured worlds channel agency, but they also provide a platform for the exercise of agency. As individuals master the skills and knowledge associated with a figured world, they frequently innovate behavior and manipulate social interaction so as to advance their own ends (Holland et al. 1998).

Feasts are popular venues for learning and shaping figured worlds. This is because feasts attract crowds. Feasts bring together critical masses of knowledge-able practitioners so that figured worlds can be evoked. Furthermore, feasts are a sensuous activity. Taste, smell, and bodily sensation give an aura of substance to otherwise imagined worlds (Kus 1992). In addition, feast foods are derived from plant and animal species which are rich in symbolic meanings suited to a range of metaphoric statements (Douglas 1966; Lévi-Strauss 1962). Finally, in Central Mexico especially, feasting was, and is, a central metaphor for sociability. Giving one's food to others is considered the ultimate altruistic act, the act upon which all enduring human relationships are based (Monaghan 1955:37).

Can these figured worlds be studied by archaeologists working in the prehistoric past? Perhaps they can. DeMarrais et al. (1996) point out that cultural ideas are forceful only when they are given suitable material expression. Holland et al. agree, emphasizing the dependence of figured worlds upon artifacts. Artifacts are "the means by which figured worlds are evoked, collectively developed, individually learned, and made socially and personally powerful" (Holland et al. 1998:610). If feasts are a primary locus for the construction of figured worlds, then the serving vessels used in feasts might communicate narratives which are central to those figured worlds. Pliant in form and having surfaces which can bear plastic or painted designs, ceramics can be made to embody what Joyce (1996:176–178), citing Barthes (1977), calls the "pregnant moment," a static image that recalls an entire narrative by evoking the actions that led up to and followed from the moment that is captured in the image.

Because feasting was very popular in Postclassic Mesoamerica, the possibilities of using ceramics to reconstruct the figured worlds of Postclassic Mesoamerica seem especially great. Feasting occurred at many levels of society in a wide variety of social contexts. According to the ethnohistoric sources, both commoners and elites used feasts to mark the births, marriages, and deaths of household members (Sahagún 1950–1982: bk. 4:97, 122, bk. 8:129–130; Durán 1967: II:123, 297; Durán 1971:122). Feasts were also held in homes and palaces on many religious occasions, including some celebrations in the solar calendar, some sacrifices to patron deities, and upon the successful completion of religious vows (Sahagún 1950–1982: bk. 2:49, 84, 153, 160, bk. 4:56, 87, bk. 9:48). Archaeologically, exten-sive feasting at all levels of society resulted in the use and discard of large amounts of decorated pottery. At Postclassic sites in the Basin of Mexico, decorated serving vessels constitute more than 30 percent of all ceramic material (Brumfiel 1987, in press; Evans 1988).

Feast sponsors controlled the types of ceramics they used in feasts. Because ceramics were made by craft specialists who sold their products in the marketplace

(Sahagún 1950–1982: bk. 10:83), consumers could always choose the kinds of vessels that they wished to purchase. Chemical analyses of the clays used in Post-classic ceramics from the Basin of Mexico show that the ceramics at any individual site represent a number of different production centers, which indicates the existence of consumer choice (Nichols et al. 2002; see Chapter 11). Given this choice, feast sponsors could acquire the decorated ceramics that best expressed the collective understandings that gave meaning to their lives.

Postclassic Mexico was rich in visual symbolism. Symbolically complex designs appeared not only on ceramics, but on textiles, war shields, mural paintings, sculpture, and pictorial documents. Moreover, texts from the early colonial period provide guidance for the meaning of many of these symbols. This symbolic wealth makes it possible to work across media and with surviving texts to decipher a number of the key narratives that guided people's understandings, values, and decision-making.

In the remainder of this chapter we will examine the symbolism of pottery from three different locales. First, we will examine symbolism at El Volador, a Late Post-classic cache of ceramics from the heart of the Aztec capital, Tenochtitlan. We begin with the Late Postclassic material because these designs can be most confidently interpreted using pictorial documents and written descriptions of Aztec culture dating from just after the Spanish Conquest. Second, we turn to ceramics recovered from (presumably) domestic contexts in Early/Middle Postclassic Culhuacan. The differences between these ceramics and those from El Volador suggest a basically different world-view in pre-imperial Mexico. Third, we examine a cache of ceramics accompanying a Middle Postclassic burial at Xaltocan. These ceramics suggest that a world-view emphasizing warfare and human sacrifice was not the invention of the Late Postclassic Aztecs. This militaristic world-view was popular in Xaltocan during its political ascendance in the Middle Postclassic, but it lost popularity when Xaltocan was subordinate the Aztecs. Thus, the ceramic data suggest a link between identity, agency, and world-views on the one hand and wider economic and political circumstances on the other.

From Ceramic Types to Figured Worlds: Methodological Strategies

In moving from ceramic types to figured worlds, archaeologists can examine five dimensions of variation.

The first is design motif. Pictorial documents accompanied by Spanish glosses enable archaeologists to identify some design motifs. For example, the glyphs associated with the 260-day ritual almanac are named in several early colonial documents (e.g. Berdan and Anawalt 1992: III:10; Boone and Nuttall 1983: II:9–11; Quiñones 1995:19). The Codex Magliabecchiano provides the names of textile designs (Boone and Nuttall 1983: II:3–9). The Codex Mendoza includes many place glyphs and associated place names (Berdan 1992). The Matrícula de Tributos provides names for the costumes worn by Aztec warriors (Anawalt 1992). Finally, specialized studies of particular domains of Postclassic culture have

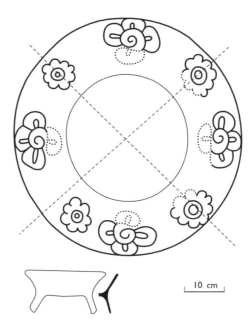

Figure 10.2. Aztec IV Black-on-Orange tripod dish from the Basin of Mexico with design motifs distributed in the four quarters of the vessel (after Vega 1984: Lámina 2)

isolated the symbols that represented these domains. For example, Anawalt (1993) describes the symbolism attached to *pulque,* the principal intoxicant of Central Mexico, made by fermenting parts of the maguey plant.

The second aid to identifying the narratives communicated by Postclassic ceramics is design composition. Vega (1984) demonstrates that the decoration on Late Postclassic vessels is organized in quadripartite patterns, with design motifs distributed symmetrically in the four quarters of the vessels (Fig. 10.2). These quadrants, Vega argues, represent the four quarters of the universe, which are defined by the points where the sun rises and sets at the summer and solstices. Thus, she concludes, the composition of Late Postclassic vessels indicates an awareness of and concern for solar cycles. Vega's association of quadripartite division with solar cycles is supported by the glyph of the sun as it appears in the *Codex Mendoza.* This glyph features a circular disk with four rays oriented to the cardinal directions and four flowers radiating out to the inter-cardinal directions (Berdan 1992:220).

The third aid to identifying narratives is vessel form and function. For example, Lind (1994) suggests that differences in the most common forms of elite polychrome vessels from Cholula, the Mixteca, and Oaxaca imply differences in the focus of elite ritual. More than half of the elite polychromes from Cholula are shallow tripod bowls designed for ritual offerings. In contrast, 80 percent of the polychromes from the Mixteca and Oaxaca are designed for serving beverages such as chocolate and pulque. On this basis, Lind proposes that elite ritual in Cholula emphasized sacrificial offerings to the gods while elite ritual in the Mixteca and

Oaxaca featured royal feasts. These two forms of ritual imply different orienting narratives. In Cholula, the need for sacrifice probably evoked myths of successive creations (Nicholson 1971:398–399), while in the Mixteca, royal feasts were events for recalling lineage origins by reciting origin myths preserved in pictorial codices and mural paintings (Pohl 1999; see Chapter 9).[2]

The fourth aid to identifying narratives is the combinations of vessels used in feasts. Feasts often consist of established sequences of foods, requiring the use of vessels of specific shapes and designs in prescribed sequences (Sherratt 1991:54). As discussed below, ceramic caches from the Middle and Late Postclassic Basin of Mexico regularly include two distinctive kinds of vessels, Black-on-Orange vessels and Red Ware vessels. Both were probably required to create a proper feast. The contrasting properties of these wares help to identify the oppositions that structured the narratives of Postclassic feasts and gave them meaning.

The fifth aid to identifying narratives is vessel origin (Spielmann 2002). Narratives are often attached to particular sacred or exotic locales (Helms 1993). Ceramics from these locales, or in the styles of these locales, may evoke tales of epic journeys by culture heroes (Helms 1988), stories of the rise and fall of ancient centers of power (Umberger 1987), foundational myths of political and/or religious movements (Spielmann 2002), or the identity of political allies (Schortman et al. 2001). Any of these might provide the central narrative of a figured world evoked at a feast. For example, much of the early Black-on-Orange pottery at the Basin of Mexico site of Xaltocan was manufactured in Culhuacan (Nichols et al. 2002). The use of this pottery, and Aztec I ceramics in general, may have invoked the prestige associated with Culhuacan as an heir to Toltec power, as well as the narrative of the glory of Tollan and its destruction (Alva Ixtlilxóchitl 1975–1977: I:274–285).

These dimensions of variation can generate converging lines of evidence which archaeologists use to bolster confidence in their interpretations (Wylie 1985).

Serving Vessels in the Basin of Mexico Postclassic: An Overview

At Postclassic sites in the Basin of Mexico, serving vessels include relatively thin-walled, well-finished containers in a number of different forms: bowls, basins, plates, dishes with tripod supports, and dishes with tripod supports and striated bottoms (*molcajetes*). Sixteenth-century pictorial documents from central Mexico (Smith et al. in press) indicate that these vessel forms were used as containers for food (plates, dishes, and molcajetes) and drink (bowls and basins). Postclassic decorated serving vessels include three distinctive wares: Black-on-Orange, Chalco-Cholula Polychrome, and Red Ware.

Black-on-Orange pottery has a bright orange base color (the natural color of the clay fired in an oxidized atmosphere) overlain by black painted designs. It was made over a very long period of time and went through a sequence of four distinct subtypes: Aztec I, Aztec II, Aztec III, and Aztec IV (see Fig. 10.1).

The earliest, Aztec I, vessels, have bold designs painted in a wide, heavy line. Complex curvilinear or symbolic designs appear on the vessel walls, and the inte-

Figure 10.3. *top*: Aztec II Black-on-Orange tripod dish from Xaltocan; *bottom*: Aztec II Black-on-Orange plate from Xaltocan

rior base is covered with a large, elaborate floral or zoomorphic motif, most commonly, the stylized head of a caiman[3] or a large flower with multiple petals (Brenner 1969[1931]:40, 59, 78, 82; Séjourné 1970:211). In Central Mexico, the caiman (*cipactli*) was the patron of the 260-day ritual almanac (Arellano 1999), and the flower was a symbol of the sun (Vega 1984:127).

Chalco-Cholula Polychrome pottery resembles Aztec I pottery in many ways, but it is more elaborately decorated. Like Aztec I, Chalco-Cholula Polychrome forms include dishes, plates, and bowls, and many of the dishes have tripod supports. The interior walls of dishes and plates bear complex curvilinear or symbolic motifs, and a glyph-like image (a day glyph from the Aztec calendar, a god, a skull, or some other complex image) appears on the vessel floor. Designs are painted red, orange, yellow, black, gray, and white, and on many vessels the paint is burnished to a high luster.

During the Middle Postclassic period, Aztec II Black-on-Orange vessels and Red Ware bowls replaced Aztec I Black-on-Orange and Chalco-Cholula Polychrome.

Figure 10.4. *top*: Black-and-White-on-Red bowl with a triangular design from Xaltocan; *bottom*: Black-and-White-on-Red bowl with vertical stripes and a spiral design from Xaltocan

Aztec II vessels continue the tradition of black-painted designs on natural orange surfaces, but Aztec II decoration is more complex (Fig. 10.3). The walls of Aztec II vessels bear broad decorative panels containing rows of horizontal lines, loops, spirals, and concentric circles. Stylized glyphs (e.g., a cipactli head, a day symbol, a feather, the four directions) are sometimes inserted among these geometric or calligraphic designs. Interior bases are plain or bear a snake motif, or are crossed by a series of parallel lines joined by spirals (Franco 1945; Griffin and Espejo 1947, 1950; Hodge 1991; Parsons 1966).

Red Ware vessels have a base color of highly burnished bright red paint. The red is overlain by complex designs in black, or black and white, or by incised designs. Incised Red Ware often bears a series of cane-like scrolls. Black-on-Red vessels have glyph-like motifs. Black-and-White-on-Red vessels feature bold triangular, vertical, and diagonal designs in chalky white paint on their red exteriors (Fig. 10.4). Up to 90 percent of all Red Ware vessels are simple rounded bowls, but drinking goblets and plates also occur (Minc 1991).

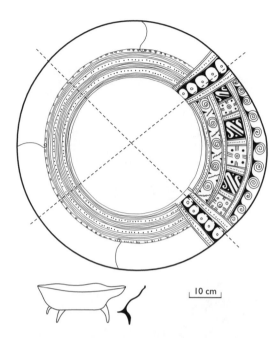

Figure 10.5. Aztec III Black-on-Orange tripod dish from the Basin of Mexico with horizontal lines and dots interrupted by a vertical panel bearing complex glyphic motifs (after Vega 1984: Lámina 6)

During the Late Postclassic period, Black-on-Orange and Red Ware continued to dominate. Aztec III Black-on-Orange vessels are defined by their thin, hard walls and by designs executed in a very fine line. Decoration is more simplified, consisting of rows of horizontal lines, dots, or dashes. The horizontal design is sometimes interrupted by a wide vertical panel bearing complex glyphic motifs (Fig. 10.5). Aztec IV vessels (Fig. 10.6), dating to the decades just before and after the Spanish Conquest, feature distinctive naturalistic motifs including flowers, birds, leaves, and feather balls on their vessel walls (Hodge 1991; Parsons 1966). Also during this time, new motifs occur on Red Ware bowls. These include the "wing-like" or "half-flower" motif and the "cable" or "intertwined undulating band" motif (Minc 1991:165, 204; Vega 1984:159) (Fig. 10.7).

The Narrative Content of Late Postclassic Black-on-Orange Vessels I: Solar Cycles

Constanza Vega Sosa (1984) has analyzed the importance of solar symbols and solar cycles in the composition and design motifs in Late Postclassic pottery. She uses 13 Late Postclassic vessels to illustrate her discussion. Five of these are Aztec III and IV Black-on-Orange dishes, and eight are Red Ware bowls. Vega shows that the decoration on all of these vessels is organized in a quadripartite pattern, with designs distributed symmetrically in the quarters of the vessels (Figs. 10.4, 10.5, 10.6).

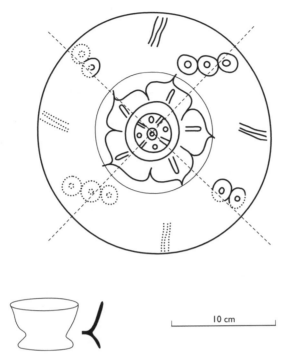

Figure 10.6. Aztec IV Black-on-Orange annular base bowl from the Basin of Mexico with naturalistic motifs (after Vega 1984: Lámina 4)

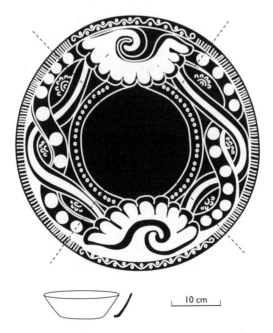

Figure 10.7. Black-and-White-on-Red bowl from El Volador with half-flower and intertwined undulating band motifs (after Vega 1984: Lámina 13)

These quadrants, Vega argues, represent the four quarters of the earth, the conventional way of thinking about space in Mesoamerica. She further argues that the four quarters are defined by lines radiating from the inter-cardinal directions, or, more precisely, the four points where the sun rises and sets at the summer and winter solstices. Thus, the composition of Late Postclassic vessels expresses awareness of and concern for the solar cycles of day and night, summer and winter.

Vega also finds that many of the design motifs on these vessels symbolize the sun and its cyclical movement. For example, flower motifs are found on five of the vessels under consideration. Some of these flowers have centers of concentric circles, some have spiral centers, and some have double spiral (S-spiral) centers. Although flowers had many symbolic associations in Aztec Mexico (see Heyden 1985), Vega suggests that associations with the sun were among the most prominent. To support this assertion, she cites evidence from the Codex Magliabecchiano (Boone and Nuttall 1983: II:8), which illustrates a textile bearing a design of a single central flower motif and accompanied by a gloss in Spanish which identifies this textile as the "cloak of the sun." Vega suggests that flowers with centers of concentric circles represent the sun without reference to its movement, while flowers with spiral centers represent the sun moving in its daily cycle. Flowers with double spiral centers symbolize the sun's passage from south to north and back again in its movement between the summer and winter solstices. Vega also suggests that the half-flower motif with a spiral center represents the sun, half hidden by the horizon at sunrise and/or sunset (Fig. 10.7).

Vega does not explore the narratives that might have been associated with these ceramics, but narratives concerning solar cycles lay at the heart of Aztec state religion. Aztec religion claimed that the daily and yearly cycles of the sun which sustained agriculture and human life were the uncertain outcome of a cosmic battle between the sun and the forces of darkness. Each day was a drama of struggle, with the sun rising victorious in the morning, driving off the moon and stars to capture the daytime sky. But the sun's victory was only provisional, for each afternoon and evening it sank in weary defeat as the moon and stars took back the heavens. According to the Aztec state, the sun's success in this daily struggle depended upon its being nourished with the hearts and blood of sacrificial victims, preferably vigorous enemy warriors captured in warfare.

This cosmology inspired young men to engage in the dangerous business of military conquest:

> Each prisoner taken by the Aztecs was a star that was to be sacrificed to the sun to nourish him with the magical sustenance that represents life and to fortify him for the divine combat . . . Hence the pride of the Aztec, who looked upon himself as a collaborator of the gods . . . In a sense the universe depended upon him for its continued existence; upon him depended food for the gods, upon him depended the beneficence of the gifts which they showered upon mankind. (Caso 1958:93)

In light of these narratives, it is significant that in Vega's sample the six vessels bearing half-sun designs all came from El Volador in Mexico City, an offering of over 900 vessels deposited in a rectangular platform adjoining the Aztec ruler's palace (Solís and Morales 1991). This offering dates to the early sixteenth century. The vessels it contains were probably similar to those used in state-sponsored feasts (Olson and Smith 2000). Such vessels, depicting the sun in its most embattled state, half-overwhelmed by the forces of darkness, must have made a powerful statement to all who attended royal feasts about the necessity of warfare and the nobility of military service.

The Narrative Content of Late Postclassic Red Ware Vessels II: Impending Chaos

In addition to the half-sun motif identified by Vega, many of the Red Ware bowls from El Volador were painted with images of human skulls and crossed long bones (Solís and Morales 1991). This design seems to communicate an explicit interest in human sacrifice. The skulls and long bones of sacrificial victims were trophy items. Skulls were placed on display on skull racks or *tzompantli*, located in the civic-ceremonial precinct at the heart of Tenochtitlan (Sahagún 1950–1982: bk. 2:183, 186, 189), and a femur from each sacrificed captive was kept as a trophy in the house of his captor (Sahagún 1950–1982: bk. 2, ch. 22). In addition, the skull and crossed bones design may have recalled the narrative of human creation: Quetzalcoatl journeyed to the underworld to gather the bones of past generations; sprinkling them with his own blood, he brought humanity to life. This established human sacrifice as part of the cosmic order: "Since man was created by the sacrifice of the gods, he must reciprocate by offering them his own blood in sacrifice . . . Man must nourish the gods with the magic sustenance of life itself, found in human blood and in the human heart" (Caso 1958:12).

In general terms, the underworld was the abode of the dead and a repository of human bones within the bowels of the earth. It existed in complementary opposition to the heavens, which were filled by the sun, shedding light and life-giving heat-energy (*tonalli*) on the living. During the night, the sun traveled through the underworld, emerging from it at sunrise. Thus, the underworld was linked with darkness and night. Night was a time when the earth might be plunged into destructive chaos, signaled by the descent of menacing star demons (the *tzitzimime*), with their faces of fleshless bone (Boone 1999). The tzitzimime were defeated only by the rising sun, strengthened by human sacrifice. Thus, the skull and crossed bone motif, like the half-sun motif, made a powerful statement about the necessity of warfare and the nobility of military service to guests at state-sponsored feasts.

Red Ware vessels can also be linked to the narrative of the forces of darkness, based on their function and the colors used in their decoration. The colors on Red Ware bowls parallel those of Omacatl, the Aztec god of hospitality. Describing Omacatl's costume, Sahagún (1950–1982: bk. 1:34) states, "His warrior's cape was red-bordered, with eyelets . . . He had fragments of mirror-stone [painted] on his face . . . His shield was chalky." Aztec mirrors were made of black stone. Thus, Omacatl's costume contained red, black, and white, the colors on many Red Ware bowls. "Chalky" is a good description of the dull, thick, white paint that appears on Red Ware vessels. Also, early Red Wares in the Basin of Mexico bore a graphite black paint, giving the impression of being painted with "mirror-stone" (i.e., magnetite) fragments. Finally, Omacatl's cape, red-bordered with white eyelets on a black band, is similar to the white circles on black bands that are a common motif on Red Ware bowls. Thus, the bowls might stand for Omacatl and evoke successful hospitality. But Omacatl was a variant of the more important Postclassic deity Tezcatlipoca, who was the god of darkness, night, discord, and warfare (Nicholson 1971:412; Sahagún 1997:113).[4]

Red Ware vessels were containers for drink, most probably pulque. By the rules governing Aztec feasts, food was served during the day, and pulque was served at night (Sahagún 1950–1982: bk. 4:118). Pulque was associated with the moon, the night, disorderly conduct, and the descent of tzitzimimes (Anawalt 1993; Taube 1993). One stone pulque vessel examined by Taube (1993:4) bears the image of the sun partially covered by a lunar crescent and menaced by tzitzimimes.

Thinking of the El Volador collection as set of vessels used in feasting provides additional evidence relating these ceramics to a narrative of cosmic warfare. The deposit contained over 900 vessels, including 175 Black-on-Orange vessels and 701 Red Ware vessels. These wares seem to exist in complementary opposition. They differ significantly in terms of vessel forms. Black-on-Orange forms are containers for food; they include 150 tripod double plates and 15 molcajetes. Red Ware vessels are containers for drink (pulque); they include 557 goblets (*copas*) and 114 flaring bowls. Black-on-Orange vessels are bright orange, and they bear the images of complete suns in design compositions that suggest orderly solar cycles; Red Ware vessels are darker and they bear images of half-suns, skulls and crossed bones, and the underworld. I would suggest that Black-on-Orange pottery symbolized the sun and its orderly movement while Red Ware vessels symbolized the night, a time when the orderly rule of the sun was threatened. Thus, the assemblage of feast ceramics taken as a whole rehearses the narrative of opposition between the orderly, life-giving sun and the destructive forces of darkness.

Taken together, these feast vessels evoked themes of cosmic warfare, embattled suns, the necessity of warfare and human sacrifice, the life path of the Aztec warrior of the sun, and the nobility of that figured world.

The Narrative Content of Aztec I Serving Vessels: The Ritual Almanac

Aztec I ceramics from domestic refuse at Culhuacan (Brenner 1969 [1931]; Séjourné 1970) show significant differences from the Late Postclassic vessels we have just examined. While Aztec I vessels, like the Late Postclassic vessels, bore sun motifs, they seem to imply a different narrative, one that was not so narrowly focused on the cosmic battle of light and darkness, order and chaos.

Aztec I dishes most often feature flowers and caimans on their interior bases. As mentioned above, flower motifs denote the sun. However, Aztec I dishes lack the motifs (spiral and double spiral centers) that Vega (1984) associates with solar motion. In addition, Aztec I vessels lack the quadripartite division that typifies later Black-on-Orange styles. Instead, the central flower on the floor of Aztec I vessels is often enclosed by concentric circles, wavy lines, scallops, or rays. These concentric motifs might suggest the radiation of the sun's heat and/or light, but not the movement of the sun through daily and seasonal cycles.

In Aztec I assemblages, a stylistic opposition between vessels used to serve food and those used to serve drink is missing. Aztec I vessel forms include both tripod dishes for food and round-sided bowls for drink, and Red Ware does not occur. Instead, Aztec I vessels are found with Chalco-Cholula Polychromes which are fancier than Aztec I vessels, but have similar vessel forms and thus seem to serve equivalent functions. Thus, Aztec I assemblages do not appear to evoke narratives of orderly solar cycles and destructive darkness. Instead, the focus of attention is upon the individual day, and the fate that it cast over individuals and their activities.

Tonalli, a key concept in central Mexico, was closely associated with the sun and its heat. Tonalli is derived from the Nahuatl verb tonal, "to irradiate," and depending on its context, it had the following meanings:

> *a.* irradiation; *b.* solar heat; *c.* summer; *d.* day; *e.* day sign; *f.* the destiny of a person according to the day of his birth; *g.* "the soul and spirit" (Molina: totonal); *h.* something meant for, or the property of, a certain person (Molina: tetonal). (López Austin 1988:204–205)

Central Mexican people conceived of each day, each new rising of the sun, as a period of time influenced by a unique conjunction of supernatural forces. These forces determined both the outcome of activities undertaken on any particular day and the endowment of children born on that day. The character of each day was recorded in a 260-day almanac, *tonalamatl*, which when read by a trained specialist would foretell the outcome of undertakings or a newborn's fate. In all, some 260 life paths were laid out. Children born on the day Seven Flower were destined to become accomplished craft specialists, while those born on the day Two Rabbit would become drunkards. Men born on the day Ten Eagle would be great warriors (Sahagún 1950–1982: bk. 4:7, 11–13, 38). Births, marriages, and deaths, and the success or failure of military campaigns or trade expeditions, all occurred according to the fate of the days as influenced by the gods.

This 260-day cycle of fate was called the *tonalpohualli*, the count of the days, and the caiman (cipactli) was its patron (Arellano 1999). The cipactli, representing the tonalpohualli, and the flower, representing the sun/day as a unique conjunction of supernatural forces, were appropriate symbols for vessels used in feasts that celebrated the life crises of household members and the economic activities undertaken by the household group. Aztec I vessels from domestic contexts seem to affirm the existence of an array of figured worlds and possible life paths rather than concentrating upon the world of the embattled suns and their warrior allies.

Politics, Feasts, and Cultural Change

The differences between Aztec I pottery from Culhuacan and Late Postclassic pottery from El Volador suggest significant differences in the figured worlds evoked during feasts during the Early and Late Postclassic periods. Why do figured worlds change over time? Why do people begin to find some figured worlds less compelling? Where do new figured worlds come from? These are questions that Holland and her colleagues, taking a short-term ethnographic approach to the subject, do not explore. Analysis of a cache of 54 complete vessels from Xaltocan, in the northern Basin of Mexico, provides some insight into these issues.

This cache was discovered by a crew of local workers who were in the process of grading a road. It was associated with a burial, probably of a woman.[5] This cache contained 29 Aztec II Black-on-Orange vessels, 12 Black-and-White-on-Red vessels, assorted plain orange pitchers and bowls, and a red burnished brazier. The cache dates to the Middle Postclassic, specifically Phase 3 in Xaltocan which spans the fourteenth century (Brumfiel in press). The cache may represent a full feast vessel assemblage.

This cache is similar to both the Culhuacan and El Volador assemblages, but it resembles the latter much more than the former. First of all, the design motifs and composition of the 26 Black-on-Orange vessels in the collection suggest a greater concern with solar cycles than with the ritual almanac. In terms of design elements, 14 of the 26 vessels bear spiral (solar cycle) motifs. On six of these vessels (all plates), the vessel floor is crossed by a series of widely separated parallel lines, joined by small spirals placed between the lines. These might depict the vault of the heavens, crossed by the sun along different paths, according to the season.[6] In terms of composition, 13 of the 26 vessels have a quadripartite division typical of Aztec III–IV vessels, and 12 of these bear spiral motifs (Fig. 10.3). Seven vessels have an unsegmented design composition such as that found on Aztec I vessels, and none of these have a spiral motif (Fig. 10.8). Three of the vessels have an anomalous tripartite division. All three of these vessels have spiral motifs. Three miniature vessels have dual symmetry, perhaps a consequence of small vessel size. All three of these vessels have floors crossed by broad decorative bands, possibly representing the vault of the heavens. Thus, almost half of the collection bears both the spiral symbols and the quadripartite divisions that, according to Vega, symbolize solar cycles. Another fourth have design motifs that might be linked to solar cycles and heavenly vaults. And only a fourth of the collection bears the unsegmented composition of stationary suns typical of older Aztec I vessels.

In addition, this cache contains both Black-on-Orange and Red Ware vessels, and different vessel forms are associated with the two wares. Black-on-Orange vessels include plates, tripod dishes, miniature dishes, small jars, and one basin with lug handles. Most of these would have been used for serving food. The Red Ware vessels include nine bowls and three small plates. Most of these would have been used for serving drink. Thus, this assemblage seems to contain some elements of the day/night opposition that characterized the El Volador collection.

Figure 10.8. *Top*: Aztec II Black-on-Orange plate from Xaltocan with an unsegmented design; *bottom*: Aztec II Black-on-Orange tripod dish from Xaltocan with an unsegmented design

However, the black, white, and red decorations on Red Ware vessels do not make explicit references to warfare and sacrifice as seen in the El Volador collection. The half-sun motifs, and the skulls and crossed bones present at El Volador are all absent from the Xaltocan cache;[7] instead, the Red Ware plates are decorated with black and red concentric circles (representing the nighttime, or subterranean, sun?) (Fig. 10.9). The Red Ware bowls feature bold triangular, vertical, and diagonal designs on their red exteriors outlined by wide black bands and filled with chalky white paint. Two bowls bear large S-spiral motifs (Fig. 10.4(b)). We might judge this collection to express the beginnings of a concern with solar cycles and cosmic warfare, but without the extensive design element vocabulary used by the later Aztec state.

It is significant that this cache dates from the fourteenth century, a time when Xaltocan was at the height of its political power. At this time, Xaltocan was the capital of an autonomous kingdom that controlled over 49 towns in southern Hidalgo and the northern basin, with tribute fields in 24 communities (Nazareo

Figure 10.9. Black-and-White-on-Red plate from Xaltocan with a concentric circle motif

1940). As a tribute-receiving capital, Xaltocan was at the height of its prosperity, as indicated by very high ratios of decorated to undecorated serving vessels (Brumfiel in press). Xaltocan was also engaged in a lengthy war against its neighbor Cuauhtitlan. These conditions may have contributed to the development of an ideology of warfare and human sacrifice at Xaltocan. Even before the Aztecs, the rulers of powerful tribute-collecting centers used their wealth to sponsor architecture, sculpture, and costuming that emphasized the importance of warfare and human sacrifice for cosmic order and human life. Rulers used these ideologies to inspire young men to engage in military conquest, and so to increase the ruler's wealth and his ability to reward his army (Brumfiel 1998, 2001).

Allusions to themes of solar cycles and cosmic warfare on the Xaltocan ceramics, presumably purchased in the market by commoners for use in their own feasts, suggest that commoners in fourteenth-century Xaltocan had at least partially adopted this militaristic world-view as their own. It is, perhaps, significant (although not totally persuasive) that a fourteenth-century deposit of domestic refuse at Xaltocan yielded two notched human femurs, which Seler (1992) places within the cult of warfare and sacrifice. In fact, the ceramic cache from Xaltocan described above may under-represent the popularity of the cult of warfare and sacrifice at fourteenth-century Xaltocan. Whereas Aztec II Black-on-Orange vessels outnumber Red Ware vessels in the cache (perhaps because they accompany the burial of a woman rather than a man), Red Ware vessels outnumber Aztec II Black-on-Orange vessels for the site as a whole by a ratio of 7:3. The high proportion of Red Ware vessels at Xaltocan may indicate widespread preoccupation with the threat of chaos and darkness and a high valuation of the warrior's role.

Ceramics suggest that in 1430, when Xaltocan became a part of the Aztec empire, popular interest in cosmic warfare and human sacrifice waned. Feasting became less popular under Aztec rule: decorated pottery declined from 33 percent of all pottery at the height of Xaltocan's power to only 28 percent in Xaltocan under

Aztec rule. And under Aztec rule, Red Ware became much less popular: it declined from 69 percent of all decorated pottery at the height of Xaltocan's power to only 53 percent of all decorated pottery in Xaltocan under Aztec rule. Overall, the frequency of Red Ware vessels declined by about 33 percent. This suggests that under conditions of political domination, the people of Xaltocan were slightly less interested in feasting in general, but markedly less interested in ideologies that emphasized the need for warfare and human sacrifice.

Rulers in imperial provinces like Xaltocan had no incentive to actively promote the cult of warfare and human sacrifice, unless they were planning rebellion. Young men from subordinate communities might fight for personal glory and for the rewards that they received from Aztec rulers, but their actions only swelled the tribute rolls of the Aztec capital. They did not increase the wealth of rulers in secondary centers such as Xaltocan. This is consistent with other evidence from Xaltocan and other provincial centers in the Aztec empire. Ceramic figurines suggest no tendency to emphasize the image of the male warrior during the period of Aztec rule; in fact, the ratio of female to male figurines increases from approximately 1:1 in pre-Aztec times to 3:1 under Aztec rule (Brumfiel 1996). Furthermore, when compared to rituals in the Aztec capital of Tenochtitlan, rituals in the provincial center of Tepepolco featured less human sacrifice, fewer mock battles, and less prominent roles for successful warriors (Brumfiel 2001).

Without substantial investments by wealthy local rulers in items of splendid dress, and flashy rituals that established the social worth of the warrior's role, that role with its attendant suffering and danger no longer seemed compelling to the people of Xaltocan. In Xaltocan, the figured world of the noble warrior was no longer being properly materialized, and the benefits of the warrior's life no longer outweighed its costs.

Conclusions

This analysis offers both methodological and theoretical conclusions. Archaeological methods are the techniques that archaeologists use to move from artifacts to reconstructions of ancient societies. Anthropological theory attempts to understand or make sense of human behavior.

In terms of methods, our analysis suggests that archaeologists can (sometimes) use ceramics (and other artifacts) to understand both the content and the distribution of the narratives that were at the core of identity for prehistoric peoples. The idea that ceramics (and other artifacts) sometimes alluded to narratives is not a new discovery. Some years ago, Michael Coe (1973) recognized the correspondence between the scenes on Classic Maya funerary pots and the adventures of the Maya Hero Twins in the land of the dead, as recorded in the sixteenth-century Maya text, the Popul Vuh. Similarly, Matos (1987) pointed out that the snake sculptures that lie of the base of the Aztec Great Temple were intended to evoke the tale of primeval warfare at Coatepec (Snake Mountain), a narrative preserved in several versions in early colonial texts. More recently, Joyce (1996) has called attention to the narratives implicit in Classic Maya sculpture. What is new in the present chapter is the suggestion that the Aztec narratives discussed were invoked not just to legitimate actions by appealing to tradition, but to provide orienting models of the way that the world should and did operate and to provide focus for the formation of identity and the exercise of agency in ancient populations.

Usually, identifying the thematic content of ceramic design will require familiarity with full narrative texts appearing in ethnohistoric or ethnographic sources, but occasionally a very full pictorial narrative, such as the Mixtec codices (Pohl 1994; see Chapter 9), will enable archaeologists to make the linkage between pottery designs and narratives. When such linkages can be made, archaeologists will be able to reconstruct:

1   the meaning of pottery designs, and
2   the narrative topics and structures that oriented people's self-identity and actions in a given prehistoric period.

Even without full knowledge of narrative content, archaeologists can use the distribution of pottery designs to study how different orienting narratives are distributed among social groups and across time. Correlating this variation with archaeological indicators of economic and political change, archaeologists can investigate how identity and agency are affected by structural change and, in turn, produce it.

Our analysis also suggests that narratives are encoded in the design elements, in design composition, and the make-up of whole ceramic assemblages. But archaeologists have often overlooked the latter two attributes. Archaeologists usually recover fragments of discarded pottery from household debris, and on small potsherds design elements are evident while design composition is not. When archaeologists have the opportunity to work with whole vessels, i.e., those recovered from burials or ritual offerings, they tend to continue to work with design elements and not exploit the full analytical potential of design composition. Particularly in Mesoamerica, where space is used to express time and vice versa (Gossen 1974), and where historical narratives were rendered in cartographic form (Boone 1996), design composition might contain important narrative elements. Similarly, archaeologists have expended tremendous energy in defining and describing individual ceramic types, but they have not been equally energetic in asking why two or more different types regularly co-occur. Archaeologists have not examined the meaning of symbolic oppositions that might exist between co-occurring types, nor how these oppositions might symbolize the tension between opposing forces that animates narratives of change.

In terms of theory, our analysis suggests some of the factors that guide prehistoric people to opt for one orienting narrative or another. To a great extent, given an array of possible figured worlds, people opt for the one that gives them the greatest chances for security and respect. Thus, their decisions have much to do with political economy, i.e., the distribution of economic and cultural capital in a society and the kinds of social groups (alliance networks) that control these resources.

For Postclassic Mexico, the attractiveness of the figured world of the warrior varied according to the amount of tribute collected by a tribute-receiving center. Young men who lived in tribute-receiving capitals received direct rewards for their participation in warfare. In addition, the rulers of these capitals invested in public dances and rituals that would make the warrior's role glamorous and appealing. Success in warfare also benefited the entire populations of tribute-receiving capitals because tribute wealth stimulated the local economy. Rulers and noble warriors used their tribute wealth to buy luxury goods from local craft specialists and long-distance traders; this created a flourishing market which attracted more market activity. Thus, success in warfare yielded a whole series of social, economic, and cultural benefits which inclined young men to accept their fate as warriors of the sun. However, the young men of subordinate communities had less access to tribute wealth, the rulers of these communities had less to invest in glamorizing the warrior's roles, and the diversion of tribute wealth from local to imperial rulers impoverished the local economy (Brumfiel in press). Small wonder, then, that the people of Xaltocan became focused on narratives of solar cycles and cosmic warfare when Xaltocan was a regional capital while the people of Xaltocan under Aztec rule found the warrior's role less appealing.

Tracing figured worlds from narratives to feasts to ceramic vessel designs has enabled us to reconstruct the identities elected by commoners in Postclassic Mexico. Placing the growth and decline these worlds in the long-term histories provided by archaeology, we are able to see how personal identities are shaped by and respond to political and other changes in the wider world.

NOTES

1 Culhuacan is conventionally considered to be a Middle Postclassic site, dating A.D. 1150–1350. However, recent carbon dates from Ch-Az-195 and Xaltocan suggest that Aztec I Black-on-Orange, which is abundant at Culhuacan, dates to the tenth century (Parsons et al. 1996).

2 Lind's interpretation based on vessel form and function is also supported by different symbolic motifs appearing on polychrome vessels in the two regions.

3 This motif is called the "serpent-head profile" by Brenner (1969[1931]:40, 59, 78, 82) and the "triangle with a solar eye" by Séjourné (1970:211).

4 Black, white, and red also connoted the warrior's life. Warriors who died on the battlefield or in sacrifice were pictured with white stripes on their bodies, black paint around their eyes, and red paint around their mouths (Seler 1992:68–69). White, black, and red are also the dominant colors on the mural of war shields adorning a palace room in Tehuacan (Sisson and Lilly 1994a, 1994b).

5 Although the road crew saved the ceramic artifacts that accompanied the burial, they did not save the bones themselves. I tentatively identify this burial as gendered female because it contained a female figurine and two large spindle whorls.

6 In three other cases, the vessel floor is crossed by a broad band containing a snake-like motif, perhaps a representation of the sky serpent.

7 However, some sherds with half-sun motifs have been recovered from other Phase 3 contexts at Xaltocan.

REFERENCES

Alva Ixtlilxóchitl, F. de, 1975–77 *Obras históricas*. E. O'Gorman, ed. Mexico: Universidad Nacional Autónoma de México.

Anawalt, P. R., 1992 A comparative analysis of the costumes and accoutrements of the Codex Mendoza. In *The Codex Mendoza*. F. F. Berdan and P. R. Anawalt, eds. Vol. 1, pp. 103–150. Berkeley: University of California Press.

—— 1993 Rabbits, *pulque*, and drunkenness. In *Current Topics in Aztec Studies: Essays in Honor of Dr. H. B. Nicholson*. A. Cordy-Collins and D. Sharon, eds. Pp. 17–38. Museum of Man Papers 30. San Diego: Museum of Man.

Arellano Hernández, J. A., 1999 Gusanos de piedra: Dioses creadores. In *Chalchihuite: Homenaje a Doris Heyden*. M. de Jesús Rodríguez-Shadow and B. Barba de Piña Chán, eds. Pp. 109–146. Mexico City: Instituto Nacional de Antropología e Historia.

Armillas, P., 1964 Northern Mesoamerica. In *Prehistoric Man in the New World*. J. D. Jennings and E. Norbeck, eds. Pp. 291–329. Chicago: University of Chicago Press.

Barthes, R., 1977 Diderot, Brecht, Eisenstein. In *Image–Music–Text*. S. Heath, trans. Pp. 69–78. New York: Noonday Press.

Bender, B., 1985 Prehistoric developments in the American midcontinent and in Brittany, northwest France. In *Prehistoric Hunter-Gatherers: The Emergence of Cultural Complexity*. T. D. Price and J. A. Brown, eds. Pp. 21–59. Orlando: Academic Press.

Berdan, F. F., 1992 The place-name, personal name, and title glyphs of the Codex Mendoza. In *The Codex Mendoza*. F. F. Berdan and P. R. Anawalt, eds. Vol. 1, pp. 163–238. Berkeley: University of California Press.

Berdan, F. F., and P. R. Anawalt, eds., 1992 *The Codex Mendoza*. Berkeley: University of California Press.

Boone, E. H., 1996 Manuscript painting in service of imperial ideology. In *Aztec Imperial Strategies*. F. F. Berdan et al. Pp. 181–206. Washington, DC: Dumbarton Oaks.

—— 1999 The "coatlicues" at the Templo Mayor. *Ancient Mesoamerica* 10, 189–206.

Boone, E. H., and Z. Nuttall, 1983 *The Codex Magliabecchiano*. Berkeley: University of California Press.

Brenner, A., 1969[1931] *The Influence of Technique on the Decorative Style in the Domestic Pottery of Culhuacan*. New York: AMS Press.

Brumfiel, E. M., 1983 Aztec state making: Ecology, structure, and the origin of the state. *American Anthropologist* 85, 261–284.

—— 1987 Consumption and politics at Aztec Huexotla. *American Anthropologist* 89, 676–686.

—— 1988 Huitzilopochtli's conquest: Aztec ideology in the archaeological record. *Cambridge Archaeological Journal* 8, 1–13.

—— 1996 Figurines and the Aztec state: Testing the effectiveness of ideological domination. In *Gender and Archaeology*. R. Wright, ed. Pp. 143–166. Philadelphia: University of Pennsylvania Press.

—— 2001 Aztec hearts and minds: Religion and the state in the Aztec empire. In *Empires: Perspectives from Archaeology and History*. S. E. Alcock, T. N. D'Altroy, K. D. Morrison, and C. M. Sinopoli, eds. Pp. 283–310. Cambridge: Cambridge University Press.

——in press Ceramic chronology at Xaltocan. In *Production and Power at Postclassic Xalto-can*. E. M. Brumfiel, ed. Memoirs in Latin American Archaeology. Pittsburgh and Mexico: Department of Anthropology, University of Pittsburgh; Instituto Nacional de Antropología e Historia.

Carrasco, P., 1978 La economía del México prehispánico. In *Economía política e ideología en el México prehispánico*. P. Carrasco and J. Broda, eds. Pp. 15–76. Mexico: Nueva Imagen.

Caso, A., 1958 *The Aztecs: People of the Sun*. L. Dunham, trans. Norman: University of Oklahoma Press.

Clark, J. E., and M. Blake, 1994 The power of prestige. In *Factional Competition and Political Development in the New World*. E. M. Brumfiel, ed. Pp. 17–30. Cambridge: Cambridge University Press.

Coe, M. D., 1973 *The Maya Scribe and his World*. New York: Grolier Club.

DeMarrais, E., L. J. Castillo, and T. Earle, 1996 Ideology, materialization, and power strategies. *Current Anthropology* 37, 15–31.

Dietler, M., 1996 Feasts and commensal politics in the political economy. *Food and the Status Quest*. P. Wiessner and W. Schiefenhövel, eds. Pp. 87–125. Providence, RI: Berghahn.

Dietler, M., and B. Hayden, eds., 2001 *Feasts*. Washington, DC: Smithsonian Institution.

Douglas, M., 1966 *Purity and Danger*. New York: Praeger.

Durán, D., 1967 *Historia de las Indias de Nueva España*. Mexico: Porrúa.

——1971 *Book of the Gods and Rites and the Ancient Calendar*. F. Horcasitas and D. Heyden, eds. Norman: University of Oklahoma Press.

Evans, S. T., 1988 *Excavations at Cihuatecpan*. Publications in Anthropology 36. Nashville, TN: Vanderbilt University.

Franco, J. L., 1945 Comentarios sobre tipología y filogenía de la decoración Negro sobre Color Natural del Barro en la cerámica Azteca II. *Revista Mexicana del Estudios Antropológicos* 7, 162–208.

Friedman, J., 1975 Tribes, states, and transformations. In *Marxist Analyses and Social Anthropology*. E. M. Bloch, ed. Pp. 161–202. London: Tavistock.

Garraty, C. P., 2000 Ceramic indices of Aztec eliteness. *Ancient Mesoamerica* 11, 323–340.

Gero, J., 1992 Feasts and females: Gender ideology and political meals in the Andes. *Norwegian Archaeological Review* 25, 1–16.

Godelier, M., 1977 The concept of "social and economic formation": The Inca example. In *Perspectives in Marxist Anthropology*. R. Brain, trans. Pp. 63–69. Cambridge: Cambridge University Press.

Gossen, G. H., 1974 *Chamulas in the World of the Sun: Time and Space in a Maya Oral Tradition*. Cambridge, MA: Harvard University Press.

Griffin, J. B, and A. Espejo, 1947 La alfarería correspondiente al último período de ocupación Nahua del Valle de México, I. *Tlatelolco a Través de los Tiempos* 9, 16–25.

———1950 La alfarería correspondiente al último período de ocupación Nahua del Valle de México, II. *Tlatelolco a Través de los Tiempos* 11, 15–66.

Hayden, B., 1990 Nimrods, piscators, pluckers, and planters: The emergence of food production. *Journal of Anthropological Archaeology* 9, 31–69.

Helms, M. W., 1988 *Ulysses' Sail*. Princeton: Princeton University Press.

——1993 *Craft and the Kingly Ideal*. Austin: University of Texas Press.

Heyden, D., 1985 *Mitología y simbolismo de la flora en el México Prehispánico*. Mexico: Instituto de Investigaciones Antropológicas, Universidad Nacional Autónoma de México.

Hicks, F., 1982 Tetzcoco in the early sixteenth century: The state, the city and the *calpolli*. *American Ethnologist* 9, 230–249.

—— 1986 Prehispanic background of colonial political and economic organization in central Mexico. In *Supplement to the Handbook of Middle American Indians*, vol. 4: *Ethnohistory*. R. Spores, ed. Pp. 35–54. Austin: University of Texas Press.

Hodge, M. G., 1991 Aztec II, III, and IV Black/Orange type descriptions. Appendix 3. In *Aztec-Period Ceramic Distribution and Exchange Systems*. M. G. Hodge and L. D. Minc. Pp. 109–155. Final Report Submitted to the National Science Foundation for Grant BSM-8704177.

Hodge, M. G., and L. D. Minc, 1990 The spatial patterning of Aztec ceramics: Implications for Prehispanic exchange in the Valley of Mexico. *Journal of Field Archaeology* 17, 415–437.

Holland, D., W. Lachicotte Jr., D. Skinner, and C. Cain, 1998 *Identity and Agency in Cultural Worlds*. Cambridge, MA: Harvard University Press.

Joyce, R. A., 1996 The construction of gender in Classic Maya monuments. In *Gender and Archaeology*. R. P. Wright, ed. Pp.167–195. Philadelphia: University of Pennsylvania Press.

Kus, S., 1992 Toward an archaeology of body and soul. In *Representations in Archaeology*. J. C. Gardin and C. S. Peebles, eds. Pp. 168–177. Bloomington, IN: Indiana University Press.

Lévi-Strauss, C., 1962 *Totemism*. R. Needham, trans. Boston: Beacon.

Lind, M. D., 1994 Cholula and Mixteca polychromes: Two Mixteca-Puebla regional sub-styles. In *Mixteca-Puebla*. H. B. Nicholson and E. Quiñones Keber, eds. Pp. 79–99. Culver City: Labyrinthos.

López Austin, A., 1988 *The Human Body and Ideology*. T. Ortiz de Montellano and B. Ortiz de Montellano, trans. Salt Lake City: University of Utah Press.

Matos Moctezuma, E., 1987 The Templo Mayor of Tenochtitlan: History and interpretation. In *The Great Temple of Tenochtitlan*. J. Broda, D. Carrasco, and E. Matos. Pp. 15–60. Berkeley: University of California Press.

McVicker, D., ed., 1992 *México: La visión del cosmos*. Chicago: Mexican Fine Arts Center Museum.

Minc, L. D., 1991 Black/Red type descriptions. Black/Red Incised type descriptions. Black-and-White/Red type descriptions. In *Aztec-Period Ceramic Distribution and Exchange Systems*. M. G. Hodge and L. D. Minc. Pp. 156–222. Final Report Submitted to the National Science Foundation for grant BSM-8704177.

Monaghan, J., 1995 *The Covenants with Earth and Rain*. Norman: University of Oklahoma Press.

Nazareo de Xaltocan, Don Pablo, 1940 Carta al Rey Don Felipe II. In *Epistolario de Nueva España*. F. del Paso y Troncoso, ed. Vol.10, pp.109–129. Mexico, DF: Antigua Librería Robredo.

Nichols, D. L., E. M. Brumfiel, H. Neff, M. Hodge, T. H. Charlton, and M. D. Glascock, 2002 Neutrons, markets, cities, and empires: A thousand-year perspective on ceramic production and distribution in the Postclassic Basin of Mexico. *Journal of Anthropological Archaeology* 21, 25–82.

Nicholson, H. B., 1971 Religion in pre-hispanic Central Mexico. In *Handbook of Mesoamerican Indians*, vol. 10: *Archaeology of Northern Mesoamerica*, part 1. G. F. Ekholm and I. Bernal, eds. Pp. 395–445. Austin: University of Texas Press.

Noguera, E., 1932 Extensiones cronológico-culturales y geográficas de las cerámicas de México. Paper presented to the 25th International Congress of Americanists, La Plata, Argentina. Mexico: Talleres Gráficos de la Nación.

Olson, J., and M. Smith, 2000 After the feast is over: Culinary remains for Aztec archaeological sites. Paper presented at the 65th Annual Meeting, Society for American Archaeology, Philadelphia.

Parsons, J. R., 1966 The Aztec ceramic sequence in the Teotihuacan Valley, Mexico. Ph.D. dissertation, Department of Anthropology, University of Michigan.

Parsons, J. R., E. Brumfiel, and M. Hodge, 1996 Developmental implications of earlier dates for Early Aztec in the Basin of Mexico. *Ancient Mesoamerica* 7, 217–230.

Pohl, J. M. D., 1994 *The Politics of Symbolism in the Mixtec Codices*. Publications in Anthropology 46. Nashville, TN: Vanderbilt University.

——1999 The lintel paintings of Mitla and the function of the Mitla palaces. In *Mesoamerican Architecture as a Cultural Symbol*. J. K. Kowalski, ed. Pp. 177–197. Oxford: Oxford University Press.

Quiñones Keber, E., 1995 *Codex Telleriano-Remensis*. Austin: University of Texas Press.

Sahagún, B. de, 1950–82 *Florentine Codex*. A. J. O. Anderson and C. E. Dibble, eds. Santa Fe and Salt Lake City: School of American Research and University of Utah.

——1997 *Primeros Memoriales*. T. Sullivan, trans. Norman: University of Oklahoma Press.

Sanders, W. T., J. R. Parsons, and R. S. Santley, 1979 *The Basin of Mexico: Ecological Processes in the Evolution of a Civilization*. New York: Academic Press.

Schortman, E. M., P. A. Urban, and M. Ausec, 2001 Politics with style: Identity formation in Prehispanic southeastern Mesoamerica. *American Anthropologist* 103, 312–330.

Séjourné, L., 1970 *Arqueología del Valle de México I: Culhuacan*. Mexico: Instituto Nacional de Antropología e Historia.

Seler, E. G., 1992 Ancient Mexican bone rattles. In *Collected Works in Mesoamerican Linguistics and Archaeology*. Vol. 3, pp. 62–73. Culver City, CA: Labyrinthos.

Sherratt, A., 1987 Cups that cheered: The introduction of alcohol to prehistoric Europe. In *Bell Beakers of the Western Mediterranean*. W. Waldren and R. Kennard, eds. Pp. 81–106. British Archaeological Reports, International Series 311. Oxford.

——1991 Sacred and profane substances: The ritual use of narcotics in Later Neolithic Europe. In *Sacred and Profane*. P. Garwood, D. Jennings, R. Skeates, and J. Toms, eds. Pp. 50–64. Archaeology Monographs 32. Oxford: Oxford University Press.

Sisson, E. B., and T. G. Lilly, 1994a The mural of the Chimales and the Codex Borgia. In *Mixteca-Puebla*. H. B. Nicholson and E. Quiñones Keber, eds. Pp. 25–44. Culver City, CA: Labyrinthos.

——1994b A codex-style mural from Tehuacan Viejo, Puebla, Mexico. *Ancient Mesoamerica* 5, 33–44.

Smith, M. E., 1984 The Aztlan migrations of the nahuatl chronicles: Myth or history? *Ethnohistory* 3, 153–186.

——1987 Household possessions and wealth in agrarian states: Implications for archaeology. *Journal of Anthropological Archaeology* 6, 297–335.

Smith, M. E., J. Wharton, and J. M. Olson, in press Aztec feasts, rituals and markets: Political uses of ceramic vessels in a commercialized economy. In *The Archaeology and Politics of Food and Feasting in Early States and Empires*. T. Bray, ed. Kluwer Academic.

Solís, F., and D. Morales, 1991 *Rescate de un rescate: Colección de objetos arqueologicos de El Volador, Ciudad de México*. Mexico: Instituto Nacional de Antropología e Historia.

Spielmann, K., 2002 Feasting, ceramics, and exchange. Paper presented at the Southwest Symposium, Tucson, AZ.

Taube, K. A., 1993 The Bilimek pulque vessel: Starlore, calendrics, and cosmology of Late Postclassic central Mexico. *Ancient Mesoamerica* 4, 1–15.

Umberger, E., 1987 Antiques, revivals, and references to the past in Aztec art. *Res* 13, 63–105.

Vega Sosa, C., 1984 El curso del sol en los glifos de la cerámica azteca tardía. *Estudios de Cultura Náhuatl* 17, 125–170.

Wylie, A. M., 1985 The reaction against analogy. *Advances in Archaeological Method and Theory* 8, 63–111.

11

The Rural and Urban Landscapes of the Aztec State

Deborah L. Nichols

The Aztec empire in the early sixteenth century was the largest state in the history of prehispanic Mesoamerica. Its heartland (Fig. 11.1) was the Basin of Mexico, a $7,000\,km^2$ mountain basin in Central Mexico with a population of between 800,000 and 1.25 million people (Sanders et al. 1979:218). Although the basin had one of the largest urban concentrations anywhere in the early sixteenth century, centered on the Aztec imperial city of Tenochtitlan-Tlatelolco, half of the Aztecs[1] lived in rural villages and hamlets. The landscape of the Aztec state was both rural and urban.

Aztec archaeology lagged behind investigations of earlier civilizations in Central Mexico, and before the mid-twentieth century investigations of Aztec remains were limited in number and scope and mostly focused on culture history and aesthetics (Sanders et al. 1979:161). Characterizations of Aztec society were largely from the viewpoint of city-dwellers, especially elites, who were treated as if they were typical of everyone in this complex society. Rural peasants barely received attention from archaeologists (Smith 1996a).

The reorientation of archaeology in the Basin of Mexico to a broader anthropological perspective employing a problem-oriented, social science approach, and the associated shift from elite to middle-class perspectives, began in the 1940s and 1950s (Nichols 1996). At this time, archaeologists began to focus their research on understanding the development of stratification, state formation, and urbanism, reflecting a broad interest in anthropology of the time in cultural evolution and in cultural ecology. Systematic regional settlement pattern research played an especially important role in shaping anthropological archaeology in the Basin of Mexico and has been one of the region's major contributions to archaeology. The Basin of Mexico settlement pattern project has proven to be "among the most successful large-scale regional archaeological studies anywhere" (Blanton 2002:402). The project was foundational in the development of methods and analytical procedures and in helping to frame major theoretical issues and debates in Aztec archaeology of the late twentieth century.

Figure 11.1. Postclassic sites in the Basin of Mexico

This chapter focuses on problem-oriented archaeological research on the Aztecs. I discuss the development of the Basin of Mexico regional settlement pattern project and subsequent archaeological research, and interpretations of the rural and urban landscapes of the Aztec state. It is not a comprehensive review of Aztec archeology (see especially Charlton 2000; Charlton and Nichols 1997a; Hodge 1998; Hodge and Smith 1994; Nichols and Charlton 2001; Smith 1996b for recent excellent synthesis, including major research projects outside the basin).

Foundations

Especially influential in changing the direction of archaeology in Mexico were the ideas of V. Gordon Childe, Julian Steward, Karl Wittfogel, and Pedro Armillas. Childe (1951) introduced the idea that human history had been shaped by two revolutionary changes: the development of food production, or the "Neolithic Revolution," and the formation of cities, the "Urban Revolution." Julian Steward's (1955) concept of cultural ecology drew attention to "relationships between environment, technology, settlement pattern and social organization" (Wolf 1976:2). Karl Wittfogel (1957) offered an elaborate theory about the relationship between irrigation agriculture and the centralization of state power (for a summary see Sanders and Price 1968:177–178).

Social and political turmoil and wars in Europe also influenced the reorientation of archaeology in Central Mexico. The Spanish Civil War and the rise of Nazism prompted the emigration of European archaeologists to Mexico. World War II and subsequent social changes brought together the discoveries and ideas of Mexican, North American, and European archaeologists. For instance, Wittfogel's ideas were introduced to Mexico by Paul Kirchoff, who fled to Mexico from Nazi Germany and taught at the Escuela Nacional de Antropología e Historia (ENAH). Attending Kirchoff's classes at ENAH was another émigré, archaeologist Pedro Armillas, who came to Mexico from Spain following the Spanish Civil War (Wolf 2001:41).

Armillas was strongly critical of archaeology's emphasis in Mexico on monumental architecture, and he was an early proponent of pedestrian archaeological survey. Independently of Julian Steward (whose work is more widely known among US anthropologists), Armillas (1948) developed a materialist approach to cultural evolution that is widely acknowledged as instrumental in moving Mexican archaeology in a new direction (Bernal 1980:12, 1983:391): "Pedro Armillas was a pioneer in the truest sense of the word. Few of those who heard his discussions and presentations in the late forties and fifties will ever forget the impact of his statements on his listeners. To him, above all, is owed the reorientation of work in the Mexican highlands" (Wolf 1976:3). Even late in his career in the 1970s, when I met Armillas, his charismatic personality and his intellectual grasp of Mexican archaeology were impressive.

Among those Armillas influenced was William Sanders, who studied with Armillas at ENAH. Following his 1946 landmark settlement pattern survey of the Viru Valley in Peru, Gordon Willey organized a symposium on settlement patterns in the

Americas at Harvard University (Willey 1956). In this symposium, William Sanders (then a graduate student of Willey's) laid out the conceptual framework that would structure the Basin of Mexico settlement pattern project. Sanders (1956) defined an 25,000 km² area of Central Mexico comprising the Basin of Mexico, the modern states of Morelos and Tlaxcala, western Puebla, and southern Hidalgo as a nuclear area for the formation of Mesoamerican cities and states. He called this the "Central Mexican Symbiotic Region" because of the environmental complementarity between the *tierra fria* (cool lands) of northern Central Mexico and the warmer, frost-free *tierra templada* (warm lands) of southern Central Mexico.[2]

Sanders attributed the early development of states and cities in the region to two features. He argued that the semi-arid climate with its marked year-to-year fluctuations in rainfall (and a frost season in northern Central Mexico) prompted the early development of intensive agriculture and specialized agricultural adaptations able to support large dense populations. The work of Esther Boserup (1965) led Sanders and his colleagues to modify the model and posit population pressure as a major factor behind agricultural intensification. They also considered how the growth of cities, such as Tenochtitlan-Tlatelolco, causes intensification (Jacobs 1969; Sanders et al. 1979; Sanders and Santley 1983).

The cultural ecological model also proposed that micro-geographic variations in agricultural and other resources encouraged trade, specialization, and economic interdependence or "symbiosis." Incorporating the theory of ethnographer Robert Carneiro (1970), circumscription, competition, and differential access to strategic resources were seen as the basis for the development of stratification and social classes, market exchange, and tribute extraction and political centralization. To test this cultural ecological model knowledge of the agricultural and population history of the basin would be required. However, documentary sources provided only limited information on Aztec rural settlements. Sanders saw Willey's settlement survey method as way to test these ideas by doing "a prehistoric cultural geography," and as a means to measure the centralization of political authority and internal differentiation on a large regional scale from an explicitly materialist, cultural-ecological framework (Sanders 1999:13, 2001a:889; Sanders et al. 1979:4).

The Basin of Mexico Surveys

In 1960 scholars interested in the ancient civilizations of Central Mexico gathered at a conference to chart directions for future archaeological research in the basin (Wolf 1976). Following the conference, Sanders (1965, 1999, 2001a) began the regional settlement pattern survey in the Teotihuacan Valley, where he focused on rural areas while René Millon directed efforts at mapping the Classic period city of Teotihuacan (see Chapters 4 and 5). Sanders intended the Teotihuacan Valley Project to be the first in a series of long-term cultural-ecological studies of the entire Central Mexican symbiotic region. The research strategy included ethnographic studies of contemporary agriculture and settlement to define material culture patterns to help understand the archaeological record. Research on Colonial period documents provided additional important information, both for model-building and on the Aztecs (e.g., Charlton 1986; Sanders et al. 2001).

Today, the regional settlement pattern survey is a fundamental archaeological method, but in 1960 when Sanders began the Teotihuacan Valley Project, strategies for how to conduct systematic surveys had to be devised for the first time (Nichols 1996; Parsons 1972; Sabloff and Ashmore 2001; Sanders 1999). Willey had used aerial photographs to identify sites in his survey of Peru's Viru Valley, which biased his survey toward sites with visible architecture. This approach is not possible in Central Mexico because sheet erosion of hill slopes, deposition of eroded soil on basin/valley floors, and plowing have reduced most prehispanic architecture to mound remnants, artifact scatters, and artifact concentrations. Fortunately, Jeffrey Parsons was able to translate his experience from geological surveys, using aerial photographs for orienteering and mapping surface features to archaeology, as he notes that "at that time, there were only about a dozen archaeologists in the entire world who were doing this kind of research" (Parsons n.d.:5).

In the Viru Valley, Willey had faced "a bewildering array of architectural forms (Willey 1999:10). In the Teotihuacan Valley survey, crews confronted a very different problem: "we located numerous mounds of varying size, form, and height, but we had no clear idea as to their original architectural characteristics, their plan, function and construction techniques" (Sanders 1999:14). To address this problem and overcome inadequacies in the available ceramic sequence (Charlton 1968; Parsons 1966), Sanders added an excavation program to the project, which included the horizontal exposure of house remains (see Sanders and Evans 2000). Today, we call investigations focused on the household as the unit of analysis "household archaeology." Prior to this project there had been *no* published excavations of a rural Aztec house. George Vaillant had dug portions of an Aztec palace or noble residence at Chiconautla (Fig. 11.2), an Aztec city-state capital in the Teotihuacan Valley (see Elson 1999). But the systematic investigation of rural Aztec households was an innovation of the Basin of Mexico project.

Following completion of the Teotihuacan Valley Project (Evans and Sanders 2000; Sanders and Evans 2000, 2001), surveys of other sections of the basin were undertaken in stages, and completed in the mid-1970s (Blanton 1972; Nichols 1980; Parsons 1971; Parsons et al. 1982; Sanders and Evans 2001; Sanders et al. 1979). The western basin could not be surveyed because it is covered by Mexico City, and the continued growth of the basin's population and associated construction has destroyed many of the sites recorded by the surveys in other parts of the basin.

Aztec Population

A major challenge in the 1970s for testing cultural ecological models was to reconstruct the size of the Aztec population. There are no Aztec census records and the first relatively accurate census by the Spanish colonial administration was not taken

NORTH TRAVERSE HOUSE

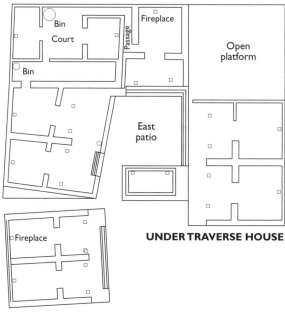

UNDER TRAVERSE HOUSE

CENTRAL TRAVERSE HOUSE

D. F. Levett Bradley, 1938   **SOUTH TRAVERSE HOUSE**

Figure 11.2. Plan of Aztec palace at Chiconautla as excavated by George Vaillant

until the 1540s, more than two decades after the introduction of European epi-
demic diseases caused a catastrophic decline in population. Sanders and his
colleagues took a twofold approach to the problem of estimating the size of the
Aztec population in the early 1500s (Sanders 1970; Sanders and Evans
2001:937–943; Smith 1996b). First, they considered a range of factors to estimate
a rate of decline from European diseases to make a conservative pre-contact population estimate. Second, from their ethnographic studies of contemporary settlement patterns they developed a graduated scale for prehispanic sites, relating
artifact densities and population. Because many archaeological sites in the basin

consist of concentrations of artifacts and building rubble visible on the surface, whole sites, not individual mounds representing buildings, became the unit of analysis. Parsons (1971:16–17) further refined the site typology, method of population estimation, and survey procedures in his survey of the Texcoco region in the eastern basin. Following completion of the surveys, Sanders, Parsons, and Santley (1979) generated the first large-scale archaeological population estimate in Mesoamerica (Smith 1996:378). The independently derived archaeological population estimates were then compared against the estimates from documentary data. The survey procedures and methodology of population estimation devised in the basin have served as a model for surveys in other parts of highland Mexico and in other world regions (Nichols 1996; Parsons 1972).

The Basin of Mexico survey project not only introduced a regional perspective to Aztec archaeology but it anticipated later trends in ethnoarchaeology, household archaeology, and historical archaeology. A most surprising and important discovery of the surveys was the high density of Aztec sites, both rural and urban. Forty percent of all the recorded sites in the basin date to the Late Postclassic period, a span of less than 200 years (Sanders et al. 1979:161).[3] The total population of the basin in the early sixteenth century has been conservatively estimated at between 800,000 and 1.25 million people – four times larger than during any previous period (Sanders et al. 1979:162). The survey data indicate that the basin's population grew rapidly during the thirteenth and fourteenth centuries. Although population relocations took place, in Sanders' view the archaeological survey data from the basin do not indicate the occurrence of large-scale migrations as described in native histories (Sanders and Evans 2001; compare Smith 1984). The rate of growth and the sheer size of the basin's population had social as well as ecological ramifications.

Aztec Urban Settlement Patterns

Aztec sites vary considerably in size and form, and include salt-making stations, special-purpose camps, hamlets (small and large), dispersed and nucleated villages, towns, and cities of various sizes. The surveys showed that, although urbanization long pre-dated the Aztec empire in the basin, it intensified during the Late Postclassic (A.D. 1350/1400–1521) when Tenochtitlan-Tlatelolco became (through immigration, as well as natural population increase) the largest city in the history of prehispanic Mesoamerica with a population of 150,000 to 200,000 people.

Archaeologists could not survey the Tenochtitlan-Tlatelolco area because it underlies Mexico City. However, details about the city's organization from Edward Calnek's (1972, 1976, 1978) archival research influenced how archaeologists interpreted Aztec urban settlement patterns. Causeways connected the island city of Tenochtitlan-Tlatelolco to the mainland where another 200,000 people lived in a dense band of settlements along the adjacent lake shore, making this one of the most urbanized areas anywhere in the sixteenth-century world. Nearly 20 percent of the people in the basin lived in Tenochtitlan-Tlatelolco (ca. 150,000–200,000 people). The city was laid out in a regular grid plan of streets and canals, with closely spaced houses grouped around patios; small *chinampa* plots were used for household gardens (Calnek 1972, 1976). Specialists in a particular craft tended to reside together in same ward (Nichols 1994; Sanders 1981:192). The marketplace at Tlatelolco, where goods could be obtained from throughout the Aztec empire and beyond, was visited by 20,000 to 50,000 people each day (Berdan 1982:26–28). A walled ceremonial precinct of major temples and altars lay at the heart of the city, and adjoining it were the palaces of Aztec rulers, noble residences, and administrative buildings (Berdan 1982:10–14; Calnek 1972). The exceptional size and complexity of Tenochtitlan-Tlatelolco was tied to its status as the Aztec imperial capital, along with economic factors including the growth of the market (Nichols et al. 2002; Sanders and Santley 1983; Smith and Montiel 2001).

The historical development of the Aztec empire had occurred only a short time before the Spanish first entered Tenochtitlan. After two centuries of intense political fragmentation, by A.D. 1400 the Acolhua of Texcoco in the eastern basin, and the Tepenaca of Aztcapotzalco in the western basin, had each formed fragile tributary empires (Charlton and Nichols 1997a:199). In 1428 the Mexica of Tenochtitlan broke away from the Tepenaca and created a military alliance with Texcoco and the small city-state of Tlacopan to defeat the Tepenaca. After consolidating control over city-states in the basin, the Aztec empire began to conquer areas outside the basin, starting in Morelos immediately south, and over the next 80 years extended their conquests to the Pacific and Gulf coasts and the southern highlands of Mexico (Davies 1973; Hassig 1988). The Mexica dominated this "Triple Alliance," but the Acolhua of Texcoco maintained strong control over an area of 3,000–4,000 km^2 with a population of 300,000. The Acolhua capital, Texcoco, while much smaller than Tenochtitlan-Tlatelolco, with 40,000 people, was nonetheless one of the largest cities in Mesoamerica (Sanders and Evans 2001:933).

Tributary empires like the Aztec empire developed from existing political units. The most stable polity throughout the Postclassic was the city-state (*altepetl* in Nahuatl). Both archaeological and ethnohistoric data indicate the existence of Aztec city-states by ca. A.D. 1200, if not earlier (Charlton and Nichols 1997a:199–202; Hodge 1994, 1997). Each city-state was ruled by a hereditary lord (or lords), the *tlatoani*. Each altepetl consisted of a rural hinterland with dependent villages organized around a central town or city that held the ruler's palace, major temples, and marketplace. Marriage and noble dynastic ties, noble gift exchanges, commercial trade, a shared "Great Tradition" of language, writing, calendrics, religion and rituals, and architecture, as well as military alliances and wars linked city-states. Between 3,000 and 6,000 people lived in most city-state capitals, although some were larger, with populations of over 10,000 (Sanders 1981:189). City-states became semi-autonomous administrative units under the Aztec empire (Bray 1972, 1983). The size hierarchy of Aztec urban centers – ranging from the small capital cities and towns of city-states to centers of larger confederations (e.g. Aztcapotzalco and Texcoco), to the imperial city of Tenochtitlan-Tlatelolco – mirrors the political hierarchy the Aztec state had developed by the early sixteenth century (Smith et al. 1994:8–9).

Based on the limited archaeological data from the city-state centers that could be surveyed, Sanders et al. (1979:163) thought that Late Postclassic Aztec provincial city-state capitals mimicked Tenochtitlan in their configuration but on a much smaller scale. In this concentric zone model, a dense nucleated core of plazas, palaces, temples and related buildings, and closely spaced high-status residences, is surrounded by a zone of less dense but still nucleated houses, which in turn are encircled by a zone of outlying dispersed houses. Full-time craft specialists concentrated in urban centers resided in wards or *calpolli* ("big houses") according to their specialty, while rural specialists were part-time. There is much debate about the nature of the Aztec calpolli. It was a territorially based corporate group that was internally stratified with its own lord that held land, paid tribute, performed military service and labor taxes, along with other political and religious functions (Berdan 1982:18; Carrasco 1971:365–366, Gillespie 2000; Lockhart 1992:17–18).

In the economic symbiotic model, the entire populace of the city-state was integrated into "a single trading system focused on the town market, which in turn was one link in chain of urban markets that made Central Mexico a symbiotic region" (Sanders 1965:67). At Otumba, one of the few Aztec city-state capitals in the Teotihuacan Valley not obscured by modern settlements, the survey found dense concentrations of ceramic and lithic workshop debris, lending support to the economic symbiotic model (see summary in Charlton et al. 2000a, 2000b).

Aztec Rural Settlement Patterns

Rural Aztec settlements were dispersed but densely distributed over an intensively cultivated landscape. The Aztecs grew hundreds of varieties of crops, but most important were maize, beans, squash, chia, amaranth, and maguey. Maguey, used for fibers as well as food, is especially well suited to growing in the drier northern Central Mexico. In the Late Postclassic maguey cultivation and fiber production was a specialty of the northern and eastern basin. Cotton, which does not grow in the basin, was imported principally from Morelos.

The Aztecs practiced a variety of agricultural land-use systems, and farmers had brought most arable land in the basin under cultivation by the end of the fifteenth century (Doolittle 1990; Nichols and Frederick 1993; Sanders et al. 1979). Terracing of piedmont hillslopes expanded significantly during the Middle and Late Postclassic. Where possible farmers supplemented the seasonal rainfall with irrigation. Seasonal runoff from summer storms was diverted through floodwater irrigation networks to water terraced fields and alluvial plains. All the freshwater perennial springs and rivers were tapped to supply water for relatively large-scale permanent irrigation networks.

The most intensive and impressive type of agriculture practiced by the Aztecs was their system of *chinampas*. Chinampas are fields constructed in shallow-water areas by digging soil from one area, creating canals, and placing it in another location, until the ground surface is above water. Between 1965 and 1967 Pedro Armillas (1971) conducted an archaeological survey of the Aztec chinampa zone in the southern Basin of Mexico. He found that in the fifteenth century the chinampas were expanded by constructing elaborate networks of drainage ditches, canals, and dikes to lower and regulate the water level of the shallow freshwater Lake Chalco-Xochimilco. The regularity of the chinampa plots, and the size of the area involved (9,500 ha), indicate that this was a coordinated, planned, large-scale project (Parsons 1991). Through this project, most of the western shore of Lake Texcoco and southern shore of Lake Chalco-Xochimilco were converted to chinampas producing an annual surplus of 16,500 metric tons of maize that was distributed through the marketplace (González 1992; Parsons 1976:252). Although constructing and maintaining chinampas requires substantial labor, they may be kept in continuous cultivation, producing up to seven crops each year, out-producing any other possible form of agriculture in the same area.

Armillas' chinampa survey was an early application of landscape archaeology. Armillas felt that the concept of "site" used by archaeologists was too limiting, especially to understand large-scale landscape modifications. Influenced by the work of British geographers, he saw "landscape archaeology" as offering a broader conceptual framework, where the cultural landscape – including field systems, roadways, and waterways that link regional systems, as well as settlements – reflects "the interplay between the environment and the technology, structure, and values of the society that shaped it" (Armillas 1971:654).

The expansion of the chinampa system in the southern basin and the terracing of hillsides was associated with a pattern of dispersed rural settlement. This rural pattern of "broadly and continuously distributed settlements over the landscape" is unique to the Late Postclassic, as is the high density of the rural population (Sanders et al. 1979:163–164). In the southern basin, *chinampero* families lived in houses built directly on chinampa plots that often belonged to noble estates (Parsons 1976). The creation of these estates was one of the ways Aztec rulers consolidated the allegiances of elites to the imperial government. On the piedmont slopes of the northern and eastern basin, rural settlements formed an almost continuous "blanket of dispersed households and terraces, with only occasional ceremonial centers breaking the continuity of what looks like essentially a single, large rural community" (Sanders et al. 1979:251). Aztec rural households had "very close, sustaining relationships with particular parcels of land" because the intensity of chinampa and terrace cultivation required farmers to live nearby their fields (Sanders and Evans 2001:969).

City-States, Political Economy, and Agency

The high density of both the rural and urban Aztec settlements of the early sixteenth century revealed by the archaeological surveys reshaped contemporary views of the Aztec landscape. The correlation between the great increase in the size of the Aztec population and the intensification of agriculture that included large-scale land modifications seemed to lend support to the cultural-ecological model proposed by Sanders and his colleagues. However, by the mid-1970s adaptational models of sociocultural evolution were increasingly criticized for being too deterministic and not comprehensive enough (e.g. Zeitlin and Zeitlin 1980). In recent decades archaeologists working in the basin have broadened their theoretical frameworks to include modifications of world systems theory, political economy, agency, history, and feminist theory, often incorporating a regional perspective.

Richard Blanton (1976a, 1976b, 2002:404; Blanton and Feinman 1984), for example, who surveyed the Ixtapalapa peninsula in the eastern basin before going on to work in the Valley of Oaxaca, felt that a more robust theory that builds on cultural ecology was necessary to understand how processes of local change at the level of households and villages shape and are shaped by change on an increasingly larger spatial scale and over longer distances. He and his colleagues have advocated a regional analysis approach (Blanton et al. 1993[1981]). Blanton credits Armillas' concept of landscape archaeology as an important early influence on his ideas (Blanton 1978:xxii). Paralleling trends in the social sciences in the 1970s emphasizing quantification and formal model-testing, archaeologists and geographers recognized that the Basin of Mexico survey data offered a valuable long-term data set on the spatial patterning of human settlements and an opportunity to apply models and methods of analysis from geography, such as rank-size, Central Place Theory, and catchment analysis (Blanton 1976a, 1976b; Brumfiel 1976a; Evans 1980; Evans and Gould 1982; Gorenflo 1996; Gorenflo and Gale 1986, 1990; Sanders et al. 1979; Smith 1979, 1980). Despite disagreements about which models are most appropriate for precapitalist societies, these studies demonstrate that the systematic regional survey data can be used to address questions never considered in the original research design.

Results of these analyses, in some cases, directly challenged the cultural ecological model of socio-political evolution in the basin, and fueled debates about the causes and consequences of population change, the importance of market dynamics, ecology, ideology, and politics in the development of Aztec city-states, urban centers, and exchange relations (see summary in Charlton and Nichols 1997a, 1997b; Nichols 2000). The settlement data could be interpreted in several ways, partly because of limited surveys of Aztec urban sites (Parsons 1990; Sanders et al. 1979:161).[4] Moreover, relevant information from documentary sources on many city-state centers, as well as rural settlements, is often very incomplete or even missing. Archaeologists had to employ other research strategies, involving intensive survey and surface collection, household archaeology, materials analysis, and ethnoarchaeology. The investigation of the impact of Aztec imperialism also was expanded to other parts of Central Mexico (see summary in Smith 1996) The most striking finding from the recent and ongoing research is the heterogeneity of Aztec city-states and their socio-economic complexity.

For her doctoral research Elizabeth Brumfiel (1976b) undertook a test of the symbiotic model at the site of Huexotla, an important city-state capital in the eastern basin, using intensive surface collections and a probabilistic sampling design. Her investigations did not find evidence of wards of craft specialists. Nor did she find such evidence in her subsequent work at Xico, in the southern basin, or at Xaltocan, an island capital of an important Otomi state in the northwestern basin (Brumfiel 1980, 1983, 1986, 1987a, 1987b). In contrast to the symbiotic model, she argues that politics played a more important role in shaping the urban landscape and in rural–urban relations. She proposes that, as the flow of tribute goods increased into Tenochtitlan-Tlatelolco and Texcoco, this encouraged people in other city-states to focus on agricultural production. Full-time craft specialists were to be found only in the imperial cities (see also Hassig 1985).

Thomas Charlton's (1978) survey of trade routes leading out of the northeastern Basin of Mexico traversed three city-states – Tepeapulco, Tulancingo, and Otumba – each of which has a long history of involvement in the obsidian industry. But he found that the organization of the obsidian industry and the impact of Aztec imperialism differed in each case (Charlton 1994; Parry 2002).

At Otumba, the capital of the largest Aztec city-state in the Teotihuacan Valley, Charlton and I directed a project of intensive surface collection and excavations in the nucleated core of Otumba, and of several workshops. The Otumba Project also intensively surveyed and made surface collections of a sample of rural sites in the city-state. Our investigations confirmed abundant evidence of craft specialization in several industries (Charlton et al. 1991; Charlton et al. 2000a, 2000b; Nichols 1994; Otis Charlton et al. 1993). Household-based workshops in the town mass-produced mold-made figurines used in household rituals, cotton and maguey spindle whorls, a local style of Red Ware pottery, marbles, stamps, whistles, censers, and other pottery molds. Although the Otumba obsidian source area lies in the city-state's domain, all but one of the obsidian core-blade workshops made obsidian tools from green obsidian imported from the Pachuca source area farther to the north (Parry 2000). Used prismatic cores from the core-blade workshops were recycled by lapidaries, who in their own workshops made lip plugs, ear spools, and other ornaments of obsidian and rare stones, using basalt grinding tools also made at Otumba (Biskowski 2000; Otis Charlton 1993, 1994). We also documented the first maguey fiber workshops that, in addition to processing maguey, spinning fibers, and presumably weaving and perhaps dying cloth, also mass-produced spindle whorls from molds (Nichols et al. 2000).

The development of specialized urban workshops for processing, spinning, and weaving maguey at Otumba was part of a broader trend of intensification of maguey cultivation in the drier northern basin. Ethnoarchaeological studies by Jeffery and Mary Parsons (1990) and research by Evans (1990; Sanders and Evans 2001) has led to a new appreciation that maguey likely complemented maize as a staple crop in the piedmont villages of the northern basin.

In contrast to the restructuring of city-state economies in the core of the basin to emphasize agricultural production, craft specialization intensified at Otumba in the Late Postclassic (Charlton 1994; Charlton and Nichols 1997a:202–203; Charlton et al. 1991, 2000a; Hodge, in press; Minc et al. 1994; Nichols et al. 2002). However, Otumba diverged from the economic symbiotic model in other respects (Nichols 1994; Sanders et al. 1979). Craft workshops were not restricted to the nucleated core of Otumba. Most workshops are in the dispersed residential zone, where some industries (e.g. figurines and maguey fiber processing and spinning) occur in clusters suggestive of wards or calpolli organization. Other craft workshops are scattered in different parts of this zone. Excavations in the core of Otumba suggest the presence of open spaces and more widely dispersed residences than previously thought.

Fred Hicks (1982) argues from research on Texcoco that, beyond a small nucleated core containing the rulers' palace(s), temples, and marketplace, most Aztec urban centers consisted of a dispersed residential zone where specialists' and non-specialists' houses were commingled. He thinks that the nucleation and barrio organization of craft specialists in Tenochtitlan-Tlatelolco was exceptional. Christopher Garraty's (2000) recent analysis of the Teotihuacan Mapping Project collections suggests that wealthy families were dispersed in different parts of Aztec Teotihuacan, as were obsidian core-blade workshops (Spence 1985).

Clearly, city-state urban centers varied in population size and density and in their spatial organization, as well as in the degree and kind of commercial activities taking place in them. Beyond a nucleated core of public buildings – rulers' palace, *calmecac* (school), marketplace, and ceremonial enclosure with the major temple and shrines – Aztec cities in the basin do not seem to follow a single canon in their layout. Nor did Aztec imperial rulers impose a standardized layout. Although some city-state capitals may be nucleated, current evidence suggests that a more dispersed residential urban landscape was common, with houselot gardens and, in some cases, workshop areas surrounding individual houses.

All Aztec city-states shared the basic structure of an urban center and an intensively cultivated hinterland with villages and hamlets (Bray 1972, 1983; Hodge 1984). In the symbiotic model, trade linked the hinterland and center of individual city-states and linked city-states into a larger network that integrated the ecological diversity of Central Mexico. Some archaeologists attribute the dominance of the city-state form during the Postclassic to the growth of the market that inhibited strong political centralization above the city-state level (Blanton et al. 1993:156, 216). Other archaeologists stress the importance of politics in the political economy (see summary in Nichols et al. 2002).

Materials Analysis

In the 1980s Mary Hodge and her colleague Leah Minc developed a new approach to analyzing the impact of politics on Aztec market exchange networks with a regional perspective. Sanders et al. (1979:161) had observed from the settlement surveys that the standardization in vessel form and decoration of Late Postclassic (Aztec III) pottery was greater than in any previous period. They attributed this to much tighter political and economic integration. Despite this standardization, Hodge's analysis of decorated pottery from survey collections of sites in the southern and eastern basin revealed spatial patterns in the distribution of certain motifs and styles (Hodge 1992; Hodge and Minc 1990, 1991). She and her colleagues compared these stylistic variants with the composition of pottery pastes and clays determined by instrumental neutron activation analysis, or INAA (Hodge et al. 1992, 1993; Minc et al. 1994). The research showed that Aztec pottery production took place in multiple centers. Hodge and Minc suggested that the development of a fully integrated regional market system was actually inhibited by political boundaries between confederations of city-states, and that these effects persisted even after the entire basin was integrated into the Aztec empire.

Building on this research, Charlton and I have directed a complementary project of INAA of ceramic and lithic artifacts focused on the northern and northeastern basin. Ceramics produced in the Otumba workshops were consumed within the city-state but also traded to other city-states, primarily in the eastern and northeastern basin (Charlton et al. 2000a; Neff et al. 2000; Nichols and Charlton 2001). INAA results from three sites in other parts of the basin with long Postclassic occupations, Chalco, Cerro Portezuelo, and Xaltocan, show that city-states were linked in complex exchange networks that pre-date the Aztec empire. Whether or not a fully integrated regional market system developed in the basin by the early sixteenth century remains an open question (Nichols et al. 2002:30).

Aztec State

Despite the impressive size and imperial status of Tenochtitlan-Tlatelolco, the Late Postclassic settlement system was not a primate pattern such as that associated with Teotihuacan in the Classic period. Administrative, economic, and ideological state functions were more decentralized in the Aztec state. The sheer size of the Late Postclassic population, and its socio-economic heterogeneity, precluded such centralization, and the dependence of rulers and other elites on the market inhibited it as well (Charlton and Nichols 1997a:204). Under the Aztec empire, city-state capitals usually retained important political-administrative and religious functions.

Aztec rulers were wealthy and powerful, but governance in Central Mexico emphasized corporate political-economic strategies and was not centered around a cult of the king or emperor (Blanton et al. 1996). Thus, unlike the Classic Maya, royal funerary monuments did not dominate the Aztec landscape. Nor do we find planned colonial administrative centers in the basin such as those constructed by the Inca in their Andean heartland. Aztec imperial rule was hegemonic: unless faced with strong resistance, local rulers usually retained control over the internal affairs of their city-states (Hassig 1988).

Aztec rulers, however, employed various other strategies beyond just military conquest to alter the political landscape and enhance their power (Berdan et al. 1996). Their interventions and manipulations were most direct in the Basin of Mexico. Along with requiring tribute in goods, commoners in the basin also were required to contribute labor to imperial construction projects (in addition to a rotational labor tax owed to their local lords). A separate imperial tribute system was implemented, and Aztec rulers assigned nobles estates created from appropriated lands that were dispersed throughout the basin. Marriages between the imperial and local dynasties, along with gifts to loyal nobles, feasting, and invitations to major ceremonies in Tenochtitlan sought to create a noble class or aristocracy that cross-cut city-states. Local administrative positions sometimes were eliminated and new ones created that suited Tenochtitlan's and/or Texcoco's interests. Aztec rulers would promote the growth of new market centers to undermine the political power of potential rivals (Blanton 1996:74; Hodge 1996; Sanders and Evans 2001:945). In the Teotihuacan Valley, the famous Acolhua ruler Nezahuacoyotl employed what Evans (2001a:93) calls an interdigitation strategy, where he reassigned tributary villages of one city-state to the lord of another city-state so that each ruler's tributaries were dispersed in different parts of the valley, undermining the territorial integrity and autonomy of city-states (see also Smith 2000:587).

Research on Aztec imperial strategies contributes to recent efforts by archaeologists working in different world regions to develop an archaeology of imperialism (Smith 2001). Smith and Montiel (2001) recently used Doyel's (1986) theory of empires to define archaeological correlates which they apply to the Aztecs and earlier regional states in Central Mexico. Despite the grandeur attributed to the Toltecs by the Aztecs, Smith and Montiel conclude that Early Postclassic Tula was not an empire, while Teotihuacan was. This is certain to spark debate, but it raises an important issue about the need for a long-term perspective on Aztec state development.

The Aztec empire formed in a political landscape influenced by the legacy of earlier civilizations and processes of change that operated over different time-scales (Charlton and Nichols 1997a, 1997b; Smith 1992a). Our ability to measure change, especially rapid change, in the archaeological record of the basin remains a problem, despite recent efforts to evaluate the archaeological chronology with radiocarbon dates and to develop more refined ceramic phases for the basin (Brumfiel in press; Cowgill 1996; Evans and Freter 1996; Manzanilla et al. 1996; Nichols and Charlton 1996; Parsons et al. 1996; Vaillant 1938). There remain unresolved questions about the degree of chronological overlap and geographical differences in the dating of certain key ceramic types that have important implications for our understanding of the basin's political geography during the Postclassic (Nichols and Charlton 1996). Emphasizing only comparisons between the Middle and Late Postclassic will overlook longer-term processes in the development of the Aztec state (Charlton and Nichols 1997a; Marcus 1992, 1998:71–74; Nichols et al. 2002:27; Smith 1992a, 2001).

Social Relations

As is true of tributary states in general, a major division within Aztec society was between a class of hereditary nobility, *pilli*, who were entitled to receive tribute (and other privileges) from commoners, *mayeque* and *macehual*, who comprised most of Aztec society. In between was an intermediary class of professional merchants, *pochteca*, and artisans who made luxury goods (Carrasco 1971, 1977). These divisions are evident in Aztec city-states in the quality of housing, the size of houses, and the relative proportions of luxury goods (Charlton and Nichols 1992; Charlton et al. 2000a; Smith 1987a, 1987b, 1994, 1996:134–161).

Stratification extended to the rural as well as urban landscape, and elites lived in rural villages as well as urban centers. Documenting socio-economic variability within rural communities represents one of the major contributions of recent Aztec archaeology. Susan Evans' excavations at Cihuatecpan, one of Otumba's dependencies, found remains of a village lord's or noble administrator's residence, a *tecpan* (Evans 1988, 1991, 1993). This tecpan consists of several apartment complexes arranged around a central courtyard in a smaller-scale version of larger tlatoani palaces. The multiple apartment complexes may have housed multiple wives of the resident lord, since polygyny was a measure of status in Aztec society. The countryside also included lavish pleasure parks built by imperial rulers, with palaces, shrines, baths, and aviaries, and landscaped with exotic plants (Evans 2000:216). Evans discusses how the development of these parks was a statement of dynastic status rivalry between Texcoco and Tenochtitlan. The appearance of sites like Texcotzingo, the royal retreat of Texcoco's rulers, signifies "an economic system vastly more wealthy than any previous Mesoamerican society" (Evans 2000:223).

Smith's large-scale program of Aztec household archaeology in Morelos has shown that rural areas outside the empire's core also were socially complex landscapes with considerable social and economic variation (Smith 1992b:3, 1997a; Smith and Heath Smith 1994). The social complexity of rural communities during the Late Postclassic seems greater than at any previous time. A number of factors contributed to shaping the complexity and heterogeneity of the Aztec rural social landscape: high population levels, reduced political centralization beyond the city-state level, market exchange, elite interactions, historical and cultural traditions, linguistic diversity, and conflict and political competition between factions and city-states and confederations (Brumfiel 1989, 1994; Charlton and Nichols 1997a; Nichols 2000; Smith 1997a, 1997b).

A goal of the Basin of Mexico project was to reconstruct social organization, which was seen as the second major determinant of settlement patterns, in addition to ecology. One approach has emphasized formal social structures, such as the calpolli (Garraty 2000; Sanders and Evans 2001). Complementing these studies are agency- or actor-based approaches focused on factions, gender, and individuals (Brumfiel 1992:559).

The Aztec social landscape was gendered, as well as stratified; the house was considered the domain of women, but Aztec women were not restricted to that space. The archaeological study of Aztec gender relations changed dramatically beginning in the 1990s, influenced both by theoretical developments and by the changing gender of archaeology. Women did not begin to pursue graduate study in archaeology in substantial numbers until the 1970s.[5]

There is ongoing debate about status of women in Aztec society. Did Aztec militarism and imperial ideology linking male warfare, human sacrifice, and tribute lead to a decline in the position of women? How widespread was the acceptance of the imperial ideology among women, among commoners, among people in hinterland city-states? Was gender parallelism or mutual opposition maintained? These questions relate to a larger theoretical issue of the effectiveness of ideological domination as a means of control (Brumfiel 1996:146; Conrad and Demarest 1984; Nash 1978).

One way archaeologists working in the basin have approached these questions is through the study of some common classes of ceramic artifacts: spindle whorls used in spinning thread, figurines, and to a more limited degree pottery (Brumfiel 1991, 1996, 1998, 2001, 2002; Evans 2001b; Joyce 2000:132–175; McCafferty and McCafferty 1991; Nichols et al. 2000; Otis Charlton 1994). Brumfiel and the McCaffertys stress how these objects, in their usage and symbolism, were related to women's identities and to resisting the imperial state ideology. Archaeological studies of the dynamics of gender relations in the basin are hampered by the limited range of excavated Aztec household contexts. Moreover, the relatively small number of Aztec burials has precluded analyses of paleo-pathology, nutrition, and demography and burial goods and practices that could greatly contribute to our understanding of gender relations (and many other facets of social relations) and how they were or were not impacted by the ideological and material dimensions of Aztec imperialism.

Ideology and the Ritual Landscape

The Aztecs created sacred or ritual landscapes that paralleled the complexity of human social relations (Smith 2002). The ultimate physical expression of Aztec state ideology and religion was a sacred walled enclosure in Tenochtitlan, a monumental sacred geography situated by divine direction to place the Mexica of Tenochtitlan at the center of the universe (Carrasco 1991). The Spanish constructed the administrative and religious center of their colonial capital, Mexico City, atop the ruins of the sacred enclosure. In 1978 the accidental discovery of a monumental carved stone of Coyolxauhqui initiated excavations and reconstruction of the Templo Mayor, the main Aztec temple, under the direction of Eduardo Matos Moctezuma (1988, 2000; Matos et al. 1998; see also papers in Boone 1987). The excavations also uncovered an adjoining hall for the elite military orders of the Eagle and Jaguar knights (Barba et al. 1998). A major museum presenting the history of the Aztecs using artifacts and other evidence from the excavations constructed at the site has become a national and international tourist center. Nationalism is an important dimension of Mexican archaeology, especially Aztec archaeology, because of its importance in the Spanish Conquest and the prominent place of the Aztecs in the historical charter of the modern Mexican state (Litvak King 1997).

The Templo Mayor is a twin pyramid with two shrines, one devoted to Huitzilopochtli, the Aztec's patron deity and god of war, and the other devoted to Tlaloc, the rain deity (Matos 1988; Matos et al. 1998). The pyramid symbolizes Coatepec, Serpent Hill, where Huitzilopochtli was born and successfully fought off his brothers, the stars, and his sister Coyolxauhqui, the moon. The Temple's architecture and offerings also express how Aztec state ideology built on and appropriated beliefs and rituals associated with core Central Mexican concepts that linked warfare and fertility to natural cycles and earthly renewal and the sustenance of cosmic forces through offerings (Broda et al. 1987; Manzanilla 2000; Matos 1988; Nicholson 1971). Most of the numerous offerings incorporated into the temple as it was enlarged by Aztec rulers are foreign objects from areas conquered by the Aztecs (López Luján 1993). The offerings also included heirlooms from earlier civilizations asserting the legitimacy of the Mexica of Tenochtitlan as the inheritors of the power of earlier great cities, Teotihuacan and Toltec Tula (e.g., Matos 2000; Nichols 2000). The Aztecs' sacred mission to sustain the sun and the present universe with large-scale sacrifices of enemy warriors at the Templo Mayor carried both political and religious meanings (Berdan 1982:111–119; Brumfiel 1998, 2001; Carrasco 1999; Wolf 1999; see also Chapter 10).

The power of the Aztec state also derived from the cultivated landscape made productive by the labor of people, and by the cosmic forces that provided light by winning the daily battle of day over night, and water from within the sacred mountains (Manzanilla 2000; Matos 1988, 2000). The sacred enclosure, as well as the grid plan of Tenochtitlan, was laid out according to astronomical alignments that had symbolic significance. The second shrine atop the Templo Mayor was dedicated to Tlaloc (associated with rain). Most Aztec monthly rituals were concerned with the agricultural cycle, also an important concern of household rituals (Brumfiel 2001:291).

The Basin of Mexico surveys recorded numerous Aztec shrines atop hills, and the Templo Mayor was linked by astronomical sightlines to the most important of these shrines on Mount Tlaloc, the highest hilltop in the eastern basin and the source of springs from which water flowed into the central Acolhua territory. On its summit, within a formally laid out enclosure, was a temple to Tlaloc. Toward the end of each dry season, the rulers of Texcoco, Tenochtitlan, and Tlacopan (the Triple Alliance capitals) and Xochimilco (an important city-state in the southern chinampa zone) made a pilgrimage to the Mount Tlaloc temple to call forth the rain from within the mountain. This ritual connected Aztec rulers with the life-giving force of water from the summer rains that renew the dry earth (Iwaniszewski and Sprajc 1987; Townsend 2000:140–148).

The symbolic analysis of the architecture and offerings of the Templo Mayor and other sacred geographies of the Aztec state exemplifies a recent focus in landscape archaeology on the social and symbolic meanings of "space and place" (Knapp and Ashmore 1999; see also Carrasco 1999:49–87 and papers in Carrasco 1991). But, how significant were the meanings of these imperial sacred geographies in the lives of most Aztecs? All city-state capitals included a ceremonial precinct and central temple, and thus were centers of state religion. There have been no recent investigations of a provincial temple and ceremonial precinct in the basin similar to the Templo Mayor project that would provide a comparable perspective on state religion at the city-state level. It has been assumed that sacrifices of warriors were made in provincial centers – a report prepared for the king of Spain in 1580 recounts such sacrifices at Acolman, a city-state center in the Teotihuacan Valley (Nuttall 1926:64–65).

Brumfiel has recently explored this issue, using ethnohistorical sources and analyses of figurines to question the assumed pervasiveness of the imperial state's warfare ideology. The widespread occurrence of ritual practices such as human sac-rifice often is taken as evidence of the dominance of Aztec state ideology. Archae-ologists working from the perspective of households and/or provincial areas suggest another alternative, that Aztec rulers appropriated and elevated "household religion in an effort to transfer sentiments from the household to the state" (Brumfiel 2001:290). For instance, although Aztec rulers claimed the New Fire ceremony as an imperial prerogative, the archaeological evidence shows that it was a widely prac-ticed household ritual before the existence of the empire (Elson and Smith 2001). Elson and Smith suggest that the form of imperial rituals was shaped by a "dialec-tic" between common household practices and new imperial strategies. Elevating the New Fire ceremony to the status of an imperial ritual "cross-cut city-states' boundaries, undermined the political power of local elites, and co-opted religious ideology for a program of imperial legitimization and glorification" (Elson and Smith 2001:171–172). Aztec rulers, in taking on essential roles in rituals performed in monumental sacred landscapes, were concerned not just to legitimize their power but also to undermine rival elites (Brumfiel 2001; Elson and Smith 2001). Appro-priating household rituals ensured that the meaning of the state-sponsored cere-monies was widely understood, and was a way of connecting the state with the ritual life of households.

Conclusions

Anthropological archaeology with a problem-oriented approach, combined with new directions in ethnohistory, has reshaped the contours of contemporary under-standings of the Aztecs. The Basin of Mexico settlement pattern project brought a regional perspective to archaeology essential to recognizing that heterogeneity, com-plexity, and scale permeated the multiple landscapes of the Aztecs. The sharp dis-tinction between rural and urban – a distinction that the Aztecs did not emphasize in their concept of the altepetl (Lockhart 1992) – has become blurred. A regional perspective has encouraged archaeologists to investigate the Aztec archaeological record from more vantage points than otherwise might have been done. Subsequent archaeological fieldwork and analyses show that the social and political landscape of the Basin of Mexico was more heterogeneous and complex during the Late Postclassic than in any previous period in Mesoamerica.

A regional perspective on households, social relations, city-states, market dynam-ics, imperialism, and ideology and ritual are critical to integrate investigations of particular sites with survey data (Hodge 1998:223). Research on the Aztecs has contributed to recent comparative work on city-states, urbanism, and imperialism and theory-building. The historical perspective of archaeology shows that some changes and developments attributed to the Aztec empire actually pre-date it and are manifestations of longer-term processes and cultural practices. Recent efforts to refine the archaeological chronology need to be continued. Household archae-ology in the basin should be expanded to a greater range of contexts, but also extended to earlier periods of the Postclassic and into the Colonial period.

Archaeologists have learned to respect the written and archaeological records as independent lines of evidence that provide different but complementary perspectives, rather than just using ethnohistory to explain the archaeological record (Charlton 2000; Hodge 1998:222–223; Nichols and Parsons 1997:162). The successful combination of archaeology and ethnohistory depends on original research in each. The reorientation of archaeology in the Basin of Mexico that began in the mid-twentieth century emphasized a regional anthropological perspective that continues to influence archaeological approaches to understanding the landscapes of the Aztec state.

NOTES

1   The term Aztec is used to refer to all the Nahuatl speakers of Central Mexico who traced their origins to a mythic place called Aztlan. The term Nahuas is now commonly used to refer to these people following the Spanish Conquest (Lockhart 1992; Smith 1996:4).

2   Felix McBryde's (1947) study of the cultural geography of southwest Guatemala inspired Sanders' symbiotic region concept (Sanders 1999).

3   The other 60 percent of sites are distributed over a 2,500-year period from ca. 1250 B.C. to ca. A.D. 1350.

4   One of the limitations of the survey procedures is that only purposive ("grab") collections of diagnostic ceramics were collected from sites for dating purposes. The grab samples are of limited use in assessing site function or in refining population estimates on sites with multiple occupations. Subsequent regional and site-specific surveys in Central Mexico have employed various combinations of probabilistic and purposive sampling of surface artifacts.

5   To the best of my knowledge no woman archaeologist working in the Basin of Mexico yet has held a tenured academic position in a U.S. university with a major graduate program in anthropological archaeology. When women with doctorates began to enter the job market in significant numbers in the 1980s, tenure-line positions were very limited.

REFERENCES

Armillas, P., 1948 A sequence of cultural development in Meso-America. In *A Reappraisal of Peruvian Archaeology*. W. C. Bennett, ed. Pp. 105–111. Memoirs of the Society for American Archaeology 13/4. Menasha, WI.

——1971 Gardens on swamps. *Science* 174, 653–661.

Aveni, A., E. E. Calnek, and H. Hartung, 1988 Myth, environment, and the orientation of the Templo Mayor of Tenochtitlan. *American Antiquity* 53, 287–309.

Barba, L., L. Lazos, K. F. Link, A. Ortiz, and L. Lopez Luján, 1998 Arqueometría en la casa de las águilas. *Arqueología* 7(31), 20–27.

Berdan, F. F., 1982 *The Aztecs of Central Mexico*. New York: Holt, Rinehart & Winston.

Berdan, F. F., R. E. Blanton, E. H. Boone, M. G. Hodge, M. E. Smith, and E. Umberger, eds., 1996 *Aztec Imperial Strategies*. Washington, DC: Dumbarton Oaks.

Bernal, I., 1980 *A History of Mexican Archaeology: The Vanished Civilizations of Middle America.* New York: Thames & Hudson.

—— 1983 The effect of settlement pattern studies on the archaeology of Central Mexico. In *Prehistoric Settlement Patterns: Essays in Honor of Gordon Willey.* E. Z. Vogt and R. M. Leventhal, eds. Pp. 389–399. Albuquerque and Cambridge: University of New Mexico Press; Peabody Museum of Archaeology and Ethnology, Harvard University.

Biskowski, M., 2000 Maize preparation and the Aztec subsistence economy. *Ancient Mesoamerica* 11, 293–306.

Blanton, R. E., 1972 *Prehispanic Settlement Patterns of the Ixtapalapa Peninsula Region, Mexico.* Occasional Papers in Anthropology 6. University Park, PA: Pennsylvania State University Department of Anthropology.

—— 1976a Appendix: Comment on Sanders, Parsons, and Logan. In *The Valley of Mexico: Studies of Pre-hispanic Ecology and Society.* E. R. Wolf, ed. Pp. 179–181. Albuquerque: University of New Mexico Press.

—— 1976b The role of symbiosis in adaptation and sociocultural change in the Valley of Mexico. In *The Valley of Mexico: Studies of Pre-hispanic Ecology and Society.* E. R. Wolf, ed. Pp. 181–202. Albuquerque: University of New Mexico Press.

—— 1978 *Monte Albán: Settlement Patterns at the Ancient Zapotec Capital.* New York: Academic Press.

—— 1996 The Basin of Mexico market system and the growth of empire. In F. F. Berdan, R. E. Blanton, E. H. Boone, M. G. Hodge, M. E. Smith, and E. Umberger, *Aztec Imperial Strategies.* Pp. 47–84. Washington, DC: Dumbarton Oaks.

—— 2002 Archaeologist at work. *Archaeology: Original Readings in Method and Practice.* P. N. Peregrine, C. R. Ember, and M. Ember, eds. Pp. 398–408. Upper Saddle River, NJ: Prentice Hall.

Blanton, R. E., and G. M. Feinman, 1984 The Mesoamerican world system. *American Anthropologist* 86, 673–682.

Blanton, R. E., G. M. Feinman, S. A. Kowalewski, and P. N. Peregrine, 1996 A dual processual theory for the evolution of Mesoamerican civilization. *Current Anthropology* 37, 1–14.

Blanton, R. E., S. A. Kowalewski, G. M. Feinman, and L. M. Finsten, 1993[1981] *Ancient Mesoamerica: A Comparison of Change in Three Regions*, 2nd edn. Cambridge: Cambridge University Press.

Boone, E. H., ed., 1987 *The Aztec Templo Mayor.* Washington, DC: Dumbarton Oaks.

Boserup, E., 1965 *The Conditions of Agricultural Growth: The Economics of Agrarian Change Under Population Pressure.* Chicago: Aldine.

Bray, W., 1972 The city-state in Central Mexico at the time of the Spanish Conquest. *Journal of Latin American Studies* 4, 161–185.

—— 1983 Landscape with figures: Settlement patterns, locational models, and politics in Mesoamerica. In *Prehistoric Settlement Patterns: Essays in Honor of Gordon Willey.* E. Z. Vogt and R. M. Leventhal, eds. Pp. 167–193. Albuquerque and Cambridge: University of New Mexico Press; Peabody Museum of Archaeology and Ethnology, Harvard University.

Broda, J., D. Carrasco, and E. Matos Moctezuma, 1987 *The Great Temple of Tenochtitlan: Center and Periphery in the Aztec World.* Berkeley: University of California Press.

Brumfiel, E. M., 1976a Specialization and exchange at the Late Postclassic Aztec community of Huexotla, Mexico. Ph.D. dissertation, Department of Anthropology, University of Michigan. Ann Arbor: University Microfilms.

—— 1976b Regional growth in the eastern Valley of Mexico: A test of the "population pressure" hypothesis. In *The Early Mesoamerican Village.* K. V. Flannery, ed. Pp. 234–249. New York: Academic Press.

——1980 Specialization, market exchange, and the Aztec state: A view from Huexotla. *Current Anthropology* 21, 459–478.

——1983 Aztec state making: Ecology, structure, and the origin of the state. *American Anthropologist* 85, 261–284.

——1986 The division of labor at Xico: The chipped stone industry. In *Economic Aspects of Prehispanic Highland Mexico*. B. L. Isaac, ed. Pp. 245–279. Research in Economic Anthropology, Supplement 2. Greenwich, CT: JAI Press.

——1987a Elite and utilitarian crafts in the Aztec state. In *Specialization, Exchange, and Complex Societies* E. M. Brumfiel and T. K. Earle, eds. Pp. 102–118. Cambridge: Cambridge University Press.

——1987b Consumption and politics at Aztec Huexotla. *American Anthropologist* 88, 676–686.

——1989 Factional competition and political development. In *Domination and resistance*. D. Miller, M. J. Rowlands, and C. Tilley, eds. Pp. 127–139. London: Unwin Hyman.

——1991 Weaving and cooking: Woman's production in Aztec Mexico. In *Engendering Archaeology: Woman and Prehistory*. J. M. Gero and M. Conkey, eds. Pp. 224–254. Cambridge: Basil Blackwell.

——1992 Breaking and entering the ecosystem: Gender, class, and faction steal the show. *American Anthropologist* 94, 551–567.

——1994 Factional competition and political development in the New World: An introduction. In *Factional Competition and Political Development in the New World*. E. M. Brumfiel and J. W. Fox, eds. Pp. 3–13. Cambridge: Cambridge University Press.

——1996 Figurines and the Aztec state: Testing the effectiveness of ideological domination. In *Gender and Archaeology*. R. Wright, ed. Pp. 144–166. Philadelphia: University of Pennsylvania Press.

——1998 Huitzilopochtli's conquest: Aztec ideology and the archaeological record. *Cambridge Archaeological Journal* 8, 3–13.

——2001 Aztec hearts and minds: Religion and the state in the Aztec empire. In *Empires: Perspectives from Archaeology and History*. S. E. Alcock, T. N. D'Altroy, K. D. Morrison, and C. M. Sinopoli, eds. Pp. 283–310. Cambridge: Cambridge University Press.

——2002a Performing gender in early Mesoamerica. *Current Anthropology* 43, 519–520.

——2002b Origins of social inequality. In *Archaeology: Original Readings in Method and Practice*. P. N. Peregrine, C. R. Ember, and M. Ember, eds. Pp. 409–422. Upper Saddle River, NJ: Prentice Hall.

——ed., in press *Post-Classic Xaltocan: Ecological and Social Determinants of Production in the Northern Basin of Mexico* Memoirs in Latin American Archaeology. Pittsburgh: Department of Anthropology, University of Pittsburgh.

Calnek, E. E., 1972 Settlement patterns and chinampa agriculture at Tenochtitlan. *American Antiquity* 38, 104–115.

——1976 The internal structure of Tenochtitlan. In *The Valley of Mexico: Studies in Prehispanic Ecology and Society*. E. R. Wolf, ed. Pp. 287–302. Albuquerque: University of New Mexico Press.

——1978 The city-state in the Basin of Mexico: Late Prehispanic period. In *Urbanization in the Americas from its Beginnings to the Present*. R. P. Schaedel, J. E. Hardoy, and N. S. Kinzer, eds. Pp. 463–470. The Hague: Mouton.

Carneiro, R. L., 1970 A theory of the origin of the state. *Science* 169, 733–738.

Carrasco, D. ed., 1991 *To Change Place: Aztec Ceremonial Landscapes*. Niwot, CO: University of Colorado Press.

——1999 *City of Sacrifice: The Aztec Empire and the Role of Violence in Civilization*. Boston: Beacon Press.

Carrasco, P., 1971 Social organization of Ancient Mexico. In *Handbook of Middle American Indians*, vol. 11. G. F. Ekholm and I. Bernal, eds. Pp. 349–375. Austin: University of Texas Press.

——1977 Los señores de Xochimilco en 1548. *Tlalocan* 7, 229–265.

Charlton, T. H., 1968 Post-conquest Aztec ceramics: Implications for archaeological interpretation. *Florida Anthropologist* 21, 96–101.

——1972 *Post-Conquest Developments in the Teotihuacan Valley, Mexico, 1521–1620*. Iowa City: Office of the State Archaeologist.

——1978 Teotihuacan, Tepeapulco, and obsidian exploitation. *Science* 200, 1227–1236.

——1986 Socioeconomic dimensions of urban–rural relations in the colonial period Basin of Mexico. In *Handbook of Middle American Indians*, supplement 4: *Ethnohistory*. Ronald Spores, ed. Pp. 122–133. Austin: University of Texas Press.

——1994 Economic heterogeneity and state expansion: The northeastern Basin of Mexico during the Late Postclassic period. In *Economies and Polities in the Aztec Realm*. Mary G. Hodge and Michael E. Smith, eds. Pp. 221–256. Albany and Austin: Institute for Mesoamerican Studies, SUNY-Albany and University of Texas Press.

——2000 The Aztecs and their contemporaries: The central and eastern Mexican highlands. In *The Cambridge History of the Native Peoples of the Americas*, vol. 2: *Mesoamerica*, part 1. Richard E. W. Adams and Murdo J. Macleod, eds. Pp. 500–558. Cambridge: Cambridge University Press.

Charlton, Thomas H., and Deborah L. Nichols, 1992 Late Postclassic and Colonial period elites at Otumba, Mexico: The archaeological dimension. In *Mesoamerican Elites: An Archaeological Assessment*. Diane Chase and Arlen Chase, eds. Pp. 242–258. Norman: University of Oklahoma Press.

——1997a Diachronic studies of city-states. Permutations on a theme: Central Mexico from 1700 B.C. to A.D. 1600. In *The Archaeology of City-States: Cross-Cultural Approaches*. Deborah L. Nichols and Thomas H. Charlton, eds. Pp. 169–208. Washington, DC: Smithsonian Institution Press.

——1997b The city-state concept: Development and applications. In *The Archaeology of City-States: Cross-Cultural Approaches*. Deborah L. Nichols and Thomas H. Charlton, eds. Pp. 1–14. Washington, DC: Smithsonian Institution Press.

Charlton, Thomas H., Deborah L. Nichols, and Cynthia Otis Charlton, 1991 Aztec craft production and specialization: Archaeological evidence from the city-state of Otumba, Mexico. *World Archaeology* 23, 98–114.

——2000a Otumba and its neighbors: Ex oriente lux. *Ancient Mesoamerica* 11, 247–265.

——2000b The Otumba Project: A review and status report. In *The Teotihuacan Valley Project Final Report*, vol. 5: *The Aztec Period Occupation of the Valley*, part 2: *Excavations at T. A. 40 and Related Project*. William T. Sanders and Susan Toby Evans, eds. Pp. 841–887. Occasional Papers in Anthropology 26. University Park: Pennsylvania State University.

Childe, V. Gordon, 1951 *Social Evolution*. New York: Henry Schuman.

Conrad, Geoffrey W., and Arthur A. Demarest, 1984 *Religion and Empire: The Dynamics of Aztec and Inca Expansionism*. Cambridge: Cambridge University Press.

Cowgill, George, 1996 A reconsideration of the post-Classic chronology of Central Mexico. *Ancient Mesoamerica* 7, 325–332.

Davies, Nigel, 1973 *The Aztecs*. Norman: University of Oklahoma Press.

Doolittle, William E., 1990 *Canal Irrigation in Prehistoric Mexico: The Sequence of Technological Change*. Austin: University of Texas Press.

Doyel, M. W., 1986 *Empires*. Ithaca: Cornell University Press.

Elson, Christina M., 1999 An Aztec palace at Chiconautla, Mexico. *Latin American Antiquity* 10, 151–167.

Elson, Christina M., and Michael D. Smith, 2001 Archaeological deposits from the Aztec new fire ceremony. *Ancient Mesoamerica* 12, 157–174.

Evans, Susan T., 1980 Spatial analysis of Basin of Mexico settlement: Problems with the use of the central place model. *American Antiquity* 45, 866–875.

—— 1990 The Productivity of maguey terrace agriculture in Central Mexico during the Aztec period. *Latin American Antiquity* 1, 117–132.

—— 1991 Architecture and authority in an Aztec village: Form and function of the Tecpan. In *Land and Politics in the Valley of Mexico: A Two-Thousand Year Perspective.* Herbert R. Harvey, ed. Pp. 63–92. Albuquerque: University of New Mexico Press.

—— 1993 Aztec household organization and village administration. In *Prehispanic Domestic Units in Western Mesoamerica: Studies of the Household, Compound, and Residence.* Robert S. Santley and Kenneth G. Hirth, eds. Pp. 173–189. Boca Raton: CRC Press.

—— 2000 Aztec royal pleasure parks: Conspicuous consumption and elite status rivalry. *Studies in the History of Gardens and Designed Landscapes* 20, 206–228.

—— 2001a Aztec period political organization in the Teotihuacan Valley: Otumba as a city-state. *Ancient Mesoamerica* 12, 89–100.

—— 2001b Aztec noble courts: Men, women, and children of the palace. In *Royal Courts of the Ancient Maya,* vol. 1: *Theory, Comparison, and Synthesis.* Takeshi Inomata and Stephen D. Houston, eds. Pp. 237–273. Boulder: Westview Press.

Evans, Susan T., ed., 1988 *Excavations at Cihuatecpan: An Aztec Village in the Teotihuacan Valley.* Publications in Anthropology 36. Nashville: Department of Anthropology, Vanderbilt University.

Evans, Susan T., and AnnCorinne Freter, 1996 Teotihuacan Valley Mexico, Postclassic chronology: Hydration analysis of obsidian from Cihuatecpan, an Aztec-period village. *Ancient Mesoamerica* 7, 267–280.

Evans, Susan T., and Peter Gould, 1982 Settlement models in archaeology. *Journal of Anthropological Archaeology* 1, 275–304.

Evans, Susan T., and William T. Sanders, eds., 2000 *The Teotihuacan Valley Project Final Report,* vol. 5: *The Aztec Period Occupation of the Valley,* part 1: *Natural Environment, Twentieth-Century Occupation, Survey Methodology, and Site Descriptions.* Occasional Papers in Anthropology 25. University Park: Pennsylvania State University.

Garraty, Christopher P., 2000 Ceramic indices of Aztec eliteness. *Ancient Mesoamerica* 11, 323–340.

Gillespie, Susan D., 2000 Rethinking Ancient Maya social organization: Replacing "lineage" with "house." *American Anthropologist* 102, 467–484.

González, Carlos Javier, ed., 1992 *Chinampas Prehispanicas.* Mexico, DF: Instituto Nacional de Antropología e Historia.

Gorenflo, Larry J., 1996 Regional efficiency in prehispanic Central Mexico: Insights from geographic studies of archaeological settlement patterns. In *Arqueología Mesoamericana: Homenaje a William T. Sanders,* 2 vols. A. Guadalupe Mastache, Jeffrey R. Parsons, Mari Carmen Serre Puche, and Robert S. Santley, eds. Vol. 1, pp. 135–160. Mexico, DF: Instituto Nacional de Antropología e Historia.

Gorenflo, Larry J., and Nathan Gale, 1986 Population and productivity in the Teotihuacan Valley: Changing patterns of spatial association in Prehispanic Central Mexico. *Journal of Anthropological Archaeology* 5, 199–228.

———— 1990 Mapping regional settlement in information space. *Journal of Anthropological Archaeology* 9, 240–270.

Hassig, Ross, 1985 *Trade, Tribute, and Transportation*. Norman: University of Oklahoma Press.

——1988 *Aztec Warfare: Imperial Expansion and Political Control*. Norman: University of Oklahoma Press.

Hicks, Frederic, 1982 Tetzcoco in the early 16th century: The state, the city and the *calpolli*. *American Ethnologist* 9, 230–249.

Hodge, Mary G., 1984 *Aztec City States*. Museum of Anthropology Memoir 18. Ann Arbor: University of Michigan.

——1992 The geographical structure of Aztec Imperial period market systems. *National Geographic Society Research and Exploration* 8, 428–445.

——1994 Polities composing the Aztec empire's core. In *Economies and Polities in the Aztec Realm*. Mary G. Hodge and Michael E. Smith, eds. Pp. 43–72. Albany and Austin: Institute for Mesoamerican Studies, SUNY-Albany and University of Texas Press.

——1996 Political organization of the Central Provinces. In *Aztec Imperial Strategies*. Frances F. Berdan, Richard E. Blanton, Elizabeth Hill Boone, Mary G. Hodge, Michael E. Smith, and Emily Umberger, eds. Pp. 17–45. Washington, DC: Dumbarton Oaks Library and Collection.

——1997 When is a city-state? Archaeological measures of Aztec city-states and Aztec city-state systems. In *The Archaeology of City-States: Cross Cultural Approaches*. D. L. Nichols and T. H. Charlton, eds. Pp. 209–228. Washington, DC: Smithsonian Institution.

——1998 Archaeological views of Aztec culture. *Journal of Archaeological Research* 6, 197–238.

Hodge, Mary G., ed., in press *Place of Jade: Society and Economy in Ancient Chalco*. Department of Anthropology Memoirs in Latin American Archaeology. Pittsburgh: University of Pittsburgh.

Hodge, Mary G., and Leah Minc, 1990 The spatial patterning of Aztec ceramics: Implications for prehispanic exchange systems in the Valley of Mexico. *Journal of Field Archaeology* 17, 415–437.

————1991 *Aztec-Period Ceramic Distribution and Exchange Systems*. Final Report to the National Science Foundation, Washington, DC.

Hodge, Mary G., H. Neff, M. J. Blackman, and L. D. Minc, 1992 A compositional perspective on ceramic production in the Aztec empire. In *Chemical Characterization of Ceramic Pastes in Archaeology*. H. Neff, ed. Pp. 203–231. Monographs in World Archaeology 7. Madison: Prehistory Press.

——————1993 Black-on-Orange ceramic production in the Aztec empire's heartland. *Latin American Antiquity* 4, 130–157.

Hodge, Mary G., and Michael E. Smith, eds., 1994 *Economies and Polities in the Aztec Realm*. Albany: Institute for Mesoamerican Studies, SUNY-Albany.

Iwaniszewski, Stanislaw, and Ivan Sprajc, 1987 Archaeology and archaeoastronomy of Mount Tlaloc, Mexico: A reconsideration. *Latin American Antiquity* 5, 158–176.

Jacobs, Jane, 1969 *The Economy of Cities*. New York: Random House.

Joyce, Rosemary A., 2000 *Gender and Power in Prehispanic Mesoamerica*. Austin: University of Texas Press.

Knapp, A. Bernard, and Wendy Ashmore, 1999 Archaeological landscapes: Constructed, conceptualized, and ideational. In *Archaeological Landscapes*. Wendy Ashmore and A. Bernard Knapp, eds. Pp. 1–32. Oxford: Blackwell.

López Luján, Leonardo, 1993 *Las ofrendas del Templo Mayor de Tenochtitlan*. Mexico, DF: Instituto Nacional de Antropología e Historia.

Litvak King, Jaime, 1997 Mexican archaeology: Challenges at the end of the century. *Society for American Archaeology Bulletin* 144, 10–11.

Lockhart, James, 1992 *The Nahuas after the Conquest.* Stanford: Stanford University Press.

Marcus, Joyce, 1992 Political fluctuations in Mesoamerica: Cycles of Mesoamerican states. *National Geographic Research and Exploration* 8, 392–411.

——1998 The peaks and valleys of ancient states: An extension of the dynamic model. In *Archaic States.* G. M. Feinman and J. Marcus, eds. Pp. 59–94. Santa Fe: School of American Research.

Manzanilla, Linda, 2000 The construction of the underworld in Central Mexico: Transformations from the Classic to the Postclassic. In *Mesoamerica's Classic Heritage: From Teotihuacan to the Aztecs.* Davíd Carrasco, Lindsay Jones, and Scott Sessions, eds. Pp. 87–116. Niwot: University of Colorado Press.

Manzanilla, Linda, Claudia Lopez, and AnnCorinne Freter, 1996 Dating results from excavations in quarry tunnels behind the Pyramid of the Sun at Teotihuacan. *Ancient Mesoamerica* 7, 245–266.

Matos Moctezuma, Eduardo, 1988 *The Great Temple of the Aztecs.* New York: Thames & Hudson.

——2000 From Teotihuacan to Tenochtitlan: Their great temples. In *Mesoamerica's Classic Heritage: From Teotihuacan to the Aztecs.* Davíd Carrasco, Lindsay Jones, and Scott Sessions, eds. Pp. 185–194. Niwot: University of Colorado Press.

Matos Moctezuma, Eduardo, Francisco Hinojosa, and Jálvaro Barrera Rivera, 1998 Excavaciones arqueológicas en la Catedral de México. *Arqueología* 631, 12–19.

McBryde, Felix W., 1947 *Cultural and Historical Geography of Southwest Guatemala.* Smithsonian Institute of Social Anthropology Publication 4. Washington, DC: Smithsonian Institution.

McCafferty, Sharisse D., and Geoffrey G. McCafferty, 1991 Mexican spinning and weaving as female gender identity in Post-Classic Mexico. In *Textiles and Traditions of Mesoamerica and the Andes.* Margot Blum Schevil, Janet Catherine Berlo, and Edward B. Dwyer, eds. Pp. 19–44. New York: Garland.

Minc, Leah D., Mary G. Hodge, and M. James Blackman, 1994 Stylistic and spatial variability in early Aztec ceramics: Insights into pre-imperial exchange systems. In *Economies and Polities in the Aztec Realm.* Mary G. Hodge and Michael E. Smith, eds. Pp. 133–174. Albany and Austin: Institute for Mesoamerican Studies, SUNY-Albany and University of Texas Press.

Nash, June, 1978 The Aztecs and the ideology of male dominance. *Signs* 4, 349–362.

Neff, Hector, Michael D. Glascock, Thomas H. Charlton, Cynthia Otis Charlton, and Deborah L. Nichols, 2000 Provenience investigation of ceramics and obsidian from Otumba. *Ancient Mesoamerica* 11, 307–321.

Nichols, Deborah L., 1980 Prehispanic settlement and land use in the northwestern Basin of Mexico, the Cuautitlan region. Ph.D. dissertation, Department of Anthropology, Pennsylvania State University, University Park. Ann Arbor: University Microfilms.

——1994 The organization of provincial craft production and the Aztec city-state of Otumba. In *Economies and Polities in the Aztec Realm.* Mary G. Hodge and Michael E. Smith, eds. Pp. 175–193. Albany and Austin: Institute for Mesoamerican Studies, SUNY-Albany and University of Texas Press.

——1996 An overview of regional settlement pattern survey in Mesoamerica. In *Arqueología Mesoamericana: Homenaje a William T. Sanders,* 2 vols. A. Guadalupe Mastache, Jeffrey R. Parsons, Mari Carmen Serre Puche, and Robert S. Santley, eds. Vol. 1, pp. 59–96. Mexico, DF: Instituto Nacional de Antropología e Historia.

——2000 Archaic states. *Journal of Field Archaeology* 27, 354–359.

Nichols, Deborah L., Elizabeth M. Brumfiel, Hector Neff, Mary Hodge, Thomas H. Charlton, and Michael D. Glascock, 2002 Neutrons, markets, cities, and empires: A 1,000-year perspective on ceramic production and distribution in the Postclassic Basin of Mexico. *Journal of Anthropological Archaeology* 21, 25–82.

Nichols, Deborah L., and Thomas H. Charlton, 1996 The Postclassic occupation at Otumba: A chronological assessment. *Ancient Mesoamerica* 7, 231–244.

——2001 Central Mexico Postclassic. In *Encyclopedia of Prehistory*, vol. 5: *Middle America*. Peter N. Peregrine and Melvin Ember, eds. Pp. 22–52. New York: Kluwer Academic/Plenum.

Nichols, Deborah L., and Charles D. Frederick, 1993 Irrigation canals and chinampas: The development of hydraulic agriculture in the northern Basin of Mexico. In *Water Management*. Barry L. Isaac and Vernon Scarborough, eds. Pp. 123–150. Research in Economic Anthropology Supplement 7. Greenwich, CT: JAI Press.

Nichols, Deborah L., Mary Jane McLaughlin, and Maura Benton, 2000 Production intensification and regional specialization: Maguey fibers and textiles in the Aztec city-state of Otumba. *Ancient Mesoamerica* 11, 267–291.

Nichols, Deborah L., and Jeffrey R. Parsons, 1997 Mary G. Hodge: 1946–1996. *Ancient Mesoamerica* 8, 161–164.

Nicholson, H. B., 1971 Religion in pre-hispanic Central Mexico. In *Handbook of Middle American Indians*, vol. 10: *Archaeology of Northern Mesoamerica*, part 1. Ignacio Bernal and Gordon F. Eckholm, eds. Pp. 395–446. Austin: University of Texas Press.

Nuttall, Zelia, trans., 1926 *Official Reports on the Towns of Tequizistlan, Tepechpan, Acolman, and San Juan Teotihuacan Sent by Francisco de Castañeda to his Majesty, Philip II and the Council of the Indies, in 1580*. Papers of the Peabody Museum of American Archaeology and Ethnology 11(2). Cambridge, MA: Harvard University.

Otis Charlton, Cynthia, 1993 Obsidian as jewelry: Lapidary production in Aztec Otumba, Mexico. *Ancient Mesoamerica* 4, 231–243.

——1994 Plebeians and patricians: Contrasting patterns of production and distribution in the Aztec figurine and lapidary industries. In *Economies and Polities in the Aztec Realm*. Mary G. Hodge and Michael E. Smith, eds. Pp. 195–220. Studies on Culture and Society 6. Albany and Austin: Institute for Mesoamerican Studies, SUNY-Albany and University of Texas Press.

Otis Charlton, Cynthia, Thomas H. Charlton, and Deborah L. Nichols, 1993 Aztec household-based craft production: Archaeological evidence from the city-state of Otumba, Mexico. In *Household, Compound, and Residence: Studies of Prehispanic Domestic Units in Western Mesoamerica*. Robert S. Santley and Kenneth G. Hirth, eds. Pp. 141–171. Boca Raton: CRC Press.

Parry, William J., 2000 Production and exchange of obsidian tools in late Aztec city-states. *Ancient Mesoamerica* 12, 101–111.

——2002 Aztec blade production strategies in the eastern Basin of Mexico. In *Pathways to Prismatic Blades: A Study in Mesoamerican Obsidian Core-Blade Technology*. Kenneth Hirth and Bradford Andrews, eds. Pp. 39–48. Los Angeles: UCLA Institute of Archaeology.

Parsons, Jeffrey R., 1966 The Aztec ceramic sequence in the Teotihuacan Valley, Mexico. Ph.D. dissertation, Department of Anthropology, University of Michigan. Ann Arbor: University Microfilms.

——1971 *Prehistoric Settlement Patterns in the Texcoco Region, Mexico*. Museum of Anthropology Memoir 3. Ann Arbor: University of Michigan.

——1972 Archaeological settlement patterns. *Annual Review of Anthropology* 1, 127–150.

——1976 The role of Chinampa agriculture in the food supply of Aztec Tenochtitlan. In *Cultural Change and Continuity*. Charles E. Cleland, ed. Pp. 233–262. New York: Academic Press.

——1990 Critical reflections on a decade of full-coverage regional survey in the Valley of Mexico. In *The Archaeology of Regions: A Case for Full-Coverage Survey*. Suzanne K. Fish and Stephen A. Kowalewski, eds. Pp. 7–32. Washington, DC: Smithsonian Institution Press.

——1991 Political implications of prehispanic chinampa agriculture in the Valley of Mexico. In *Land and Politics in the Valley of Mexico*. H. R. Harvey, ed. Pp. 17–42. Albuquerque: University of New Mexico Press.

——n.d. Geological mapping with Rob Scholten in the Beaverhead Range, S. W. Montana and adjacent Idaho, summer 1960. Unpublished paper in possession of author.

Parsons, Jeffrey R., Elizabeth Brumfiel, and Mary Hodge, 1996 Developmental implications of earlier dates for early Aztec in the Basin of Mexico. *Ancient Mesoamerica* 7, 217–230.

Parsons, Jeffrey R., and Mary H. Parsons, 1990 *Otomí Maguey Utilization: An Ethnoarchaeological Perspective*. Museum of Anthropology Papers 82. Ann Arbor: University of Michigan.

Parsons, Jeffrey R., Mary H. Parsons, and David J. Wilson, 1982 *Prehispanic Settlement Patterns in the Southern Valley of Mexico: The Chalco-Xochimilco Region*. Museum of Anthropology Memoir 14. Ann Arbor: University of Michigan.

Sabloff, Jeremy A., and Wendy Ashmore, 2001 An aspect of archaeology's recent past and its relevance in the new millennium. In *Archaeology at the New Millennium: A Sourcebook*. Gary M. Feinman and T. Douglas Price, eds. Pp. 11–32. New York: Kluwer Academic/ Plenum.

Sanders, William T., 1956 The Central Mexican symbiotic region. In *Prehistoric Settlement Patterns in the New World*. Gordon R. Willey, ed. Pp. 115–127. Viking Fund Publications in Anthropology 23. New York.

——1965 *Cultural Ecology of the Teotihuacan Valley*. University Park: Department of Sociology and Anthropology, Pennsylvania State University.

——1970 The population of the Teotihuacan Valley, the Basin of Mexico and the Central Mexican symbiotic region in the 16th century. In *Teotihuacan Valley Final Report*, vol. 1: *The Natural Environment, the Contemporary Occupation and the 16th-Century Population of the Valley*. William T. Sanders, ed. Pp. 385–452. Occasional Papers in Anthropology 3. University Park: Pennsylvania State University.

——1976a The natural environment of the Valley of Mexico. In *The Valley of Mexico: Studies of Pre-hispanic Ecology and Society*. Eric R. Wolf, ed. Pp. 59–68. Albuquerque: University of New Mexico Press.

——1976b The agricultural history of the Basin of Mexico. In *The Valley of Mexico: Studies of Pre-hispanic Ecology and Society*. Eric R. Wolf, ed. Pp. 101–160. Albuquerque: University of New Mexico Press.

——1981 Ecological adaptation in the Basin of Mexico: 23,000 B.C. to the present. In *Handbook of Middle American Indians*, supplement 1: *Archaeology*. Jeremy A. Sabloff and Patricia A. Andrews, eds. Pp. 147–197. Austin: University of Texas Press.

——1999 Three valleys: Twenty-five years of settlement archaeology in Mesoamerica. In *Settlement Pattern Studies in the Americas: Fifty Years Since Virú*. Brian R. Billman and Gary M. Feinman, eds. Pp. 12–21. Washington, DC: Smithsonian Institution.

——2001a Preface. In *The Aztec Period Occupation of the Valley*, part 3: *Syntheses and General Bibliography*. William T. Sanders and Susan Toby Evans, eds. Pp. 889–890. Occasional Papers in Anthropology 27. University Park: Pennsylvania State University.

——2001b Pre-Aztec occupation of the Teotihuacan Valley. In *The Aztec Period Occupation of the Valley*, part 3: *Syntheses and General Bibliography*. William T. Sanders and Susan Toby Evans, eds. Pp. 1080–1130. Occasional Papers in Anthropology 27. University Park: Pennsylvania State University.

——ed., 1970 *The Natural Environment: Contemporary Occupation and 16th-Century Occupation*. Occasional Papers in Anthropology 3. University Park: Pennsylvania State University.

Sanders, William T., and Susan Toby Evans, eds., 2000 *The Teotihuacan Valley Project Final Report*, vol. 5: *The Aztec Period Occupation of the Valley*, part 2: *Excavations at T. A. 40 and Related Projects*. Occasional Papers in Anthropology 26. University Park: Pennsylvania State University.

————2001 The Teotihuacan Valley and the Temascalapa region during the Aztec period. In *The Aztec Period Occupation of the Valley*, part 3: *Syntheses and General Bibliography*. William T. Sanders and Susan Toby Evans, eds. Pp. 931–1079. Occasional Papers in Anthropology 27. University Park: Pennsylvania State University.

Sanders, William T., Susan Toby Evans, and Thomas H. Charlton, 2001 Colonial period cultural geography of the Teotihuacan Valley and Temascalapa region. In *The Aztec Period Occupation of the Valley*, part 3: *Syntheses and General Bibliography*. William T. Sanders and Susan Toby Evans, eds. Pp. 889–930. Occasional Papers in Anthropology 27. University Park: Pennsylvania State University.

Sanders, William T., and Barbara Price, 1968 *Mesoamerica: The Evolution of a Civilization*. New York: Random House.

Sanders, William T., Jeffrey R. Parsons, and Robert S. Santley, 1979 *The Basin of Mexico: Ecological Process in the Evolution of a Civilization*. New York: Academic Press.

Sanders, William T., and Robert S. Santley, 1983 A tale of three cities: Energetics and urbanization in Pre-hispanic Central Mexico. In *Prehispanic Settlement Patterns: Essays in Honor of Gordon R. Willey*. E. Z. Vogt and R. M. Leventhal, eds. Pp. 243–291. Cambridge and Albuquerque: University of New Mexico Press and Peabody Museum of Archaeology and Ethnology.

Smith, C. A., 1976 Regional economic systems: Linking geographical models and socioeconomic problems. In *Regional Analysis*, vol. 1: *Economic Systems*. C. A. Smith, ed. Pp. 3–63. New York: Academic Press.

Smith, Michael. E., 1979 The Aztec marketing system and settlement pattern in the Valley of Mexico: A central place analysis. *American Antiquity* 44, 110–125.

——1980 The role of the marketing system in Aztec society and economy: Reply to Evans. *American Antiquity* 44, 110–124.

——1984 The Aztlan migrations of the Nahuatl Chronicles: Myth or history? *Ethnohistory* 31, 153–156.

——1987a Archaeology and the Aztec economy: The social scientific use of archaeological data. *Social Science History* 11, 237–259.

——1987b Household possessions and wealth in agrarian states: Implications for archaeology. *Journal of Anthropological Archaeology* 6, 297–335.

——1992a Rhythms of change in Postclassic Central Mexico: Archaeology, ethnohistory, and the Braudelian model. In *Archaeology, Annales, and Ethnohistory*. A. B. Knapp, ed. Pp. 51–74. Cambridge: Cambridge University Press.

——1992b *Archaeological Research at Aztec-Period Rural Sites in Morelos*, vol. 1: *Excavations and Architecture*. Memoirs in Latin American Archaeology 4. Pittsburgh: University of Pittsburgh.

——1994 Social complexity in the Aztec countryside. In *Archaeological Views from the Coun-*

tryside:Village Communities in Early Complex Societies. Glenn Schwartz and Steven Falconer, eds. Pp. 143–159. Washington, DC: Smithsonian Institution Press.

——1996a The silent majority: William T. Sanders and the study of Aztec peasantry. In *Arqueología Mesoamericana: Homenaje a William T. Sanders,* 2 vols. A. Guadalupe Mastache, Jeffrey R. Parsons, Mari Carmen Serre Puche, and Robert S. Santley, eds. Vol. 1, Pp. 375–386. Mexico, DF: Insituto Nacional de Antropología e Historia.

——1996b *The Aztecs.* Oxford: Basil Blackwell.

——1997a Life in the provinces of the Aztec empire. *Scientific American* 277(3), 56–63.

——1997b The Mesoamerican urban landscape from Teotihuacan to the Aztecs. Paper presented at the Conference on Archaeology of Complex Societies: Centripetal and Centrifugal Forces. California State University San Bernardino.

——2000 Aztec city-states. In *A Comparative Study of Thirty-City-State Cultures.* Mogens Herman Hansen, ed. Pp. 581–595. Copenhagen: Royal Danish Academy of Science and Letters.

——2001 The Aztec empire and the Mesoamerican world system. In *Empires: Perspectives from Archaeology and History.* Susan E. Alcock, Terence N. D'Altroy, Kathleen D. Morrison, and Carla M. Sinopoli, eds. Pp. 128–154. Cambridge: Cambridge University Press.

——2002 Domestic ritual at Aztec provincial sites in Morelos. In *Domestic Ritual in Ancient Mesoamerica.* Patricia Plunket, ed. Pp. 93–114. Cotsen Institute of Archaeology Monograph 46. Los Angeles: UCLA.

Smith, Michael E., and C. Heath-Smith, 1980 Waves of influence in Postclassic Mesoamerica? A critique of the Mixteca-Puebla concept. *Anthropology* 4, 15–50.

——————1994 Rural economy in Late Postclassic Morelos. In *Economies and Polities in the Aztec Realm.* M. G. Hodge and M. E. Smith, eds. Pp. 349–376. Albany: Institute of Mesoamerican Studies, SUNY-Albany.

Smith, Michael E., Cynthia Heath-Smith, Ronald Kohler, Joand Odess, Sharon Spanogle, and Timothy Sullivan, 1994 The size of the Aztec city of Yautepec, Morelos, Mexico. *Journal of Field Archaeology* 15, 349–358.

Smith, Michael E., and Mary Hodge, 1994 An introduction to Late Postclassic economies and polities. In *Economies and Polities in the Aztec Realm.* M. Hodge and M. E. Smith, eds. Pp. 1–42. Albany: Institute for Mesoamerican Studies, SUNY-Albany.

Smith, Michael E., and Lisa Montiel, 2001 The archaeological study of empires and imperialism in Pre-hispanic Central Mexico. *Journal of Anthropological Archaeology* 20, 245–284.

Steward, Julian, 1955 *Theory of Culture Change.* Urbana: University of Illinois Press.

Spence, M. W., 1985 Specialized production in rural Aztec society: Obsidian workshops of the Teotihuacan Valley. In *Contributions to the Archaeology and Ethnohistory of Greater Mesoamerica.* W. J. Folan, ed. Pp. 76–125. Carbondale: Southern Illinois University Press.

Townsend, Richard F., 2000 *The Aztecs,* rev. edn. New York: Thames & Hudson.

Vaillant, George C., 1938 A correlation of archaeological and historical sequences in the Valley of Mexico. *American Anthropologist* 40, 535–573.

Willey, Gordon R., 1953 Prehistoric settlement patterns in the Virú Valley Peru. *Bureau of American Ethnology Bulletin* 155. Washington, DC: Smithsonian Institution.

——ed., 1956 *Prehistoric Settlement Patterns in the New World.* Viking Fund Publications in Anthropology 23. New York.

——1999 The Virú Valley Project and settlement archaeology: Some reminiscences and contemporary comments. In *Settlement Pattern Studies in the Americas: Fifty Years Since Virú.* Brian R. Billman and Gary M. Feinman, eds. Pp. 9–11. Washington, DC: Smithsonian Institution.

Wittfogel, Karl A., 1957 *Oriental Despotism*. New Haven: Yale University Press.

Wolf, Eric, 1976 Introduction. In *The Valley of Mexico: Studies of Pre-hispanic Ecology and Society*. Eric R. Wolf, ed. Pp. 1–10. Albuquerque: University of New Mexico Press.

——1999 *Envisioning Power: Ideologies of Dominance and Crisis*. Berkeley: University of California Press.

——2001 Armillas, Pedro. In *Archaeology of Ancient Mexico and Central America: An Encyclopedia*. Susan Toby Evans and David L. Webster, eds. P. 41. New York: Garland.

Zeitlin, Robert N., and Judith Francis Zeitlin, 1980 Sociocultural evolution in Mesoamerica. *Science* 207, 396–398.

12

Postclassic and Colonial Period Sources on Maya Society and History

Julia A. Hendon

Introduction

In Chapter 7 Wendy Ashmore notes that the complex political landscape of the Maya lowlands underwent an important change during the Terminal Classic period, or the ninth to tenth centuries A.D. This period of political and social upheaval is often referred to as the "Classic Maya collapse." The term collapse suggests a complete, sudden, and uniform process and this is how the events of the Terminal Classic period looked to the earliest archaeologists working on the Maya (Chase and Rice 1985; Joyce 1999). The southern Maya lowlands, and especially the major city-states of the Peten lowlands in Guatemala, such as Tikal and Palenque, and western Honduras, such as Copan, were thought to have been abandoned completely. The next period defined by archaeologists, the Postclassic, was seen as a time of reduced settlement, Mexican invasion, and loss of a distinctively Maya identity. Two lines of evidence contributed to this interpretation. A limited amount of excavation and settlement pattern research meant that large areas of the lowlands were incompletely surveyed and therefore seemed to be devoid of occupation. The second kind of evidence was documents, written in a conventionally European manner or in an equally conventional but quite different Maya manner, that date from the very end of the Pre-Columbian era or from the Colonial period after the Spanish Conquest. Interpretation of these sources is difficult due to differences in cultural perspective, not only between us, as modern researchers, and late medieval to early Renaissance Spaniards or between us and fourteenth- to nineteenth-century Maya, but also between Spaniard and Maya, even when contemporary with one another and communicating face to face. As I discuss in more detail later in this chapter, many of the more historical sources (or what seem to us as approximating more closely our idea of history) attribute the abandonment of cities and the founding of new ones to the invasions of foreigners and the migrations of peoples. Taking these sources at face value, coupled with an apparent lack of archaeological evidence for settlement, suggested to early researchers not just change but in fact the overthrow and destruction of Classic period kingdoms and of the very nature of Maya society.

However, as our information about Classic, Terminal Classic, and Postclassic Maya settlement and society has increased exponentially over the years through the location and excavation of many sites of differing sizes and types, as our ability to interpret Maya hieroglyphic writing has improved, and as our understanding of the historical documents has become more analytically critical, it has become clear that the Terminal Classic period represents a much more varied and complex set of events and that the Postclassic Maya societies of the northern Yucatan peninsula, the southern Maya lowlands, southeastern Honduras, and the highlands of Guatemala and southwestern Mexico were neither merely pale reflections of a once great society nor completely Mexicanized hybrids (Culbert 1973a; Rice et al. 2003). The expansion of research has also shown that we need to look at the individual histories of polities rather than searching for a single explanation that accounts for all events and changes.

This chapter has two goals. The first is to summarize the current view of the processes contributing to the transition from Classic to Postclassic Maya society. The second is to introduce the documentary sources and to provide a sense of their strengths and weaknesses through a general overview and a specific case study. The case study uses the most important written source on Maya society from a Spanish perspective, *Relación de las cosas de Yucatán* (Account of the Things of Yucatan) written around 1566 by the bishop of Yucatan, Diego de Landa, to consider Maya gender relations and the role of women in Maya society.

The Postclassic Period and the Question of the Maya "Collapse"

By arguing, as I do above, that the Maya "collapse" does not mean that the Maya disappear, devolve, or otherwise cease to exist as a people, I do not want to give the impression that nothing changes. The mere fact that archaeologists have decided that the ninth to tenth centuries deserve their own time period (Terminal Classic) and that after A.D. 1000 another time period (the Postclassic) needs to be defined, indicates clearly that something has happened, since archaeologists define new time periods in order to reflect changes in the archaeological record of sufficient scale to suggest important changes in the societies being studied. The key question, though, is what changes?

In this chapter, I will emphasize three changes: changes in the density of *human settlement*, an increase in *militarism*, and the emergence of a *pan-regional elite identity* (sometimes referred to as the Mixteca-Puebla style or the Postclassic Religious style). All of these are changes in degree rather than kind, that is to say, they can be shown to relate to and develop out of Classic period conditions rather than representing a sharp break. These changes are best viewed in the context of a continuing process of realignment of the *political landscape* in the Maya area, in the Valley of Mexico, and more broadly in Mesoamerica as a whole. These realignments, driven by a combination of ecological, demographic, political, and social factors, result not only in abandonment of existing Maya settlements but also in the continued occupation of others, and the development of new cities and towns. Taken together, these three processes result in the redistribution of settlement and different political groupings throughout the Maya-speaking region.

Shifts in the location of settlement

Abandonment of existing settlements is the process most often assumed to be the dominant one during the Terminal Classic. Although abandonment really refers to the movement of people away from a town or city, and thus needs to studied using settlement data, abandonment has often been assumed based on a very different kind of evidence – the fact that many major Classic period cities stop erecting dated hieroglyphic monuments (especially stelae) on a regular basis after A.D. 790 (9.18.0.0.0 in the Maya Long Count calendar). Construction of monumental architecture in the royal precincts of such sites also came to an end or was much reduced. But monumental art, writing, and architecture in these areas of Classic Maya cities such as Tikal or Palenque are practices associated with and reflective of the concentration of political power in the hands of a ruling family. Thus, changes in these practices relate more directly to changes in the political and social structure of the society. Such changes may result from economic, ecological, military, and demographic changes, but do not of themselves tell us what those changes were.

Studies of the distribution of settlement across the landscape reveal several patterns of change. Certain prominent Classic period polities did suffer a drastic reduction in population during the ninth century. Tikal is perhaps the best example. Its population loss has been estimated to be as high as 90 percent, based on the dating of residential and public structures (Culbert 1973b; Culbert et al. 1990). Even here, however, social differentiation continued, with a Terminal Classic elite living in the center and erecting a stela and altar in A.D. 869 (10.2.0.0.0).

Abandonment in terms of settlement, then, seems in most cases to have been gradual (see Culbert and Rice 1990). Copan provides a well-studied example of this process. The nobles living in the area right around the center (including the Sepulturas zone discussed in Chapter 6), and the farmers and artisans living in the valley, stayed put for about a century after the ruling family lost power (Webster 1999). Few new monuments were erected, but a ballcourt in the elite living area was renovated and continued to be used even as the larger one in the royal precinct fell into disuse (Fash and Lane 1983).

While changes like those at Tikal are dramatic, it is important to put them in a longer-term historical context. Shifts in population and the abandonment of particular settlements were not unique to the Terminal Classic period. Such changes occurred throughout the Pre-Columbian era, both before and after the time of the "collapse." Demarest (1992) has argued that Maya political systems were inherently unstable, not because of cultural decay that peaked in the ninth century A.D., but because of the competing interests of rulers, elites, and commoners in an ecologically diverse and fragile environment.

Even as some settlements declined in size and political importance during the Terminal Classic, others continued to flourish. Small settlements around Tikal, for example, grew and became more prominent politically as Tikal's control waned. Some of these settlements, such as Jimbal and Ixlu, even began putting up their own carved and dated monuments depicting local nobility and describing their importance in hieroglyphic texts (Rice 1986). Cities such as Uxmal, Coba, and Chichen Itza in northern Yucatan became powerful polities (Robles Castellanos and Andrews 1986). Xunantunich in Belize and Quirigua in Guatemala initiated new large-scale construction projects and erected dated monuments, while their population did not show the kind of decline seen at Tikal (LeCount et al. 2002; Sharer 1985). Cities and smaller settlements that did continue to be occupied beyond the date of the "collapse" varied in how long they were occupied, of course, since, as noted above, Maya polities were unstable. Once a settlement successfully negotiated the realigned political landscape of the Terminal Classic, it might be occupied up to the time of the Spanish colonization or fall victim to political, economic, or ecological stresses of the post-A.D. 1000 Maya world. In general, it is the core area of the Peten lowlands, where large and powerful Classic period polities were concentrated, that saw the most severe disruption in occupation, whereas Belize, southeastern Guatemala and western Honduras, and northern Yucatan were the location of the most successful Terminal Classic and Postclassic polities (Joyce 1999). Lamanai and Santa Rita Corozal, both in Belize, are two of the best studied examples of continuity. Santa Rita Corozal was occupied through the Late Postclassic period (Chase and Chase 1988), whereas Lamanai was still a functioning town at the time of Spanish contact and became part of the Spanish colony. Not only did Maya continue to live in this community during the so-called collapse, but they continued to build and trade, and maintained the same kind of social divisions evident in the Classic period (Pendergast 1985).

As the preceding discussion suggests, new settlements also appeared. Such settlements are a logical consequence of the abandonment of existing settlements. If people have left their old towns and cities, they must either move to an existing settlement or build a new one. New settlements are even found in the Peten lowlands, demonstrating that Maya did not abandon this region completely (Rice 1986), as well as in northern Yucatan and the Guatemalan highlands. One of the best known is the city of Mayapan (Fig. 12.1), which was the pre-eminent northern Yucatecan polity in the Late Postclassic period, but which was abandoned in the fifteenth century, before contact with the Spanish (Brown 1991).

Increased militarism and conflict

Part of the changing political landscape is a rise in militarism, as seen in art, and, by implication, of military conflict between city-states. During the Classic period, the role of warrior, usually defined as someone who takes prisoners in battle, was

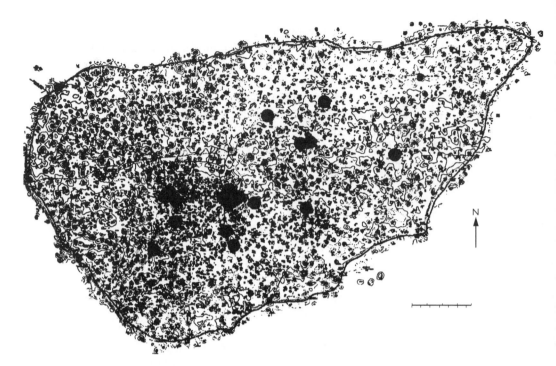

Figure 12.1. Settlement map of the walled city of Mayapan. The city walls enclose 4 km² of closely spaced houses

one of several standardized elite identities or actions represented in monumental art. Male, and sometimes female, elites had themselves depicted carrying weapons or standing on bound prisoners. Less commonly, male elites were shown actually engaged in combat, as on Yaxchilan Lintel 8 (Tate 1992). Such images were complemented by hieroglyphic texts in which an individual's capture of a prisoner was recorded. A ruler or member of the elite might add the name of a particularly high-status captive to his titles, memorializing himself as "captor of X." Texts also recorded the occurrence of conflicts with other Maya city-states, such as the one discussed by Ashmore between Quirigua and Copan.

Terminal Classic and Postclassic large-scale art shows a greater emphasis on this particular elite role and activity, often at the expense of the depiction of other important elite actions, such as making religious offerings, taking office, designating an heir, or playing the ballgame. Murals at Chichen Itza depict extensive battle scenes in which villages are burned (Fig. 12.2), whereas Classic period murals from Bonampak show only a mass combat between elite warriors and the sacrifice of those captured in battle (Joyce 2000; Miller 1993; Webster 1993). Sculpture of groups of warriors becomes more common than in the Classic period, when the armed ruler standing by himself or with a few other warriors was the rule. Associated with this change in elite representations is a decline in the number of images of noble or royal women (Joyce 2000).

Figure 12.2. Warriors sack a town. Mural from west wall, south section, Upper Temple of the Jaguars, Chichen Itza. Detail from figure 60 of Alfred M. Tozzer, *Chichen Itza and its Cenote of Sacrifice: A Comparative Study of Contemporaneous Maya and Toltec.* Memoirs of the Peabody Museum of Archaeology and Ethnology, vols. 11, 12 (1957). Used with permission

Postclassic pan-regional elite identity

Maya societies of the Terminal and Postclassic periods participated in long-distance exchange networks that connected them with other groups in Mesoamerica, most notably in the western and central Mexican highlands and to the southeast into Honduras (Fox et al. 1992; Joyce 1986; Sharer 1985; Smith and Heath Smith 1980). One of the most debated questions about the Maya collapse and developments from the Terminal Classic to Postclassic is to what degree they resulted from contact with the societies of Central Mexico, either directly, or by way of Gulf Coast Maya societies who were seen as "Mexicanized" (e.g., Thompson 1970). "Mexicanized" means that such Maya societies had adopted certain religious practices and social customs once thought to be more common among the prehispanic societies of the Valley of Mexico. In particular, earlier archaeologists pointed to the use of human sacrifice for religious purposes and the emphasis on militarism and conflict as new practices introduced from elsewhere. This notion has become less tenable as increased study of Classic period Maya groups has shown that human sacrifice and militarism were present prior to the collapse and were integral to the maintenance of elite power. Interpretation of the Colonial period written sources, which speak in terms of invasion, conquest, and loss of political control, has been

Figure 12.3. Mixteca-Puebla-style pottery vessel from Honduras. Photograph courtesy of Russell N. Sheptak; used with permission

used to bolster the idea of foreign practices introduced via the intrusion of foreign peoples. Such sources were written after the fact and after the imposition of a new religious and political order (Catholicism and the Spanish colony), an issue discussed below in greater detail. Although we should not ignore these sources, they must be assessed in light of the archaeological evidence which reflects the actual practices and beliefs of Terminal Classic and Postclassic societies.

What, then, do we see in the archaeological record that suggests interaction with, or influence from, or conquest by, societies of Central Mexico, keeping in mind that economic, political, and artistic influences have flowed between Central Mexico and the Maya lowlands since the Formative period? As with the collapse itself, much of the evidence cited to support Mexican invasion is artistic and comes in three forms. First is the use of a "collection of standardized religious symbols that were popular throughout Mesoamerica" during this time period (Smith and Heath-Smith 1980:15). Second are similarities in the style of certain kinds of polychrome pottery vessel that were widespread in Mesoamerica at this time (Fig. 12.3). Third, in the Late Postclassic, is the appearance of a particular style of mural painting

Figure 12.4. Mixteca-Puebla mural from Santa Rita. After Bureau of American Ethnology Nineteenth Annual Report (1900), plate XXX

(Fig. 12.4). Smith and Heath-Smith have termed the standardized religious symbols the Postclassic Religious style, while Nicholson (1982) coined the term Mixteca-Puebla style for the whole complex, reflecting what was then the presumed origin of many of the objects, including those found in the Maya area.

In fact, it is now clear that objects made in this style were produced in a number of different places and exchanged. The archaeological context of the objects and symbols that comprise this apparently Mexican complex do clearly show that Terminal Classic and Postclassic Maya nobility expressed their status and political power in part through the incorporation of foreign symbols and materials into their costume, buildings, burials, and religious practices. Because of the variety of materials and because research has shown that objects were produced in a number of areas and exchanged widely, it is helpful to differentiate four kinds of objects that formed part of the material culture of Terminal Classic and Postclassic Maya nobles.

The first group of objects is imported items that were used to decorate the noble person or in the religious and social events important to the affirmation of elite status. While it is not always clear exactly where these objects came from, the consensus view is that many were manufactured in central or western Mexico, including the Mixtec area discussed by John Pohl in Chapter 9. Finely made metal objects of copper or gold, often decorated with mosaics of turquoise, shell, and other precious materials, represent very distinctive examples of such imports that have been found in elite burials, including those at Late Postclassic Santa Rita Corozal (D. Chase 1992:127; see Chase and Chase 1988). Metalwork became part of the elite person in the most direct sense as something worn as jewelry or incorporated into clothing. Other materials that were widely exchanged include certain types of pottery vessels, especially Plumbate, and green obsidian.

The second group of objects consists of locally made monumental stone sculptures in new forms, in style and motifs distinctive from, although rooted in, earlier Maya art (Miller 1993). Three well-known monument types, familiar to anyone who has visited Chichen Itza, are the figures known as "chac mools," "banner carriers," and "atlantean figures." Chac mools, reclining humans (or human-like deities) holding a bowl on their stomach, are also found in contemporary and later sites in Central Mexico, but do not necessarily originate there. Other motifs, such as jaguar and eagle warriors and feathered serpents, with precedents in Classic Central Mexican iconography, become more prominent in Postclassic Maya sculpture.

The third category of objects is another example of locally produced artwork, the Mixteca-Puebla-style murals found at some Late Postclassic Maya sites. Mural painting itself has a long history in the Maya area, although few examples have survived into the present day. Stylistically distinct Mixteca-Puebla-style murals have been documented in Belize at Santa Rita Corozal, in northern Yucatan at Tulum, and in the Guatemalan highlands at Utatlan (Chase and Chase 1988; Fox et al. 1992; Miller 1982). Despite the differences in style, however, these Late Postclassic International-style murals, like their Classic period predecessors, often include Maya hieroglyphic writing.

The fourth group of objects that formed part of the material culture of Terminal Classic and Postclassic Maya nobles consists of locally produced objects that share formal or stylistic properties that affiliate them with the style of imported objects and locally produced art in the new styles. One of the best examples of this category is certain pottery vessels in types such as Altar and Silho Fine Orange, which scientific analysis has demonstrated were produced at sites in the Maya area (Sabloff et al. 1982).

Some archaeologists initially argued that the introduction of this material culture and symbolism marked the invasion of new groups of people from the Gulf Coast or Central Mexico. Such groups, sometimes referred to as Toltecs, sometimes as Putun, were seen as conquering weakened Maya polities or taking over abandoned areas. Chichen Itza is the most often cited example of such a supposed invasion. Here, it has been argued, one can see a superposition of Toltec architecture and art, in the form of chac mools and atlantean figures, on top of the earlier Maya city. More recent archaeological work at Chichen Itza, however, has demonstrated that this neat sequence does not work and that, in fact, the art and architecture at Chichen Itza represents an amalgam of the continuation of Classic period styles with the emerging International style (Lincoln 1986). Ringle (1990) has argued that the hieroglyphic texts carved on ninth-century lintels at Chichen Itza commemorate the actions of people who were members of three families that also figure prominently in Spanish accounts from the time of conquest and colonization in the fifteenth and sixteenth centuries, suggesting continuity in elite identity rather than the introduction of a new, foreign elite.

More broadly, archaeologists point to three lines of evidence for rejecting the argument of a large-scale intrusion of a new ethnic and linguistic group in the Maya area. First, the elements listed above do not necessarily appear all at once at a site,

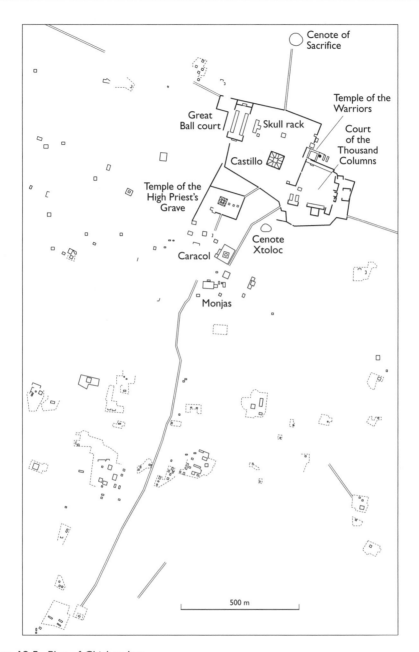

Figure 12.5. Plan of Chichen Itza

nor do most sites have all of the features. Chichen Itza (Fig. 12.5) is one site where all, or almost all, of these features can be documented. Different communities exhibited a greater or lesser degree of adoption of such objects and art as part of local decision-making. Second, even at sites where groups were very interested in acquiring and displaying these objects, foreign elements are integrated into local traditions of material culture and social practices. For example, despite the reduction in the carving of texts on monuments, a practice which disappears by the Late Postclassic period, neither the knowledge nor the use of Maya hieroglyphic writing disappears as attested by Spanish accounts of the large quantities of codices, or books, most burned as part of the conversion process (Tozzer 1941). Third, the use of artistic styles, symbolism, and certain kinds of material culture to reflect local elites' awareness of larger trends and their ability to interact with powerful foreign polities was hardly a new phenomenon in Mesoamerica. The art style we call Olmec (see Chapter 3) became a way for Formative period emerging elites to show their connections to ideas, peoples, and regions outside of their own. Classic period Maya polities traded with the city of Teotihuacan, adopted aspects of its iconography, and played up their ties to its rulers (see Chapters 4, 5 and 7).

Postclassic Maya elites participated in exchange networks that helped create a pan-regional sense of elite identity that reinforced their status and power at home. They were "cosmopolitan Maya people solidly entrenched in a Pan-Mesoamerican system of exchange and well aware of outside innovations" (Chase and Chase 1988:83). Nor should we assume that involvement in trade networks and the incorporation of new ideas or symbols were limited to the elite. Based on excavations at a small settlement in Belize, Laguna de On, that was occupied in the Late Classic through the Middle Postclassic, Masson (1997) has shown that, even at the level of day-to-day practice, farmers shifted their "emulation spheres" in response to realigned economic and political realities.

Continuities despite change

Archaeologists now recognize that, despite alteration in settlement, political structure, and the degree of conflict, the people living in these ongoing and new places in northern Yucatan, the southern Maya lowlands, and the Guatemalan highlands shared a *cultural and linguistic tradition* that allows us, as present-day archaeologists, to continue to identify the people as Maya and to recognize that the indigenous Maya-speaking peoples living in contemporary Mexico and Central America are the descendants of these Classic and Postclassic period societies. This cultural tradition is expressed through material culture and represents a continuation of ideology and practices that characterized Maya societies of the Classic period. Cultural traditions are reproduced through practice and day-to-day interactions of the sort described by Cynthia Robin in Chapter 6 and Linda Manzanilla in Chapter 5 (see also Masson 1997). Thus, even at Terminal Classic Tikal, with its shrunken population and less powerful elite, Culbert (1973b) was able to point to the continuation of household religious rituals as evidence of a continued Maya occupation. It is thus crucial when discussing Maya history to distinguish political entities (Maya kingdoms or states) which rise and fall, expand and contract, and their associated settlements, some of which are occupied for longer spans of time than others, from cultural traditions which have a greater continuity, change at a slower rate, and connect people who are members of different communities or states.

Assertion of social distinction and of differences in social status continued into the Postclassic period as well. These assertions drew on the same vocabulary of symbolism and material culture as discussed by Robin in Chapter 6: the location, size, and scale of residences; the construction, use, and control of public architecture; hieroglyphic writing; and the themes of monumental art. Of these practices, the carving of texts on monuments and buildings became less widespread than in the Classic period, although, as discussed below, the use of images and writing did not disappear. Although the reduced use of hieroglyphic writing was once seen as further evidence of Maya devolution (Willey 1986), analysis of the content of late inscriptions indicates that changes in how writing was used were connected to changes in the structure of the political system. Whereas Classic period political structure made the ruler the focal person and therefore the living symbol of the state, Postclassic polities seem to have moved to a more oligarchic form of political control in which the life, deeds, and ancestry of one particular person were no longer celebrated (Joyce 2000; Ringle 1990).

Documentary Sources and the Historiography of Maya History

The participation of Postclassic Maya elites in this pan-regional identity can be seen through the analysis of material culture and artistic style – tangible objects which were exchanged and used by people living in a number of communities throughout Mesoamerica. In the Maya area, members of the nobility or elite used or displayed these objects or works of art as part of the assertion of their importance and power. By looking at these objects in context, archaeologists have been able to study the ways that imported and locally produced materials became part of the daily life and special events that together help construct social identity through practice.

As noted earlier, the interpretation of the changes from Classic to Postclassic period as the result of outside invasion came primarily from a different kind of data: written or documentary sources. Such sources, because they are written documents, may seem to us to fall into the province of historical rather than archaeological research and, in fact, it is the case that here we encounter one of the boundaries between academic disciplines. The boundary has proved to be a porous one in that archaeologists and historians have made use of each other's data (compare Chapter 9). Perhaps because of the primacy we accord in our own society to the written record, however, in Maya archaeology it has been archaeologists who have been most successful at considering both lines of evidence and in using archaeological data to help assess the usefulness of the documentary sources.

In the remainder of this chapter, I discuss the documentary sources in order to explore the wealth and variety of written materials available, as well as to raise issues that influence their usefulness. While, as will become clear, these sources do have limitations, there is no question of not using them. We cannot throw away information, particularly when dealing with time periods and cultures about which so much information has already been lost inadvertently or destroyed on purpose.

Nevertheless, one cannot extract information from the documentary sources without first considering the questions of bias and purpose. This is something one needs to do with all kinds of evidence, but it sometimes seems that we have done a better job of this when dealing with archaeological data than with written sources, perhaps because we are more accustomed to information conveyed through writing and therefore tend to give greater weight to written records. Many of the documentary sources were written by Europeans conditioned by a model of how to record information and of what history should be that, at first reading, seems more compatible with our own definition of history. Furthermore, the written sources are so rich in terms of what they describe and the range of information covered that it is tempting to use them uncritically.

The Spaniards who began arriving in Mesoamerica in the early sixteenth century encountered Maya societies living in socially stratified polities in northern Yucatan, the highlands of Guatemala and Mexico, eastern Guatemala, and western Honduras, and even the Peten lowlands. The political landscape that confronted the Spaniards was fragmented into multiple polities. Out of the complex interactions between European and Indian emerged a large and diverse body of written records and texts which reflect the literate traditions of two very different cultures. As earlier chapters in this book make clear, the use of writing and a sense of history were integral to the cultural traditions of many Mesoamerican peoples, including the Maya, Zapotec, Mixtec, Aztec, and possibly the inhabitants of Teotihuacan. Writing was integrally linked to image in a way very different from our own notion of images as mere illustrations. The introduction of a new orthography, or way of writing – the Roman alphabet used by the Spanish – and new languages, including Spanish and Latin, expanded further the ways for indigenous groups in Mesoamerica to record information and ideas, creating the conditions for the recording of competing accounts, histories, and ideas. Control over and interpretation of the written word continue to be as important to Maya peoples today as it does to the nation-states in which they live (Sullivan 1989).

Types of documentary sources

Before turning to the case study of Maya gender relations, let me review the kinds of sources we have available to us. Documentary sources may be grouped together based on a variety of characteristics. I find it useful to classify written sources five ways.

1   *Authorship.* Some, although by no means all, surviving documents have been attributed to specific individuals whom we can identify as the author of the work. More broadly, though, authors may be divided into two groups – indigenous or European. This division is not merely an ethnic one but also reflects the very different cultural traditions and social and political positions of colonized and colonizer. Within these two categories, one may also distinguish authors by their social position, occupation, degree of interaction with the subject of study, and gender.

2   *Date.* Since writing and written records pre-date the advent of Europeans in some areas of Mesoamerica, it is important to distinguish between pre-contact and post-contact sources. As noted in Chapters 6 and 7, hieroglyphic texts carved on stone monuments are a defining feature of the Maya Classic period. Our focus here, however, is on materials written either in the Late Postclassic period, before Spanish contact, or during the Colonial period.

3   *Language and Orthography.* Late Postclassic texts use only indigenous languages and ways of writing those languages. Maya texts from this time period transcribe one of the several different Mayan languages using the hieroglyphic system of writing. After the conquest, especially during the first 70 years of the new colony, the dream of early Spanish missionaries to establish a native clergy gave some native people, usually members of noble families, instruction in Latin, Spanish, and the writing of their own languages using the Roman alphabet (see Burkhart 1989).

4   *Style.* The two categories here are written or pictorial. These are somewhat misleading terms since the pictorial documents are not just pictures but do indeed contain text. However, they also represent a Mesoamerican type of document that is gradually replaced by a European style of document that consists entirely or mostly of writing with few or no pictures – and those pictures are reduced in their importance to illustrations. The Maya, like the Mixtec discussed by Pohl (Chapter 9), had their own tradition of handwritten and painted books which have been called codices. Only a few pre-conquest codices have survived. Some have been lost due to natural processes of decay, but most were burned by the Spanish in an attempt to separate indigenous peoples from their non-Christian religious beliefs. Three of the four surviving codices from the Maya area come from the Yucatan peninsula and are known as the Codex Dresden, the Codex Madrid, and the Codex Paris (Glass and Robertson 1975).

      The term codex has been applied to manuscripts of various formats and materials produced both before and after the conquest (see Glass 1975 for a detailed discussion). The preferred prehispanic method was to fold a long sheet of bark paper or animal skin into a fan-like arrangement, coat the paper with a thin layer of lime stucco, and paint the imagery and texts in several colors, including black, red, and blue. The surviving Maya codices deal with religious, calendrical, astronomical, and agricultural matters rather than historical or economic information. Unlike Central Mexico, where the Spanish commissioned reproductions of important Aztec codices, the Maya area did not produce such copies. Nevertheless, the term codex has been applied to some post-conquest Maya-language documents written in the Roman alphabet and on European paper. The Maya codices contain substantial hieroglyphic texts, while those from Central Mexico or the Mixtec area are predominately pictorial, reflecting the fact that the Maya employed a writing system to fully represent longer texts, while Mexican peoples evolved oral recitation with shorter, less fully developed texts.

5   *Genre.* An enormous variety of kinds of documents were produced, including histories, censuses, government reports, dictionaries, accounts of religious beliefs and ceremonies, astronomical tables, and agricultural almanacs.

Ironically, the conventional European-style histories are in some ways the most problematic precisely because their goal is to sum up and to present a comprehensive discussion. Such summarizing and comprehensiveness, however, reduce the amount of detail and increase the amount of interpretation, where assumptions based on the author's background can override the evidence. Analysis of legal documents, for example, in which indigenous people brought suits to reclaim property or made wills to pass on property, have revealed much about native kinship and inheritance rules (e.g., Witschey 1991) that is not discussed in more conventional histories of native society, which tend to assume patrilineal inheritance and primogeniture (e.g. Tozzer 1941).

Important documentary sources on or by the Maya

The surviving Pre-Columbian Maya codices, such as the Paris, Dresden, and Madrid codices, are manuals to be used by Maya ritual practitioners for divination and the carrying out of ceremonies (Love 1994). They contain almanacs and tables that may be used to calculate the occurrence of astronomical and calendrical events, such as the beginning of the new year, eclipses, equinoxes, and solstices, and the cycles of the moon and planets such as Venus (Thompson 1972). Using the almanacs and tables effectively would have required a thorough knowledge of the calendars, especially the 260-day cycle, and a good understanding of mathematics. Deities are named in the hieroglyphic texts and appear in the associated pictures either as personifications of these events or as the supernatural beings associated with the events or dates in the 260-day calendar. Although the entries cover periods of time, they are not historical in a linear sense and thus do not correspond to a European notion of history. But they do indicate the kinds of knowledge the Maya considered significant and allow us to consider the symbolism of ritual and astronomical matters.

The mission to convert and minister to the Maya of the Yucatan resulted in the destruction of many other codices, but did prompt Diego de Landa, a Franciscan and bishop of Merida, to write an account of Maya society, a partial copy of which is available to us as the *Relación de las cosas de Yucatán*. Other Spaniards also wrote accounts, including Bernardo de Lizana (1988), Diego López de Cogolludo (1971), Fray Alonso Ponce (Noyes 1932), and Pedro Sánchez de Aguilar (1937). However, Landa's account has emerged as the most commonly used because it is believed to have been written early in the Colonial period and has been translated into English in several different editions.

Landa is thought to have written his history sometime during the 1560s–1570s. He returned to Spain in the 1560s after 17 years of service in Yucatan to answer accusations of having exceeded his authority while Provincial of the Franciscan order in Yucatan (Karttunen 1994:97–105). The check on his career was short-lived, and by 1573 Landa had been appointed bishop of Yucatan. He died in Merida in the Yucatan peninsula in 1579. The text that modern scholars study is based on an incomplete and probably rearranged seventeenth-century version that postdates

Landa's death and may contain sections interpolated from other sources (Restall and Chuchiak 2002). As known to us, the *Relación* combines an account of pre- and post-conquest historical events in the northern Yucatan peninsula, with a discussion of Maya society prior to Spanish contact and a description of the natural setting. It is ironic that the most widely used historical source on the Maya, a source that shapes, to one degree or another, all our reconstructions of prehispanic Maya society, should have been written by one of the men most responsible for the destruction of indigenous writings. As Landa wrote, "We found a large number of books . . . and as they contained nothing in which there were not to be seen superstition and lies of the devil, we burned them all, which [the Maya] regretted to an amazing degree, and which caused them much affliction" (Tozzer 1941:169).

Despite this destruction, Maya continued writing into the Colonial period, often on subjects that Landa would have considered idolatrous and heathen. The texts scholars call the Books of Chilam Balam were written by Yucatec Maya using the Roman alphabet (see Gibson and Glass 1975:379–387; Sullivan 1989). *Chilan* (or *chilam*) was, according to Landa, a particular category of religious practitioner who served as an oracle or prophet (Tozzer 1941:111–112). The books vary in content and organization, and include information on Maya history both before and after the conquest, prophecy, religion, astronomy, and other topics. They also include information derived from contact with Spaniards, and Christian ideas and concepts to a greater or lesser degree.

The Books of Chilam Balam, especially those from Tizimin and Chumayel (Edmonson 1982; Roys 1967), have been the main source of the accounts of Mexican or Mexicanized Maya invasions of Yucatan, along with briefer information from Landa. According to the Chilam Balams, such foreigners (sometimes referred to as the Itza) waged war and introduced new religious and even sexual practices. As discussed earlier, archaeological evidence and translation of Classic period hieroglyphic texts have established that human sacrifice and military conquest were integral to Maya civilization throughout its history and cannot be attributed to the influx of new peoples. The Chilam Balams could be describing in poetic terms great changes that took place in Maya history, as the power of different sites waxed and waned, including, but not limited to, the events archaeologists recognize as the transformation from Classic to Postclassic periods.

Most sources authored by Spaniards that have been widely used by archaeologists focus on the Maya of northern Yucatan, but indigenous texts are known from highland Guatemala. One much-studied text from this region is the Popol Vuh, which offers a Maya version of the creation of the universe that takes us from the first beginnings of the world to after the Spanish Conquest. It is known to us only through an early eighteenth-century copy made by Francisco Ximénez, priest to the Quiche Maya (Tedlock 1985:23–65). Tedlock has argued that internal evidence indicates that the text Ximénez copied was first written between 1554 and 1558, possibly as part of an attempt by the Quiche elite to regain their pre-conquest economic and social rights.

Translation and interpretation of the Books of Chilam Balam and of the Popol Vuh have proved difficult but rewarding. They seem to modern eyes an uneasy mix of myth and history in that all link their mythological narratives with the origins of historically attested groups of people. Edmonson (1982:xi), writing of the Chilam Balam of Tizimin, calls it "history in the Mayan manner . . . dominated by a sense of cyclical repetition and by a profound faith in the predictive force of the calendar." The books were written to preserve knowledge not condoned by Spanish religious or secular authorities and therefore are marked by the use of highly symbolic and metaphoric language to conceal meaning from outsiders. For the Maya, the opposition between myth and history is a false one. In their view, "the mythic and historical parts of [the] narratives . . . [belong] to a single, balanced whole" (Tedlock 1985:63) that together justify the social order and political relations of the Quiche or the Yucatec Maya at the time of the Spanish Conquest. This process provides a social charter or at the least an explanation of current circumstances.

The written sources most used by archaeologists and historians to understand the pre-contact situation were written during the first 70 years of Spanish control, when Spanish interest in native culture was strong and survivors of the conquest still alive. But this was also a period of rapid and major cultural change during which indigenous people found themselves incorporated violently into a new political order, converted, often with equal violence, to a new, exclusionary religion, subjected to the demands of a new economic system, and dying in large numbers from introduced European diseases and general abuse. The repudiation of certain practices such as bloodletting and human sacrifice, by displacing them on to putative foreigners, makes sense in the context of the disruption caused by colonization and this desire to explain current circumstances.

Many of these documentary sources reflect, to some degree, the changes resulting from the Spanish Conquest and the efforts of indigenous peoples to come to terms with those changes, through accommodation and resistance. With Landa's *Relación*, the native voice is almost entirely submerged. Although it is clear that not all of Landa's information can have come from his own observation of or participation in events, he identifies only one Maya person, Juan Nachi Cocom, and no Spanish ones, as sources (Tozzer 1941:vii). Landa skims over his own role in the destruction of Maya culture (Karttunen 1994:107). Clendinnen (1987:125–126) and Karttunen argue that it is against the backdrop of Landa's involvement in the rooting out of religious backsliding in 1562 that one must view the *Relación*. As with other Spanish writers, Landa saw native history and life very much through the lens of his own culture, judging Maya behavior and beliefs in terms of his own religious concepts and moral standards. Thus, the Maya are inevitably morally deficient by virtue of their idolatrous religious beliefs and practices, beliefs and practices explained by the Spanish (using their own cultural categories) as the result of the devil's work (Frost 1993).

The accretion of interpretations that have accumulated around these sources is another issue influencing their use. The standard English-language edition of Landa is an example. It was translated by Alfred M. Tozzer and published in 1941. More than just a translation of the 1616 copy, the edition contains over a thousand footnotes by Tozzer that explain and expand on Landa's text by drawing on archaeological, ethnohistorical, ethnographic, and linguistic scholarship. The footnotes, although a tribute to Tozzer's erudition, at times overwhelm the text, occupying all or most of a page. Tozzer's annotation represents one of the great scholarly achievements in Mesoamerican studies. Yet the length and depth of the commentary creates a new, hybrid text, a Landa–Tozzer. Tozzer's footnotes, by expanding on Landa, provide the reader with an impressive overview of ideas on the Maya circa 1941. But in the process, Landa comes to us filtered through Tozzer (Joyce 1992, 2000). In drawing on Landa for information on ancient Maya society, we must keep Landa and Tozzer separate and focus on what Landa himself says rather than on Tozzer's interpretation of Landa's meaning.

Case study: The gendering of religious participation in Postclassic Maya society

All these documents, then, must be read critically, but cannot be ignored. In order to demonstrate a critical use of these sources, I close with a case study of gender relations and the role of women in Postclassic Maya society that shows the value of using multiple lines of evidence, including documentary, archaeological, and visual sources. Gender relations and the role of women are by no means the only subject on which Landa has been interrogated. Diane Chase (1992) has discussed the ways that Landa's description of Maya towns, such as Mayapan, does not represent the only way that Late Postclassic settlements were arranged spatially or socially. I have chosen to consider the participation of women in religious ritual in Postclassic Maya society because of the strong influence interpretations of Spanish documents have had on models of social relations surrounding gender. It has been suggested, based on Landa's account, that women were considered impure, did not participate in community-sponsored rituals in temples, and that Maya attitudes toward women's bloodletting became more restrictive over time (Clendinnen 1982).

Let us begin by looking at how Landa writes about women and what this tells us about his attitudes. Like most of the written sources, he never incorporates women's voices explicitly. Landa assumed that men represented the active and meaningful segment of society and were morally and intellectually best suited to the conduct of public affairs (see Frost 1993). Thus, Landa's descriptions of "typical" Maya life are really based on his interpretation of men's experiences: "The vices of the *Indians* were idolatries and repudiation of their wives" (Tozzer 1941:72–73; emphasis added). In describing the appearance of the "Indians of Yucatan," Landa writes, "They did not grow beards . . . They wore their hair long like women . . . They bathed frequently without taking the trouble to hide their nakedness from the women" (Tozzer 1941:87–89).

Landa's discussion of women centers on their appearance, sexuality, temperament, reproductive capabilities, and domestic chores (e.g., Tozzer 1941:125–129). "The Indian women of Yucatan are generally better looking than Spanish women and larger and well made . . . They are very productive and have children very early. And they are excellent nurses for two reasons: first, because the warm drink which they take in the morning gives a good flow of milk; and secondly, the continual grinding of maize and not keeping their breasts tightly pressed makes them have very large ones, from which cause it happens that they have a great deal of milk" (Tozzer 1941:127–128).

The idea of women as active participants or agents receives less attention or is treated pejoratively. The gender roles and categories of native society were interpreted through the filter of European and Christian points of view. In order to make the native conception of the domestic role of women match their own, for example, the missionaries had to ignore or deride the economic and symbolic meaning of women's work and religious participation (Hendon 1999). Women, as the supposed weaker sex, were dangerous because of their susceptibility to sin and the devil, and direct interaction between men in religious orders and native women was discouraged (Burkhart 1997). Religious, economic or political practices of women that moved them outside of their proper role, that of the hard-working, fertile, and submissive wife and mother, were considered strange and dangerous, precisely the sort of beliefs and actions the missionaries needed to change. Consequently, Landa cannot be treated as a disinterested reporter of the reality of gender roles and activities.

Nor was he a simple reporter when he discussed religion. We need to consider both how Landa interprets Maya religious practices and how he describes those practices since, as noted above, the descriptions often contain details that the author himself overlooks when providing an explanation for those practices. In discussing religion, it is useful to distinguish between different levels of interaction and sponsorship, differences which in turn imply different functions for ceremonies and other ritual observances. On the one hand, we have society-wide or community-wide ceremonies which involve members of the priesthood and the political leadership as well as specific social group such as nobles, artisans, and commoners. Many of these ceremonies took place in public spaces – streets or plazas – while others were set in the temples or other religious buildings built with communal labor under the control of the government. Such ceremonies, often tied to the calendar, fostered a sense of social identity that transcended family or status. Although presented as benefiting society as a whole, they served as an important source of power for the elite. The active role played by the nobility, either as priests or in their capacity as political leaders, ensured their control of official religious doctrine and practice. Ceremonies of this sort described by Landa represent another line of continuity between Classic and Postclassic period Maya society.

On the other hand, we have the daily observances and life-cycle rituals that involved a much smaller segment of society. The rituals attendant on birth, baptism, coming of age, marriage, and death were household-centered. Such rituals commonly required bloodletting, sacrifice, and feasting set within houses or other parts of the living area, space controlled by the household. Some of these life-cycle events might be folded into society-wide ceremonies or require the participation of priests. But households took responsibility for the ceremonies which served primarily to foster a sense of social identity and integration among members of these smaller social groups. In addition to these special events, people at all levels of society had ritual obligations that they fulfilled through ceremonies at home involving praying,

Figure 12.6. Group of four female figures participating in mortuary and accession rituals, comparable to women described by Landa as participants in New Year's rituals. South roof vault inside the North Ballcourt Temple, Chichen Itza. After Wren and Schmidt (1991: fig. 9.7). Drawing by Linnea Wren after Peter Schmidt. Reprinted with the permission of Linnea Wren

incense-burning, and making offerings of food and blood (Fig. 12.6). These obligations applied to men and women, adults and children. Archaeological evidence for such household-based religious practices comes from Classic and Postclassic period living areas (see Chapter 6; Masson 1997).

Landa never says whether women held priestly office and thus had an official, institutionalized role in community-wide ceremonies as some women did in the contemporary Aztec empire (McCafferty and McCafferty 1988). He does state that women were not allowed in the temples (Tozzer 1941:152), in contrast to men. He also notes another apparent difference in religious practices between Maya men and women. Landa makes much of the constant and ubiquitous self sacrifice of Maya men (Tozzer 1941:184–185; see also Sánchez de Aguilar 1937:133–134). Maya women, according to Landa (Tozzer 1941:114), followed a completely opposite course. They "did not practice this shedding of blood, though they were great devotees," using instead blood of birds, animals, or fish as offerings.

Here we must pause for a moment and consider Tozzer's contribution to this issue. Tozzer interpreted Landa's statements about bloodletting and lack of access to temples as evidence that women, and their blood in particular, were considered unclean. "The very common idea among many people of the ceremonial uncleanness of women is brought out clearly by Landa as regards the Maya. Not only are they not allowed, with one exception, in the temples, but . . . their blood as sacrifice is not acceptable to the gods" (Tozzer 1941: footnote 596). Tozzer starts with a statement that he believes represents a cross-culturally valid generalization. His interpretation has been widely accepted for the Maya (e.g., Thompson 1970:184). More recent research on the symbolic meanings associated with bodily fluids, blood, and in particular menstrual blood, has demonstrated that this cross-cultural generalization is not valid (Buckley and Gottlieb 1988). One needs to demonstrate that a particular culture holds such a view on impurity before using such beliefs as an explanation for specific practices. Note that Landa does not say that women were considered unclean, that they were prohibited from bloodletting (only that they did not do so), or that their blood was unacceptable as an offering.

Institutionalized roles for women may be demonstrated through analysis of Landa's description of two ceremonies. The first took place in the month of Yaxkin and is a good example of a society-wide ceremony. Boys and girls were brought to the temple where they were struck gently nine times on the backs of their hands. The blows were to ensure "that they might become skillful workmen in the professions of their fathers and mothers" (Tozzer 1941:159). A woman called *ix mol* ("the conductress"), dressed in a special costume, administered the blows to the girls. Although not stated explicitly, Landa's description implies that a different person, presumably male, was responsible for the boys. Sets of tools associated with different occupations were covered in blue pigment and offered to the deities as a sacrifice. The position of *ix mol* sounds very much like an institutionalized religious position (Joyce 1992). The conductress not only has a specific role and ceremony to carry out but she wore a special feather costume and carried an insignia, "the feather of her office" (Tozzer 1941:159). Furthermore, the ceremony is set in a temple, yet a woman not only attended but carried out the ceremony.

Ceremonies that were located in household space, yet which had larger implications for social integration, occurred in the month of Zip for people with specific occupations: hunters, healers, and fishermen (Tozzer 1941:155–156). It is clear from Landa's description of the events that the ceremonies must have involved not only the hunter, healer, or fisherman, but also the person's spouse. Hunters and their wives made offerings to the patron deities, including their own blood through auto-sacrifice. As in the Yaxkin ceremony, arrows used in hunting were imbued with sacred power through the application of blue pigment. The participants then danced and feasted. The fishermen and their wives carried out a very similar ritual, culminating in a communal feast of fish. Although to Landa the focus of the ceremony may have been the hunter or fisherman, with the wife as an adjunct, indigenous texts and art make it clear that husband and wife formed a complementary and interdependent unit. Such a unit is more properly referred to as a mother–father pair and represents a basic element of Maya gender symbolism. In Maya cosmogony, the ultimate or primary creative force is made up of both male and female principles, sometimes represented as a single divine entity, more often as a male and female pair. Creation begins in the Popol Vuh with the thoughts and words of a series of deities who are "modelers," associated with the male gender, and "makers," associated with female gender (Recinos 1950:78; Tedlock 1985:71–72, 347). Creator deities in the Dresden Codex are also depicted as male and female pairs (Thompson 1972:43, 9c). Such economically and ritually significant pairing receives ritual validation in the ceremonies described during the month of Zip.

Based on Landa's descriptions and supplemented by information in other Spanish-authored accounts, Maya women took part in the preparations for and the celebration of public and household rituals. They raised animals, wove cloth, and prepared food and drink to be used as offerings, gifts, and for feasts. They served food and drink and got drunk with their guests. They participated in the dances and processions that made up a large part of the cycle of festivals (Noyes 1932:339; Sánchez de Aguilar 1937:133–134; Tozzer 1941:92, 94, 105–107, 127–128, 143–147, 151).

Landa's claim that women were not allowed in temples is contradicted in part by his own descriptions of certain ceremonies, such as the Yaxkin ceremony described above, when young girls and the conductress entered the temple. Ceremonies in celebration of the New Year included a group of women who danced in the temple precincts wearing a special costume (Joyce 1992). These women, described as "old," were carrying out a socially accepted and institutionalized role that required them to weave cloth for the ceremonies as well as dance (Tozzer 1941:128–129, 143, 145, 147, 152). Other Spanish-authored accounts of Yucatec Maya life also suggest women's participation in temple rites. Lizana (1988:56) writes that everyone, men and women, made offerings in the temples, while López de Cogolludo (1971 vol. 1:231, 257) states that the Maya assigned young girls to serve in the temples for a period of time before marriage.

Finally, we come to the issue of whether women's blood was an acceptable offering to deities. Images of men and women engaged in self-sacrifice establish that both men and women let blood during the Classic period. Lintels from the site of Yaxchilan show that women of highest social rank engaged in self-sacrifice in order to carry out religious rituals (Tate 1992). It has been suggested that Maya attitudes toward women's bloodletting became more restrictive over time. There is evidence, however, that dates from the Postclassic period itself to show that bloodletting was thought of by the Maya as something that both sexes did.

In the Madrid Codex, a document created during the Postclassic period by the very Mayan society Landa tries to reconstruct after the fact, a young female deity lets blood from her ear on page 95a in the company of three male deities. This is, in fact, the only depiction of self-sacrifice in the codex, and it involves deities of both genders (Codex Tro-Cortesianus 1967:95a). While it is possible that female deities may do things that mortal women cannot, in Mesoamerica divine action serves as a model for human action. Deities in the codices undertake many actions that human beings would regularly engage in, such as planting, fighting, weaving, spinning, making offerings, writing, painting, and carving. Showing the deities engaged in these activities provides a supernatural mandate or justification for such activities (Hendon 1997; Reents-Budet 1994:36–46).

Looking at another text that offers a more Maya point of view, we see that the blood of female sacrifices was as acceptable as that of male victims as an offering. In the Popol Vuh, Blood Woman, a daughter of one of the underworld deities, is intended as a sacrifice. Her father, in anger at her pregnancy, orders that her heart be cut out and burned as an offering to him and his fellow deities. The heart in Mesoamerican thought is the center of life and the most worthy offering (López Austin 1973:124). Blood Woman averts her own death by substituting a lump of red tree resin. The smell of the burning resin so enchants the deities that they fail to notice the trick (Tedlock 1985:115–117). While the sacrifice is meant as a punishment, her heart is as acceptable as that of a male victim.

The Late Postclassic Maya society described by Landa considered human sacrifice an important part of its religion (Tozzer 1941:115–121). In one ceremony,
the celebrant "wounded the victim with an arrow in the parts of shame, *whether it
was a man or woman*, and drew blood and . . . anointed the faces of the idols with
it" (Tozzer 1941:118; emphasis added), thus demonstrating that women's blood
was acceptable as an offering (see also Lizana 1988:58; López de Cogolludo 1971
vol. 1:251). Landa also records the practice of drowning people in the *cenotes*, or
wells, of Yucatan as an offering to the rain deities (Tozzer 1941:54). Archaeological
evidence confirms this as a Postclassic practice. Dredging of the cenote at Chichen
Itza in the early twentieth century recovered skeletons of men, women, and children, along with a multitude of objects thrown in as offerings (Hooton 1940). To
modern eyes the opportunity to be a sacrificial victim may not seem a particularly
enviable one. The point to remember, however, is that women were deemed worthy
to be offerings as much as men.

Clearly, some women did play roles in religious life in Postclassic Maya society.
That not all women were so engaged reminds us that, in a complex society, people's
participation varies according to many different distinctions. We have little information on how participation in ritual by men broke down along lines of class, age,
marital state, occupation, or other social categories. What hints Landa does give
indicate that being male was not sufficient to ensure participation in all aspects of
religious life. Adults, nobles, and priests had greater responsibilities than children,
commoners, or laymen. Other criteria no doubt intervened as well. Such differentiation as we can disentangle from Landa echoes that evidenced in Classic period
Maya society. It therefore seems reasonable to suggest that Landa's blanket statements fail to cover the complex reality of either men's or women's religious life.

Conclusions

The sources available to us for understanding Postclassic Maya society are limited
but varied in their format and the kinds of information they present to us. Archaeological research, analysis of art, and study of written documents need to be used
together as multiple and intersecting lines of evidence, as demonstrated in the case
study of women's religious roles and practices. Rather than assuming that the
written texts are in some way a better source of information, we need to recognize
that they offer certain kinds of information but that archaeology and art can offer
equally useful insights. This chapter has focused on the Maya collapse and the
Terminal and Postclassic periods because our understanding of these processes and
time periods has been shaped and to a certain extent distorted by Colonial period
written documents. The view of the collapse as a sudden and large-scale event has
given way to an understanding of it as a process of political realignment and
settlement relocation. The idea that the Maya area was invaded by a foreign group
in the Postclassic that brought with it a set of artistic and material cultural
elements has given way to a notion of continuity and change in Maya society as
economic ties readjusted themselves and elites adopted material markers of a

pan-regional elite identity. While these changes may have included changes in gender relations, the sharp break suggested by Landa's account (and Tozzer's interpretation) between Classic and Postclassic society is not borne out by Landa's own descriptions of particular events, by other Spanish accounts, or by the Maya documents.

REFERENCES

Brown, C. T., 1991 Ich Noh Cah Mayapán: Organización social yucateca del Postclásico tardio. *Boletín, Consejo de Arqueología* 19–23.

Buckley, T., and A. Gottlieb, 1988 A critical appraisal of theories of menstrual symbolism. In *Blood Magic: The Anthropology of Menstruation*. T. Buckley and A. Gottlieb, eds. Pp. 1–52. Berkeley: University of California Press.

Burkhart, L. M., 1989 *The Slippery Earth: Nahua–Christian Moral Dialogue in Sixteenth-Century Mexico.* Tucson: University of Arizona Press.

——1997 Mexica women on the home front: Housework and religion in Aztec Mexico. In *Indian Women of Early Mexico*. S. Schroeder, S. Wood, and R. Haskett, eds. Pp. 25–54. Norman: University of Oklahoma Press.

Chase, A. F., and P. M. Rice, eds., 1985 *The Lowland Maya Postclassic.* Austin: University of Texas Press.

Chase, D. Z., 1992 Postclassic Maya elites: Ethnohistory and archaeology. In *Mesoamerican Elites: An Archaeological Assessment*. D. Z. Chase and A. F. Chase, eds. Pp. 118–134. Norman: University of Oklahoma Press.

Chase, D. Z, and A. F. Chase, 1998 *A Postclassic Perspective: Excavations at the Maya Site of Santa Rita Corozal, Belize.* Monograph 4. San Francisco: Pre-Columbian Art Research Institute.

Clendinnen, I., 1982 Yucatec Maya women and the Spanish Conquest: Role and ritual in historical reconstruction. *Journal of Social History* 15, 427–442.

——1987 *Ambivalent Conquests: Maya and Spaniard in Yucatan, 1517–1570.* Cambridge: Cambridge University Press.

Codex Tro-Cortesianus/Codex Madrid, 1967 Museo de América Madrid. Graz: Akademische Druck- und Verlagsanstalt.

Culbert, T. P., ed., 1973a *The Classic Maya Collapse.* Albuquerque: University of New Mexico Press.

——1973b The Maya downfall at Tikal. In *The Classic Maya Collapse*. T. P. Culbert, ed. Pp. 63–92. Albuquerque: University of New Mexico Press.

Culbert, T. P., L. J. Kosakowsky, R. E. Fry, and W. A. Haviland, 1990 Population of Tikal, Guatemala. In *Precolumbian Population History in the Maya Lowlands*. T. P. Culbert and D. S. Rice, eds. Pp. 103–121. Albuquerque: University of New Mexico Press.

Culbert, T. P., and D. S. Rice, eds., 1990 *Precolumbian Population History in the Maya Lowlands.* Albuquerque: University of New Mexico Press.

Demarest, A. A., 1992 Ideology in ancient Maya cultural evolution: The dynamics of galactic polities. In *Ideology and Precolumbian Civilizations*. A. A. Demarest and G. Conrad, eds. Pp. 135–157. Santa Fe: School of American Research Press.

Edmonson, M., trans., 1982 *The Ancient Future of the Itza: The Book of Chilam Balam of Tizimin.* Austin: University of Texas Press.

Fash, W. L., and S. Lane, 1983 El juego de Pelota B. In *Introducción a la arqueología de Copán, Honduras*, vol. 2. C. Baudez, ed. Pp. 501–562. Tegucigalpa: SECTUR.

Fox, J. W., D. T. Wallace, and K. L. Brown, 1992 The emergence of the Quiché elite: The Putun–Palenque connection. In *Mesoamerican Elites: An Archaeological Assessment*. D. Z. Chase and A. F. Chase, eds. Pp. 169–190. Norman: University of Oklahoma Press.

Frost, E. C., 1993 Indians and theologians: Sixteenth-century Spanish theologians and their concept of the indigenous soul. In *South and Meso-American Native Spirituality: From the Cult of the Feathered Serpent to the Theology of Liberation*. G. Gossen, ed. Pp. 119–139. New York: Crossroad.

Gibson, C., and J. B. Glass, 1975 A census of Middle American prose manuscripts in the native historical tradition. In *Handbook of Middle American Indians*, vol. 15: *Guide to Ethnohistorical Sources*, part 4. H. F. Cline, ed. Pp. 322–400. Austin: University of Texas Press.

Glass, J. B., 1975 A survey of native Middle American pictorial manuscripts. In *Handbook of Middle American Indians*, vol. 14: *Guide to Ethnohistorical Sources*, part 3. H. F. Cline, ed. Pp. 81–252. Austin: University of Texas Press.

Glass, J. B., and D. Robertson, 1975 A census of native Middle American pictorial manuscripts. In *Handbook of Middle American Indians*, vol. 14: *Guide to Ethnohistorical Sources Part Three*. H. F. Cline, ed. Pp. 81–252. Austin: University of Texas Press.

Hendon, J. A., 1997 Women's work, women's space, and women's status among the Classic-period Maya elite of the Copan valley. In *Women in Prehistory: North America and Mesoamerica*. C. Claassen and R. A. Joyce, eds. Pp. 33–46. Philadelphia: University of Pennsylvania Press.

——1999 Multiple sources of prestige and the social evaluation of women in prehispanic Mesoamerica. In *Material Symbols: Culture and Economy in Prehistory*. J. E. Robb, ed. Pp. 257–276. Occasional Paper 26. Carbondale: Center for Archaeological Investigations.

Hooton, E. A., 1940 Skeletons from the Cenote of sacrifice at Chichen Itzá. In *The Maya and their Neighbors*. Pp. 272–280. New York: D. Appleton-Century.

Joyce, R. A., 1986 Terminal Classic interaction on the southeastern Maya periphery. *American Antiquity* 51, 313–329.

——1992 Images of gender and labor organization in Classic Maya society. In *Exploring Gender through Archaeology: Selected Papers from the 1991 Boone Conference*. C. Claassen, ed. Pp. 63–70. Monographs in World Archaeology. Madison: Prehistory Press.

——1999 El colapso del clásico. In *Historia general de Guatemala*, vol. 1: *Epoca precolombina*. M. Popenoe de Hatch, ed. Guatemala: Asociación de amigos del país, Fundación para la cultura y el desarollo.

——2000 *Gender and Power in Prehispanic Mesoamerica*. Austin: University of Texas Press.

Karttunen, F., 1994 *Between Worlds: Interpreters, Guides, and Survivors*. New Brunswick: Rutgers University Press.

LeCount, L. J., J. Yaeger, R. M. Leventhal, and W. Ashmore, 2002 Dating the rise and fall of Xunantunich: A Late and Terminal Classic Maya center. *Ancient Mesoamerica*, 13, 41–63.

Lincoln, C. E., 1986 The chronology of Chichen Itza: A review of the literature. In *Late Lowland Maya Civilization: Classic to Postclassic*. J. A. Sabloff and E. W. Andrews V, eds. Pp. 141–196. Albuquerque: University of New Mexico Press.

Lizana, B. de, 1988 *Historia de Yucatán*. F. Jiménez Villalba, ed. Crónicas de América 43 Madrid: Historia 16.

López Austin, A., 1973 *Hombre–Dios: Religión y política en el mundo Náhuatl* [Man–God: Religion and Politics in the Nahuatl World]. Serie de Cultura Náhuatl Monografía 15. Mexico: Universidad Nacional Autónoma de México, Instituto de Investigaciones Históricas.

López de Cogolludo, D., 1971 *Los tres siglos de la dominación española en Yucatán o sea historia de esta provincia* [The Three Centuries of Spanish Domination in Yucatan, or: The History of this Province], 2 vols. Graz: Akademische Druck- und Verlagsanstalt.

Love, B., 1994 *The Paris Codex: Handbook for a Maya Priest.* Austin: University of Texas Press.

Masson, M. A., 1997 Cultural transformation at the Maya Postclassic community of Laguna de On, Belize. *Latin American Antiquity* 8, 293–316.

McCafferty, S. D., and G. G. McCafferty, 1988 Powerful women and the myth of male dominance in Aztec society. *Archaeological Review from Cambridge* 7, 45–59.

Miller, A. G., 1982 *On the Edge of the Sea: Mural Painting at Tancah-Tulum, Quintana Roo, Mexico.* Washington, DC: Dumbarton Oaks.

Miller, M. E., 1993 On the eve of the collapse: Maya art of the eighth century. In *Lowland Maya Civilization in the Eighth Century A.D.* J. Sabloff and J. S. Henderson, eds. Pp. 355–413. Washington, DC: Dumbarton Oaks.

Nicholson, H. B., 1982 The Mixteca-Puebla concept revisited. In *The Art and Iconography of Late Post-Classic Central Mexico.* E. H. Boone, ed. Pp. 227–254. Washington, DC: Dumbarton Oaks.

Noyes, E., trans., 1932 *Fray Alonso Ponce in Yucatán 1588.* Pp. 297–372. Middle American Research Series 4. New Orleans: Tulane University.

Pendergast, D. M., 1985 Lamanai, Belize: An updated view. In *The Lowland Maya Postclassic.* A. F. Chase and P. M. Rice, eds. Pp. 91–103. Austin: University of Texas Press.

Recinos, A., 1950 *Popol Vuh: The Sacred Book of the Ancient Quiché Maya.* D. Goetz and S. G. Morley, trans. Norman: University of Oklahoma Press.

Reents-Budet, D., 1994 *Painting the Maya Universe: Royal Ceramics of the Classic Period.* Durham: Duke University Press.

Restall, M., and J. F. Chuchiak, 2002 A reevaluation of the authenticity of Fray Diego de Landa's *Relación de las cosas de Yucatán. Ethnohistory* 49, 651–669.

Rice, D. S., P. M. Rice, and A. A. Demarest, eds., 2003 *The Terminal Classic in the Maya Lowlands: Collapse, Transition, and Transformation.* Boulder: University of Colorado Press. In press.

Rice, P. M., 1986 The Peten Postclassic: perspectives from the Central Peten lakes. In *Late Lowland Maya Civilization: Classic to Postclassic.* J. A. Sabloff and E. W. Andrews V, eds. Pp. 251–299. Albuquerque: University of New Mexico Press.

Ringle, W. M., 1990 Who was who in ninth-century Chichen Itza. *Ancient Mesoamerica* 1, 233–243.

Robles Castellanos, F., and A. P. Andrews, 1986 A review and synthesis of recent Postclassic archaeology in northern Yucatan. In *Late Lowland Maya Civilization: Classic to Postclassic.* J. Sabloff and E. W. Andrews V, eds. Pp. 53–98. Albuquerque: University of New Mexico Press.

Roys, R. L., 1967 *The Book of Chilam Balam of Chumayel.* Norman: University of Oklahoma Press.

Sabloff, J. A., R. L. Bishop, G. Harbottle, R. L. Rands, and E. V. Sayre, 1982 Analyses of fine paste ceramics. In *Excavations at Seibal, Department of Peten, Guatemala.* G. R. Willey, ed. Pp. 265–343. Peabody Museum Memoir 15/2. Cambridge: Peabody Museum of Archaeology and Ethnology.

Sánchez de Aguilar, P., 1937 *Informe contra Idolorum Cultores del Obispado de Yucatán* [Report against the Worship of Idols in the Bishopric of Yucatan], 3rd edn. Merida: E. G. Triay.

Sharer, R., 1985 Terminal events in the southeastern lowlands: A view from Quirigua. In *The Lowland Maya Postclassic*. A. F. Chase and P. M. Rice, eds. Pp. 245–253. Austin: University of Texas Press.

Smith, M. E., and C. M. Heath-Smith, 1980 Waves of influence in Post-Classic Mesoamerica? A critique of the Mixteca-Puebla concept. *Anthropology* 4, 15–50.

Sullivan, P., 1989 *Unfinished Conversations: Mayas and Foreigners Between Two Wars*. Berkeley: University of California Press.

Tate, C. E., 1992 *Yaxchilan: The Design of a Maya Ceremonial City*. Austin: University of Texas Press.

Tedlock, D., trans., 1985 *The Popol Vuh: The Maya Book of the Dawn of Life*. New York: Simon & Schuster.

Thompson, J. E. S., 1970 *Maya History and Religion*. Norman: University of Oklahoma Press.

——1972 *A Commentary on the Dresden Codex: A Maya Hieroglyphic Book*. Philadelphia: American Philosophical Society.

Tozzer, A. M., ed. and trans., 1941 *Landa's Relación de las cosas de Yucatan*. Papers of the Peabody Museum of American Archaeology and Ethnology 18. Cambridge: Peabody Museum.

Webster, D., 1993 Study of Maya warfare: What it tells us about the Maya and what it tells us about Maya archaeology. In *Lowland Maya Civilization in the Eighth Century A.D.* J. Sabloff and J. Henderson, eds. Pp. 414–444. Washington, DC: Dumbarton Oaks.

——1999 The archaeology of Copán, Honduras. *Journal of Archaeological Research* 7, 1–53.

Willey, G. R., 1986 The Postclassic of the Maya Lowlands: A preliminary overview. In *Late Lowland Maya Civilization: Classic to Postclassic*. J. Sabloff and E. W. Andrews V, eds. Pp. 17–51. Albuquerque: University of New Mexico Press.

Witschey, W. R. T., 1991 Maya inheritance patterns: The transfer of real estate and personal property in Ebtun, Yucatan, Mexico 1560–1830. *Estudios de Cultura Maya* 18, 395–416.

Wren, L. H., and P. Schmidt, 1991 Elite interaction during the Terminal Classic period: New evidence from Chichen Itza. In *Classic Maya Political History: Hieroglyphic and Archaeological Evidence*. T. P. Culbert, ed. Pp. 199–225. Cambridge: Cambridge University Press.

Glossary

agency The ability of person to choose to act in one way, given the possibility of alternative forms of action. Not all action is agency, and not all agency is consciously strategic.

agent A person exercising *agency*, including both strategic action and the active reproduction of *structure*.

aggrandizers *Agents* who aggressively pursue fame and fortune through culturally acceptable means within the constraints of an *egalitarian* society.

agricultural intensification Actions taken to increase the productivity of farming. In Mesoamerica, these include construction of terraces, raised fields, and irrigation systems, as well as changes in the means of clearing land for planting and the cycle of land use.

almanac Text tracing a pattern of dates and associating those dates with astronomical events, often providing guidelines for ritual practices.

altepetl Word in Nahuatl, the language of the people who dominated the Aztec state, used to designate a *city*. Composed of the words for water and mountain.

ancestors Those predecessors from whom living people trace their descent. In Mesoamerica, ancestors continued to influence the actions of their living descendants.

arboriculture The cultivation of trees, which may be brought into domestication through this process.

archaeoastronomy The study of the astronomical knowledge and practices of past societies through the physical remains they left behind, including observatory buildings, buildings and monuments aligned with astronomical phenomena, and texts recording astronomical data.

axis mundi Literally 'world axis,' a term that refers to the idea held by many ancient peoples that there was a central point in the universe that linked different levels of creation. In Mesoamerica, this center was associated with the color green, the central hearth, and the *Old Fire God*.

bajo Literally 'low,' a term used in Maya archaeology for low basins where water collects during the rainy season in the Central Maya lowlands. Some Maya specialists argue that bajos were sites of *agricultural intensification.*

ballcourt A special architectural complex arranged to facilitate playing a variety of games using a native rubber ball. Ballcourts are found in the southwest United States and the West Indies, in addition to Mesoamerica. The defining features of a ballcourt are a long alley bordered by at least two long buildings, with a building on at least one end optional. The long side buildings, called 'ranges,' have complex architectural profiles on the side facing the ballcourt alley. These inner profiles are usually symmetric, mirror images of each other, combining horizontal benches and sloping surfaces off which the rubber ball could be played.

barrio From a Spanish word for neighborhood, a term used especially at Teotihuacan for different areas within a site where it is believed people shared a similar way of life and may have been members of distinctive social groups like the later Aztec *calpolli.*

bone isotope Chemical elements incorporated in living bone through normal processes of growth occur in different forms, or isotopes. Study of proportions of different isotopes of some elements provides information about ancient human diet. In particular, carbon isotopes are studied to understand what forms of plants were eaten, nitrogen isotopes are informative about the sources of protein, both from plants and animals, and strontium isotopes help differentiate protein derived from different environments.

cacique Leader or chief of an indigenous society.

calpolli Word in Nahuatl, the language of the Aztecs, for a social group composed of a number of families. Spanish sources describe the calpolli of the Aztec capital, Tenochtitlan, as having occupational specializations, sharing land rights, and worshiping common deities. The extent to which similar organization was found outside Tenochtitlan and other cities is debated.

cardinal directions The main world directions, north, south, east, and west. While Mesoamerican people divided space into four cardinal directions, they based these divisions on the course of the sun, not magnetic orientation to north. From a solar perspective, east was the primary direction, and appears at the top of Mesoamerican maps. In addition, rather than conceiving of the four directions as points, Mesoamerican people represented them as lines, together forming a rectangular space.

catchment area The area around a *settlement* from which it draws the natural resources, including plants and animals, used for everyday survival.

celt A stone object, usually polished, often made of *greenstone*, shaped like a long oval. The basic shape is that of an axe or adze blade.

censer Any of a variety of vessels, most made of pottery, used to burn various kinds of materials to form scented smoke as part of rituals. Teotihuacan's theater-type censers were made by attaching individual ceramic appliqués to a framework surrounding a central figure, on one side of the chimney through which smoke would rise from the censer body. Other figural censers were created by modeling a hollow figure that sat on the lid of the vessel. Among the substances burned in censers were tree resins (copal), rubber, and paper.

Central Place Theory An approach to understanding why people live in particular spatial arrangements, based on the assumption that settlements are located to maximize such values as transportation efficiency. Applied in Mesoamerican archaeology to *settlement pattern* distributions to infer what values were most important to the people living in the sites.

ceramic sequence A set of identified types of pottery vessels, based on excavation of deposits whose sequence in time is known, that are differentiated from each other by changes in decoration, details of shape, the mixture of clay and other materials, or other visible signs of difference.

ceremonial center Concept developed in Mesoamerican archaeology in the first half of the twentieth century to describe settlements understood as sites of periodic use for ritual by populations believed to live elsewhere, primarily in small, scattered villages. Contemporary Mesoamerican archaeology suggests the idea that Mesoamerican cities are unusual because they are dominated by temples and open spaces for ritual performance, rather than being organized around a core of economic and governmental buildings.

Chicomoztoc In Aztec historical and mythical tradition, the cave where the ancestors of the peoples of the Valley of Mexico emerged onto the earth.

chiefdom The anthropological label for societies in which authority to rule is inherited, but there is relatively little class differentiation. Sometimes seen as a stage through which societies passed, following *egalitarian* society and preceding *state* society, characterized as *rank society*.

chinampa Fields constructed in shallow-water areas by digging soil from one area, creating canals, and placing it in another location, until the ground surface is above water.

Cipactli Aztec term for the crocodilian earth monster.

circumscription The concept that the area available for exploitation by a society might be limited by the presence of other societies or natural barriers, leading to pressure for changes in social organization to deal with rising population, environmental degradation, and other problems assumed to develop automatically over time.

city A central place distinguished within a region by hosting the widest possible range of activities, including craft production, economic exchanges, and religious practices. Cities are usually sites where otherwise unrelated social groups live together, managing their interactions through marketplaces, guilds, and other institutions. While cities are often assumed to require large populations, what is large will vary from one historical situation to another.

city-state A society centered around a single city, where that city is simultaneously the seat of government.

class In social theory, a term for social *status* differentiation typical of *states*, where classes are ranked, but within any class, there is no guarantee that individuals can be ranked relative to each other. Contrasts with *rank*.

Cocijo Oaxacan deity associated with storms and lighting.

codex, codices The term codex has been applied to manuscripts of various formats and materials produced both before and after the Spanish Conquest. Prehispanic codices were produced by folding a long sheet of bark paper or animal skin into a fan-like arrangement, coated with a thin layer of lime stucco, and painted in multiple colors, especially black and red.

commoner A person who was not considered to be a member of a *noble* family in the two-class system that was general in Mesoamerica. Words for commoners in Mesoamerican languages often identified them as agricultural workers.

community Used both for people in a bounded group, with a perception of social identity, of common interests, and of 'belonging,' and also for the place housing these people. Communities exist above the level of kin groups and subsume and cross-cut them.

compositional analysis The application of chemical and physical science methods to archaeological objects to determine what elements made up the raw material used. Compositional analyses can provide a 'fingerprint' of objects made from the same raw materials. When the original raw material is not altered too much, compositional analysis can match a group of objects to a source of raw materials. In Mesoamerica, compositional analysis has been used on pottery, *greenstone*, and *obsidian*.

compound Term used to label a group of buildings and their associated open working spaces that were the location of residence of a social group.

core-blade, prismatic A particular technology for producing stone tools, especially from *obsidian*, that is characterized by preparation of a lump of stone so that pressure applied to a flat side (the platform) releases a series of long blades that are triangular or five-sided prisms in cross-section.

cosmogony The actions through which the world was created.

cosmogram A representation of the entire universe through symbolic shorthand or artistic metaphor.

cosmology A set of beliefs about the structure of the material and immaterial world, its creation, and the place of humans and other beings in it.

Coyolxauhqui Aztec female deity, the older sister of *Huitzilopochtli*, who kills and decapitates her.

crocodilian Any of a group of reptiles inhabiting the rivers of Mesoamerica that resemble the crocodile. These include alligators and caimans.

cultural ecology Study of the relation of people to their environment.

cultural evolution The idea that societies pass through a series of stages, often represented as inevitable or at least tightly constrained, through which the centralization of governmental power, the intensification of agriculture and craft production, and the development of differences in status, wealth, and class identity all take form over time.

cultural history An approach typical of archaeology beginning in the first half of the twentieth century in which the goal of research was to understand the sequence of events at a particular place over time.

culture Distinctive practices by a group of people, usually living in proximity, and their descendants over time. Sometimes considered the sum total of all the practices of a group, and at other times taken to refer only to those practices that are shared. Always conceived of as distinguishing a group of people from other, similar groups.

descent Relationships recognized as kinship over time, linking living people to their *ancestors*.

domestic Concerned with the *household*.

dynasty A series of rulers over time who claim to be related through kinship.

ear spools Ornaments inserted through a hole pierced in the lobe of the ear during childhood, gradually widened to allow insertion of a tube held in place only by the weight of beads hanging from it. Made of various stones and pottery.

egalitarian Term for a society in which *status* differences are not assumed to be inherent and inherited, but are the products of individual action during life, and are subject to change or different valuation in different settings. Sometimes treated as a stage of *cultural evolution*.

elite see *noble*

empire A form of political organization in which one state has power over other states, often as a result of conquest. In Mesoamerica, the Aztecs are the only society generally conceded to have formed an empire, and some specialists debate whether the term should be applied to them.

equinox Days in the spring and fall when the sun reaches the midpoint of its apparent seasonal movement on the eastern and western horizons, marking the turn of the seasons. At this point in the year, the day and night are of equal length.

ethnoarchaeology The study of living people by archaeologists, or for the purpose of illuminating understanding of archaeological remains.

Feathered Serpent A supernatural being present in multiple versions across Mesoamerica, the Feathered Serpent is particularly prominent at Teotihuacan.

figurine A small three-dimensional representation of a human being, animal, or building, often modeled in clay, sometimes carved of stone, bone, shell, or wood.

Fine Orange A set of pottery types produced in the western Maya lowlands near the end of the Classic period and extending into the beginning of the Postclassic period.

glyph, hieroglyph Term for individual signs used in writing systems.

Great Goddess The central image in much of the mural art of Teotihuacan, a figure giving rise to water, plants, and precious things.

Great Tradition The concept that *cities* were sites of development of cultural practices and beliefs distinct from, and more encompassing than, those of surrounding villages.

greenstone Term used to label the green stones, including *jade* and *serpentine*, preferred for ornaments and ritual tools by Mesoamerican people. Emphasizes selection for color which appears more typical than selection for mineral type.

headdress The ornaments worn on the head by Mesoamerican people, sometimes mounted on a supporting structure, at other times forming freestanding helmets or hats.

heterarchy As an alternative to *hierarchy*, refers to situations in which there are multiple lines of authority associated with different practices, such as a religious hierarchy independent of a political hierarchy.

hierarchy A relationship in which one party has greater *power*, control, or *status* than another.

hinterland The area away from the central place or *city*, from which the central place draws resources.

house, household Label both for a group of people sharing most aspects of everyday life necessary to persist economically and reproduce socially, and for the physical structures in which these people live.

household archaeology The specialized study of evidence for the small-scale, day-to-day, face-to-face activities through which members of a site ensure their economic and social survival.

Huehueteotl Aztec Old Fire God, represented as elderly, seated deity supporting *censers* on his back, associated with the central world direction.

Huitzilopochtli Aztec sun deity, one of two deities honored at the main temple in Tenochtitlan. The specific patron of the Mexica, the dominant group in Aztec society.

iconography Representations believed to have highly stereotyped symbolic meaning that can be studied like a language, and the study of symbolic meaning embodied in such representations.

ideology As an aspect of *structure*, may justify or legitimate domination, although subordinates are able to see through and resist dominant ideologies to varying degrees.

INAA Instrumental neutron activation analysis, a form of *compositional analysis*.

jade A specific form of *greenstone* whose only known source identified to date is in the Motagua river valley in Guatemala.

landscape A term that embraces both the environment and human activities and settlements in the environment.

landscape archaeology The specialized study of human activity on a broad scale, with special attention to practices through which landscapes are perceived, altered, and reproduced.

lineage A specialized form of kinship group based on *descent* through a line of people, often people of one sex. A lineage joins people over time, binding *ancestors* and descendants.

Long Count calendar A specialized calendar that counted from a fixed beginning point and used place notation to create an infinitely expandable means of calculating and recording dates.

microcosm A small-scale version of the entire cosmos.

military orders Among the Aztec, men who remained as warriors full-time after their required service as youths formed permanent groups with distinctive costumes and identities, such as Eagle and Jaguar warriors.

milpa Cornfield specifically; more generally, an annually cultivated field.

monolith A large, single piece of stone.

mounds The remains of ancient buildings, collapsed and covered with accumulated dirt.

New Fire An annual ceremony among the Aztecs and probably other Mesoamerican people, when all existing fires were extinguished at midwinter and a new fire was kindled in a ritual.

noble With *commoners*, one of two strata in the fundamental two-class system characteristic of Mesoamerica. Nobles were often conceived of as different in origin or even in physical nature than commoners. *Descent* was of fundamental importance in noble identity.

obsidian Naturally formed volcanic glass used as the raw material for the cutting tools of Mesoamerican societies. Usually black, but Mesoamerican people also exploited green sources. *Compositional analysis* can identify tools from known obsidian sources.

Old Fire God Generalization of Aztec deity *Huehueteotl*.

Omacatl Aztec deity associated with drinking and feasts.

palace A residential building inhabited by *nobles*, especially rulers, often serving also as a governmental building.

pedestrian survey The practice of seeking archaeological sites by walking through fields systematically.

Plumbate A set of ceramic types made over a period beginning in the Late Classic and extending to the Early Postclassic, distinguished by a metallic orange or gray finish produced by unique chemistry of clays used. *Compositional analysis* confirms that the Pacific Coast of Guatemala was the center of production of these widely traded pottery types.

political economy The distribution of economic and cultural capital in a society and the kinds of social groups (alliance networks) that control these resources.

polity The unit of political organization of a society, such as a *city-state*.

polygyny The practice of men marrying multiple women.

Popol Vuh An early Colonial text written in the Quiche Maya language using the European alphabet, containing a description of *cosmology* and history of the rulers of the Quiche Maya state.

power The transformative capacity of an agent to achieve a desired outcome.

practice theory Social theories that attempt to join individual *agency* and *structure* in a single model, in which people reproduce the structures that limit their agency through their exercise of agency in the form of practices.

primate center A single *settlement* whose population size is of an order of magnitude larger than any others in its *hinterland*.

private Concerned with events and actions taking place outside of the public domain. Often equated with *domestic*.

public Sometimes means non-domestic, supra-household, or non-private, or restricted use. At other times signifies open to common view, common access, or shared use.

public transcripts Overt and public representations in writing, art, and architecture of the ideologies and cosmologies of society's dominant groups.

pulque An intoxicating beverage made by fermenting the hearts of the maguey plant.

rank In social theory, a term for social *status* differentiation typical of *chiefdoms*, where status is inheritable, and any two people can be placed in a relative ranking such that in theory the entire society forms a single rank series. Contrasts with *class*.

rank society A society typified by *rank* differences.

rank-size rule A means of arranging *settlements* in a hypothetical *hierarchy* based on their sizes.

ritual almanac see *almanac*

roof comb A form of ornament constructed on top of the roof of a building, especially temples in the Maya lowlands.

sedentism The quality of habitually living in one place.

serpentine A form of *greenstone*.

settlement The material traces of people's presence on the land.

settlement pattern The regularity observable in the placement of *settlements*, including relations to natural resources and the location of central places and *hinterlands*.

shamanism A form of ritual practice in which ritual specialists, through a variety of techniques including music, dance, and use of intoxicants, are able to cross boundaries between the world of everyday existence and other dimensions of the cosmos, often through the actions of a spirit capable of moving the waking body.

skull rack A platform built to support a framework of poles on which skulls of sacrificed captives were threaded and displayed.

slash and burn A technique for clearing land for agriculture, in which vegetation is cut and allowed to dry before being burned.

solstice Days in the winter and summer when the sun reaches the extreme southern and northern points of its apparent seasonal movement on the eastern and western horizons, marking the turn of the seasons. The shortest and longest days of the year.

spindle whorl A circular weight attached to a spindle to contribute to its rotation, critical to spinning fibers into thread.

state A social formation characterized by centrally administered government, and social *hierarchy*, often associated with the development of social classes, and usually tied to defined territories.

status Relative social standing. May be related to wealth or political power but can be, and often is, independent.

stela, stelae Two-sided, free-standing stone monuments placed in the open, public plazas of cities including those of the Gulf Coast of Mexico, Formative Central Mexico, Oaxaca, and the Maya lowlands.

Storm God Equivalent and predecessor at Teotihuacan of Aztec deity *Tlaloc*.

stratification The division of society into strata with differential *status* and, usually, wealth and *power*.

structure, structuration In social theory, structure is a term for those aspects of social existence that set limits to the exercise of *agency* and channel it into traditional forms. Structure is produced and transformed by the actions or practices of social agents, whose exercise of agency is simultaneously structuration.

swidden A form of agricultural production that involves cultivating fields for some years and abandoning them when productivity declines, cultivating new fields.

talud-tablero A form of architecture characteristic of, although not invented by, Teotihuacan, giving a uniform and distinctive appearance to public buildings and domestic shrines at the site. Composed of two parts, a sloping lower surface (talud) supporting a rectangular framework that usually projects far beyond the sloping apron and may contain added designs (tablero).

Tezcatlipoca The most powerful and feared Aztec deity.

Tlaloc Aztec deity of rainfall and earthly fertility, one of two deities honored at the main temple in Tenochtitlan.

tlatoani The Nahuatl term for the highest governmental authority among the Aztecs, literally meaning 'speaker.'

Tollan Nahuatl name of the site, also called Tula, that played the role of legendary source of civilized practices for the Aztecs and many other Postclassic people. Used as part of place name of numerous Postclassic sites, notably Tula in the Mexican state of Hidalgo.

Toltec A person from *Tollan*.

toponym Place name

Triple Alliance According to Aztec traditional histories, a political alliance with two neighboring *city-states* critical to their consolidation of power in the Valley of Mexico.

urbanism Form of social life dominated by *cities*, particularly large ones.

volcanic ash Used as a material added to clay during ceramic production, a form of volcanic glass with a very small particle size that when welded together forms rocks such as volcanic tuff, ignimbrite, or rhyolite.

wealth Differential economic resources.

Index

Note: Page references in italics indicate maps and figures. In the subentries, chronological periods appear (in chronological order) before general topics, which follow in alphabetical order.